Acting as Reading

Acting as Reading

The Place of the Reading Process in the Actor's Work

David Cole

Ann Arbor

THE UNIVERSITY OF MICHIGAN PRESS

Copyright © by the University of Michigan 1992
All rights reserved
Published in the United States of America by
The University of Michigan Press
Manufactured in the United States of America

1995   1994   1993   1992   4   3   2   1

Library of Congress Cataloging-in-Publication Data

Cole, David, 1941–
   Acting as reading : the place of the reading process in the actor's
work / David Cole.
     p.   cm. — (Theater—theory/text/performance)
   Includes bibliographical references and index.
   ISBN 0-472-10302-4
   1. Acting. 2. Reading. I. Title. II. Series.
PN2061.C59 1992
792'.028—dc20   92-1640
                                                  CIP

A CIP catalogue record for this book is available from the British Library.

Acknowledgments

Permission to quote from the following sources is gratefully acknowledged:

Aristophanes, vol. 2, *The Birds,* translated by Benjamin Bickley Rogers (Cambridge: Harvard University Press, 1924). Reprinted by permission of Harvard University Press and the Loeb Classical Library.

Don Quixote by Miguel de Cervantes Saavedra, translated by Samuel Putnam. Translation copyright 1949 by The Viking Press, Inc. Used by permission of Viking Penguin, a division of Penguin Books USA, Inc.

Anton Chekhov, *Best Plays,* translated by Stark Young (New York: Random House, 1956). Reprinted by permission of Flora Roberts, Inc.

Errol Durbach, editor, *Ibsen in the Theater* (New York: New York University Press, 1980). Reprinted by permission of New York University Press and The Macmillan Press, Ltd., London.

Norman N. Holland, *The Dynamics of Literary Response* (New York: Columbia University Press, 1989). Copyright © 1968, 1975, and 1989 by Norman N. Holland. Reprinted by permission of Norman N. Holland.

Constantin Stanislavski, *An Actor Prepares* (New York: Routledge/Theatre Arts Books, 1989). Reprinted with the permission of the publisher, Routledge, Chapman and Hall, New York.

Constantin Stanislavski, *Creating a Role* (New York: Routledge/Theatre Arts Books, 1989). Reprinted with the permission of the publisher, Routledge, Chapman and Hall, New York.

I want to thank the following friends and colleagues for response and advice: Herbert Blau, Eileen Blumenthal, David Bromwich, Sara Friedman, Elinor Fuchs, Don Gertmenian, Meg Gertmenian, Michael Goldman, John Leubsdorf, Richard Sewall, Kathleen Sullivan, and Glenn Young.

This book is dedicated to my wife, Susan Letzler Cole, with respect, thanks, and love.

Contents

Chapter 1

Acting as Reading

But not *only* as reading, surely?

That reading is a phase or aspect of the acting process I suppose no one would deny. The actor reads for his role (usually a "cold reading"), reads the script, attends a first reading or read-through, perhaps participates in some developmental staged readings. But all this is generally viewed as merely preliminary to "getting it on its feet," "walking through it." Only when the actor has at last *come off book* (as in "off drugs," "off the sauce"?) is the "real work" often felt to begin.

Clearly, reading is more in evidence at some stages of an actor's work than at others. Nevertheless, it is the entire acting process—from first encounter with the script through performance—that I am going to present as, essentially, a reading process. And by "reading," though eventually I shall have some things to say about reading aloud and reading to others, I mean first of all *silent, solitary reading to oneself in a chair.*

Stated in the broadest possible terms, my argument is as follows: Acting is a physicalization of the act of reading. But the act of reading which acting physicalizes was itself originally—had its origins in—a bodily process. In acting, then, what was once physical becomes physical once more. *Acting is the recovery of a "lost" physical of reading.*

What this "lost" physical is, why reading lost it, and how acting restitutes it I will attempt to show in the chapters that follow. First, though, it seems important to suggest what advantages there might be in approaching acting as reading and what answers might be made to some of the rather obvious objections that could be raised to such an approach.

It is not as if to pronounce acting "reading" immediately cleared up every difficulty about it. Reading, after all, is anything but a straightfor-

ward act. It has physiological aspects (eye, mouth, and throat movements), cognitive aspects (sign/sound matching, letter and word recognition and grouping), interpretive aspects (the discovery of literary structures and meanings), and intrapsychic aspects (the assimilation of fantasy
material). Not all these levels will be of equal concern to us: When I
speak of acting as reading I do not mean simply that actors "interpret" a
role, much less that they merely "construe" its signs (though, of course,
an actor's reading, like anyone else's, proceeds by interpretation and
construal). But, however much or little we choose to make of each, all
these levels are present in the single activity of reading.

Assuming, that is, that reading even *is* a single activity—for we call
a bewildering variety of situations by that name. Psychics and poets both
"give readings." Significance may be "read into" a book, and members
"read out of" a club. My "early reading" is a collection of books; my
"best reading" an informed guess. Someone who chooses to "read eco-
nomics" at a university has chosen more than a reading list, while someone who "reads me like a book" may never read books at all. Hunters
"read sign" (animal tracks) in the absence of a text;[1] lasers "read" video
disks in the absence of a text and reader alike;[2] and "do you read me?"
asks the pilot of the tower, meaning "can you *hear* my *voice?*" "Curiously
unreadable metaphor of reading," muses Paul de Man, "which one never
seems to want to read."[3] But perhaps the universality of the trope is
traceable back to the ancient view of the universe itself as a Book:
Dante's "single volume" in which "substances and accidents and their
relations" are "ingathered";[4] Sir Thomas Browne's "universal and pub-
lick Manuscript, that lies expans'd unto the Eyes of all."[5] If all the
world's a text, then every experience you can have of the world is
reading—which is to say, reading is no one single experience.

But even if we limit the term to its most literal sense, perusal of
print, is there some one thing you do when you comb want ads, check
ingredients, look ahead to the next line of a manuscript you are typing,
run your eye over the four of seven letters of a crossword line you have
thus far filled in?[6] "Do we read the string $30 = 50 - (4 \times 5)$? What about
the string of characters that used to be popular in comic books,
$%&&*&%$? Does reading necessarily include comprehension? If so,
what is it we do when we pronounce the letter string, hyperphractic?"[7]

Reading, in short, is every bit as great a puzzle as acting is. What
can one possibly hope to gain by offering an explanation of the actor's
work in terms of another process at least as mysterious as acting itself?

First, let me acknowledge a personal hope. I am a playwright, which is to say, a writer whose readership is composed of actors. Like any writer, I feel I have a stake in understanding how my readers read, and for a playwright this means understanding how *actors* read. Therefore, this book covertly begins, and openly ends (chaps. 6 and 7), in a meditation on the playwright-actor relation considered as a writer-reader relation.

There is, however, an argument for treating acting as reading which goes beyond my or anyone else's predisposition to do so. Reading is something that all actors actually and necessarily *do*. One can argue endlessly about whether the actor can or should or might function as a "social critic" (Brecht)[8] or "skilled worker" (Meyerhold)[9] or "secular saint" (Grotowski)[10] or "signal[er] through the flames" (Artaud);[11] but meanwhile there is no question that he *is* functioning as a reader. Every actor—whether he works for Robert Wilson or the Shubert Organization, the Royal Shakespeare Company or the high school dramatics club—*reads*.

I mean, of course, in his capacity as actor. As individuals, actors vary as much as other people in their reading habits and skills. I know actors who pride themselves on reading the *New Republic* and actors who pride themselves on reading nothing, actors who are skilled sight readers and actors who are near-dyslexics. (Indeed, I know one actor who is, clinically, dyslexic.) It must be said, however, that even a performer's most personal reading problems are likely to bear some relation to his acting process. When an actor repeatedly stumbles over a word or phrase this is often the outward sign of a difficult *acting* moment. When an actor feels (as many do) a general aversion to reading this is probably not, as is generally assumed, the result of "anti-intellectualism" but, rather, of an instinctive reluctance to squander what are unconsciously felt to be *acting* energies in the wrong place. "I never pick up a book," claims the great British actress Billie Whitelaw. "I only read what I'm working on."[12] But this perhaps is no more than to say: My work as an actor being reading, I must save myself for my work.

Still, to speak of reading as something all actors do may seem an overstatement. What about actors in non-Western performance traditions? What about actors in antitextual or nonverbal forms of contemporary experimental theater? What about actors in preliterate societies? No model of acting—not the "skilled worker" or "social critic" or "secular saint"—fits all theatrical cultures equally well, and, clearly, acting as reading fits best those that provide the actor with something to read. This, however, is far less of a limitation than might at first appear.

With certain non-Western performance traditions I confess I can do nothing. "We learn the dialogues of all two hundred and fifty plays by rote," explains an actor in the Japanese Kyogen theater. "Somewhere they are written down in a book, but we never see the book."[13] Such a practice falls outside the bounds of acting as reading, not only because the actors literally don't read but also because, as we shall see in chapters 6 and 7, it is the very essence of the actor-reader's project to be the reader in whose reading others read, whereas in Kyogen this "first reader" is always someone other than the actor.

As for the actor in contemporary nonverbal theater, his doing without a dramatic text does not necessarily mean that he does without reading. The participants in happenings and performance pieces work from instruction sheets or scenarios. And even when no script, however rudimentary, is in evidence, reading—displaced from scripts to other kinds of texts—quite possibly still forms the basis of the actor's work. In such cases the script-surrogate may be a manifesto or theoretical document: The antitext enthusiasts of the 1960s read to pieces their copies of *The Theatre and Its Double*. Or it may be an acting manual. Viola Spolin's "theatre games" method of actor training is the last thing from text-oriented. Yet her highly structured book of acting exercises, *Improvisation for the Theater,* itself presents the actor with, in Spolin's own words, "a full text . . . a charted course" of "activity that brings about spontaneity."[14] As this last example suggests, even the *improvising* actor may be, in some degree, a reader—if only of his improvisation handbook. Managers of commedia dell'arte troupes counseled their players to read widely in dramatic and other literature so as to deepen their stock of usable material.[15] Indeed, I shall suggest in chapter 4 that improvisation itself may best be understood as a limiting case of acting as reading, in which the actor simultaneously "writes" what he "reads."

Actors in preliterate societies seem excluded by definition from the ranks of actor-readers. Yet even here there is some overlap. If in *The Theatrical Event* I was able to offer a shamanistic model of the actor's transaction with a text, this is because the two phases of the shaman's trajectory—the exploratory *(shamanic)* and the self-abandoning *(hunganic)*—correspond, as we shall see in chapter 4, to phases of the reading process. Perhaps not even the Kyogen actor, who "never see[s] the book," is on a wholly different path from that of the actor-reader. For, as a nonreader, he "must absorb the movements physically,"[16] and reading itself, we shall find, originally was, and in acting once more becomes, a process of physical absorption.

But even granting that the literacy of actors places some limits on a view of acting as reading, the limits are not, at least so far as Western theater is concerned, very constricting ones: As far back as we choose to look, it seems that actors could read. While it is just barely possible that the citizen-members of the Greek tragic chorus were taught their roles orally,[17] present-day authorities on Greek literacy take it for granted that the actors themselves could read.[18] (For one thing, we know that Greek singers were literate—they are depicted on Attic vase paintings performing from book rolls that "no doubt would have contained both text and musical notation"[19]—and actors in the Theater of Dionysus sang their roles.) One might not suppose the medieval townsmen who put on the Corpus Christi cycles were as well educated as their Athenian counterparts, and indeed the roles they played, being both brief and rhyming, could certainly have been imparted "by ear." Nonetheless, the town archives of both York and Coventry contain records of payment for the copying out and delivery of parts to actors.[20] Two such copies of parts, one from the fourteenth century and one from the fifteenth, survive to the present day.[21]

From the sixteenth century on, the literacy of actors may be taken for granted. Of course, the mere fact that actors *could* read in a particular society is no evidence that reading was regarded by that society as germane to the acting process. Nor will direct evidence on such a point be soon forthcoming. Most earlier periods did not even possess the conception of an "acting process," never mind issue statements as to what constituted it. There are, however, three types of indirect evidence which suggest that the link between acting and reading is a long-standing one: (1) early endorsements of the value for actors of supplementary reading; (2) early instances of reading rehearsals; and (3) the role of the lector ("reader") in the development of medieval liturgical drama.

1. *Supplementary reading.* That reading has at least an ancillary contribution to make to the work of the actor has long been recognized. I have already mentioned the commedia-master's recommendation of "outside reading" to his troupe as a source of improvisatory material. In the first full-length acting manual in English (1710), Thomas Betterton urged upon actors the study of moral philosophy as an aid to character analysis. Garrick recommended to a colleague the perusal of "other

books besides plays." (Salvini and Bernhardt thought the study of historical works especially useful.)[22] And in our own day Uta Hagen exhorts her students to acquire "a thorough education in history, literature, English linguistics,"[23] while Joseph Chaikin encourages the members of the Open Theater "to read material on wild and isolated children" in preparation for their portrayal of such figures in *The Mutation Show*.[24]

2. *Reading rehearsals.* A clear indication of the importance a given era attaches to reading in acting is the emphasis it places on reading as a rehearsal technique, i.e., on "reading rehearsals." Rehearsal "at the table" is sometimes thought to be an innovation of the Moscow Art Theatre.[25] But Goethe had pointed out the usefulness of "book rehearsals" over a hundred years before Stanislavski.[26] And in Leone di Somi's *Dialogues on Stage Affairs* we have an account of a reading rehearsal which dates from the mid-sixteenth century:

> First I have all the parts carefully copied out and then . . . gather [the actors] all together in one room and give each one that part for which he is most fitted. I get them, after that, to read the whole play in order that they . . . may learn the plot, or at least that portion which concerns them, impressing on all their minds the nature of the characters they have to interpret.[27]

3. *The lector.* From earliest times the reading of biblical passages has figured in the worship of the church, and from the second century on such reading was the province of a special reader, distinct from the mass-celebrant.[28] As early as the eighth century, these readings *(lectiones)* began to be chanted or sung, and the lectors who chanted or sang them to be chosen specifically for their performance skills. Eighth-century Roman lectors, for example, had to pass a singing audition administered by the Pope himself.[29]

But the lector was not only a performer; he performed in those very antiphonal exchanges between a choir and a soloist which some regard as the origin of medieval drama.[30] Furthermore, his performance in these antiphons was not purely musical but at least prototheatrical. By the early ninth century lectors were varying their voices to distinguish one biblical character from another. It is even possible that different lectors were employed to sing different "roles."[31] And even when, over the course of the centuries, lection singing passed to other functionaries (e.g., subdeacons and priests), these were obliged to stand where the lector had formerly stood, dress as the lector had formerly dressed, and be summoned by name to their task, as the lector had formerly been summoned[32]—as if in acknowledgment that, when one takes one's place as a performer, it is the place of a reader one takes.

Yet, after all, the lector is more a symbolic precursor of the actor-reader than his literal origin. It is really only in our own time, in fact with Stanislavski, that reading begins to be consciously understood as the essence of the acting process. Although, or perhaps because, his own view of reading was a paradoxical one,[33] Stanislavski never wearies of stressing the ties between reading and acting.[34] He compares learning to act with learning to read:

> This ABC and grammar of acting are, comparatively speaking, not difficult, although in the majority of cases they take years to acquire. Without them, it is impossible to live on the stage. . . . How can anyone read fluently and feel it, when the letters and commas keep distracting his attention?[35]

He associates bad acting with perfunctory reading:

> Now let us compare our method with what is done in any theatre of the ordinary type. There they read the play, hand out the parts with the notice that by the third or the tenth rehearsal everyone must know his role by heart. They begin the reading, then they all go up on the stage and act, while holding the script. . . . At the predicted rehearsal the books are taken away.[36]

And he identifies progress in acting with progress in reading:

> [The script] must be read over and over, and with each additional reading we must guide ourselves by what was established the time before.[37]

Of these many readings that the actor is presumed to bestow on the script, the first—i.e., the one that is most purely a *reading*—has, Stanislavski repeatedly asserts, a special significance: "This all-important moment can be likened to the first meeting between a man and a woman . . . destined to be . . . lovers or mates." Consequently, "the external circumstances for the first reading . . . should be properly set. . . . The occasion should be accompanied with a certain ceremoniousness." The first reading is accorded this degree of importance by Stanislavski because he looks upon it not as a mere preliminary to acting but as already part of the acting process—"the first stage of creativeness." Listening to the play being read aloud, the actors are already in motion:

> They are carried away by the reading. They cannot control the muscles of their faces, which oblige them to grimace or mime in accordance with what is being read. They cannot control their movements, which occur spontaneously.[38]

But, if the first reading stands at the origins of acting, it also stands for its eventual goal:

> In the beginning, when they [the actors] read the play, the words, both their own lines and those of the others who play opposite them, seem interesting, new.[39]

"Interesting" and "new" is what the words of the script must one day seem again—in performance. That "first time," the illusion of which acting tries to recover, is the time of first reading,[40] at which, in the words of Stanislavski's American disciple Lee Strasberg, "actors can give you such wonderful results that the problem becomes, 'How do you keep this?' "[41] The work of the actor is born of, and aspires back to, that lost paradise of fresh imaginative response which was formerly his as a reader. For Stanislavski it is scarcely an exaggeration to say that acting begins and ends in reading.

I therefore naturally find the Stanislavskian account of acting a congenial one. But to rest the case for acting as reading solely on Stanislavski may seem to prejudice the outcome. Of course, Stanislavski, with his emphasis on interiority and process in acting, stands ready to welcome into acting the interior process of reading. The surprise is that, when we turn to acting approaches far less hospitable to inwardness than Stanislavski's, we still find reading accorded a prominent place. Brecht, for example, views reading as a means of preserving rather than abolishing emotional distance between actor and role—and therefore welcomes it into an acting technique whose aim is to preserve just this distance:

> To safeguard against an unduly "impulsive," frictionless and un-
> critical creation of characters and incidents, more reading rehearsals
> can be held than usual. The actor . . . should go on functioning as
> long as possible as a reader (which does not mean a reader-aloud).[42]

But even in approaches to acting which openly denigrate reading,
reading may find a place. Artaud and Grotowski, for example, in leaving
so little place for the text, would seem to be leaving none at all for the
actor-reader. And yet, the audacities these innovators contemplate
against the text are audacious acts of reading. Grotowski defines his
theatrical enterprise as "confrontation with myth." But what exactly are
the myths to be confronted? "In the theatre," Grotowski asserts, "the
text has the same function as the myth had for the poet of ancient
times."[43] Our myths are *texts*—the numinous, daunting masterpieces of
earlier dramatic literature—and one confronts a text by reading it. As I
have argued in *The Theatrical Event,* all such confrontational productions, with their foregrounding of certain motifs at the expense of others,
their search for acceptable contemporary "meanings," etc., are, in effect,
onstage critical readings—even those productions that imagine that it is
the impossibility of reading they confront.[44] "The library at Alexandria
can be burned down," declares Artaud, who, however, has only read
about the library of Alexandria in a volume that escaped the blaze. The
Artaudian production of a classic play, "stripped of [its] text," "without
regard for text,"[45] not only presupposes a reading of that play, it *is* a
reading of that play.

The indisputable involvement of acting of most sorts with reading
of some kind, the mass of historical evidence which suggests that the
acting-reading tie is a long-standing one, the centrality accorded reading
by some of acting's most important practitioner-theorists—all these
seem good reasons for venturing upon a consideration of acting as reading. And yet, whatever the advantages, there also appear to be some
very evident objections to such an approach. There are, after all, so
many ways in which readers are *not* like actors: immobilized, silent,
self-absorbed, solitary, passive. But it turns out that each of these "unac-
torlike" characteristics of reading may, under certain circumstances,
characterize acting itself. Let us consider each in turn.

1. *The reader is immobilized.* So is the actor playing Beckett's Winnie
or Aeschylus' Prometheus. So is an actor working on such exercises as
this of Viola Spolin:

Have student-actors sit quietly concentrating on the profession each
has chosen—nothing more. If concentration is complete, what he
needs for the problem will arrive for his use.[46]

Or this of Stanislavski:

Let us do a little play. This is the plot. . . . The curtain goes up, and
you are sitting on the stage. You are alone. You sit and sit and
sit. . . . At last the curtain comes down again. That is the whole play.

Stanislavski's answer to the student who complained that this was "not
action" may also serve as a reply to those who raise the present objection
to a view of acting as reading:

The external immobility of a person sitting on the stage does not
imply passiveness. You may sit without a motion and at the same
time be in full action. Nor is that all. Frequently physical immobility is the direct result of inner intensity.[47]

Moreover, if we ask why readers tend to immobilize themselves
while reading, the explanation is such as to suggest a further tie with
acting. People stay still when they read because there seems to be an
"intimate connection between motor inhibition and regression into fantasy."[48] But actors also seek to regress into fantasy—and to do so by this
very means. For *motor inhibition* is only another term for relaxation of
muscles, the precondition for any fruitful work on an actor's part:

Muscular tautness interferes with inner emotional experience. As
long as you have this physical tenseness you cannot even think about
delicate shadings of feeling or the spiritual life of your part.[49]

No less for the performer than for the reader is motor inhibition conducive to a "regression into fantasy."

2. *The reader is silent.* He has not always been, as we shall see in
chapter 3. But grant that he is: So is a mime. So are actors doing an
Emotion Memory or mirror exercise. So is the actress playing Miss Y
in Strindberg's *The Stronger* throughout her role—or any actor playing
any role through large sections of it.

3. *The reader is self-absorbed.* But self-absorption is also a possible

state for the actor—arguably, the ideal state: "Forget about the public. Think about yourself. . . . If you are interested, the public will follow you."[50] One might argue that an actor's "self-absorption" is really only in the interest of subsequent public performance. But, of course, the solitary reader, too, may aim at eventual performance for others: Consider a student reading poems so as to impress his poetry professor or a lawyer reading precedents so as to sway a court. Conversely, there are acting practices that, not being meant to issue in public performance, may, like solitary reading, benefit only those who participate in them: the closed workshop investigation, for example, or the Brechtian *Lehrstück* ("teaching play").

4. *The reader is solitary*. Not necessarily. One can read to oneself in a library or a restaurant or a train. Of course, in such situations one is not especially concerned with, or even aware of, the other library patrons, diners, or passengers: Such reading is a form of "solitude in public." But this is Stanislavski's very term for the actor's ideal work state:

> It is what we call Solitude in Public. You are in public because we are all here. It is solitude because you are divided from us by the small circle of attention.[51]

Moreover, even when a reader is literally alone, he is only apparently so. We read a novel or poem as members of a "company of readers"[52] (the actual or intended audience for such texts) and as members of an "interpretive community"[53] (those whose reading strategies and assumptions we share). Clearly, the actor, too, reads as a member of an interpretive "community" or "company": the other actors working with him on the show. If an actor is a reader, another actor is *another* reader—a simple fact that, as we shall see in chapter 4, makes it possible to extend the "one-person" model of acting as reading to the work actors do with one another.

Now, while communities of readers sometimes actually convene (say, in a classroom or discussion group), companies of actors are far more likely to do so: They convene at every rehearsal. Still, the contrast in question is between the literal and merely implicit presence of other readers, not between solitude and society.

What further complicates the distinction between *reading alone* and *acting with others* is that much of the actor's work, too, goes forward in solitude. Character workups, "beat" and "through line" analysis, and,

of course, line memorization are all solitary labors—and, not coinciden-
tally, all labors of reading. "It's good to be here with you, my friends,"
muses a vacationing actress in Chekhov, "delightful listening to you,
but . . . sitting in my hotel room, all by myself, studying my
part . . . how much better."[54] To yearn to act is, among other things, to
yearn for a reader's solitude. Not only is the actor often solitary, he is
often a solitary reader.

But, even if we concede that, as is obviously the case, readers spend
a good deal more time alone with texts than actors do, there still remains
the question: How alone is one when one is "alone" with a text?

Not very, according to a long tradition that views the text as, in
some sense, "another." Everyone from Plato to the New Critics has
assured us that a text is "a sort of living organism,"[55] "formed out of
living matter . . . an organic web."[56] Texts, in other words, are bodies
("the text is . . . a verbal body . . . that can be sounded, weighed")[57] or,
at any rate, *have* bodies ("every discourse . . . like a living creature . . . has
a body of its own").[58] These textual bodies may possess *minds* ("the book
faces us like the body of another mind")[59] and even *souls* ("the whole of
the law seems . . . to resemble a living being, with the literal command-
ments for its body, and for its soul the invisible meaning stored away in
its words").[60] But to conceive the text as a body-mind or body-soul
amalgam is, in effect, to have conceived it as "a sort of human being"[61]—
indeed, as a *self,* for a text conceived in such terms *"acts* or *works* like a
self."[62] This, in turn, suggests that texts are capable of standing in all the
sorts of relations to their readers that one self may stand in to another—
for example, that of *friend:*

> [Books] are the one set of friends of whom, quite often, we take
> our leave with feelings of regret. And when we have left them we
> are oppressed with none of those thoughts that spoil friendship—
> what did they think of us?—didn't we behave rather tactlessly?—did
> they like us?—or with the fear that we may be forgotten by some-
> one. All such agitations expire on the threshold of the pure, un-
> ruffled friendship which is what reading really is.[63]

Or *therapist:*

> The prior text . . . becomes rather like a sympathetic psychothera-
> pist who helps us bring to consciousness repressed thoughts we had

never dared avow openly, and hence to recover energy previously wasted in repression.[64]

Or *lover:*

The text you write must prove to me *that it desires me.*[65]

Reading a good book is not much different from a love affair, from love, complete with shyness and odd assertions of power. . . . One can marry the book . . . add it to one's life, live with it.[66]

To the extent that texts are experienced as others, reading tends to be experienced as interpersonal encounter. One "doesn't speak *about* literature," says Julia Kristeva, one "speaks *to* literature."[67] And the literature speaks back: There arises a " 'dialogue' between text and reader," a "dyadic interaction."[68] In short, "the pleasure of the text is the pleasure of meeting another self."[69] And, one must add, the challenge of the text is the challenge of meeting another self. For the "dialogue" is also a confrontation ("even the most competent reader before a text is, finally, one self confronting another self")[70] and, like any confrontation, may issue in violence, in a "psychic warfare between . . . texts and readers."[71]

Any full explanation of *why* encounters with texts should seem like interaction with others must await the detailed account of the reading process to be given in chapters 3 and 4. What concerns us at present is the challenge that their seeming so poses to any straightforward conception of a solitary reading contrastable with acting. The figure of the reader may at first appear an obvious image of solitude, self-communion, even isolation. (We speak of being "lost" or "buried" in a book.) And yet, of course, the text is the work of another, tells of others, is even, as we have just been seeing, likely to be experienced as *itself* "another." The "solitude" of the solitary reader is therefore a problematic one, for reading is both a solitude and its interruption. The person with a book in his hand holds off a world he holds converse with, holds converse with a world he holds at bay.

To be "alone" with a text, in other words, is to be already *interacting with others.* The very phrasing of this statement suggests what might be the effect of taking it as a statement about the actor. The "(inter)acting with others" which seems to commence only when the actor's solitary reading is interrupted—i.e., when he comes to rehearsal—is "already in progress" in, is already the nature of, solitary reading itself. If, then, acting with others cannot ultimately be contrasted with reading in solitude, this is not merely because the actor is, at some moments, a solitary reader but also because solitary reading is, at all moments, interaction with "others"—others who (and it is on this score alone that the actor-reader's case is a special one) ultimately present themselves in the guise of literal other people: his fellow cast members, at the first rehearsal.[72] The communality of theater work is not the antithesis of solitary reading but, rather, the staging of it.

5. *The reader is passive.* Here, I think, we touch on the objection that underlies all the rest: a nagging sense that, after all, reading (especially reading silently to oneself) is a passive taking in; acting, a getting up and doing.

But, in fact, this is a simplification all around. Acting is not all active: It is also surrender (to the role, to directorial intent, to one's own impulses). And reading is not all intake: It is also structuring, comparing, decoding . . . in short, activity (chap. 2), even a kind of displaced or suppressed *physical* activity (chap. 3), whose suppression acting repeals (chap. 4). Indeed, even considered as a taking in, reading is not wholly passive: To take in is to receive, but it is also to consume, to incorporate, to *take* in. In fact, acting and reading are most alike on the score of this supposed "contrast." *Each* is a problematic mix of active and passive, of self-assertion and self-surrender.[73]

Granted that the actor is a reader—or, at least, not distinguishable from a reader on any of the "obvious" grounds just discussed—he is still bound to appear a rather limited one, reading as he does (1) only from a single point of view (his character's) and (2) only up to a certain point (the moment of his coming off book). But once again the implied distinctions between actors and other sorts of readers are not so clear-cut as they appear.

To distinguish the actor's from a more general reading on the grounds that actors do their reading from within role is to simplify the reading process of actors and readers both. General readers are notorious for identifying more with one character than others. Critics write essays on a particular character's experience or function in a work. While neither of these practices is equivalent to the actor's "taking on" of a role, they do suggest that a reader's sympathies are not necessarily any more uniformly distributed over a spectrum of characters than an actor's are. More important, the mere fact that actors read from within role does not sever their ties with general reading. On the contrary, as we shall see in chapter 4, the process of reading from within role—otherwise known as characterization—consists largely in an attempt to endow one's character with the inner life of the general reader one has had to leave off being in order to play him, an attempt that ultimately involves the actor in claiming a privileged "first-reader" status usually associated with a text's author but claimable by actors because, in dramatic texts, it resides not in some authorial function or consciousness but, rather, in (each) role. (The conflict between the mirroring claims of actor and author to be, each, the text's "first reader" is, as we shall see in chapter 7, basic to any understanding of the actor-playwright relation.)

That the actor, however much of a reader he may have been in rehearsal, eventually *stops* reading seems indisputable. Just when actors come off book may vary, but surely by the time of performance reading has been left behind—or, rather, if any reading is going on in performance, it is being done by the audience: They "read" the production. I dispute this line of argument on two grounds. First, I question whether what an audience does at a performance can in any useful sense be called "reading." And, second, I deny that an actor who *performs* thereby ceases to *read*. The two points are, we shall find, related.

We owe the conception of theatergoing as reading primarily to the semioticians, for whom a theatrical production is a "text," composed of "signs" and therefore requiring to be "read." For all my interest in establishing ties between theater and reading this is one connection I cannot muster much enthusiasm for. It seems to me at best no more than a trope for audience experience and in some ways, as I shall argue in chapter 6, a highly misleading one. Basically, though, I am unhappy with the view that audiences read performances less for what it says about audiences than for what it fails to say about performances, namely, that in them the actor *has not ceased to read.*

Performance and reading are not necessarily incompatible, or even distinguishable, activities. The performer of music, for example, is generally reading the score he performs in the moment of performing it. And perhaps it is for this reason that one commonly speaks of, say, the New York Philharmonic's "reading" of the Bruckner Eighth, meaning their performance of it. Furthermore, it is not at all unusual for an act of reading to be offered as, itself, a kind of performance. Writers' public readings of their works, for example, frequently tend, for reasons we shall consider in chapter 7, to take on a theatrical dimension ("The *reading* of the story," observed a member of Dickens's audience, "was altogether a truly artistic *performance*")[74] and to take place in theatrical venues.

In particular, the reading of actors is often offered as a performance. In the nineteenth century famous actors gave one-man or one-woman readings of entire plays; Mrs. Siddons, for example, performed *Othello* in this manner and Charles Kemble, *Cymbeline*. Such solo readings are currently out of fashion. But "book in hand" performance is more widespread than ever. We see it in such "stands and stools" productions as *The Hollow Crown* and *Don Juan in Hell*.[75] (To read from scripts on music stands is perhaps implicitly to claim for theater that simultaneity of the reading and performance moments generally conceded to music.) We see it in the many contemporary experimental pieces that foreground their own activity of reading.[76] And, of course, we see it in the innumerable public "readings," staged and unstaged, by which, increasingly, new scripts are tried out before audiences. It is customary to bemoan how little of the play can be "there" in a reading, what with actors who may barely have had time to peruse the text sitting around in chairs or, at best, awkwardly "walking through it," script in hand. But I have always been struck by how much more performance-like these occasions seem than they have any right to, how much of the life of a script they seem able to find and release. This surprising reversal of expectation, many times repeated (for, like most American playwrights, I have even more experience of staged and unstaged readings than I could wish), is certainly one of my starting points for the present inquiry. Having time and again witnessed the liberation of acting energies through these "mere" acts of reading, I began to wonder whether the acting and reading processes themselves might not be more intimately related than is commonly thought.

Of course, it is possible to argue that script-in-hand performances of any kind are the exception—that in the vast majority of cases a performing actor's book has "disappeared." Obviously, this is so, but one must still ask whether performance can always be distinguished from reading by the mere disappearance of the book. I would argue that it cannot, for three reasons.

1. *The book can "disappear" in reading as well as in performance.* Let my absorption in a text deepen beyond a certain point, and:

> where is the book I held in my hands? It is still there, and at the same time it is there no longer, it is nowhere. . . . That thing made

of paper . . . is no more, or at least it is as if it no longer existed, as long as I read the book. For the book is no longer a material reality. It has become a series of words, of images, of ideas which in their turn begin to exist. And where is this new existence? Surely not in the paper object. Nor, surely, in external space. There is only one place left for this new existence: my innermost self.[77]

In reading, as in acting, there is a moment when one comes off book.

2. *Insofar as the "disappearance" of the book in performance refers to its memorization by the actor, performance raises the same questions as does any act of memorized reading.* When I come out with a text I have learned by heart am I, in any sense, reading? It does not *feel* like reading; I have no sensation of scanning a page. Wittgenstein, however, calls attention to an instructive middle case:

> Try this experiment: say the numbers from 1 to 12. Now look at the dial of your watch and *read* them—What was it that you called "reading" in the latter case? That is to say: what did you do, to make it into *reading?*[78]

While an actor is not very often called upon to read a watch dial, he is quite often required to read, or simulate reading, some text that his character is supposed to be reading from at that moment. An example would be Hotspur reading aloud and commenting on the letter in act 2, scene 3 of *Henry IV,* part 1. In all likelihood the actor playing Hotspur will have memorized the letter; it is, after all, part of his role. But it is also likely that, either as an aide-mémoire or from naturalistic scruple, he will have the text of the letter written out on the prop parchment he carries—in which case, we are back with Wittgenstein and the watch dial. Is the actor who "reads off" the letter, which he has in fact memorized, still reading?

Now, of course, reading off the watch dial and reading off Hotspur's letter are each rather a special case. The point is that they are the *same* special case. The challenge memorization poses to a concept of acting as reading is the same difficulty it creates for any act of reading. If I am not, in fact, reading the memorized text that I am, to all appearances, reading off, "what would I have to do to make it into reading?" I do not know the answer to this question, but I know that the question is the same for reader and actor: Is it reading when memorized? Is it acting-as-reading when memorized by an actor?

3. *Insofar as the "disappearance" of the book in performance refers to acting's "going beyond" reading into physicality, performance represents a return to the (original) condition of reading itself.* As I will show, the physical dimension that acting seems to "add" to reading is in fact no addition but, rather, a restitution. Acting restores to reading—in fact, can virtually be *defined* as the return to reading of—a "lost" physical dimension that reading has had to forgo in order to *become* reading.

The reason why reading cannot be clearly distinguished from, or viewed as merely preliminary to, performance becomes apparent the moment one asks: What is performance the performance *of*? If we answer: "of roles, of plays," we skip over the greater part of the actor's work. What is the action of the Royal Shakespeare Company's production of the novel *Nicholas Nickleby*? Not, surely, "the action of *Nicholas Nickleby*" but, rather, "a theater company reads a novel." The RSC actors *perform their reading* of *Nicholas Nickleby*. This "special case" is in fact the general case. All theatrical performance is the performance of reading. His reading is what an actor performs.

It is from this perspective that I reject, not as "wrong" (how can a trope be wrong?) but as misleading, the semiotic description of performance as a reading *by* the audience *of* the stage action. If what the actor performs is his reading, then audiences are having reading performed *for* them *by* actors. While to attend theater may in some extended sense be "to read action," it is in a quite literal sense to be read *to*, to be present at or to the reading of another, to read in others' reading.

This has rather a paradoxical ring. Isn't theater supposed to offer the unmediated presence of imaginative events? (I have myself described it as doing so in *The Theatrical Event*.)[79] "Reading in others' reading," on the other hand, sounds farther from presence than ever: not simply a mediation but a *mediated* mediation.

Actually, as we shall see in chapters 6 and 7, this is not so much a paradox about theater as a paradox within reading, which theater, along with so much else about reading, takes for its own. Nothing feels more immediate to me than my solitary encounter with a text. And yet, if the structuralists and poststructuralists have taught us anything, it is that

we never really confront a text immediately, in all its freshness as a thing-in-itself. Rather, texts come before us as the always-already-read; we apprehend them through sedimented layers of previous interpretations, or—if the text is brand-new—through the sedimented reading habits and categories developed by those inherited interpretive traditions.[80]

All reading is in others' reading. What theater does is to bring this home to us by making the inevitable prior readers present in the person of the actors. But to be the prior reader through whom later ones read is to stand as an intermediary between the text and them, even if, as happens to be the case with the actor, one stands there in the flesh. Acting offers its audience the unmediated presence of mediators and the immediate experience of acts of mediation. The flesh-and-blood event with which theater presents us, and to which theater makes us present, is a flesh-and-blood act of reading.

The earliest known reference to private reading occurs in the opening scene of Aristophanes' *The Frogs*. There one of the characters relates how, as he sat alone perusing a book, he was suddenly seized by an impulse to set out in search of the book's author:

> DIONYSUS: So then I'm sitting on deck, see, reading this new
>   book:
> *Andromeda,* by Euripides: all of a sudden it hits me
> Over the heart, a craving, you can't think how hard
>
> . . . .
> A craving for Euripides.[81]

In chapter 5 we shall learn to take occurrences of reading in plays (including a couple of plays by Aristophanes) as images of the actor's reading-encounter with the script. And certainly the present passage invites interpretation along such lines. That the first mention ever of solitary reading should occur in a play already hints at a link between acting and the reading process. But further, the solitary reader who tells the tale is Dionysus, the god of theater and acting. What he has been reading is a script, Euripides' *Andromeda*. The subject of this script is release of a "lost" physical life (that of Andromeda, chained to her rock), and the effect on Dionysus of reading it is to send him off in search of the "buried" physical source of his reading experience (Euripides, recently dead and confined to Hades).[82]

I offer this moment in Aristophanes as an emblem, not an argument, but it is an emblem of the argument I wish to make. At the moment we first come upon the figure of the solitary reader it is already the figure of the actor, of Dionysus, we have come upon. Already the text he holds in his hands is a script. Already the promise of the script is of a "lost" life waiting to be restored, and already the actor has set forth on a quest after the "lost" bodily origins of his reading experience. This is also our journey, and it is time we set forth after him.

Chapter 2

The Reader as Actor

Why, however, begin with the literary critics? One would not go to Lee Strasberg or Uta Hagen for help with Keats's *Ode to a Nightingale*. Why turn, as I will do repeatedly in this chapter, to the likes of Roland Barthes, Stanley Fish, etc., for enlightenment on the actor's work? True, literary critics have said many good things about the reading process (although no one has said better things about reading than Wittgenstein and Proust). But why start with anyone's statements *about* reading? Theoretical speculation of any kind seems to lie at an immense distance from what I called at the end of the last chapter the "flesh-and-blood acts of reading" which actors perform. By what, however, if not its remoteness from the goal, may one expect to recognize a starting point? "At a distance from the physical" is where reading, consisting as it does in the *opening* of that distance, the *loss* of that physical, always finds itself—and therefore where acting, which seeks to *close* the distance and *recover* the loss, always initially finds itself. To start "far from the physical" is to start where acting starts.

As for starting with the speculations of literary critics, it is not as if writers of this sort aspired to enlighten us about acting. In fact, most of the critics I shall discuss show no particular interest in dramatic literature or theory. What concerns—indeed, obsesses—these authors is the reading process. Yet, time and again, *setting out to construct the figure of the reader, it is the figure of the actor which they produce.* How is it that the description literary critics offer of the reading that absorbs them makes it sound like nothing so much as the acting of which they never think? Such inability on the part of a critic to stop linking acting and reading seems to me better evidence of their relatedness than any conscious attempt to relate them could provide. It is for this reason that I begin my account of acting as reading with a discussion of writers who think of nothing less than to give an account of acting.

It sometimes seems as if, over the past forty years or so, the study of literature has been redefined as the study of reading.[1] This is the declared position of the so-called reader-response critics (Stanley Fish, Wolfgang Iser), for whom a text only comes into being in and through an act of reading. But it is an emphasis no less evident in the work of the phenomenological critics (Georges Poulet, Jean-Pierre Richard), for whom the critical act has become narration of the adventures of a reading consciousness; or in the "influence criticism" of Harold Bloom, with its central concept of "strong misreading"; or in the resurgence of interest in hermeneutics (Hans-Georg Gadamer, Paul Ricoeur), which offers itself as a sort of metalogic of reading. Within psychoanalytic criticism the ascendancy of Jacques Lacan, for whom "the unconscious is not only *that which must be read,* but also, and primarily, *that which reads,*"[2] has focused new attention on the reading process; while in the work of Norman Holland, emphasis has visibly shifted from study of the author's fantasy material, as reflected in the text, to study of the reader's fantasy processes, as reflected in his reading activity. The structuralists are much concerned with the nature of the process—variously known as "decoding," "naturalization," or "actualization of virtual semantic properties"[3]—by which readers "recuperate" sense from signs. Deconstruction, with its insistence on "the necessary *unreadability* of the text,"[4] might at first seem to be an exception to the trend. But an "unreadable" text turns out to be not one that cannot be read but, rather, one that "produces . . . readings that are incompatible."[5] The central question for deconstruction thus emerges as "How can we read the unreadable?"[6]— emerges, that is to say, as a question about reading.

All this is supposed to be by way of a break with the New Criticism of the 1940s and 1950s, which is remembered as having exalted the literary text as a self-sufficient object, prior to, and independent of, any reader's encounter with it. But, in practice, the New Critics were forever appealing to the "experience of reading" and, indeed, characterized their method as "close reading," or *"reading in slow motion."* It is amusing to watch this last New Critical catchphrase be successively reinvented, as descriptive of *their* respective approaches, by the reader-response critics:[7]

> Essentially what the method does is *slow down* the reading experience. . . . It is as if a slow-motion camera with an automatic stop action effect were recording our linguistic experiences.[8]

And by the structuralists:

> The *step-by-step* method . . . is never anything but . . . a *slow motion,* so to speak, neither wholly image nor wholly analysis.[9]

The history of this term is, in little, the history of modern criticism's recurring rediscovery of reading as, if not its actual subject matter, certainly its central theme.

Now, if discussions of reading are ubiquitous in contemporary criticism, suggestions of a link between reading and acting are ubiquitous in these discussions. The clearest evidence of this is the pervasive use of acting, by critic after critic, as a metaphor for the act of reading:

> Literature of the first order calls for lively reading; we must almost act it out as if we were taking parts in a play.[10] (Reuben Brower)

> But Sterne not only proposes an identity, or several identities, for the reader, he asks the reader to impersonate them. He gives him a part to play and lines to speak. . . . And in this way he very effectively symbolizes the reader's essential relationship to what he reads: he is in effect defining the reader as a kind of actor.[11] (John Preston)

> The reader—every reader [of Hemingway] is being cast in the role of a close companion of the writer.[12] (Walter J. Ong)

> The *actors,* or the agents of this textual action, are indeed the readers and the critics no less than the characters. Criticism . . . here consists not of a statement, but a performance. . . . Reading here becomes not the cognitive observation of the text's pluralistic meaning, but its "acting out."[13] (Shoshana Felman)

In some cases, as in the passages by Felman and Preston (from whom I have borrowed the title of this chapter), the acting-reading comparison is consciously elaborated. More often, though, as in the Ong and Brower excerpts, it seems to reflect an instinctive awareness of affinity between the two activities, the more noteworthy for being at most half-conscious.

But theatrical metaphors are, for reasons that I suspect do not reflect very favorably on theater, endemic to our cultural discourse. What is more striking is how often in contemporary critical accounts of reading,

even where there is no reference to (and, one presumes, no thought of)
theater, *it sounds like acting that is being described*. For example:

> Reading . . . is the very practice in which we can be assured that
> other minds and feelings can inhabit us as surely as any thought or
> emotion of our own. In reading, I can be here and elsewhere, myself
> and another.[14]

> Thoughts which are part of a book I am reading . . . are the thoughts
> of another, and yet it is I who am their subject. . . . I am thinking
> the thoughts of another. Of course, there would be no cause for
> astonishment if I were thinking it as the thought of another. But I
> think it as my very own. . . . Because of the strange invasion of my
> person by the thoughts of another, I am a self who is granted the
> experience of thinking thoughts foreign to him. I am the subject of
> thoughts other than my own. My consciousness behaves as though
> it were the consciousness of another.[15]

> It is in the reader that the text comes to life, and this is true even
> when the "meaning" has become so historical that it is no longer
> relevant to us. In reading we are able to experience things that no
> longer exist and to understand things that are totally unfamiliar to
> us.[16]

> We read to usurp. . . . Usurp what? A place, a stance, a fullness, an
> illusion of identification or possession; something we can call our
> own or even ourselves.[17]

None of these passages is from a work of dramatic criticism or by an
author especially interested in theater. The first is taken from a book
about Montaigne; the second and third, from theoretical studies of reading; the last from an essay on "revisionism and critical personality."
Yet, in each case, if *actor* and *script* are substituted for *reader* and *book,* the
result is a series of instructive, even illuminating, comments on acting.

Any critic who thus formulates perceptions about reading in imagery either drawn from, or evocative of, the acting process implicitly
refers reading to acting, as if to its prototype. "Only have understood
acting," such formulations seem to promise, "and you will find you
understand reading as well." But this is an extraordinary promise; what

can possibly be the grounds for it? On what basis is such a by no means obvious equivalence being affirmed? Two assumptions seem to me to be in play here: first, that reading and acting are both forms of activity; and second, that the particular activity that reading most resembles is an actor's "realization" of a script. Let us look at each of these in turn.

The critics' specific equation of reading to acting rests upon a more general conception of reading as *active,* as *action,* as *activity.* "I have to do my reading," says the student; is reading, then, something that we *do?*[18]

> He read . . . as if he were guiding something, or wheedling a large flock of sheep, or pushing his way up and up a single narrow path; and sometimes he went fast and straight, and broke his way through the bramble, and sometimes it seemed a branch struck at him . . . ; but he was not going to let himself be beaten by that; on he went. . . .[19]

The driven Mr. Ramsay of *To the Lighthouse* is scarcely a typical reader. Yet the impression that reading gives in him of being an intensely active occupation is confirmed by the researches of cognitive psychologists (who find in it a whole series of interrelated active processes: searching, scanning, comparing, selecting, grouping, etc.) and by the statements of literary critics of every stripe. "Reading is . . . activity,"[20] and not necessarily of an especially innocent or virtuous sort:

> Reading . . . is not less aggressive than sexual desire, or than social ambition, or professional drive.[21]

The reader "confronts," "moves into,"[22] in a word, "is a participant in,"[23] the action of the text—possibly even its hero:

> There is still another hero to be noted in the universe of *Paradise Lost*—the reader.[24]

> Eventually it dawns on us that it is *the reader* [of *Finnegan's Wake*] who achieves the quest.[25]

> When these marks [on the page] become words . . . or characters or events, they do so because the reader plays the part of a prince to the sleeping beauty.[26]

If this sounds glamorous, it is first of all hard work:

> Reading is not a parasitical act. . . . It is a form of work. . . . To read,
> in fact, is a labor of language.

For the active reader is "no longer a consumer, but a producer of the
text."[27] He *constructs*,[28] *builds his own structures*,[29] *composes from supplied
elements*—even *achieves the work for himself.*[30] No wonder critics are
more interested in the reader than they used to be: He is where the action
is.

As the variety of terms in the preceding paragraph suggests, opin-
ions as to exactly *what* activity reading is vary from critical school to
critical school. Structuralist readers "decode" messages. Bloomian
strong readers "contest" with predecessors. Phenomenological readers
"deliver [works] from their . . . immobility . . . release[] the book from
its speechlessness."[31] Readers of the (misnamed!) reader-response school
"concretize" the text's potential.[32] Deconstructive readers "traverse the
text without finalizing a . . . construction."[33]

Now there is not one of these descriptions of reading activity which
does not also describe some aspect of the actor's work. The actor, too,
"contests," "concretizes," "decodes," "delivers from immobility [and]
speechlessness," "traverses . . . without finalizing." Indeed, one might
go farther and see specific styles of acting as each carrying into action a
particular critical model of the reading process. For example, the structuralist reader, with his view of the work as a self-abiding system of
relations awaiting decipherment, would correspond to the "British," or
"technical," actor ("it's all in the text"). The reader of the phenomenolo-
gists, who seeks to "summon back [the work] by placing my own consciousness at its disposal,"[34] suggests the Stanislavski actor. While the
deconstructive reader, compelled "to move, to shift systems whose perspective ends neither at the text nor at the 'I,' "[35] recalls the actor-stage-
hand of performance art: a pusher-around of isolated signs that can neither be taken *in* (as text) nor taken *on* (as role) and to which the only
possible relation is therefore that of external manipulator. "Because his
job is to put things on stage, he is onstage himself," might be a verdict
on the status of the actor in certain experimental theater pieces. It is,
however, a statement of Derrida's on the status of the reader vis-à-vis
certain experimental texts.[36]

Active reading, then, can be likened to any number of different activities, each in turn comparable to some different style or aspect of acting. Is there, beyond this diversity, some one underlying similarity between active reading and acting which would account for the former's being so persistently written about in terms of the latter? I believe that there is and that it can be stated as follows: *Readers are like actors because what an actor does to a script is what any reader must do to any text—"realize" it, "actualize" it, make it happen as an event.* In passage after passage the critics we are concerned with hint at an equivalence between reading and acting on just this basis:

> The role of the text is to "designate *instructions* for the *production* of the signified." . . . The relation is one of script to performer.[37]

> For me, reading (and comprehension in general) is an event . . . , the actualization of meaning.[38]

> The strong reader and the strong poet know only . . . a reading which is a relational event.[39]

> The reader . . . activates the text in the present moment.[40]

Plays, it is customary to say, are texts that "are only realized in performance." But if, as reader-oriented critics contend, *all* texts are only realized in the performance of them by active readers, then acting becomes the inevitable metaphor for reading as such.

The view that it is readers who "produce" or "actualize" texts has led some reader-response and deconstructive critics to see a text's reader as, in some sense, its "author":

> The distinction between author and reader is one of the false distinctions that the reading [of Proust] makes evident.[41]

> The reader writes the text.[42]

> I write my reading.[43]

Certainly, if what readers do is *compose from elements, build structures,* etc., then it is possible to claim not only, in Emerson's famous phrase, that "there is creative reading as well as creative writing,"[44] but even that

"*each* act of reading . . . makes something new."[45] Some have found the
attribution of creativity to mere readers unwarranted. What is unwarranted, however, is not the claim that reading is creative but, rather, the
assumption, especially common among reader-response and deconstructive critics, that the form of creativity involved must be that of a *writer*.[46]

For in what does this process of "concretization" or "realization"
actually consist? The reader-oriented critics tend to conceive texts as
sequences of "indeterminate areas"[47]—"gaps" or "blanks"[48]—which at
most hint at the lines along which they might be filled in and joined but
leave the actual filling and joining to the reader. Thus challenged by the
text to provide "connectability [of segments]"—or, as the gestalt psychologists call it, "good continuation"—the reader is stirred into performing "acts of consistency-building."[49] These are the acts in which his
activity as a reader, and hence his status as an active reader, consist.

> To end, to fill, to join, to unify—one might say that this is the basic
> requirement of the *readerly,* as though it were prey to some obses-
> sive fear: that of omitting a connection.[50]

Such a process of filling in preexistent blanks does not sound much like
writing—which, one might say, is more a matter of laying out the
blanks. What it does sound like is a certain kind of *acting*.[51]

> [The playwright] often says nothing at all about what has happened
> to his characters while they have been in the wings, and what makes
> them act as they do when they return to the stage. We have to fill
> out what he leaves unsaid. Otherwise we would have only scraps
> and bits to offer out of the life of the persons we portray. You
> cannot live that way so we must create for our parts comparatively
> unbroken lines.[52]

In Stanislavski's "obsessive fear . . . of omitting a connection" (otherwise
known as the search for a "through line of action"), we recognize a
process akin to the active reader's quest for "connectability of segments." And in the active reader's confidence that he can "supply what
is meant from what is not said,"[53] we catch an echo of the Stanislavski
actor's faith in a "subtext that makes us say the words we do in a play."[54]
So near does active reading draw to acting in this regard that one might

be hard put to say which of the following passages is literary criticism
and which is acting theory:

> A: *I am out of petrol.*
> B: *There is a garage round the corner.*
> (Story: A needs petrol and B wants to help him. B knows that A
> knows that usually garages sell petrol, knows that there is a garage
> round the corner, and knows (or hopes) that this garage is open and
> has petrol to sell. So he informs A about the location of the garage.
> Will or will not A follow successfully the suggestion of B?)[55]

> We bring to life what is hidden under the words; we put our own
> thoughts into the author's lines, and we establish our own relation-
> ships to . . . characters . . . ; we filter through ourselves all the mate-
> rials that we receive from the author.[56]

(In fact, the first passage is from a structuralist study of reading; the
second is from *An Actor Prepares*.)

In a word, any time we hear a contemporary critic proclaim something along the lines of *"in the text, only the reader speaks,"*[57] we are
certainly right to feel that the reader has received a promotion—but not
a promotion to author. There is, indeed, a text in which "only the reader
speaks": the performed script. Not like the writer but "like the actor [the
reader] has to help the . . . work into existence."[58] If the "active reader"
of contemporary literary criticism seems always to be coming before us
tricked out in the rhetoric of acting, this is because it is in the work of
the actor that active reading itself finds a prototype.[59]

A prototype, however, which the active reader would appear to
realize only up to a certain point. The actor does not merely "fill in the
blanks" of the text with imagined connections; he fills in the blank of the
role with himself. The actor does not merely "make the text actual" in
the "event" of reading; he makes of the text an actual event. The active
reader, by contrast, is active *only* as a reader; "active," in his case, means
no more than active-*minded*. For even the most active reading stops short
of the body. Or so it may appear.

In fact, I am going to argue that at the heart of reading lies an
activity no less physical than acting itself, and that it is of this "lost"
physical dimension that the literary-critical ideal of the active reader
preserves a reminiscence.

What evidence is there for any such "lost" physical dimension of reading? What is it? How was it lost? These are questions to which I shall turn in the next chapter.

They are not just questions about reading. For it is precisely as reinstatement of this "lost" physicality of reading that the physicality of acting proposes itself. Acting is not a new venture for reading but, rather, the process by which reading relearns its origins in the body. The active reader of the literary critics is not a dream of what never was; it is a dream of restoration.

Chapter 3

The "Lost" Physical of Reading

The clearest evidence that some physical dimension has been "lost" from reading is that it has not been wholly lost.

Probably most people can recall moments when a book they were reading seemed to be having a physical effect on them: changing the rate at which their breath came or their pulse beat, putting them strangely at one, or strangely at odds, with the surrounding scene. In all likelihood such physical "side effects" of reading are more frequent and more varied than we realize. You have only to leaf through André Kertész's photographic studies of all sorts of people reading under all sorts of conditions[1]—indeed, you have only to look around you in the subway or the library to see how many different ways the body has of disposing itself to meet a text and of receiving a text's impact.

No doubt the degree of physical susceptibility to texts varies from reader to reader, and no doubt actors are among the more susceptible:

> They are carried away by the reading. They cannot control the muscles of their faces, which oblige them to grimace or mime in accordance with what is being read. They cannot control their movements, which occur spontaneously.[2]

It is true that, as we shall see in the next chapter, actors are to an unusual degree "whole-body readers," but they could not be so unless it were possible to "read with the body" in the first place. Certainly, it is not *only* actors who have testified to the possibility of such reading:

> One reads poetry with one's nerves.[3] (Wallace Stevens)

If I read a book and it makes my whole body so cold no fire can ever warm me, I know it is poetry. If I feel physically as if the top of my head were taken off, I know this is poetry.[4] (Emily Dickinson)

The sentences [of Fontenelle, Aristophanes, and Rabelais] would resist me the way objects resist.[5] (Jean-Paul Sartre)

I read sentences of Goethe as though my whole body were running down the stresses.[6] (Franz Kafka)

Of course, all these statements were made by writers—i.e., by people who, to an even greater extent than actors, live and breathe language—and one may, therefore, question how general a tendency they evince. Where is the warrant for so broad a claim as Stanley Burnshaw's?

In the reading of a poem, the motions and attitudes of the muscles in all the bodily structures—not only those of the face...but equally those hidden from view—"translate" into physical motion the psychological impressions and ideas and feelings evoked in the reader.[7]

If there is any such extensive involvement of the body in reading, it does, indeed, remain "hidden from view":

On the outside...the reader has rotated his eyes a few millimeters and [if reading aloud] he has begun to move his mouth. But on the inside, there has been a rapid succession of intricate events.[8]

Are there, among these presumably cognitive "events," any physical ones?

Well, there are those rotating eyeballs. Let us begin by looking at them—since, after all, they are there to be looked at. However much else of the "lost" physical of reading may have vanished within, the reading eye is still visibly in motion. Moreover, the motion is such as to suggest that, in it, a quite specific aspect of the reading process is finding physical expression.

Instrument-assisted study of the eye movements of readers has revealed that reading is not the steady linear "scan" one might suppose it but, rather, proceeds in a stop-and-start, forward-and-back rhythm built up out of three distinct elements: *"saccades,"* or "leaps ahead" to the next segment of text, during which little or no information is acquired;[9] brief *fixations* on particular chunks of text, during which most of the actual intake occurs; and periodic *regressions* back over already examined portions of text, which serve to verify predictions and build up context.[10]

Now, while all visual activity involves eye movements of some sort, the particular sequence *saccade-fixation-regression* is unique to reading. This suggests that such a movement pattern physically carries out some aspect of the reading process, a conjecture confirmed by the correlation that seems to exist between an individual's eye movements and his reading skills. (The better the reader, the longer his saccades, the fewer his fixations and regressions.)[11] But to what aspect of reading does a pattern of *approach, register,* and *pull back* movements give expression?

Georges Poulet suggests an answer to this question when he compares the hermeneutic circle to a "dance" in which the interpreter alternately approaches and withdraws from the text.[12] *Approach-register-pull back* is the rhythm of interpretation. The characteristic eye movements of reading perform the hermeneutic circle as a physical circling. In the dancing eyes of the proficient reader Poulet's dance of interpretation is visibly in progress.[13]

Another kind of evidence for bodily involvement in reading is the involvement of voice. Though to us "reading" means primarily silent reading, it is only in the last few centuries that reading has become a silent occupation, and physiological tests reveal traces of covert muscular activity in the vocal apparatus even of silent readers. The "lost" physical of reading is not simply a lost voice. But loss of voice is certainly one of its more obvious symptoms.[14] And, therefore, it seems worth considering the evidence that reading has only recently fallen silent—and never altogether silent, at that.

It is not true, as used to be thought, that all reading prior to the late Middle Ages was reading aloud; considerable evidence for silent reading in antiquity has recently come to light.[15] Still, as even the chief collector of these counterexamples acknowledges, for ancient readers "the normal way to read a literary text . . . was out loud."[16] The most striking evidence for this remains the passage in the *Confessions* where St. Augustine notes with wonder how, when his teacher St. Ambrose read, "his eyes went over the pages and his heart looked into the sense, but voice and tongue were resting."[17] To us, it is Augustine's comment, not Ambrose's behavior, that evokes wonder; silence on the part of a solitary reader is nothing more nor less than we would expect. Yet, so odd does Augustine find the practice that he feels compelled to suggest three or four different possible reasons for it: Perhaps Ambrose is maximizing his study time? signaling a wish for privacy? conserving his voice? Apparently, in the ancient world the spectacle of a man "reading always to himself and never otherwise" was unusual enough to warrant, and mysterious enough to defy, explanation.[18]

Augustine was writing in the late fourth century A.D. But we have evidence for the normality of solitary reading aloud that reaches back at least as far as the New Testament era (c. A.D. 100). In chapter 8 of the Acts of the Apostles Philip comes upon a eunuch of Ethiopia sitting *alone* reading in his chariot (vv. 27–28) and *hears* the man reading from the Book of Isaiah (v. 30): This solitary reader is clearly reading aloud.

And so solitary readers continued to read all through the medieval period, "not as today, principally with the eyes, but with the lips, pronouncing what they saw, and with the ears, listening to the words pronounced, hearing what is called the 'voices of the pages' [*voces paginarum*]."[19] St. Benedict (sixth century A.D.) urges the monk who desires to read during rest hours to "read to himself in such a way as not to disturb anyone else"[20]—an injunction that only makes sense on the assumption that "reading to oneself" meant reading aloud, possibly in a whisper or murmur. And in various medieval languages words meaning "read" were consistently used in ways that imply that the reading in question was out loud. To cite a Middle English example:

> For when I of their loving read,
> *Mine ear* with the tale I feed.[21]

Contemporary usage also retains traces of this earlier state of affairs. Consider the French idiom *entendre l'allemand*, "to understand German." Although the verb *entendre* means literally "to hear," the expression as a whole may denote comprehension of either spoken or *written* German and thus betrays its origins in a culture where to understand-by-reading was also a matter of hearing.[22] Similarly, the contemporary English idiom "to *audit* accounts" now describes a silent scrutiny but clearly "points to a time when 'auditing' was as much a matter of ears as of eyes."[23]

Why should readers have clung so tenaciously to a practice that, one feels, can only have slowed and wearied them? H. J. Chaytor claims that it was a matter of shaky skills: "The medieval reader . . . was in the stage of our muttering childhood learner; each word was for him a separate entity and at times a problem, which he whispered to himself when he had found the solution."[24] But it is a little difficult to imagine Dante or St. Bonaventure with a learning disability. More probable, and more germane to the argument I am making in this chapter, is the suggestion of Jean Leclercq that, to the ancient and medieval mind, reading is a form of meditation *(meditatio)* and that "to meditate is to read a text . . . with one's whole being"—with the memory and understanding and will, to be sure, but also "with the body, since the mouth pronounced it."[25] This seems to me to get the emphasis right. "Reading aloud" is not the main, or even a separate, issue. The role accorded bodily voice in the reading process is, as we shall presently see, only a reflection of the role accorded the body as such in it.

When, in the later Middle Ages, reading finally began to fall silent, the body did not give up its prerogatives without a fight. A would-be silent reader of the transitional period complains:

> Oftentimes when I am reading straight from the book and in thought only, as I am wont, they [devils] make me read aloud word by word, that they may deprive me so much the more of the inward understanding thereof . . . the more I pour myself out in exterior speech.[26]

Thus, reading protests against the suppression of its physicality: With diabolical persistence the "lost" voice clamors to be heard.

And, indeed, all these centuries later, with silent reading long since established as the norm, the clamor continues, though now often only detectable by instruments in the form of electromuscular activity in the vocal apparatus.

With poor and beginning readers an audible undercurrent of involuntary whispering or muttering seems to dog every attempt at silent reading. This reading under the breath, or *subvocalizing,* as psychologists call it, is not to be confused with intentional reading aloud: For one thing, in subvocalization words may be skipped or slurred or have only their first letter or two pronounced.[27]

Clearly, subvocalizing retards and fragments reading. And, while it may be a necessary stage in learning to read, anyone who persists in it seems destined to remain on the level of the child reader or the medieval reader, whose out-loud, word-at-a-time realization of the text subvocalization recalls. It therefore comes as something of a surprise to learn that *all* readers, to some extent, subvocalize—that there is *no such thing as absolutely silent reading.* "The reader normally does not want to make sounds, but at some level he does." Though the volume may vary "from audible sounds (e.g., whispering) to movements of the speech musculature which must be highly amplified to be detected," in all likelihood "every reader is producing some surrogate for sound detectable by microphones [in the form of] amplified electropotentials of the speech musculature."[28] That is, if electrodes are attached to the skin directly overlying a reader's vocal organs, leaps in electrical activity, indicative of some degree of "speech" activity on his part, will be found to occur even during silent reading. Thus, if one reads silently a word that, read aloud, would require unusually vigorous lip movements (e.g., *bomber* or *waffle*), an electrode on the lips records a jump in electrical activity *just as if the word had been read aloud.*[29] What is more, electrical activity in the speech musculature increases proportionately with the conceptual difficulty of the material read.[30] Intellectual comprehension seems the very type of a "purely mental" activity, yet, apparently, laboring to understand a text is also, in some degree, physical labor.

Those not inclined to trust the word of experimental psychologists in such matters may be reassured to find the existence of an inner voice of reading confirmed by Proust, who in his splendid essay "On Reading" recalls how, as a child, he would always find it necessary, upon reaching the end of a book, to "check my voice which had been soundlessly following the words." Proust further implies, however, that the soundlessness of this inner voice is at any moment reversible. Only let there occur an officious interruption,

> and, merely in order to say, "No, thank you very much," I had to stop what I was at, and *summon from afar* my voice which, silently and to myself, was forming the words spread out before my eyes. I had to stop and *make it audible,* if only to say, "No, thank you very much," had to make it seem alive, to give it that intonation of response which it had lost.[31]

Proust's emphasis on what an unpleasant experience this was should not obscure the fact that it was, nonetheless, a possible one. The inner voice *can* be "summoned from afar" and "made audible" again. The "lost" physical of reading is, it seems, retrievable—at least insofar as it is a question of lost physical *voice*.

Let me repeat, however, that the silence of reading is only the most evident sign of a more fundamental curtailment of its physicality. Back when it was still reading aloud (in antiquity and the Middle Ages), reading was considered "an activity which . . . requires the participation of the whole body." Ancient physicians "used to recommend reading to their patients as a physical exercise on an equal level with walking, running or ball-playing"[32]—a recommendation that might not have surprised Montaigne, who likened reading to tennis ("the historians come right to my backhand"),[33] or Thoreau, who believed that "to read well . . . requires a training such as the athletes underwent,"[34] and which perhaps finds a distant echo in the publicity for a present-day book club which claims to provide "aerobics for the mind."

Montaigne and the Literary Guild are speaking figuratively—it is only our minds we must "stretch" if we do not wish to "miss points"— but in earlier periods it seems clear that reading was experienced as making distinct physical demands. "When Peter the Venerable was suffering from catarrh, not only was he no longer able to speak in public, but he could no longer perform his *lectio* [private religious reading]. And Nicholas of Clairvaux noticed that, after being bled, he lacked the strength to read." To us, who bring our friends books and magazines in the hospital, this seems odd. But reading, as the Middle Ages understood it—i.e., as *meditatio*—entailed vigorous physical involvement. For while "meditation" has since acquired quietistic overtones, the Latin verb *meditari* means "to practice" and was as readily applied to military or athletic exercise as to a kind of reading which aimed to "inscribe . . . the sacred text in the body."[35]

The physicality of reading, conceived in such terms, obviously goes far beyond its being physically voiced. And loss of voice, while a telling symptom, is by no means the full extent of the loss. What else, then, has "dropped out"? What is the "lost" physical of reading?

If we turn for guidance to the literary critics who were our guides in the last chapter, we find ourselves overwhelmed with suggestions. Harold Bloom has defined critics as "people in search of images for acts of reading."[36] It is not surprising that the imagery favored by these partisans of the active reader is, almost without exception, an imagery of physical activity—for example, *motion through space*. The reader is

imagined as moving out of himself[37]—this may initially entail some
"movement within oneself"—into a text that lies before him as a
"world" or "territory," which he must "journey into and explore."[38]
The journey may be a voyage of discovery on the scale of Da Gama's
or Magellan's,[39] or the reader may just decide to "explore down . . . side
roads."[40] The manner of his advance may be choreographed ("The
reader must execute a *lateral dance of interpretation*")[41] or casual ("The
Model Reader is allowed to take inferential walks");[42] may reflect the
utmost skill ("the acrobatics in which [the text] involves him")[43] or the
utmost randomness ("we read . . . the way a fly buzzes around a room:
with sudden, deceptively decisive turns, fervent and futile").[44] As this
last example suggests, a view of reading as motion does not necessarily
imply that the reader is getting anywhere. He may turn out to be traveling in the wrong direction ("to read . . . is . . . to retreat from name to
name").[45] He may go into "a kind of metonymic skid."[46] Indeed, he may
not even make it out the door: "The reader . . . will pass through doors
only to find himself in the room he has just left."[47]

Another form of physical activity to which "active reader" critics
tend to liken reading is physical contact between people.[48] Readers are
described as having sex with texts ("the deconstructive reader is an amo-
rous desiring body, seeking pleasure and bliss in an excess of polymor-
phous play");[49] as giving them medical treatment (the reader is "a kind
of physician, a body probing another body");[50] or as locked in combat
with them, a "hand-to-hand struggle in which the reading mind engages
the living, feeling, resisting [text]."[51]

When the active reader is not physically interacting *with* the text-as-
other, he is likely to be physically acting *upon* the text-as-object, whether
in the manner of a natural force:

> Reading transforms a book the same way the sea and the wind
> transform the works of men.

or an artist:

> Reading endows the book with the kind of sudden existence that the
> statue "seems" to take from the chisel alone.[52]

or a mere manipulator:

> To read . . . is to fold the text according to one name and then to unfold it along the new folds of this name.[53]

The reader "sculpts." And "folds." And "walks" and "skids" and "fights" and "journeys" and "dances." What an immense nostalgia for the physical is revealed in this blizzard of proposed critical analogies. Might some one or another of them by any chance *be* the "lost" physical of reading? And, if so, how would we know when we had it? All are suggestive, none definitive. There are, perhaps, moments when reading feels like each of them. But none seems clearly to have it over all the rest. And, in any case, we do not seek a "best physical analogy" but, rather, an actual physical basis, which, presumably, all the analogies are just so many attempts to name.

I think we would do well to seek it in the reading theory of Norman Holland, as presented in his 1968 study, *The Dynamics of Literary Response*. Though sometimes classified as a reader-response critic—I have myself cited him among the "active reader" critics in chapter 2—Holland can be distinguished from Stanley Fish or Wolfgang Iser by the distinctly psychoanalytic approach he takes to reading activity. This psychoanalytic bent inclines Holland to see mental processes as the survival, the "displacement upward," of what were once bodily processes. He is thus encouraged to seek a "lost" physical basis for the mental process of reading, and the solution he comes up with is, if not the "right" one in any absolute sense, certainly the right one for our purposes. For what Holland supplies is not only the "lost" physical itself but also an explanation of why it should ever have been lost—and a hint as to how acting might prove the means of its recovery.

Like other psychoanalytic critics, Holland assumes that an author's repressed fantasy material finds expression in the texts he produces but that there must first occur "a transformation of the fantasy at the core of [the] literary work into terms satisfactory to an adult ego." (Holland gives as an example Chaucer's *Wife of Bath's Tale,* in which boyhood fears of castration at the hands of an offended mother have been transformed into a high-toned parable of the wisdom of submission to feminine values.)[54]

How can texts defend against awareness of the very impulses that lead to their composition? By means, Holland argues, of their *form.* Form can fulfill this defensive function because, Holland claims, formal devices are "analogous to the defenses one would find in a man's

mind"[55]—that is, to the so-called mechanisms of defense enumerated
by Anna Freud (reversal, reaction-formation, projection, etc.), by which
the ego protects itself against awareness it does not wish to acknowledge.[56] Thus,

> Irony [in a text] looks like [the defense mechanism of] reversal or
> reaction-formation; omission looks like repression or denial; im-
> probable causality . . . resembles projection; pointing a moral seems
> like rationalization, and so on.

Very roughly, then, "form in a literary work corresponds to defenses;
content, to fantasy or impulse." This means that the work as a whole,
conceived as some sort of balance between form and content, both "em-
bodies and evokes . . . a central fantasy" and "manages and controls that
fantasy."[57]

Holland's originality—and his usefulness for our purposes—lies in
his now going on to ask what all this means *for the reader*. Readers, too,
after all, have fantasies that they would both gratify and conceal from
themselves. And, if readers are attracted to a text, must not this be,
Holland asks, because they see in the text's balance of control and
gratification a solution that they might appropriate for themselves?

> The literary work manages . . . fantasy in two broad ways: by shap-
> ing it with formal devices which operate roughly like defenses; by
> transforming the fantasy toward ego-acceptable meanings—some-
> thing like sublimation. The pleasure we experience is the feeling of
> having a fantasy of our own and our own associations to it managed
> and controlled but at the same time allowed a limited expression and
> gratification.[58]

But how is such an appropriation of a text's balancing act possible?
The text and I may share the same fantasies, and, given the equivalence
between (my) defense mechanisms and (its) formal devices, we may be
said to share the same techniques for managing those fantasies. Nevertheless, it is always "the text and I." Even a text conceived, as we saw
in chapter 1 a text *may* be conceived, along the lines of another person
is still *another* person. How can its solutions be mine, any more than
your solutions can be mine? In order to "feel the ordering and structuring
powers of literature . . . as though they were our own," one would have

to be functioning in a mode where there was no more "other" or "own" but, rather,

> the mental process embodied in the literary work somehow becomes a process inside its audience. What is "out there" in the literary work feels as though it is "in here," in your mind or mine.[59]

Now, of course, we all *have* known a time "when self and object [were] still not clearly differentiated," when it was still possible to "experience a total unity of self and nurturing environment."[60] As the word *nurturing* suggests, this was the time of the "oral phase," the infant at the breast. And, Holland argues, it is precisely this era of boundless oral receptivity that reading reinstates: "The literary work . . . finds in us a matrix reaching back through many, many experiences of gratification in fantasy to our earliest experience of passive satisfaction." In part, this is an effect of its subject matter: "Of all the different levels of fantasy in literature, the oral is the most common. . . . No matter what other issues from later stages appear in a literary work, one almost always finds at the core some fantasy of oral fusion and merger."[61] But, more basically, it results from the structure of the reading experience itself, which, Holland claims, is essentially "the experience of passively being fed by a loving mother":[62]

> We come to a literary work with two conscious expectations: first, that it will give us pleasure (of an oral, "taking in" kind); second, that it will not require us to act on the external world.[63]

(The "not require us to act" part does not seem to bode too well for a view of *acting* as reading but, as we shall presently see—as Holland himself helps us to see—even impulses "of an oral, 'taking in' kind" seek enactment.)

Once reading is conceived in such terms the question of how a text's solution of its fantasy-management problem can become a *reader's* solution is solved—or, rather, need never arise. Insofar as the encounter with a text consists in "regression to our earliest oral experience . . . in which we are merged with the source of our gratification,"[64] there is no question of the reader having to "appropriate" anything. What the text I read does for itself it does for me, because it is, for the nonce, indistinguishable from me.

Is there any evidence that people actually experience their reading as eating? Holland points to the ubiquitous use of eating terms to characterize reading experience. "We call a man who 'devours books' a 'voracious' reader. . . . A certain novel may be a 'treat.' A parody may be 'delicious'."[65] Some readers are "omnivorous"; others only have a "taste" for science fiction—or, possibly, an "insatiable appetite" for it, in which case they are likely to "consume" vast quantities. Whereas a reader "hungry" for good writing—one who "relishes" wit, "savors" ambiguities, etc.—may not be able to subsist on a "diet" of such "pap."[66] The Middle Ages knew what it was doing when it nicknamed its most admired biblical scholar Peter "Comestor": Peter "the Eater" had "digested" the whole of Scripture.[67]

As this last example suggests, while the psychoanalytic understanding of such a vocabulary may be recent, the vocabulary itself has long been in use.

For books are as meats and viands are; some of good, some of evill substance; . . . Wholesome meats to a vitiated stomack differ little or nothing from unwholesome; and best books to a naughty mind are not unappliable to occasions of evil.[68] (Milton, late seventeenth century)

Some books are to be tasted, others to be swallowed, and some few to be chewed and digested.[69] (Bacon, early seventeenth century)

Read, mark, learn and inwardly digest.[70] (Book of Common Prayer, sixteenth century)

[In the Middle Ages] reading and meditation are sometimes described by the very expressive word *ruminatio*. . . . It means assimilating the content of a text by means of a kind of mastication which releases its full flavor. It means, as St. Augustine . . . and others say . . . to taste it with the *palatum cordis* [palate of the heart] or *in ore cordis* [in the mouth of the heart].[71]

"But," you reply, "I wish to dip first into one book and then into another." I tell you that [it] is the sign of an overnice appetite *(fastidientis stomachi)* to toy with many dishes; for when they are manifold and varied, they cloy but do not nourish.[72] (Seneca, first century A.D.)

For Milton, for Bacon, for Augustine, for Seneca, reading is a kind of eating.

Only, to be sure, a metaphorical kind: We do not literally snack down the wood pulp and specks of dried carbon.[73] Rather, we "introject" or "incorporate" the fantasy material they record. But the psychic mechanisms of introjection and incorporation are, as the very etymologies of the words suggest, themselves survivals on the mental plane of what were once physical processes. *Introjection* and *incorporation* are the "displacement upward" of feeding and digestion, respectively. What is now trope was once event. *The "lost" physical of reading is eating.*

What, then, of all the other physical activities with which, as we have seen, reading can be metaphorically identified, or of which, in the case of eye movements, it preserves actual traces? In the case of subvocalization there is no conflict but, rather, confirmation: The throat-and-mouth region in which physical activity persists is the very area that, on a view of reading as eating, would originally have been involved. But the pattern of eye movements we saw to be characteristic of reading seems to bear little relation to eating, and the various physical activities with which critics have metaphorically identified reading (movement in space, manual labor, etc.), even less. Actually, as we shall see in the next chapter, *all* physical activity has its roots in orality—specifically, in the orally active behavior of late infancy (biting, spitting, etc.), as whose "spread" to the organism as a whole bodily action must be understood. But, beyond this, there is reason to see a link between orality and the very sorts of actions to which we have found reading most often likened. The nature of the link is suggested by Susan Isaacs:

> The instinctual drive towards taking things into [the infant's] mind through eyes and fingers (and ears, too), towards looking and touching and exploring, satisfies some of the oral wishes frustrated by his original object. . . . Hand and eye retain an oral significance throughout life, in unconscious phantasy and often . . . in conscious metaphor.[74]

If "looking" (which includes eye movements) and "touching and exploring" (which include most of the other physical activities invoked by critics as metaphors for reading) are all displaced forms of orality—i.e., all just so many ways of vicariously "satisfy[ing] . . . oral wishes frustrated by [the] original object"—then Holland's identification of reading with eating is not refuted by but, in fact, receives unexpected support from the proliferation of apparent "alternatives" to itself.[75]

Which is not, of course, to say that it is immune to challenge on other counts. On the contrary, Holland's model of the reading process has come under attack from many quarters. Lacanians, deconstructionists, and opponents of reader-oriented approaches generally have all written against him. If I feel no overwhelming impulse to rise to the defense, this is partly because Holland has shown himself well able to answer his own opponents[76] but also, frankly, because it seems to me his opponents are often right. I know of at least three arguments against Holland which I do not know how to refute (which of course is not to say that Holland himself would not know how to refute them).[77]

I suppose this should cause me some concern, since, after all, I am heavily indebted to Holland, not only for my basic model of the reading process but also for the specific conception of character on which my discussion of the actor's work of characterization rests. But it does not cause me much concern. This is partly because the most acute negative criticism of Holland has focused on his conception of "identity themes"[78]—characteristic strategies of anxiety-management which individual readers bring to, and impose upon, the texts they read—and I will not have much recourse to identity themes,[79] or, in general, to the post-1968 writings in which Holland shifts his focus to individual readers, except insofar as these works elaborate positions set forth in the earlier *Dynamics of Literary Response*. But the main reason I do not feel more troubled by Holland's errors is that, where others see mistakes, I see possible applications to theater (which is not to say that I do not also see mistakes). Holland, it seems to me, errs with the theater. His errors, if errors they be, are the "errors" of theater itself, as I think will become clear if we examine each of them in turn.

General mutterings against psychoanalytical reductiveness aside, the account of reading offered in *The Dynamics of Literary Response* seems vulnerable to criticism on at least five counts:

1. Holland gives reading the structure of a neurotic process.
2. Holland reduces mental activity to bodily activity.
3. Holland confuses persons with texts.
4. Holland reduces reading to a solipsistic rediscovery of the self's concerns everywhere.
5. Holland's reading self is the discredited self of ego psychology.

In each case my procedure will be not to refute the charge but, rather, to show how a reading theory vulnerable to such a charge is only that much the more serviceable to theater.

1. *Holland gives reading the structure of a neurotic process*—that is, reduces it to the gratification/concealment of a single unconscious wish. The assumption that the most disparate moments of an individual's behavior can all be understood as either overt or, more likely, disguised expressions of some one unspoken wish may not be very flattering to readers or to human nature generally. But it is just the assumption that an actor reading his role needs to be able to make, as at once becomes apparent if we give the single unspoken wish its theatrical name of "through line" or "superobjective," and the disparate moments of behavior *their* theatrical name of "units" or "beats."

2. *Holland reduces mental activity to bodily activity.* Well, so do physicalization exercises, image-work, blocking. The "reduction" of mental activity to bodily activity is the very essence of the actor's work and, indeed, of the entire production process, conceived as getting a text on its—i.e., on the actor's—feet.

3. *Holland confuses persons with texts.* As we have seen, this "confusion" is pervasive in recent criticism, which persists in regarding texts as their readers' "partners," "lovers," "foes," etc.—in short, as persons. Admittedly, such a perspective is especially crucial to Holland, who must be able to speak of a text as "having fantasies," "defending against awareness," etc. But there is another enterprise than Holland's to which such a perspective is crucial. What is the central myth of theater if not that texts are persons unaccountably (and temporarily) bewitched into textual form, of whose "lost" physicality the actor may aspire to make a recovery? What is acting itself but the (mis)representation of texts as persons?

4. *Holland reduces reading to a solipsistic rediscovery of the self's concerns everywhere.* As one opponent of "the reader-oriented criticism practiced by Wolfgang Iser, Stanley Fish, and Norman Holland" puts it:

> The . . . critic did not prove the power of his personality by mastering a difficult text, but rather by finding the text *to be his personality* projected into an objective form. When he reads a text, a reader-response critic looks forward to the pleasure of witnessing the dissolution of the distinction between himself and the work.[80]

But to an *actor*-reader, whose eventual aim is to refashion the role out of the self's materials, what could be more useful than a solipsistic confidence that *I will find nothing in the text that I do not already find in myself.* On this point Norman Holland and Stanislavski, respectively, are at one:

> What is "out there" in the literary work feels as though it is "in here," in your mind or mine.[81]

> You cannot easily distinguish where the actor begins or his character ends. When you are in that state you come closer and closer to your part, you feel it inside you and feel yourself inside it.[82]

And sardonic objections to the critical approach of the former ("finding the text *to be his personality,*" "looks forward to the pleasure of witnessing the dissolution of the distinction between himself and the work") sound like nothing so much as neutral descriptions of the rehearsal procedures of the latter.

5. *Holland's reading self is the discredited self of ego psychology.* Holland is generally seen as working in the tradition of ego psychology and is consequently often dismissed by those who dismiss the ego psychological "fiction" of a coherent self. These include especially the deconstructionists, for whom a person (and a fortiori a reader) "is a place of intersecting roles, forces, languages, none of which belong to him alone,"[83] and, of course, the Lacanians, for whom the ego is not at all that "sturdy, helpful being" posited by Anna Freud or Heinz Hartmann[84] but, rather, a "ghostly entity,"[85] "built out of alienating identifications" with others (including one's own mirror image *as* other),[86] in that early phase of infant development which Lacan calls the "mirror stage."[87]

I suppose an argument could be made that Holland is something less than an orthodox ego psychologist—that, indeed, on some points he is rather closer to Lacan. Certainly, Holland's conception of an ego desperate at all costs to keep its own desires from itself (while gratifying them) bears some resemblance to the Lacanian view of the ego as "bearer of neurosis and . . . center of all resistance to the cure of symptoms."[88] Moreover, Holland's correlation of particular psychic processes with particular rhetorical figures (noted earlier) finds an echo in Lacan's identification of Freudian condensation and displacement with metaphor and metonymy.[89] There is, however, no disputing that, in his central vision of the ego set in a posture of defensive adaptation vis-à-vis the unconscious, Holland stands squarely in the tradition of ego psychology.[90]

It is certain that Holland is some sort of ego psychologist, and it is possible, as the Lacanians argue, that ego psychology is some sort of mistake about the self. If I, nonetheless, have recourse to Holland, this is because it seems to me that *ego psychology is the mistake about the self which acting needs to make.* Jonathan Culler may be right to protest that "people . . . are not harmonious wholes whose every action expresses their essence,"[91] but I doubt he will find many actors to join him in his protest. The assumption of a coherent self may be only a fiction—but it is a useful one to those whose job is to assume coherent fictional selves. A Lacanian analyst writes: "The ego is not the subject, it is closer to the persona, to appearance, to a role than to consciousness or subjectivity. . . . *The ego is the site of the subject's imaginary identifications.*"[92] This language is meant, as theatrical language is so often meant, to *signal* inauthenticity—in this case, the inauthenticity of a self that can be adequately characterized in such terms. In the theater, however—where literal "personas" or "roles" frankly offer themselves as "sites of . . . imaginary identification"—a verdict on the self as "mere assumed role" is no worse than the fact of the matter. Acting, unlike the rest of experience on a Lacanian view, is a search for a fictional self that *knows* itself to be searching for a fiction. Here the illusory quest may become a conscious quest *after* illusion, the "mirror stage" be safely staged as a mirror exercise.

In short, I think I might be more deterred from applying Holland's theories by objections I do not know how to refute if the objections themselves did not already sound so much like the applications I wish to make. To "endow a self with coherence that it does not possess" or "confuse texts with persons" or "reduce the mental to the bodily"—each of these constitutes a pretty fair description of acting. This is what I mean by saying that Holland errs, if he errs, *with* the theater, which I take as an indication that he *thinks* with the theater—which is how I, too, desire to think.

And what is "thinking with the theater"? To me, it is a thinking that seeks not to be free of imperfections but to be shot through with the same imperfections as theater itself. I do not aspire to be "more right" than theater, never mind "right" where theater is "wrong." I want to make all the "mistakes" theater does. While this can no doubt be achieved in other ways than by making all the mistakes Norman Holland does, Holland's views on reading suggest answers to some of the most basic questions we face.

For example: To recognize the "lost" physical of reading as eating is to understand why it should ever have been lost. Reading, as Holland presents it, satisfies a powerful but regressive fantasy—to be fed without having to work for it[93]—and toward the possibility of such regressive satisfactions, our attitude is likely to be an ambivalent one: We want them, and we don't want to have to *know* that we want them. Thus, the conflict between simultaneous impulses to suppress and gratify the same fantasy, which Holland finds to be at work in texts and in readers, reappears in the "history" of the reading process itself.

The physical basis of reading is "lost"—i.e., lost to consciousness, *repressed*—because only through that repression can reading constitute itself. Reading's "loss" of its physical dimension must not, therefore, be viewed as some kind of misfortune it undergoes but simply as the precondition for its emergence as a distinct activity. To become a matter of texts and minds it has had to give over being a matter of food and mouths—which includes giving over all recollection of ever having *been* a matter of food and mouths. Reading cannot afford a knowledge of its origins. To continue, it must continue in ignorance.

(Here, incidentally, is an explanation of why the literary critics, so quick to intuit the presence of *some* physical activity behind reading, nevertheless do not get it right. How can these partisans of "active reading" be expected to rest content with a theory that seems to reduce reading activity to intake and critical judgments to food preferences?)

How does reading push away awareness of its own physicality? First, it falls silent. "When he was reading," Augustine writes of the first (or first recorded) silent reader, "his . . . voice and tongue were resting."[94] Since, as I pointed out above, the muscle areas involved in reading aloud are (roughly) the same ones involved in chewing and swallowing, their immobilization (that "resting" voice and tongue) amounts to a denial that any sort of eating-related behavior is in progress. It is because it enacts such a denial, and not merely because speech is "more physical" than silence, that the historical transition from audible to silent reading marks a first stage in the "loss" of reading's physicality.

But, since the ties between reading and orality go beyond voice, the denial of those ties must inevitably go beyond silence. In order for the reader to hold his awareness of reading's physical basis successfully at bay, there must arise a sort of reaction-formation whereby the recognition *when I read, I eat,* is allowed into consciousness only in the inverted form: *my reading and eating exclude each other;* and ultimately: *reading and eating are at odds.* Of our first silent reader we are told: "He was *either* refreshing his body with necessary food *or* his mind with reading."[95] And, ever since, his successors have tended to preserve these alternatives as if they *were* alternatives.

Of that unhappy reader Emma Bovary we are told: "It was above all . . . meal-times that were unbearable to her"; for at meals with her husband, Charles, "all the bitterness of life seemed served up on her plate." As a countermeasure, "she . . . brought her book to the table, and turned over the pages while Charles ate." By this gesture Emma thinks to set her craving for higher things against the coarse hunger of Charles, a nonreader, who takes what life dishes out. But, all too clearly, Emma—who is described as "devouring" the Paris society pages and who seeks in the novels of Balzac and Georges Sand "imaginary satisfaction for her own desires"—is no less than Charles *indulging an appetite.*[96] She must, however, refuse all knowledge of the mortifying equivalence. And it is this refusal to acknowledge what is, literally, staring her in the face, that Flaubert conveys by the tableau of Reader and Eater at table. Reading is set down before, is literally brought face to face with, its prototype—and persists in seeing only a crude alternative to itself.

The most sustained example I know of reading's refusal to look on its origins is the opening section of Proust's essay "On Reading." In this memoir of childhood reading and eating are made out to be in perpetual rivalry. One reads under constant threat of interruption by meals, by those who serve them, by other diners:

> Some, without waiting for the meal to begin, would take their accustomed seats at once about the table. That was the worst of all, for it would have the horrible effect of making late arrivals think that noon had struck, and say, too soon, to my parents the fatal words: "Time to shut up books: luncheon's just coming in."

Eating displaces reading ("luncheon . . . would put an end to reading") and is displaced by reading in its turn ("I would cut short the picnic tea which had been brought in baskets and distributed to us children on the grassy riverbank where my book lay, though I was strictly forbidden to return, yet a while, to my reading"). Even more categorically than in

Madame Bovary, reading here will know itself only as the negation of eating and will see in eating nothing but the negation of itself:

> Our thoughts, while we ate, were wholly of the moment when, the meal at long last ended, we should be free to go upstairs, there to finish the interrupted chapter.[97]

In such extreme terms is the conflict posed that one begins to suspect it of being only a stand-in for some other, deeper-lying tension. What is really at issue here?

To be summoned from the book he is devouring to do some actual devouring disturbs Proust because it reawakens his awareness of the essential *continuity* between the two activities, an awareness that he, like any reader, has sought to suppress. (Both the awareness and its suppression are reflected in his choice of a reading site: the *dining* room table *between* meals, i.e., swept clear of all visible trace of eating or food.)[98] To be compelled to leave off the eating-which-is-reading to come and eat is, all too clearly, to go on doing the same thing. By the usual reaction-formation, *when I read, I eat* has entered consciousness in the form *I am forever having to leave off reading to eat.* Now the dinner bell sounds and finds me . . . already at table. The "interruption" only underlines that there has been no interruption—or, rather, if anything has been interrupted, it is the hold of a successful repression.[99]

I set out to argue that acting is the recovery of a "lost" physical dimension of reading. One might well question, however, whether the identification of that "lost" physical dimension with *eating* brings its recovery any closer. In some ways we appear to be worse off than before. Eating may or may not seem a very promising basis for the work of the actor: too passive, etc. But, even if it were the ideal basis, how would one go about establishing the acting process on such a basis? Once orality has been "displaced upward" to the level of mental functions, how does acting propose to bring it down to gut level again? What's the actor supposed to do—eat the book?

Chapter 4

Acting as the Recovery of the "Lost" Physical of Reading

How can acting "recover" a lost physical of reading understood as eating? Obviously, it is not a question of closing the book and opening the fridge. The problem is to recover eating *within* and *for* reading, as a potentiality *of* reading. Eating is physical intake of physical content. Reading is mental intake of mental content. It would seem that once the content has ceased to be physical—once, that is, eating has "passed upward" into introjection and reading—the *mode* of intake must cease to be through the body. A text cannot, except metaphorically, "go back" to being food. How, then, can reading go back to being bodily intake?

And when I looked, behold, an hand was sent unto me; and, lo, a roll of a book was therein. And he spread it before me; and it was written within and without: and there was written therein lamentations, and mourning, and woe. Moreover he said unto me, Son of man, eat that thou findest; eat this roll, and go speak unto the house of Israel. So I opened my mouth, and he caused me to eat that roll. . . . and it was in my mouth as honey for sweetness.[1]

And the voice which I heard from heaven spake unto me again, and said, Go and take the little book which is open in the hand of the angel which standeth upon the sea and upon the earth. And I went unto the angel, and said unto him, Give me the little book. And he said unto me, Take it, and eat it up; and it shall make thy belly bitter, but it shall be in thy mouth sweet as honey. And I took the little book out of the angel's hand and ate it up; and it was in my mouth sweet as honey; and as soon as I had eaten it, my belly was bitter.[2]

It turns out that the rather desperate-sounding formulation we were driven back upon at the close of the previous chapter is, in fact, an ancient and vivid trope for a kind of reading which has recovered (or never lost) its dimension of bodily intake. These biblical passages differ from the instances of digestive imagery we looked at in chapter 3 in that here it is no longer a matter of eating metaphors but of eating as an actual, if highly symbolic, event. The difference between reading as an "inward digesting"[3] and the actual digestion of parchment and ink reflects the distance between the ordinary and the prophetic reader. A prophet can "take in" the word of God directly. Others read and are "nourished"; the prophet *eats the book.*

Is anything like this unmediated reception of text into the body a possibility for acting? Clearly, there is a certain *kind* of acting—or a certain moment in all acting—which corresponds to this infinite availability of the prophet to the Word:

> [The actors] are carried away by the reading. They cannot control the muscles of their faces, which oblige them to grimace or mime in accordance with what is being read. They cannot control their movements, which occur spontaneously. They cannot sit still, they push closer and closer to the person reading the play.[4]

Note that the receptivity to language of these actors described by Stanislavski is accompanied by a passivity, a helplessness, even ("cannot control their muscles," "cannot sit still") which, as we saw in the last chapter, comes over into reading from reading's origins in the oral phase, that time when—like the unworthy prophet who, through no effort or merit of his own, is given the book to eat—one was fed without having to work for it.[5] (In Dürer's woodcut for our Revelation passage the book that John eats is twisted around into something like the shape of a breast and nipple.)[6] Stanislavski's actors, indeed, are spared even the cognitive labor of doing their *own* reading: They are read *to,* "fed text."[7]

In the preceding chapter I cited Norman Holland's characterization of orality as a state in which one is (dismayingly for our purposes) "not required to act." But in another passage, also quoted earlier, Holland, following Freud, points to the "intimate connection between motor inhibition and regression into fantasy"[8]—a connection whose usefulness for acting is also reflected in Stanislavski's emphasis on relaxation of muscles as the precondition for good imaginative work. Taken together, these two insights suggest how the kind of reading represented by *eating the book* might issue in a kind of acting. The actor who is "fed text," either by being read to or by one of the other techniques to be discussed in a moment, is thereby encouraged to regress to an orally passive state of "motor inhibition," where he is "not required to act." But it is precisely in such a regressed state that his body is most responsive to the fantasy material of the text, with the result that, as in the Stanislavski passage, his responses act *him.*

These days the practice which Stanislavski describes of a reader delivering the entire script to the assembled company is out of favor. There is, however, a contemporary rehearsal and training technique that also involves reading to actors and which also reflects the assumption that direct bodily availability to a text can result in, can *be,* acting. I refer to the sorts of exercises, sometimes called "image-work," where an actor is told to open himself to a moment of language—to just "let it happen" to him. When the actor is further instructed to "take the word in on your breath" the specifically oral nature of the technique becomes apparent. And of an exercise such as the following "eating (or: being fed) the book" could stand as an almost literal description:

> We drop the word [i.e., each successive word of a Shakespeare speech] into the actor and let it come up on the outgoing breath.[9]

Though their principal use is as a rehearsal or training device, such exercises do sometimes become the basis for performance, especially in film and television acting, where the performer may be told not to try to "do" anything beyond "taking in" the script moment: The small muscular changes that result will be enough of an event for the camera. Beautiful as such work can often be, to take in and perform—or, rather, *to offer the traces of one's taking in as already the performance*—is obviously not all there is to acting. What has become of the whole *interpretive* side of the actor's work: analyzing motivation, setting objectives, looking for subtexts, fixing beats, etc.? Clearly, it is absent, not because orality and interpretation exclude each other—on the contrary, as we shall see, interpretive activity is itself enactment of an oral process—but because the oral process in question here is of a wholly passive, taking-in variety. There can be no effort of interpretation when texts are swallowed whole. To wish for the sort of unmediated receptivity to texts implied by *eating the book* is thus to wish away reading—and perhaps, ultimately, to wish away texts themselves. (These are, of course, possible wishes—although, as we shall see later in this chapter, even the actor who chooses to work improvisationally strains to a paradox but does not thereby step free of an involvement with reading and texts.)

Ultimately, then, *eating the book* amounts to a denial of the ties between eating and reading as emphatic as that of Emma Bovary or of Proust in the "Reading" essay. For Emma and for Proust, to read a book is precisely *not* to have to eat. For Ezekiel and St. John, to eat a book is precisely *not* to have to read. It is instructive to see how, over the course of the centuries, educational and ritual practices founded upon this trope have foundered upon this difficulty.

> There was a medieval custom, at the commencement of the Jewish education of the child, of smearing with honey a slab on which were inscribed . . . letters of the Hebrew alphabet and some Biblical verses, "which the child might lick off and taste, as it were, the sweetness of instruction." The Rabbis of old . . . knew of the value of associating early impressions of Jewish experience with oral satisfaction.[10]

Apparently, they did—and yet the very need to "associate" reading and eating testifies to a felt distance between them. The child licks the honied slab and only then (if then) turns his attention to the letters written thereon.

In Catholic ritual the priest kisses the volume from which he is about to read the day's gospel selection[11]—an action the oral overtones of which Stephano, in *The Tempest*, makes explicit ("Kiss the book," he commands Caliban, passing him the bottle),[12] but whose orality is in fact already acknowledged in the verbal formula that originally accompanied it: "Hail, you words of the holy gospel, which *fill up/make full* the entire world."[13] (The Latin word for "make full/fill up" is *replestis*, as in *replete, repletion*.) Here the act of reading implied by the moment of oral contact at least ensues upon it. But to kiss or, like the medieval Jewish schoolchild, lick a text need not necessarily lead on to reading it. That resolute nonreader Sancho Panza runs his tongue over a packet of letters because they smell of cheese—then forwards them unread.[14]

The colonial American custom of baking the letters of the alphabet into gingerbread for schoolchildren[15] seems to close the loophole in the

Jewish practice, but not really. The child cannot decipher the bits of gingerbread while they are between his teeth. If the Jewish pupil must eat before he reads, his Puritan counterpart is obliged to read before he eats. What matters, however, is not the order in which the two actions are performed but, rather, the fact that there are two actions. Whether one first *construes the letters* and then *consumes the snack* or vice versa, the implication is still: Eating is not reading; the sign is not the treat.

Thus, these quaint attempts to make little St. Johns and Ezekiels out of beginning readers only call attention to a fissure already present in the great originals. Eating the book or honied slab or gingerbread—each of these intended demonstrations of the oneness of eating and reading turns out to demonstrate instead the apparent inability of eating and reading to coincide in a single act.

Does this mean we must abandon eating as the "lost" physical of reading? What we must abandon is an oversimple view of eating as mere intake. As verbs like *consume, devour, put away,* and *wolf down* should remind us, a human being eating is not a pail being filled. The question was raised in chapter 3 whether eating is enough of an *activity* to be at the root of acting. Maybe (passive) eating can be the basis of a (likewise passive) reading, but how can passive reading serve as the basis of the actor's work? But as I pointed out in chapter 1, acting and reading are, in fact, both mixtures of active and passive, and in nothing more clearly than this do they display their common oral heritage. Indeed, their being, each, such a mixture is traceable to their having, both, such a heritage. For as we shall now see, the orality in which eating originates, and which acting reoriginates, not only contains an active as well as a passive tendency but is most fundamentally *structured* as a conflict between active and passive tendencies, between taking in and being taken in, between aggressive and defensive modes of engaging the world. What is more, such a tension can, on closer inspection, already be made out even within the (as we have thus far treated it) unequivocally passive image of *eating the book.*

For, if one thinks about it, not even assimilation of a text one "eats" directly can be a wholly untroubled flow. In part this is owing to the nature of texts. As we saw in the last chapter, a text is a tense balance between an impulse to indulge and an impulse to deny a single desire—between, in Holland's terms, "fantasy" and "fantasy-management." When we take in a text "it is this transformational process, this management of fantasy, that we take into ourselves."[16] On this view to "eat a book" is not to down a simple substance but, rather, to internalize a conflict, swallow a warfare.

Furthermore, a reader is himself a balance of fantasizing and defensive impulses and comes to a text largely in the hope of "recreating . . . [his] own defenses from [its] materials,"[17] thereby warding off the anxiety that awareness of his fantasies might otherwise cause him.[18] The defense/drive conflict he internalizes along with the text is, thus, in some measure already his own—only with the fantasies at once more satisfyingly indulged and more efficiently managed—and has, indeed, been internalized for this very reason. Reading is, thus, not an openness (on the part of the reader) meeting an openness (on the part of the text); it is more like one set of barriers going up against another—"defensive warfare," as Harold Bloom calls it.[19]

For such a process as this *eating the book* may now begin to seem a hopelessly undialectical description: all fantasy-flow and no fantasy-management; a premature recovery of a misconceived physical; half the story at best. And yet, if we look more closely, *eating the book* is, as a figure, scarcely innocent of those tensions within reading which it seems designed to bypass. Both Ezekiel and John, it will be recalled, compare the book they eat to honey (Ezekiel: "in my mouth as sweet as honey for sweetness"; John: "in my mouth sweet as honey"). By itself, this comparison (which was to have a long subsequent history in Western literature)[20] seems to carry to an extreme the view of reading as effortless intake: honey is smooth, good tasting, "slides right down," etc. But this assumes that the honey is already there waiting to be effortlessly taken in, and in reading—as Proust, with his characteristic mistrust of facile eating-reading connections, is quick to point out—this is not the case. Truth, Proust cautions, is "not . . . a material *object* which exists between the pages of a book, *like honey made by others,* to be possessed merely by stretching out our hands to a bookshelf and *passively digesting* it in a mood of bodily and mental torpor."[21] If a text is in any sense "honey," it is, as Montaigne had long since maintained, honey that the active reader *produces* through his own digestive process:

> The bees plunder the flowers here and there, but afterward they make of them honey, which is all theirs; it is no longer thyme or majoram. Even so with the pieces borrowed from others; [the reader] will transform and blend them to make a work that is all his own.[22]

Where there is digestion, even of honey, there is the potential for indigestion—as the biblical authors themselves seem well aware. "As soon as I had eaten it," says John of his honey-sweet book, "my belly was bitter." And, apparently, Ezekiel, too, finds the divine text a little hard to swallow, for in the verse just preceding those I quoted, he has to be badgered into eating it:

> But thou, son of man, . . . Be not thou rebellious like that rebellious house: open thy mouth, and eat that I give thee.[23]

To some extent the digestive problems each prophet experiences can be explained by the contents of the text he must assimilate. Ezekiel's book contains "lamentations, and mourning, and woe"; John's tells of the coming tribulations of the church. "Taking in" the contents of a troubling book may be painful for a reader; "internalizing" a "meaty" role is almost always so for an actor-reader. Nevertheless, it is not altogether a matter of content. Eating a book is likely to be hard on the digestive system, no matter what the book is about. Paper, parchment, and vellum are not very digestible substances and can be made so only by considerable biting, gnawing, tearing—in short, by a kind of oral behavior far more active than any we have yet associated with this trope.

Thus, *eating the book,* which began by seeming so clearly a metaphor for reading as unobstructed intake, is in fact already structured as a tension between aggressive and receptive impulses. Moreover, the sort of acting which most resembles eating the book—image-work—likewise displays at least the outlines of a rudimentary active-passive tension. For, if to work in this manner is passively to allow the events of the text to happen in your body, it is also actively to supplant the text as site of the text's own events. The conflict between active and passive is present here only as a kind of clash of implications but will assume more overt forms as we move on to more complex methods of taking text into the body.

It is important to recognize that this tension between active and passive does not first arise in the moment when eating passes over into eating the book. It is already present in the structure of eating itself—*always already present,* one feels tempted to say, though, strictly speaking, this is not the case. The eating that, as the "lost" physical of reading, acting sets out to recover was, indeed, an untroubled flow, but the experience of eating upon which the actor must draw in pursuing this aim is one of an eating already divided against itself.

To see why this should be so we must go back to the time when eating did, in fact, display the character of a boundless receptivity—back, that is, to the early oral phase, when the "infant at the breast does not as yet distinguish his ego from the external world as the source of the sensations flowing in upon him."[24] In this paradisiacal state there is obviously no problem about intake because there is no awareness of anything external to the self which need be taken in nor of a "self" to which other things might be external. *But this is as much as to say there is no awareness in, or of, such a state.* To "know" a time when there was no boundary between a (pre)self and a (not yet) other is to know oneself already past that time, for the self-that-knows has only constituted itself by drawing that boundary:

> Only by being able to wait for, expect, trust in, the reappearance of a nurturing other, does [the infant] begin to sense that there is a world which is not part of himself. Only by recognizing that other as a being separate from himself does he recognize himself as a bounded entity.[25]

Thus, while there is such a thing as unbounded receptivity, there can be no possible *experience* of such a thing. To know that one eats is to know that one eats something else, that there *is* something else, a world *and* a self, between which there may henceforth be any degree of commerce, interchange, union (as well, of course, as less harmonious relations), but never again undifferentiated flow. The sort of unobstructed intake of text represented by *eating the book* could only happen to one who was unaware anything was happening (which explains why it *does* sometimes happen to actors—on occasions when, as with imagework, the language is "in" before there is time to think about it—and also why it cannot be counted on to provide a regular basis for their work).

Nevertheless, I maintain that it is this boundariless state—unable to distinguish "in here" from "out there," knowing nothing of any "you" or "me" or "it"—which, as the original physical form of eating, lies at the origins of reading:

> You are inside it [the book]; it is inside you; there is no longer either outside or inside.[26]

and which acting, therefore, seeks to recover:

You feel it [your role] inside you and feel yourself inside of it.[27]

It can, however, no longer be recovered directly. Why not? The *need* for boundarilessness is as strong as ever. Only one now "knows too much"—simply in knowing oneself to *be* a self—to experience that need without anxiety. The self's desire for such a total commingling with another is necessarily an ambivalent one, for such a union, if realized, might mean the end of the self. Eating as "boundariless flow" becomes a rather sinister proposition when there are two distinct parties and no way of determining the direction of the flow. Who can say, under such circumstances, that to merge or fuse *with* the other might not take the form of being engulfed *by* the other—of being devoured? From now on the *wish* to eat must always be accompanied by a *fear* of being eaten in one's turn.

But this new ambivalence that the child feels *toward* eating he can only express *through* eating. He cannot stop eating or displace his feelings onto some other activity: All he "does" is eat. If formerly he manifested his dependency through oral behavior, he must now likewise assert his newfound independence in an oral mode. He must, so to speak, "eat back." So the passive oral phase is succeeded by a more active one, the so-called oral-sadistic phase, in which the child, now fearing fusion with the mother as well as longing for it, begins to defend against as well as desire her; to bite and gnaw and tear as well as suckle; to spit out and turn away as well as to draw in.[28]

Thus, the child's newfound ambivalence toward eating *splits eating itself* into passive-receptive and hostile-rejecting elements. The once un-bounded receptivity has become "a fusion of loving and destructive impulses."[29]

As we shall see, the tensions that thereby arise within eating, eating "passes on" to each of the "higher" activities that derive from it: introjection, reading, and, ultimately, acting. And, as we shall also see, on each level the conflict grows more acute.

How could it be otherwise? Once such a fundamental breach has appeared in consciousness it can never simply be rescinded or healed; it can only deepen, widen, run its course. I have said that boundarilessness cannot be recovered in any direct way, leaving open the question of whether it can be recovered at all. I now want to propose, and in the

remainder of this chapter will attempt to show, that the original boundariless state (the "lost" physical of reading) can be recovered out of the
jaws of—indeed, *through an appropriation of*—this deepening division itself, and can best be recovered by *acting* precisely because in acting this
division is at its sharpest. As the gap between active and passive impulse
can only widen, it must somehow make of its widening a way back to
the unity it began by shattering and is even now moving farther from.

How is this possible? Because at every level, from eating on up, the
very widening of the gap between active and passive impulse provokes
increasingly urgent efforts to recover the lost boundarilessness *as a relation between*—as a paradoxical "setting equal" of—the particular forms
of active and passive impulse at work on that level. On the level of eating
itself, for example, the conflicting active and passive oral impulses and
the paradoxical "setting equal" that their conflict provokes can be stated
as follows:

Eating

Orally Active Impulse: I resist being taken in (eaten) by mother.
Orally Passive Impulse: I gladly take in (eat) mother.
"Setting Equal": I enact within my mode of taking in *from* mother
   my resistance to being taken in *by* mother (i.e., I bite, gnaw, tear,
   turn away, etc.).

As with eating, so on each subsequent level (introjection, reading,
acting): Something like the original indissoluble unity is recovered in the
form of an unresolvable paradox. Or more accurately: On each level
within conscious experience the closest model of the indissoluble unity
with the other that *precedes* experience turns out to be a paradoxical
"setting equal" of whatever unresolvable active and passive oral impulses
toward the other are at work on that level—until finally acting, as the
most unresolvable of the paradoxes, turns out to provide the most thor-
oughgoing of the recoveries.

In the pages that follow I will trace this active-passive conflict from
its origins in eating up through each of its successively "higher" transfor-
mations into introjection, reading, and acting, in each case identifying
the form that the active and passive impulses assume and the resolution
that they find on that level. The *motive* for each successive rise in level
is to gain additional power: One can introject objects one can't eat;

achieve, through a text's fantasy-management structure, balances one can't achieve on one's own, etc. Each of these successive gains in psychic strength, however, is paid for by a further loss of physical immediacy— eating actually takes something else into the body, introjection merely fantasizes taking something else into the body, reading is no longer even conscious of itself as introjective fantasy—until, at length, acting reinstates the whole process in the organism once more.

Since the discussion will be lengthy, it may be helpful to have the entire course of it laid out in advance:

Level	Orally *Active* Impulse	Orally *Passive* Impulse	Form in Which Active and Passive Oral Impulse Are "Set Equal" to Produce Boundarilessness
Eating pp. 59–60★	I resist being taken in (eaten) by mother.	I gladly take in mother.	I enact within my mode of taking in *from* mother my resistance to being taken in *by* mother (i.e., I bite, gnaw, tear, turn away, etc.).
Introjection pp. 62–67	I seek power over the other.	I open myself to the other.	I seek power over the other by opening myself to the other.
Reading pp. 65–78	I seek interpretive power over the text.	I open myself to the fantasy-management pattern of the text.	I give the text the solution that the text gives my fantasy-management conflicts.
Acting (general) pp. 72–84★★	I make my body the source of the text.	I open myself to the text as source of my every word and move.	I make my body the source of the text by opening myself to the text as source of my every word and move.
Acting (as orality still in the mouth: *speech*) pp. 84–88	I make my utterance the source of the text.	I open myself to the text as source of my utterance.	I make my utterance the source of the text by opening myself to the text as source of my utterance.

Continued

Level	Orally *Active* Impulse	Orally *Passive* Impulse	Form in Which Active and Passive Oral Impulse Are "Set Equal" to Produce Boundarilessness
Acting (as orality that has spread to the body: *movement*) pp. 88–99	I rise to enact my supplanting of the text.	I rise to enact my immersion in the text.	The action I take to deepen my immersion in the text supplants the text with action I take.
Acting (as improvisation) pp. 100–101	I produce (make up, "write") a text of actions.	I consume (use up, "read") a text of actions.	I consume by my actions the text my actions produce.
Acting (as a transaction with character) pp. 110–26	I impose upon my character the identity of the reader I am.	I accept as my identity that of the reader my character is.	I impose my identity as a reader upon the character from whom I accept my identity as a reader.
Acting (with other actors) pp. 126–36	I take the place of another('s) reading.	I take my place in another('s) reading.	I take the place of a reading in which I take my place.

*The occasional overlap in these page numbers is owing to certain sections of the chapter being transitional from one level to the next. Pages 65–68, for example, are given as the final three pages of Introjection and the first three pages of Reading because they are concerned with the common ground between introjection and reading.

**For the explanation of these brackets, see chapter 4 n. 87.

Having already considered the relation between active and passive elements in infant orality itself, let us see what form this conflict assumes on the next level up: introjection.

Why accord separate consideration to introjection? We seek to map the relation between three activities: *acting*, which recovers *eating* as the "lost" physical of *reading*. What is to be gained by interpolating this fourth "tier" on the chart? *Introjection* is "the unconscious fantasy of union with another by ingestion."[30] As such, it implies "oral cannibalistic incorporation of the other person."[31] Specifically, "it is often unconsciously modeled after the physical action of eating or swallowing. . . . The person . . . unconsciously imagines that he is eating or being eaten by the person with whom he becomes identified."[32] Thus, already—apart from any relation it may bear to reading but considered simply as the taking of another life into the body—introjection can be seen to play some role in the acting process. But, as we shall see, to open to the role as "another" and to read the role as a text ultimately converge back toward the same experience—and that, an introjective one.[33] Introjection spans the gap between physical and textual intake. Roughly, eating is the basis of *it,* and *it* is the basis of reading. It may be only a transitional concept, but, precisely as such, it shows how such a transition is possible. Moreover, the gains of introjection over actual eating prefigure (and to some extent provide the mechanism for) the sorts of gains which reading may expect to make over it and so illustrate the potential advantages of what might seem the wholly *dis*advantageous course (if power is the aim) of forsaking the physical realm for the mental.

What are these advantages? Eating something is obviously an effective way of asserting power over it. Thus, Cronus, in Greek myth, ensures against dethronement at the hands of his sons by devouring them.[34] The trouble is, of course, that there are distinct limits to what one can eat. In particular, one can't, like Cronus, eat other people: Even the infant's active-sadistic "eating" of mama—its biting, gnawing, tearing, etc.—is only a symbolic enactment of eating another, albeit a physical enactment. Eating "forsakes" the body to become the mental process of introjection with a view toward broadening its diet. There is almost nothing (except food) you can eat; there is nothing, and no one, you cannot introject. The "eating," of course, will now henceforth be only intrapsychic, but the loss in physicality is compensated for by the immense gain in range.

As a displaced form of eating, introjection ought to preserve the tension between active-hostile and passive-receptive impulses toward its object which, we have seen, characterizes eating itself. Does it do so?

There is a sort of transitional moment halfway between eating and introjection when children begin to put nonedible objects into their mouths: Insofar as the objects are physical, the child is still eating; insofar as they are no longer food, he has begun to introject. If we catch this process at its pivotal moment—in mid-displacement, as it were—we can see this proto-introjective behavior already showing signs of the ambivalence that marked the literal eating even now being left behind:

By making [the objects he puts in his mouth] a part of himself, [the child] ensures that they will always be with him, that they will be unable to do him harm, that they will never be there—outside.[35]

"Always be with him"/"Unable to do him harm"—both the orally passive and orally active impulses enacted by this transitional behavior will also characterize introjection itself, the former expressing itself as an *opening to* the other, the latter as a *seeking power over* the other.

And, just as in literal eating the two opposed impulses did not simply sit side by side but reached toward each other in a paradoxical effort to make of this boundless opposition a boundarilessness, so now the psychic "eating," which is introjection, strains toward a still more paradoxical "setting equal" of *its* opposed impulses. For, though technically a "defense mechanism," introjection does not simply defend against by excluding; it defends against *by taking in*. Its opening-to *is* a seeking-power-over; it safeguards the citadel by flinging wide the gates.

We have a vivid illustration of this in the Greek myth of Zeus and his first wife, the Titaness Metis, whom the king of the gods no sooner weds than swallows. This is an essentially defensive move: Like his father, Cronus, Zeus acts in response to prophecies that any offspring he sires will supplant him. But Zeus' relations with his introjected bride do not end there; she proceeds to give him counsel from inside his belly.[36] Metis is the goddess of (her name, in fact, means) "cunning" or "resourcefulness," qualities that the newly ascendant Zeus must make his own if he is to reign successfully.

> By marrying, mastering and swallowing Metis, Zeus . . . becomes more than a mere king, he becomes sovereignty itself. All the *mētis* in the world . . . [is] now inside Zeus.

But this preemptive taking in *of* Metis is also a merger or fusion *with* Metis. Zeus introjects Metis—and is himself hereafter *mētieta,* "met-isized" to the core.[37] That confusion may arise between the orally active and orally passive aspects of an introjective act is already anticipated in the very definition of introjection as the fantasy that one is "eating *or being eaten* by the person with whom [one] becomes identified." What the example of Zeus and Metis illustrates is how the confusion can, so to speak, "spread" from the act to the agents, ambiguity as to which one has incorporated the other ultimately becoming uncertainty as to where one leaves off and the other starts.

Thus, by "setting equal" the opposed tendencies within itself—eat or be eaten, take in or be taken in—introjection in its turn recreates something like the boundariless fusion-with-source of primal orality. Or to restate the situation in the form I have already employed for eating itself:

Introjection

Orally Active Impulse: I seek power over the other.

Orally Passive Impulse: I open myself to the other.

"Setting Equal": I seek power over the other by opening myself to the other.

Any such problematic fusion as this contains, as we have already seen in the case of literal eating, a terrifying potential for self-loss. And so introjective fantasies, in literature and elsewhere, often involve images of being devoured, buried alive, engulfed and, especially, *drowned*.[38] (It is no coincidence that merging Metis is the daughter of two *sea* deities and is herself associated with divination by *water*.)[39]

Such water and drowning imagery is especially significant for our purposes as we move from introjection to reading, since it is an imagery as likely to be found associated with the latter as with the former. Proust compares the mind of the reader to "a hand reposing motionless in a stream of running water," which thus receives "the shock and animation of a torrent of activity and life."[40] But, of course, the "depth" of a reader's "immersion" need not stop at the wrist—or indeed, stop at immersion. "Every good reader properly desires to drown," writes Harold Bloom.[41] And that most immersed of readers, Don Quixote, finishes his adventures at the ocean's edge—an ironic first glimpse of "shore" after his long immersion in what he himself calls "the *mare magnum* [vast ocean] of their [chivalric] histories."[42] Conversely, Dan Jacobson, a reader less eager than Quixote to "take the plunge," compares the texts that solicit him to the sea beating against a shore he is unwilling to quit:

> The more one reads [of the Old Testament prophetic books], the more one feels impelled to put up a defense against them—a kind of breakwater in the mind—to prevent oneself from being overwhelmed by the constant, unrelenting roar of verbiage, beating down upon the page with all the fury and ultimate monotony of waves on a beach.[43]

Of the texts one reads, no less than of the object one introjects and the water in which one drowns, it may be said: "In absorbing it, we become absorbed."[44]

On the basis of the similarities brought out by such imagery Norman Holland often tends to equate introjection and reading: "we introject the text," "the reader . . . introjects the literary work," etc.[45] One (fictional) reader for whom reading *is* "all introjection" illustrates the possibilities and limits of such an identification. Stephano, the perpetually drunken butler of *The Tempest,* would restore to explicit orality the somewhat denatured mass practice we examined earlier: He sends along his bottle to the next toper with the command "Kiss the book!" Now, while Stephano boasts that he is immune from drowning, he never appears to be less than full fathom five in his cups, that is to say, completely sloshed.[46] Like Holland's reader, he is "absorbed by" what he "absorbs" from his book/bottle. For introjection, to eat is to be eaten; for reading, to absorb is to be absorbed; for Stephano, to drink is to be drunk.

The words *drink, drunk,* and *drown* all derive from a common root: *To drown* is to drink, and be drunk by, the sea. Consequently, Stephano's excessive immersion in his "book" is appropriately punished by an even more excessive immersion in the horse pond. He has the tendency to drown drowned out of him. And this homeopathic cure ironically shows *The Tempest*'s other "over-absorbed" reader—Prospero, whose "library" being "dukedom large enough" initially cost him his dukedom and whose present immersion in magical texts threatens to cost him more than that—what he must do: "deeper than did ever plummet sound / I'll drown my book."[47] The entranced reader proposes to break the textual spell by doing to a book what books have (almost) done to him. That in which he might have fatally immersed himself shall now itself be fatally immersed.

Thus, in *The Tempest* an initial confident identification of reading with drinking/drunkenness/drowning issues in a watertight distinction, or even opposition, between them. The tension that afflicts this characteristically introjective imagery when applied to reading suggests that it will be the tension between its own active and passive impulses which introjection "passes on" to reading. But in what form? *I seek power over the other, I open myself to the other, I seek power over the other by opening myself to the other*—how must each of these conflicting aims and their paradoxical resolution be understood when the "other" in question is a *text*?

Part of the answer we already know. To "open to" a text means, as we saw in chapter 3, to allow the text's fantasy-management program to achieve within oneself the balance between control and gratification which it has achieved for the text—with all the blurring of "in here"/"out there" distinctions and "text"/"self" boundaries which such a process entails.

But what Stephano's experience makes clear is that to read is not merely to introject fantasy-management solutions; if it were, it would already *be* the boundariless state that, like all forms of displaced orality, it seeks a way back to. Reading is also a *cognitive* process. We must take in intellectually (i.e., comprehend) the text whose fantasies we take in (i.e., introject). An actual book is never, as in Stephano's dynamics of literary response, "all bottle." On the contrary, the more "absorbing" we find a text, the harder we are likely to have to work at "absorbing" it. This, in turn, suggests what form the more active aspect of introjection is going to assume in reading. The "power I seek over the other" when the other is a text is precisely this cognitive—or, to give it its more inclusive name, interpretive—grasp, interpretation being, as Nietzsche first noted, fundamentally a will to power over texts.[48] Whether we focus on word- and letter-grouping processes or on large-scale critical "sweeps" after structure and theme, interpretive activity always proceeds as an opening, rending, and recombining of the elements of a text. Interpretation, in other words, is the form that the active-sadistic aspect of eating assumes on the level of reading and, as such, is heir to all the violence of the original.

Does this mean that it is active orality that the active reading discussed in chapter 2 enacts? It is a tempting conclusion. If orality is the basis of reading, then, it would seem, *active* orality must be the basis of *active* reading. What is more, the imagery favored by reader-oriented critics seems, at least initially, to impute to active reading the interpretive "violence" that, I am arguing, is the mark of displaced active orality. And yet, to fill in the blanks of a text with one's own material, as well as asserting authority over the text, blurs the boundary between the blanks and him who fills them. "A reader-response critic looks forward to the pleasure of witnessing the dissolution of the distinction between himself and the text"[49]—yes, but is the anticipated "pleasure" one of self-surrender or self-will? Such expressions imply that to read actively is as much a matter of following an orally *passive* impulse to merge with the text as an orally *active* impulse to assert power or priority over it.

Active reading, then, enacts not active orality but, rather, the conflict between active and passive impulses which characterizes every type of displaced orality. And, as a single action that enacts both sides of the conflict, active reading demonstrates the possibility of active and passive orality being "set equal" in a single act of *reading*.

This, given the forms that passive and active orality assume on this level, is a possibility that needs some demonstrating. There would not seem to be much likelihood of blurring the boundaries between regressed fantasy and interpretive will. But the opposition is not so drastic as it sounds; for one thing, it is not purely an opposition. In reading, cognition *serves* fantasy.

Why, after all, does introjection "go on" to become reading? Reading's gain over introjection, like introjection's over eating, is a gain in *range*. As introjection makes it possible to "take in" things you couldn't otherwise take in, reading makes it possible to internalize fantasy-management solutions you could not otherwise "make your own" because they only occur in texts. There is no access to texts without certain cognitive skills, but the access, and hence the skills, are of value only for the sake of the fantasy solutions; in this sense cognition "serves" fantasy. Or, as Norman Holland puts it, modifying somewhat his emphasis on reading as pure introjection, the relationship is one between a "core" of regressive fantasizing and a "rind" of higher mental functions which foster and contain it.[50] (So, for example, it is Don Quixote's *memory* for chivalric texts—which is, we are told, "exceptional"[51]—which sustains him in the *fantasy* that every event that befalls him reenacts some moment from one of them.)

Cognition-at-the-service-of-fantasy is rather startlingly reflected in the external activity of reading a book. In order to get through a bound volume from page 1 to page *n,* a reader simultaneously performs two distinct motions. His eye moves over or across the surface of each page in a *scanning* movement. Meanwhile, he descends deeper and deeper into the pile of pages in a movement of *penetration*. The scanning movement—forward-moving, linear, and tending to "stay on the surface"—suggests (and, in fact, helps perform) cognitive activity upon the text. The movement of penetration—a gradual "going deeper," or "getting into," a "volume"—suggests deepening immersion in the text's fantasies. As the (literal) surface-scanning serves to make possible a (literal) penetration of the depths of the page pile, so the reader's cognitive scan is all the while bringing about a deeper penetration of the work's fantasy material. Some such awareness of this parallel between the psychological and physical acts of reading seems to inform Georges Poulet's comment that "to *penetrate* a text is . . . to *advance* into a domain without boundaries and perhaps without bottom,"[52] as well as Norman Holland's observation that New Critical reading "explores *depths* by confining itself to the *surface* verbal texture."[53] And, indeed, Holland's "rind"/"core" view of reading—relatively "superficial" cognitive scans, which nonetheless bring about immersion in the underlying fantasy—is demonstrated every time a reader comes to the end of the line and turns the page.

Though the comparison may seem an incidental, even a frivolous, one, we shall soon see that this "two-motion" model of reading bears a surprisingly close relation to the rehearsal process and so provides confirmation, from a quite unexpected quarter, of the tie between acting and reading.

But a mere relation of subordination between the cognitive and fantasizing elements in reading scarcely provides a basis for their being felt as equivalent. If cognition and fantasy can be "set equal," it is because they display a further tendency *to participate in each other's qualities*. Both, after all, share a common substratum. Being a displaced form of active orality, cognitive activity is no less clearly grounded in eating than fantasizing is, as Quintilian's account of one particular cognitive activity, memorization, reminds us:

> Just as we do not swallow our food till we have chewed it and reduced it almost to a state of liquefaction to assist the process of digestion, so what we read must not be committed to the memory . . . while it is still in a crude state, but must be softened and, if I may use the phrase, reduced to a pulp by frequent re-perusal.[54]

In particular, cognition and fantasy tend to take on each other's associations with *active* and *passive*. Thus, while cognition is, as we have seen, a largely active process, in some respects it is experienced as a passive one. I let myself be guided by the text's signs, and my eventual recognition of these, however much of an event on the neurological or information-processing levels, just seems to "happen" without any effort on my part. (We may recall in this connection that it is not during active eye movements (saccades) but at moments of eye immobility (fixations) that cognitive intake occurs.) Conversely, while fantasizing may seem a basically passive process—one "yields" to fantasies, "receives" gratification from them, etc.—it is not entirely so. For fantasy actively *seeks* its own gratification and, when it seeks it in literary works, displays something very like that will to power over texts which has so far appeared the exclusive prerogative of the interpretive will.

In this somewhat paradoxical state of affairs can be discerned the outlines of the paradoxical equivalence we seek between the active and passive aspects of reading, and, as on previous levels, to arrive at the equivalence we must develop the paradox. As we have already seen in the case of introjection, there is no taking in *of* another that is not also opening of the self *to* the other. To seek power *over* by taking *in* is, thus, inescapably to lay oneself open to the power of what one has taken in (remember Zeus and Metis). We are now in a position to understand what such statements might mean when the "other" who takes and is taken in is a text—i.e., in reading.

The power I seek over a text is power to elicit and control its meaning. The power a text has over me is power to elicit and control my fantasies. But, while one may thus speak of "powers," plural, in the act of interpretation the text's power over me and mine over it are revealed to be identical—or, at least, indistinguishable. To subject the text to my interpretive activity is to subject myself to the text's fantasy-management program—or, rather, any interpretive activity upon the text is already an expression of the text's action upon the fantasy-management system of the interpreter. Interpretation may be an active search, but what the interpreter actively seeks is to fall into the power of the text. My will to power over the text is a will to be overpowered by the text. Or to make use once again of the format employed for introjection and reading:

Reading

Orally Active Impulse: I seek interpretive power over the text.
Orally Passive Impulse: I open myself to the fantasy-management pattern of the text.
"Setting Equal": I give the text the solution that the text gives my fantasy-management conflict.

There is doubtless some blurring of boundaries in all this, but, it will be recalled, that is precisely the aim. *Uncertainty as to just where the boundaries lie* is the best approximation *within* conscious experience of that *unawareness that there are boundaries*—the original boundariless state— which *precedes* conscious experience and which reading, like all forms of displaced orality, seeks to reinstate.

Of course, one could argue that reading *already* reinstates boundari- lessness simply insofar as it produces that regressive absorption, which we found in chapter 3 to be characteristic of it. But the boundary- blurring that is the result of a wholly regressive process must at every moment fear disruption from the very cognitive activity needed to sus- tain its hold. Whereas the dynamic we have been considering brings cognitive-interpretive activity itself into play as a force in the boundary- blurring. If I experience my yielding to the text's fantasy-management program as the text's yielding to my interpretive efforts, then interpre- tive activity, far from interfering with regressive surrender, *enacts* it.

If such statements have a paradoxical ring, it is because they restate the paradox of interpretation itself. The circle they go round in is the hermeneutic one—to understand, one must interpret; to interpret, one must understand—which I am in effect restating in terms of the experi- ence of the interpreter himself, thus: I experience the text's power to elicit and control my fantasies as my power to elicit and control the meaning of the text. I experience the text's solution of my problem as my solution of the text's problem. In a word, I experience the effect of the text on me as an effect of mine on the text.

The hermeneutic circle, that most puzzling of intellectual dilemmas, thus emerges as the material out of which reading recovers a time before dilemmas. While it is one of the premises of this book that there is more to reading, especially to an actor's reading, than mere "interpretation," it is striking how, even in its purely interpretive aspect, reading points the way back to its "lost" physical origins. As the flow of a single power neither clearly that of a text over a mind nor clearly that of a mind over a text, the unending dialectical movement of interpretation models—and induces—the primal boundarilessness. For a process that cannot un- equivocally be placed "in here" (in the mind) or "out there" (in the text) tends to blur the very possibility of a distinction between "in here" and "out there." That reading can be such a process any number of readers have testified:

> Thus the reader is both inside and outside [the text]. He is helping forward the imagining of a world in which he can then see this

imagining reflected as a story. Thus the more he loses himself in the pursuit of the fiction, the more likely he is to be able to believe in his identity within that fiction.[55]

The house was quiet and the world was calm.
The reader became the book; and summer night

Was like the conscious being of the book.
The house was quiet and the world was calm.

The words were spoken as if there was no book.[56]

You are inside [the book]; it is inside you; there is no longer either outside or inside.[57]

Now, of course, such a blurring of the "in here"/"out there" boundary between reader and text can also occur when the reader is an actor and the text is a role. In fact, I have already juxtaposed the last of the above quotes with the assertion of Stanislavski (who urged "study of the role in one's self and one's self in the role") that "you feel [the role] inside you and feel yourself inside of it."[58] This suggests that whatever further ambiguities follow from the blurring of inner/outer distinctions in reading will tend to characterize acting as well, and such is indeed the case. For example, insofar as reading activity goes on "in here" (in his mind), the reader will feel like a participant; insofar as it goes on "out there" (in the text), he will feel like an observer. But, insofar as what is going on cannot clearly be *placed* "in here" or "out there," he will feel like participant and observer both:

The ability to perceive oneself during the process of participation is an essential quality of the aesthetic experience; the observer finds himself in a strange, halfway position: he is involved, and he watches himself being involved.[59]

The reader is both a participant in the action and a critic of his own performance.[60]

Now, as the imagery of the latter passage suggests, the situation is the same between the actor and his role. He, too, is both "in it" and "outside of it," and so he, too, is both participant and observer:

You can be the observer of your dream, but you can also take an active part in it—that is, you find yourself mentally in the center of circumstances and conditions. . . . In time . . . you can become the main active personality . . . ; you can begin . . . to act.[61]

Further: As *participant*, the reader feels "involved"; as *observer*, he feels detached. But, since the reader is both participant and observer, he is likely to feel both involved and detached.

While reading . . . I was acutely conscious that I was lying on the floor in my own living room, that I was brimming with anxiety and emotion, and that I was deeply and frighteningly implicated—all this at the same time that I was attending with special care to the characters and events in the book. Unquestionably, much of the power of the experience resided in some terrible tension between my involvement and my self-awareness.[62]

Again, we think of the actor—or would do so, if the reader-oriented critics had not already thought of him for us:

Like an actor, the reader is simultaneously both involved and detached, intimately engaged in creating the fiction but coolly critical at the same time, taken out of himself yet in the end in a position to find himself.[63]

"Like an actor," indeed. One's thoughts go immediately to Diderot's paradox:

[The actor] must be two people at once, the one immersed in his role and the other coolly observant and critical outside it: "[the actress Mlle. Clairon] is able, following out her memory's dream, to hear herself, see herself, judge herself and judge of the impression she will produce. In that moment, she is double: little Clairon and [her character] great Aggripina.[64]

But such a view of the actor's state—notwithstanding the stereotype of the "method" actor losing himself in his role—was also quoted approvingly by Stanislavski:

Salvini said: "An actor lives, weeps, and laughs on the stage and all the while he is watching his own tears and smiles."[65]

And it is perhaps somewhere in the background of Grotowski's definition of acting as "a passive readiness to realize an active role."[66]

In short, the *paradoxe sur le comédien* is also a *paradoxe sur le lecteur*. For the active-passive polarity from which it proceeds in acting traverses reading as well, reading and acting being both displacements of an orality itself thus divided.

Moreover, the "acting version" of this polarity preserves the tendency we have already noted within reading for such a split to become a dialectical passing over of active *into* passive, passive *into* active, by means of which something like the original boundariless flow is paradoxically modeled. At first any such interchange might seem unlikely: Insofar as the actor (or reader) is an involved participant, is he not simply active; insofar as he is a detached observer, is he not simply passive? But things are not so straightforward. The involved participant in a text, be he "absorbed" reader or "internal" actor, is one who has *opened* himself to the text's fantasy solutions, dropped his defenses; in this sense, his is the more passive relation to the text. Conversely, the detached observer of a text, be he "critical" reader or "technical" actor, is one who has *resisted* the text's fantasy solutions, kept interpretive control; in this sense, his is the more active relation to the text.

Ultimately, acting does not merely preserve the paradoxes of reading but, by bringing them to a crisis, brings about the most persuasive simulation yet of the indivisible by the unresolvable. This it achieves, as noted earlier, by letting the whole problem "break out" in the body. But before we follow it there let us look a little more closely at some of the purely psychological continuities acting displays with reading as an oral-introjective process.

One of the clearest indications we had that reading is itself such a process was its frequent association with an imagery of immersion in water: Proust's hand in the stream, Jacobson's waves on the beach, Don Quixote's *"mare magnum* of [the] histories,"* etc. An expression of Charles Dickens—whose public *readings* of his works were, by all accounts, quasi-theatrical *performances* of them—suggests that this imagery of watery fusion may carry over into acting. "Having already read two Christmas books at Birmingham," wrote Dickens to a friend, "I should like to . . . have a swim in the broader waters of one of my longer books."[67]

Do actors likewise experience their work as "a swim in . . . broader waters"? "Your head will *swim* from the excitement of the sudden and complete *fusion* of your life with your part," writes Stanislavski,[68] of one of those moments of merger/self-loss that, as we have already seen in the case of reading, tend to find expression in water images.

I must now quote a somewhat lengthy but, for our present purposes, extremely revealing use of water imagery in connection with acting by Stanislavski:

> Out of the corner of my ear I heard Tortsov make some approving comment and explain to the students that this was the right approach to the subconscious. But I no longer paid any attention to encouragement. I did not need it because I was really living on the stage and could do anything I chose.
>
> Evidently the Director, having achieved his pedagogic purpose, was ready to interrupt me but I was eager to cling to my point and I went right on.
>
> "Oh, I see," said he to the others. *"This is a big wave."* Nor was I satisfied. I wanted to complicate my situation further and enhance my emotions. So I added a new circumstance: a substantial defalcation in my accounts. In admitting that possibility I said to myself: What would I do? At the very thought my heart was in my mouth.
>
> *"The water is up to his waist now,"* commented Tortsov.
>
> "What can I do?" I said excitedly, "I must get back to the office!" I rushed toward the vestibule. Then I remembered that the office was closed, so I came back and paced up and down trying to gather my thoughts. I finally sat down in a dark corner to think things out.
>
> I could see, in my mind's eye, some severe persons going over the books and counting the funds. They questioned me but I did not know how to answer. An obstinate kind of despair kept me from making a clean breast.
>
> Then they wrote out a resolution, fatal to my career. They stood round in groups, whispering. I stood to one side, an outcast. Then an examination, trial, dismissal, confiscation of property, loss of home.
>
> *"He is out in the ocean of the subconscious now,"* said the Director. Then he leaned over the footlights and said softly to me: "Don't hurry, go through to the very end."
>
> He turned to the other students again and pointed out that, al-

though I was motionless, you could feel the storm of emotions inside of me.

I heard all these remarks, but they did not interfere with my life on the stage, or draw me away from it. At this point my head was swimming with excitement because my part and my own life were so intermingled that they seemed to merge. I had no idea where one began or the other left off. My hand ceased wrapping the string around my finger and I became inert.

"*That is the very depth of the ocean,*" explained Tortsov.[69]

I cited both this and the preceding Stanislavski passage in *The Theatrical Event,* the first apropos of the actor's possessionlike takeover by his role, the second apropos of the actor's shamanlike voyage to the "other world" of the script. (Voyages to the other world are frequently represented in shamanism as undersea journeys.)[70] I quote them again here not only because they are relevant in the present context but also because their being so suggests a continuity between the (as it otherwise might appear) irreconcilable models of acting offered in that book and the present one—and, more generally, between an antitextual theater and a theater of texts.

The Theatrical Event discusses acting within a preliterate problematic of tribal ritual (shamanism and possession experience) and is therefore primarily concerned with the script as a "realm" to visit or make present, only secondarily with the script as text. The present book, by contrast, presents acting not merely within a framework of literacy and textuality but as, in its inmost essence, a mode of engagement with texts—as reading.

That this contrast reflects a shift in my own preoccupations over the decade that separates the two books, and in particular my increasing activity as a playwright, I would not attempt to deny. But there also seems to me to be a real continuity between the actor as shaman and the actor as reader, for which the lengthy Stanislavski passage just quoted suggests the basis. The imagery of that passage represents the young actor Kostya moving (horizontally) *forward* across the ocean floor as he gets (vertically) *deeper* into his action. These are, of course, the very movements that we have found to characterize reading, considered as an amalgam of cognitive advance and fantasy penetration (recall Poulet: "to *penetrate* a text . . . is to *advance* into a domain without boundaries and perhaps without bottom")[71] and which we have even found reflected in the external physical motions of reading: *across* pages and *down into* a "volume." Kostya, too, scans (the ocean floor) so as to penetrate (the "very depths" of the role).

Kostya's sea journey, put forward by Stanislavski as an example of the actor's work process at its most fruitful, occurs at the *n*th repetition of an improvisatory exercise which Kostya and the other student-actors are heartily sick of. They have been *over and over* the material, can't *get into it,* etc. And yet it is precisely by going over it (one more time) that the actor does get into it (at last). Which is to say: Rehearsal, of which Kostya's experience is here offered as the type, has, like reading, the form of a *penetration-by-scanning*. Running over and over the lines, one at length penetrates to the core of the material.

It is, thus, no coincidence that the shaman, the reader, and the actor can all have their experience represented by the same imagery; they are all having essentially the same experience.[72] The shaman "sinking" into his "oceanic" trance state, the "absorbed" reader becoming more and more deeply "immersed" in his book, and the actor getting further and further "out in the ocean of the subconscious"—each of these *advances by engulfment,* be it into a text, a script realm, or the realm of myth. In *The Theatrical Event* I compared the dramatic text to an *illud tempus:* a mythical region or era where the events of the play are "always happening."[73] I have since learned that *"in illo tempore"* ("at that time") are the words with which it was customary to introduce the gospel-reading section of the mass.[74] To enter upon reading, it seems, is also to enter a time and realm where the events of a text are always happening.

While I would, of course, like to feel some continuity between my own earlier and present positions, I have not dwelt so long on the structural parallel between acting, shamanism, and reading simply out of a concern to harmonize *Acting as Reading* with *The Theatrical Event.* I believe that the ultimate psychological identity of these three experiences hints at a solution to—or, better, hints at the unreality of—one of the "great controversies" of twentieth-century theater. The actor-shaman seems to entail a view of theater as tribal/ecstatic/bodily; the actor-reader, a view of theater as textual/verbal/literary. We have long been accustomed to regard the opposition between these two kinds of theater as fierce and irreconcilable. Julian Beck or Jean Anouilh—whose side are you on? And yet, if the shaman, the actor, and the reader are all having, at most, differently displaced versions of the same experience, can these two visions of theater really be so implacably opposed? Can they, even, be very clearly distinguished?

I find some indication that they cannot in, of all places, *The Theatre and Its Double*. If there is any writer whom one would expect to find squarely on the side of the shamans against the readers, it is the author of "No More Masterpieces." Yet, in the very manifesto in which Artaud deplores "the theatrical superstition of the text," he speaks of the "need for theatre to steep itself in the springs [*se retremper aux sources*] of . . . a poetry realized by a return to the primitive Myths."[75] Such an image implies the ultimate identity of the world of myth ("primitive Myths") and the world of texts ("poetry"), elsewhere so sharply distinguished by Artaud, precisely on the grounds that "steeping" oneself, i.e., *advancing by engulfment,* is the appropriate means of advance through each.

The presence of immersion/engulfment imagery in the writings of Artaud and Stanislavski is certainly some indication that actors experience their work in oral terms. Are there, however, more direct indications? To employ a vocabulary of *immersion* and *engulfment* is to speak in a language with oral overtones. To what extent does eating *itself* figure among the ways in which actors experience and discuss their work? The problem here is not so much to accumulate evidence as to decide what will count as evidence. I am myself most struck by, and will presently offer examples of, statements in which actors themselves directly link their work process with eating. First, though, I want to consider three aspects of acting which seem to me to reveal its oral dimension no less clearly than does such direct testimony. These three aspects—the "childishness" of actors, the prominence of meals and eating in rehearsal, and the "hunger" of actors for audience approval—are, it may be felt, rather peripheral ones. But it is precisely at the peripheries of a practice, where nothing seems to be at stake and so defenses are down, that the hidden impulses involved in the practice are most likely to reveal themselves.

1. *"Childishness."* That actors are "like children" or, at any rate, can be "awfully childish at times" is not merely a slander dreamed up by those who do not understand or respect the acting process.[76] Acting encourages, if not actual regression to the oral stage, at least a commitment to the working out in oral terms of active-passive tensions that usually present themselves to adults in some other form. Considering this willed commitment to the psychic mode of infancy, one can only wonder that actors are not more childish than they are. For, in a very basic sense, to act is to act like a child.

2. *Rehearsal eating.* Coffee is brewed and served by a production assistant. The catered meal arrives. Or the cast spends twenty minutes discussing the merits of every lunch place in the neighborhood. Or the stage manager is sent out for sandwiches and drinks. . . .

Eating and drinking are a big part of rehearsal and apparently always have been: Medieval theater records that tell us so little else we would like to know about rehearsal procedures go into enormous detail about the supplying of the company with beverages and food.[77] Of course, actors have to eat. But the almost ritualized quality of the attention paid to meals and snacks in rehearsals hints at a more germane connection between eating and the acting process. It is as if all the evoking of displaced oral impulses which acting requires had evoked some actual oral impulses as well.

3. *"Hunger" for audience approval.* In an actor's playing before an audience, as in any form of exhibitionistic behavior, psychoanalysis teaches us to see a doubly disguised avowal of oral dependency.[78] The actor's "I want others to be avid for a view of me" is a recognizable transformation of "I am avid to be viewed by others," with the oral dependency both projected outward (*they* are hungry to see *me*)[79] and displaced upward from mouth to eye (they are hungry to *see* me).

To some it will appear that all this only links orality to the less creditable aspects of acting: childishness, time wasting, vanity. I would reply that it is, rather, a matter of linking the less creditable aspects of acting to the most central fact about it. But it is time we heard from the actors themselves.

We have seen that readers betray the unconscious link they feel between reading and eating by the use of expressions like "omnivorous," "digest," "steady diet of pap," etc., in connection with their reading activity. Do actors talk about what they do in a vocabulary drawn from eating and food?

It might seem as if only those actors committed to an internal method of work would be likely to do so. And, indeed, Stanislavski speaks of actors *"filter[ing] through ourselves all the materials* that we *receive* from the author";[80] Uta Hagen, of having *"devoured* the play for any light it could shed on 'my' [the character's] background."[81] But, in fact, an oral experience of acting is not reserved for those who "internalize." From a psychoanalytic perspective even external mimicry of another's behavior reflects the wish to make him part of oneself,[82] i.e., enacts an essentially introjective impulse. (*Introjection, incorporation,* and the far more external-sounding *identification* are, it will be recalled, all roughly equivalent terms in the psychoanalytic vocabulary.)[83] And, in practice, even the most external actor is likely to speak of a "meaty" or "juicy" role (one he can really "sink his teeth into") or to announce that he hasn't yet "got his lines down."[84]

But I would be reluctant to base my argument on the occasional stray remark, however revealing. As a more sustained example of the connections that may subsist in an actor's mind between eating, reading, and acting, consider how, in the following passage, Uta Hagen's recommendation to actors that they read shades over into a recommendation that they eat:

> (Read Ben Shahn's extraordinary book, *The Shape of Content.* He is talking about painting, and every word should be an eye-opener for the actor. Read *On Modern Art* by Paul Klee.) In comparing painting to acting I used to say that to paint an apple you have to see and sense everything about the apple before you can come to a statement about it, and that if you combined that statement with your skill you might produce a canvas that had your mark. Picasso claimed you have to *eat* the apple first. He clearly wanted to come to full grips with his material and *digest* it before he gave it shape, before his statement came into being.[85]

The shift in the passage from "see[ing] . . . the apple" to "eat[ing] the apple" charts the return of orality from its "displacement upward" in the eyes, the site of that reading which the passage begins by endorsing, back down into the mouth where it "belongs"—charts, in other words, the recovery of a "lost" physical basis of reading.

But, though Hagen is a practitioner, the foregoing recounts principles, not practice. For a firsthand account of the acting process whose language leaves no doubt that the experience involved is an oral one, I turn to some comments of the American actress Diane Venora concerning her work on the title role of *Hamlet* for a 1981 production at the New York Shakespeare Festival. At the outset of the rehearsal period Venora declares that she cannot be content with offering as her performance of Hamlet "a poetry-reading that costs nothing."[86] We may hear this as determination to offer, rather, an *actor's* reading: that is, a reading whose "lost" physical dimension has, whatever the cost, been recovered. From all we have seen of the nature of that "lost" physical the terms in which she and her director, Joseph Papp, describe its recovery should come as no surprise. Papp observes: "She's *consuming* a lot of things, not just working on the stage. She has to *absorb* the material." The oral character of Papp's language ("consuming," "absorb") is strikingly echoed in Venora's own statements about her work:

> As [the rehearsal period for] the play kept going, I had suddenly losses of appetite. I didn't feel like eating as much, playing this character.

The loss of literal appetite indicates that she is getting her nourishment elsewhere. She doesn't "feel like eating as much, playing this character" because it is already all she can do to "take in" Hamlet. But it is only at a moment of discouragement, farther along in the rehearsal period, that the full extent of the connection Venora feels between acting and eating suddenly appears:

> You give all you've got in a role. And Shakespeare says to you, "So you've given all you've got. Great. Good. Now you have to give more. Now more. Now *more*. More, damn you, more, more"— until your heart and your guts and your brain are pulp, and the part feeds on you, eating you. And that's exactly what this play does to me. It consumes me, it wastes me, and it still says: "Not enough!"

We have seen how, on every level, the original possibility of *being* eaten (by an all-absorbing maternal presence) haunts eating in the form of a sinister inversion of eating itself: Introjected Metis consumes Zeus from within; the reader becomes absorbed in the book he set out to absorb, etc. And so it is here: The very digestive mechanism of the actor is itself now threatened with digestion ("until . . . your guts . . . are pulp, and the part feeds on you"). But further: In the present bottomless hunger of the play for its player ("and it still says: 'Not enough!'") we recognize an ironic reversal of the initial state of affairs, when it was *the actor's* hunger

for (as it then appeared) an endlessly "satisfying" *role* that seemed "bottomless," that cried out "Not enough!" It is difficult to imagine more
eloquent testimony to the psychological ties that link acting and eating.

Note, however, that the danger that Venora sees herself as exposed
to from this ravenous text is by no means merely psychological: *Hamlet,*
she feels, has designs on her "heart" and "guts" as well as her "brain."
To a far greater degree than a reader or introjector the actor feels herself
to be physically at risk. One would have to go back to the infant at the
breast to find fears of engulfment quite this literal.

But, if the danger is greater for the actor, so also are the opportunities. Important as are the sorts of psychological links between acting and
orality which we have thus far considered, ultimately what gives acting
its power to recover the "lost" physical of reading is the return it man-
dates of the whole problem to the arena of the body.

This reinstatement must not be seen as the mere transposition of an
ongoing conflict from one site to another, still less as a simple "home-
coming" of what has, for all its displacements upward, never ceased to
be "of the body." The orality that returns to the body after a sojourn in
mental process is not the same orality that departed thence. To allow
eating to grow physical once more is to invite the conflict between its
active and passive elements to assume a new degree of intensity—and
this, not just because physical experience is, in some general way, more
"intense" than mental. The return to the body which acting undertakes
is not a nostalgic return to some status quo ante—not a falling back upon
(or back *into*) the body of impulses that once had bigger plans. It is,
rather, a reaching toward the most paradoxical identification yet—which
is to say, the most powerful simulation of boundarilessness yet—between a reader and a text.

Eating "left the body" so as to expand its range: Introjection made
it capable of incorporating other people; reading, of introjecting other
people's fantasy solutions. The actor, who must incorporate all sorts of
other people and make his own all manner of fantasy solutions, has every
stake in holding onto these gains in range. A recovered physicality is no
use to him if it means only reversion to an earlier, simpler time. What
he must do is recover the body in a way that preserves the gains for the
sake of which the body was left behind. Eating passed into introjection
and reading so as to expand the *scope* of its operations at the expense of
their physicality. What the actor must do is acquire the lost physicality
for the expanded operations.

The original bodily form of the relation to be recovered was, it will be recalled, *I resist being taken in (eaten) by mother, I gladly take in (eat) mother.* A return to the bodily level such as the actor contemplates must then (as Diane Venora's language suggests) somehow reinstate this eat-or-be-eaten relationship.

How does one have an eat-or-be-eaten relationship with a text? The question becomes more compassable if we confine ourselves for the moment to the power-seeking aspect of eating. We could then say: An eat-or-be-eaten relationship with a text is one in which an actor seeks *bodily* power over the text, even as the text seeks bodily power over him. What is a body's power over a text? To be the source of the text's words (not just, as in reading, of possible *meanings* for the words, but of the words *themselves*). What is a text's power over a body? To be the source of the body's words and actions (not just, as in reading, of words spoken and of actions taken *in response* to itself, but of *all* the body's actions and words).

But this exactly describes how things stand between an actor and a script. The actor may justifiably say *I was never more in control of the text:* It speaks with his voice, has its origin in his body; he makes all its moves for it. Yet at the same time the actor is obliged to concede *I was never more under the control of the text:* No word out of his mouth or movement of his muscles but is prescribed for him there.

So understood, acting fulfills the paradoxical condition without which it could never be more than a regressive surrender of ground gained. That is, acting achieves the ends that first led eating away from the body—as much as introjection, it is a taking in of another; as much as reading, it is appropriation of another fantasy/defense structure. But it achieves these ends in and through the body. From this perspective reading and introjection can begin to look like acting that was only allowed to happen up to a certain point.

Stated in the form I have previously employed for introjection and reading, the relation assumed by active and passive orality in acting is as follows:

Acting (general)

Orally Active Impulse: I make my body the source of the text.

Orally Passive Impulse: I open myself to the text as source of my every word and move.

"Setting Equal": I make my body the source of the text by opening
myself to the text as source of my every word and move.[87]

Or to phrase it in a way that suggests how much nearer to the original
boundariless flow we are brought by acting than on any previous level:
Into my body disappears the text into which I disappear.

"Become the source of a text that is one's source," "disappear into
that which disappears into you"—what actual processes lie behind such
descriptions of the actor's work? The question can best be answered in
two stages: first, with respect to the actor as *set to speaking* by a text; then,
with respect to the actor as *set in motion* by a text. This is no mere matter
of expository convenience. It's not as if the *verbal* and the *physical* were
the two "halves" of the subject, requiring to be "dealt with" in turn.
Nor, although I am a playwright, is it that I believe the verbal level of
theater in some sense "comes first": The issue is not really words or
speech as such. We are considering acting as the recovery of an essentially oral process, and recovery of the oral is first of all going to involve
the mouth. The body "comes second" in the sense that the bodily involvement of the actor can best be understood as a "spread outward" of
orality from its original site. To act is to give a fundamentally oral
process the run of the organism.

For the moment, however, let us concentrate on an orality "still in
the mouth." What form do passive and active oral impulse assume for
an actor who has been set to speaking by a text?

If acting is the return of a "lost" physicality, we would expect both
an actor's orally passive and orally active impulses toward the text he
speaks to assume a more directly physical form than is the case in introjection or reading. We have already found this to be so for the passive-
receptive side of acting: An actor's "eating the book"—his image-work
and so forth—passes immediately into physical activity. But what about
acting's version of the *active* impulse in eating? What, indeed, is acting's
version of this impulse?

The original physical prototype of active orality was, it will be
recalled, the *tearing, spitting out, turning away* behavior of the infant in the
later, or "sadistic," oral stage. Our question then becomes: How does
this pattern—resistance by mouth to an oral fusion that also is accomplished by mouth—reappear in the work of the (speaking) actor?

In the absence of a literal breast to reject or aggress against the adult may assert his independence from maternal flow by attempting to establish himself as the *source* rather than the recipient of such a flow: "A common defense against oral fusion and merger is putting something out of the mouth instead of taking something in."[88] The "something," where adults are concerned, is most likely to be sounds and words. Thus, singers, lecturers, drill sergeants, and compulsive talkers are, in effect, all proclaiming: "Not *into* my mouth, but *from* my mouth, proceeds the stream." To this list, of course, could be added writers and actors, both of whom also emit verbal streams.[89] I link the two because the psychoanalyst Edmund Bergler's explanation of writing in these terms—"writers emit words as a way of defending against the fearful desire to obliterate oneself in a total at-oneness with some primal mother"[90]—also sheds considerable light on orality in acting.

Bergler sees in writing an "attempt to exclude the giving mother and her breast by the fantasy that the writer gives himself words = milk."[91] The association of words with milk, implicit in such expressions as "a flood of words" or "fluent speech," emerges clearly in the New Testament injunction: "As newborn babes, desire the sincere milk of the word, that ye may grow thereby."[92] The writer, however, must seek to escape any such dependency on the milky word of another by himself becoming the source of an oral counterflow. "You should drink . . . from your own cistern," Erasmus advised authors, "not . . . seek help from elsewhere but rather . . . divert water from your spring into others."[93] Such seems to have been the aspiration of Rilke, who expressed to Lou Andreas-Salomé (whose "somehow lost son" he considered himself) the hope "that my mouth, when it has become a great river, may sometime flow . . . into your hearing."[94] And such, perhaps, is the unconscious symbolism involved in providing authors who read in public ("divert water from your spring into others") with water pitchers, whereby they themselves may become the "source" of their "outpourings" ("drink . . . from your own cistern"). Conversely, to lack or lose confidence as a writer is to be no longer capable of producing one's own verbal flow and so to revert to suckling status, as Dante fears he may do when faced with the challenge of rendering a direct vision of God: "Now will my speech fall more short . . . than that of an infant who still bathes his tongue at the breast."[95]

This dialectic of oral (in)dependence in writing begins to shed light on the actor's work when we take it (as I believe it must be taken) as being less about the writer's relation with his biological mother than his

relation to prior *texts,* which he both draws upon for imaginative sustenance and fears to remain too much the child of. It is against the implicit
claim of already existing texts to be all that he (or anyone) will ever need
that the writer presumes to "add to the flow."

For Americans the prime example of a writer confident of his ability
to muster a counterflow is Emerson, the champion of "self-reliance" and
"enjoy[ing] an original relation to the universe." And in Emerson, as
Barbara Packer points out, "metaphors of oral aggression . . . are always
a sign of recovered self-confidence." Thus, *The American Scholar* moves
from the passive-tending-toward-active oral imagery of:

> The books which once we valued more than the apple of the eye,
> we have quite exhausted. . . . First one, then another, we drain all
> cisterns, and waxing greater by all these supplies, we create a better
> and more abundant food.

to the fierce active orality of:

> The human mind . . . is one central fire . . . flaming now out of the
> lips of Etna . . . and now out of the throat of Vesuvius.[96]

But the transit marked by these images is not unique to Emerson. It is
the trajectory of any writer *as he passes into the act of writing*—passes, that
is, from thirsty recipient to independent source, from "drainer of cis-
terns" to "central fire," from reader to author.

It is, of course, also the trajectory of the actor as *he* passes from
recipient to emitter of text—from reader to actor. No less than the
author, the actor initially stands face-to-face with a precursor text (the
script), which offers itself as a source of words for him—even at the
moment when *he* is attempting to come into play as, himself, a source
of words. And, like the author, the actor responds to this challenge by
putting forth words out of his mouth.

There is, of course, one crucial difference. The words a writer
"comes out" with to set himself off as distinct from his source text are,
in fact, distinct from it: They are his, the writer's own, words. If they
are not, or do not seem to be, all his own, they will not confirm his
independent status; rather, they will mark him as "derivative" from his
source—the very imputation he set out to avoid. The situation of the
actor, by contrast, remains—as befits acting's claim to recover "lost"

physicality—a good deal closer to the original bodily prototype. The milk that the infant spits out to refute his dependence on the mother he has, in fact, received from the mother. Similarly, the words that the actor "spits out" to establish himself as a source of text are the very words he has taken in *from* the text.[97] Hence, the very gesture by which he seeks to enact his independence from the text necessarily also enacts his dependence on it. The actor's relation to this stream of words emanating from his lips is, thus, undecidably ambiguous. It is at once the sustaining flow from without on which he depends (he has accepted the text as source of his utterance) and the self-originating counterflow he gives forth to deny that dependency. Far more truly does Wordsworth's famous image of writing as "spontaneous overflow" characterize the creative process of the actor than the writer.[98] For an "overflow" is a state of affairs in which *flow into* and *flow out of* have become the same flow; such a "setting equal" of passive and active orality—of in-fluence and out-pouring—is characteristic only of derivative writing, but characterizes acting as such. The actor achieves the status of emitting source by accepting the text as source of his emissions.

Active and passive orality are, thus, here in far less need of "merging" or "blurring" or being *set* equal than in the case of introjection or reading. The actor's orally active and orally passive relation to the text he speaks *both* find expression in the single act of his speaking it and so tend to be experienced as the same relation. A boundariless relation with the text becomes available to the actor as a consequence of the necessary absence of any boundary between his own activity considered in one light and that same activity considered in another. The actor, one might say, "borrows" the self-identity of his own speech act with itself to be his identity with the text.

This identity between actor and text exists apart from any psychological identification with his *character* which the actor, according to his work methods, may or may not attain. Psychological identification can only be the result of prolonged exploration of the script by the actor.[99] Whereas the identity to which I refer, since it is brought into play simply by his speaking the script's words, is in force from the moment he begins to speak them. The first read-through is already what every subsequent read-through, rehearsal, and performance will be: a denial of dependency on the text, brought forth as a bringing-forth of the text. Or to restate it in our usual format:

Acting (as orality still in the mouth: speech)

Orally Active Impulse: I make my utterance the source of the text.
Orally Passive Impulse: I open myself to the text as source of my
utterance.
"Setting Equal": I make my utterance the source of the text by
opening myself to the text as source of my utterance.

I have said that the coming into play of the body in acting must be
understood as the "spread" of this essentially oral process to the organism as a whole. What evidence is there for any such mouth-to-body
sequence in the actor's work? The first thing to realize is that such a
trajectory is not unique to acting; on the contrary, in this respect acting
only reflects a general trend in human development. Infants advance
from active eating at six months to the beginnings of overall bodily
activity at eight to ten months, a pattern recapitulated in adult lovemaking, where initial oral contact (words, kisses) leads on to whole-body
involvement. When Goethe's Faust modifies his initial translation of the
Gospel according to St. John 1:1 from "In the beginning was the Word"
(oral) to "In the beginning was the Deed" (whole body), he is opting not
merely for more extensive activity but also for the usual route from less
to more extensive activity.[100]

From the initially oral to the eventual bodily is of course also the
usual trajectory of rehearsal work: You go from getting your tongue
around the words to getting the show on its feet, from read-through to
walk-through. Nor is it surprising that acting, which essays the recovery
of a "lost" physical of reading, should begin with the voice. For voice,
as we saw in chapter 3, is the first aspect of physicality to go when
reading falls silent—first to go, and first to return. But, just as in reading
loss of voice already carries within it the seeds of a more fundamental
curtailment of physicality, so the return of voice at a first read-through
already gives promise of a more extensive bodily recovery still to come:
As they read, the actors gesture, shift weight, rise, move off from the
reading table, etc. (Here, perhaps, is the explanation of the frequently
startling theatrical effectiveness of even unstaged play readings:
"Officially," they only restore voice, but to restore voice is already to
be on the way toward a more comprehensive restoration.)

Indeed, the mouth-to-body trajectory of the rehearsal process is
reflected in the very history of the word *rehearse*, which has shifted from

its now nearly obsolete meaning of *"say* (words) over" to its present-day theatrical sense of *"do* (actions) over." In actual rehearsal periods, of course, the *doing over of actions* which ensues upon the *saying over of words* also includes saying over those words. And, in general, whole-body activity does not simply supplant the oral behavior it succeeds—infants do not cease to spit and gnaw once they can crawl, nor lovers to kiss and speak once intercourse has begun—but rather preserves and extends that behavior. In fact, according to Susan Isaacs, whole-body activity can best be understood as the preservation/extension of oral behavior:

> The instinctual drive towards taking things into [the infant's] mind through eyes and fingers (and ears, too), towards looking and touching and exploring, satisfies some of the oral wishes frustrated by his original object. . . . Hand and eye retain an oral significance throughout life.[101]

That this general link between orality and bodily movement has implications for the relation between voice and movement in acting is clear from the comments of acting teacher Robert Benedetti:

> Speech forms a kind of pointing, and more specifically, a kind of grasping. You can see this in babies. . . . The word or sound becomes a way to possess, a kind of long distance tasting. Language from the beginning has this physical basis as a way of extending . . . oneself through space.[102]

These observations of Isaacs and Benedetti suggest an unexpectedly specific meaning for Grotowski's dictum that actors "speak with the body" and perhaps suggest as well an explanation for the emphasis placed, in actor-training methods of all kinds, on "freeing the voice."[103] For, if Isaacs and Benedetti are right, in freeing the voice one inevitably frees more than the voice.

The question of *why* orality "spreads" to the body needs not so much to be answered as stood on its head. *Where else* but from orality would the body have acquired its model for action? Active orality—the spitting/biting/turning away behavior of the infant at six months—is the first instance of, and as such the prototype for, all subsequent forms of active behavior.

This genesis of action in active orality appears in the etymology of the very word *action*. As Michel Serres points out, *"agere,* Latin for 'to act,' has as its first concrete and physical meaning 'expulsion.'... Action... for our immediate ancestors... was purging, banishment, eviction, rejection, elimination." And, while the Latin word *agere* does not refer specifically to theatrical acting, Serres goes on to connect the expulsive view of action which it preserves with theater: "It is not at all astonishing that the word *action* is now used in the theater. The tragedy with goat's feet expels the scapegoat."[104] But the link with theater extends well beyond the *tragos* theory of tragedy—as, indeed, the mechanics of that very theory make clear. A scapegoat is cast out so that the community will not be consumed by its sins, crimes, etc. Expulsion of the scapegoat is, thus, itself a "spitting out" against being swallowed up, just as we have found the actor's verbal counterflow to be. Stanislavski takes the final step toward identifying theatrical action with expulsion, and hence with active orality. "Scenic action," he writes, "is the movement from the soul to the body, from the center to the periphery, from the internal to the external, from the thing an actor feels to its physical form."[105] Note that it is not clear whether Stanislavski is talking about verbal utterance or physical activity or both. Once again we are brought to a perspective from which the familiar categories of "verbal" and "physical" theater begin to lose some of their force. The distinction between theater that is "full of action" and theater that is "all talk" may no longer appear terribly meaningful once one has recognized that, in the theater as elsewhere, action is only the continuation of active orality by other means. Be it vocal or bodily, theatrical "expression" (from the Latin *ex-primere,* "to press outward") is a pushing forth, an extrusion, an emitted counterflow—and, as such, finds its prototype in expulsive orality.

What form does the "spread" of oral impulse from the actor's mouth to the actor's body assume? We must not lose sight of what is spreading. In the two preceding paragraphs I have spoken almost exclusively of *active* orality. And, indeed, it might seem as if the moment of coming into action off a text were *all* active: no more depending, merging, being fed; one is now up and doing.

And yet, insofar as acting is a displaced oral process, how should it fail to carry forward orality's characteristic active-passive tension into all its moments, including the moment we are now considering? And, in fact, "coming into action" is no more a simple denial of oral dependency than a simple persistence in it. Rather, it represents the latest "outbreak"—this time on the scale of the body as a whole—of the clash within orality between the need and the refusal to depend. Orality, however far displaced, never ceases to be characterized by that warfare between active and passive impulses which is its heritage from its bodily origins—and least of all now at the moment of its return to the body. As always, we are dealing with one impulse toward ever-deepening dependence, passivity, merger and a counterimpulse toward ever greater independence, self-sufficiency, and going one's own way. The question is: What form does each of these impulses assume in the behavior of an actor rising to enact a text? I answer as follows:

The impulse toward passivity, dependence, merger finds expression in attempts to make the body ever more available to the energies of the text. The more the text is allowed, in accordance with this impulse, to act upon the body of the actor, the more bodily activity he will be in.

The contrary impulse, toward rejection and independence, finds expression in attempts to break the hold, step free of the text—to supplant the text with the body's own energies. But the more the actor seeks, in accordance with *this* impulse, to make the text's moves for it, the more bodily activity he will, once again, be in.

Thus, *both* the actor's impulse toward surrender to the text *and* his impulse toward mastery over it tend to bring his body into activity. Antithetical as these impulses may be to one another, there is only one course of bodily activity (and one body) for them both to find expression through, namely, the *rising-to-enact* itself. We have seen, on the verbal level, how the actor "borrows" the identity of his own act of speaking-the-text with itself to be his identity *with the text,* his boundariless relation with it. Similarly, here on the level of whole-body activity we find the actor borrowing the identity of a single course of bodily enactment with itself to provide a way back to "boundarilessness." In the single action of rising to enact the text—since it is both movement into which the actor *is called by* the text and movement by which the actor *takes over from* the text—active and passive oral impulses are "set equal," and a boundariless relation with the text is thereby simulated. Or to put it in our usual format:

Acting (as orality that has spread to the body: movement)

Orally Active Impulse: I rise to enact my supplanting of the text.
Orally Passive Impulse: I rise to enact my immersion in the text.

> "Setting Equal": The action I take to deepen my immersion in the
> text supplants the text with action I take.

I am now going to examine several fictional scenes of reading which
depict this paradoxically active-passive behavior of coming into action
off a text. It may be asked: Why linger over scenes of *reading* when we
are ready to pass on to acting itself? The answer, of course, is that what
one passes on to acting *from* is, precisely, a scene of reading. As for the
scenes I discuss being fictional ones, it is true that Paolo and Francesca
and Don Quixote are only characters in a story, but the "story" is, in
each case, precisely that of reading's attempt to pass over into acting.

This still leaves the question: Why focus on scenes from *narrative,*
rather than *dramatic,* fictions? If, at a critical moment in an argument
about theater, one feels one must have recourse to texts, shouldn't they
at least be theatrical texts? The avoidance may seem all the more puzzling
in that I *do* later devote consideration—in fact, I devote an entire chapter
(5)—to scenes of reading from plays. Would not such scenes reflect the
acting-reading relation we are now trying to establish? The answer is
that they reflect it all too well. Scenes of reading in plays are, in effect,
"forecasts" of what will be the actor's eventual reading transaction with
the plays that contain them. It is acting that renders such scenes intelligi-
ble, not they that explain acting, and for this reason I defer consideration
of them to a later chapter. It is only after the acting process that they
image has been presented that the manner in which they image it can be
grasped. Finally, I am under no illusion that I can shed new light on the
much commented upon fictional works I shall discuss *(The Divine Comedy, Don Quixote);* rather, I look to them to illuminate my inquiry.

> One day, for pastime, we read of Lancelot, how love constrained
> him; we were alone, suspecting nothing. Several times that reading
> urged our eyes to meet and took the color from our faces, but one
> moment alone it was that overcame us. When we read how the
> longed-for smile was kissed by so great a lover, this one, who never
> shall be parted from me, kissed my mouth all trembling. . . . That
> day we read no farther.[106]

Dante's celebrated account of Francesca da Rimini's fall into adultery with her brother-in-law Paolo Gianciotto as a consequence of their
reading together the story of Lancelot and Guinevere sums up much of

what I have been trying to say about the relation between acting and reading. We start with an experience of reading from which the dimension of physical hunger has been repressed: The soon-to-be lovers read *sanza alcun sospetto,* "suspecting nothing" (l. 129). But, like actors, these readers reopen their bodies to the energies of the text ("It is," Charles Singleton points out, "the reading itself that reveals their love to them")[107] and in so doing reopen reading to its origins in bodily experience. We actually *see* the "lost" physical of reading work its way back down from its uppermost displacement in the *eyes* ("urged our eyes to meet" [l. 130]) to the *cheeks* ("took the color from our faces" [l. 131]) to the *mouth* ("kiss my mouth" [l. 136]). And once returning physicality has reached the mouth, it stands, *as is also the case in acting,* at the propagation point from which it can "spread out" to involve the entire body—an involvement here represented as, precisely, the undoing of the initial, dephysicalized *reading*: "that day we read no farther" (l. 138).

Thus, the Paolo and Francesca episode can, in a general way, be taken as a parable of acting as reading. But at present what interests us is the unresolvably ambiguous "mix" of active and passive impulses toward a text in any enactment of it, and to this the famous litotes that ends the passage gives eloquent expression. On the one hand, Paolo and Francesca "read no farther" because they actively supplant the text of love with their own lovemaking. The textual kiss between Lancelot and Guinevere is replaced by an actual kiss between Paolo and Francesca, etc. On the other hand, this same rising-to-enact marks their total surrender to, immersion in, the fantasy material of the text. In this sense, for Paolo and Francesca to "read no farther" is to be no longer capable of the *distance* of a reader (who seeks fantasy-*management* as well as fantasy-gratification), to be "taken over" by the text to the point where they live the actions of Lancelot and Guinevere as their own experience. Thus, Paolo and Francesca's coming into action in response to their book undecidably enacts both active appropriation of and passive self-surrender to it, the very pattern I am arguing characterizes the transaction between actor and script.

As for the result: Francesca speaks the words I have quoted in a moment of respite from the perpetual whirlwind in which she, Paolo, and the other souls damned by lust endlessly revolve: "hither, thither, downward, upward, it drives them" (l. 43). In Dante's hell punishment for sinful activity consists in grotesquely literalized reenactment of that very activity; accordingly, the whirlwind of the Lustful is generally interpreted as something along the lines of "the endless cycle of desire." But, insofar as the activity that Paolo and Francesca image is acting, and specifically, coming-into-action off a text, we may want to interpret this *unbroken circling* into which they are "finally" brought by their reading as a rather sinister image of the boundariless state, attained through the "setting equal" of opposed impulses ("hither, thither, downward, upward") in a single enactment. (That the boundariless relation Paolo and Francesca attain is between the two readers as well as between each reader and the text—"this one, who never shall be parted from me" (l. 135)—has implications for the nature of the work between *actors,* a subject to which I shall return in the final section of this chapter.)

There are a number of different tacks one could take in linking Don Quixote with acting. One might point out that Quixote was an actor in his youth,[108] is still sympathetic to plays and players, and displays a strong interest in theatrical problems and dramatic theory (579). Or one might focus on how Quixote's own performance of chivalry elicits performance energies, and actual performances, from others (Sancho agrees to play his squire; the innkeeper, a castellan [36], etc.); for these counter-performances, while they usually begin in mockery, sometimes reveal a performance impulse as deep, and as crazy, as that of Quixote himself. (Thus, the bachelor Carrasco sets out on a quest after Quixote as single-minded as Quixote's own [601–2]; the Duke and Duchess pursue a charade with Quixote comparable in timescale and elaborateness to the latter's own knightly "charade" [733–832].)[109] Or one might argue, in view of the many subsequent stage adaptations Cervantes's novel has received (from Fielding and Henry Irving to Balanchine and Mitch Leigh), that "Don Quixote" is itself a great dramatic role—a role asking to be acted because it asks, *what is acting?*—which Alonso Quijano de la Mancha was only the first of many to attempt. Or, coming closer to our own perspective, it would not be difficult to find in Don Quixote a prototype of the actor as active reader, who "fills in the blanks" of the text with his own conceptions.

Don Quixote as sometime performer, as role, as evoker of acting in others, as active reader—all of these suggest the legitimacy of, but none in itself constitutes, the parallel I wish to propose, which is as follows: *Don Quixote is one who, like an actor, rises into action in response to a text that he seeks thereby simultaneously to deepen his immersion in and to supplant.*

Clearly, Don Quixote seeks to *supplant* the texts he reads; his whole career, his essential project, could be described as one long attempt to replace the texts of knightly adventure with his own adventures as a knight (an effort in which, so far as world literature is concerned, he has been successful beyond his wildest dreams). But no less obvious is his desire to *immerse* himself in the chivalric material. One of the first things we learn about him is that he has become "immersed in his reading" (27). And, in fact, his whole career and essential project could equally well be described as an attempt to deepen this readerly immersion in what he himself calls "the *mare magnum* of their histories" (696), *immersion* here implying, as it generally does in oral fantasies, total fusion or merger; ultimately, Quixote seeks nothing less than, as Mariann Regan puts it, "to become the text itself."[110] And, what is crucial to our argument, this irreducibly ambiguous impulse to supplant/immerse himself in the text time and again leads him to *rise and enact*. I will give three examples of Quixote thus called into motion by a text. "Many times," his niece recalls,

> my uncle would sit reading those impious tales of misadventure for two whole days and nights at a stretch; and when he was through, he would toss the book aside, lay his hand on his sword, and begin slashing at the walls. (50)

When this reader is moved, he is *moved*. The choice of the walls as target is also significant: Partitions and boundaries are the natural enemies of him who seeks, above all, the boundariless state.

A second example: Given the lie by a pugnacious Biscayan, "'"'You shall see as to that presently,' said Agrajes,"'" Don Quixote quoted. He cast his lance to the earth, drew his sword, and, taking his buckler on his arm, attacked the Biscayan with intent to slay him" (68). The quotation is from one of the books Quixote most desires to supplant/merge with, *Amadis of Gaul*,[111] and one suspects it is less the force of the insult than the opportunity to supplant and merge with the desired text which now brings him to his feet.

A third and particularly revealing example occurs at a moment when Quixote is more than usually immobilized, as the result of a beating he has just received:

> Seeing, then, that he was indeed unable to stir, he decided to fall back upon a favorite remedy of his, which was to think of some

passage or other in his books; . . . the story of Baldwin and the
Marquis of Mantua, when Carloto left the former wounded upon
the mountainside . . . impressed him as being especially suited to the
straits in which he found himself; and, accordingly, with a great
show of feeling, he began rolling and tossing on the ground as he
feebly gasped out the lines which the wounded knight of the wood
is supposed to have uttered. (47)

Here the mere *recollection* of a long since read text suffices to put the
deactivated knight back into action—and by what we have found to be
the usual route: from initial active orality ("feebly gasped out") to eventual whole-body involvement ("rolling and tossing").

It could be objected that in each of the three preceding examples
either the text in question has been memorized or the scene in question
is a flashback. And it is remarkable that, so far as I can remember, never
in the present of the novel do we see this voracious reader with a book
in his hand (except, in pt. 2, the book of his own pt. 1 adventures, an
exception to which I shall return). Far, however, from this being an
argument *against* Don Quixote as actor-reader, it is the confirmation of
it. For many years prior to the outset of the novel Quixote read of
enactment; now he rises to enact his reading—*and the novel begins at that
moment*. But this is as much as to say that the whole ensuing novel is
an account of a reader coming off the books he seeks to merge with and
supplant—the very description I have offered of the *actor's* work. In this
sense, the action of *Don Quixote* is acting. And the relegation of reading
to recollection or flashback is a running reminder that reading has "now"
(i.e., in the present of the novel) passed over into acting once and for all,
to the point where the richest scene of "reading" in the novel, the moment that, I would argue, conclusively sums up Don Quixote as actor-
reader, does not involve an actual book at all.

In chapters 25 and 26 of part 2 Quixote and his party witness a
puppet show, in which the attempt of a disguised knight, Gaiferos, to
rescue his wife, Melisendra, from captivity among the Moors, is depicted (675–87). All goes well until the moment when the Moorish army
sets out in pursuit of the fleeing lovers:

Upon seeing such a lot of Moors and hearing such a din, Don
Quixote thought that it would be a good thing for him to aid the
fugitives; and, rising to his feet, he cried out, "Never as long as I

live and in my presence will I permit such violence to be done to so famous a knight and so bold a lover as Don Gaiferos. Halt, lowborn rabble; cease your pursuit and persecution, or otherwise ye shall do battle with me!"

With these words he drew his sword, and in one bound was beside the stage; and then with accelerated and unheard-of fury he began slashing at the Moorish puppets, knocking some of them over, beheading others, crippling this one, mangling that one. (683)

Now, of course, there is one very obvious sense in which this episode marks Don Quixote as an actor: He sees his place as in the action, not in the audience. What concerns us, however, is not this general resemblance between Quixote's behavior and acting but, rather, the extent to which Quixote's response to the puppet play can be seen as exemplifying the actor's coming into action off a text toward which he feels conflicting impulses to merge with and supplant.

The conflicting impulses themselves are certainly present. Insofar as Quixote seeks to become personally involved in the battle, he enacts an impulse to *deepen his immersion* in the fiction. Insofar as he seeks to change the course of events, and thereby shake off the anxiety they are causing him, he enacts a need to *supplant* the fiction with activity of his own. We even find evidence of the ushering in of whole-body activity by an upsurge in active orality: Before bounding up onto the stage, sword in hand, Quixote twice verbally interrupts the exchange (681, 682).

What we don't, of course, find is *a text*. Whatever the nature of Quixote's responses, they are to a puppet show; how, then, can they be compared to—never mind seen as epitomizing—the responses of an actor-*reader* to a text?

To this I reply as follows: What Don Quixote has before him on the puppet stage is a two-dimensional, threadbare chivalric fiction, performed by automata, which he nonetheless experiences as a real event that he is able, nay obliged, to take part in. But "a two-dimensional, threadbare chivalric fiction, performed by automata, which he nonetheless experiences as a real event that he is able, nay obliged, to take part in" is what Don Quixote has before him every time he opens one of his chivalry books. The puppet show is not a book, but it is a book *as books appear to Don Quixote,* that is, to one who has, in Karlheinz Stierle's words, "lost all awareness of the text as such."[112] *But this is precisely how* his *"book" (the script) appears to the actor,* that is, as an event "already in progress" which, however, does not seem to be going too well without him—which, indeed, cries out for his prompt personal intervention.

Surely, though, an actor doesn't destroy what he intervenes in? But there is a sense in which he does exactly that. To act is to displace one mode of representation (the text) by another (the performing body). Of the actor generally, then, it might be said what can here literally be said of Quixote and the puppets: that, thanks to him, a faraway conflict now unexpectedly rages in our midst—but his efforts to bring this about have left the original representational means in a shambles. The actor is another who has "lost all awareness of the text as such."

To all this I can easily imagine a single overwhelming objection. Don Quixote is exclusively obsessed with one kind of text, and his need to enact texts of this kind is itself obsessive. How can so idiosyncratic a figure be taken as a "type" of the actor or of anything else: Of what but itself can a monomania be typical? To this I would reply that Quixote is presented as a uniquely far-gone, but by no means unique, reader—that, on the contrary, in him is portrayed a potential present in all readers, in the act of reading itself.

The world of *Don Quixote* is one where readers (not just Don Quixote) tend to be set in motion by texts (not just chivalric texts). In fact, the novel comes close to endorsing the view that the power to set its readers in motion is a property possessed by every text. When Quixote's niece recommends burning all books on the grounds that any one of them might become a script for monomania (52), the proposal appears a bit . . . quixotic. And, yet, the prediction she casually throws off:

> I shouldn't wonder at all if my uncle, after he has been cured of this chivalry sickness, reading one of these books [of pastoral poetry], should take it into his head to become a shepherd and go wandering through the woods and meadows singing and piping. (56)

eventually comes true not only for Quixote himself (949–51) but for two other sets of readers as well: the students Ambrioso and Grisóstomo, whom we see put aside their scholars' gowns for shepherds' weeds (87); and the court ladies, who, having pored over the eclogues of Garcilaso and Camões, now go about the countryside acting them out (887). At times it almost seems as if the only way to avoid being set in motion by a text is to be set in motion by *another* text. "If . . . carried away by your natural inclination, you feel that you must read of knightly exploits," the canon advises Don Quixote, "then turn to the Book of Judges in the Holy Scriptures" (438). Perhaps Quixote is recalling this advice when, on his deathbed, he expresses the wish that it were not too late to undo the bad effects of his reading—by other reading:

> I see through all the nonsense and fraud contained in [the books of chivalry], and my only regret is that my disillusionment has come so late, leaving me no time to make any sort of amends by reading those that are the light of the soul. (984)

The choice of life is a choice of reading matter—a choice, one might say, of script.

In the moment when the innkeeper brings out the book in which he keeps his hay and barley accounts, and, "reading" from it, dubs Don Quixote a knight (40), there opens before us a still more vertiginous possibility: If an account book used as a script can put you in knightly motion, perhaps *any* text can put you in *any* motion? Far from viewing Quixote as sui generis, Cervantes seems to imply that for a reader to be set in motion by a text is *always* a possible outcome between a reader and a text—any reader and any text. Acting, one might say, is *a risk reading runs.*

The point in all this is not to deny Quixote's madness but to name it. In Quixote we see the utmost development of a potential for madness in all reading. That potential is called acting. Don Quixote carries reading behavior to extremes. But acting is just such extreme behavior on the part of reading. Don Quixote has gone off the same deep end that reading goes off when it goes off to become acting. All the wondering or dismissive verdicts one might render on Don Quixote's "mad" performance in the puppet theater of reading turn out to be more or less neutral statements about the acting process. *"Quixote can't be kept down."* By his rising-to-enact the actor symbolizes the refusal of a "lost" physical of reading to be "kept down" (i.e., repressed)—symbolizes the refusal even as he begins the work of recovery. *"Quixote can't be made to understand."* As well say that the Royal Shakespeare Company "can't be made to understand" that they're not supposed to perform their reading of *Nicholas Nickleby*—or of *All's Well That Ends Well.* *"Quixote forgets himself."* But *acting* is a reading that "forgets itself" in both meanings of the term: It forgets that it is only reading—and is thereby enabled to "forget itself" in the idiomatic sense: *go too far,* rise, move.

Still, to enshrine Don Quixote as the very type of the actor, whatever other advantages it may bring, must seem to lock in once and for all what many would view as the chief limitation of the approach to acting taken in this book. If the actor is a reader, and is best epitomized by the text-obsessed Don Quixote, what about acting in the absence of texts and reading—what about improvisation? How can the entire performance tradition running from, say, the commedia dell'arte through Viola Spolin be brought within the bounds of, or even squared with, a view of acting as reading?

This is a question that seems to me worth considering in some detail, not because I consider improvisation a "difficulty" to be disposed of but because I consider it a paradoxical limiting case of acting as reading, in the light of which all the more usual cases reveal their aspiration.

The argument I intend to develop is as follows: that improvisation can best be understood not as acting without a text but as the simultaneous production ("writing") and consumption ("reading") of a text; that this production/writing and consumption/reading are the forms that active and passive orality, respectively, assume in an improvisatory context; and that their inevitable coincidence in an improvised action is improvisation's version of the boundariless state—the most persuasive version yet and, therefore, the one to which all forms of scripted acting can be seen as aspiring.

As some preliminary indication that the improvisatory impulse does not necessarily preclude text-involvement, I would point to the presence of it in none other than our paragon of text-obsessiveness, Don Quixote. In fact, the very moment we have taken as epitomizing Don Quixote as actor-reader—his coming into action off the "text" of the puppet show—itself displays an improvisatory aspect. For, while Quixote, as I have said, treats the puppet show as a "script," it is not a script that contains a role for him *until he improvises one:* that of knight-appearing-out-of-nowhere-to-save-the-day. The puppet show, I have argued, represents the chivalric literature as the chivalric literature appears to Quixote, that is, as *out before him to enter.* But no more in the chivalric literature as a whole than in the puppet show that stands for it is there a role reserved especially for Quixote. He is, in general, as here in the puppet play, going to have to *write himself in*—an essentially improvisatory project that becomes explicitly so at such a moment as the following:

And so we find our newly fledged adventurer jogging along and talking to himself. "Undoubtedly," he is saying, "in the days to come, when the true history of my famous deeds is published, the learned chronicler who records them, when he comes to describe my first sally so early in the morning, will put down something like this: 'No sooner had the rubicund Apollo spread over the face of the broad and spacious earth the gilded filaments of his beauteous locks, and no sooner had the little singing birds of painted plumage greeted with their sweet and mellifluous harmony the coming of the Dawn, who, leaving the soft couch of her jealous spouse, now showed herself to mortals at all the doors and balconies of the horizon that bounds La Mancha—no sooner had this happened than the famous knight, Don Quixote de la Mancha, forsaking his own downy bed and mounting his famous steed, Rocinante, fared forth and began riding over the ancient and famous Campo de Martiel.' "

And this was the truth, for he was indeed riding over that stretch of plain. . . .

And so he went on, stringing together absurdities, all of a kind that his books had taught him, imitating insofar as he was able the language of their authors. (31)

Now this is admittedly a rather strange "improvisation." Not that one cannot think of analogies from actual theater practice. Brecht has a detachment exercise in which the actor, exactly like Quixote here, "speaks his part not as if he were improvising it himself but like a quotation . . . using the third person and the past tense."[113] Story-theater actors often tell their action as they do it. And consider the following teaching device of Stanislavski's:

"In every *physical action,* unless it is purely mechanical, there is concealed some *inner action,* some feelings. This is how the two levels of life in a part are created, the inner and the outer. They are intertwined. A common purpose brings them closer together and reinforces the unbreakable bond between them. . . .

"I shall prove it in my own person by repeating the scene from *The Inspector General,* not mechanically but completely justified as to the physical being of the part."

Tortsov began to act and at the same time to explain his feelings.

"While I am playing I listen to myself and feel that, parallel with the unbroken line of my physical actions, runs another line, that of the spiritual life of my role. It is engendered by the physical and corresponds to it. But these feelings are still transparent, not very provocative. It is still difficult to define them or be interested in them. But that is not a misfortune. I am satisfied because I sense the beginnings inside me of the spiritual life of my part," said Tortsov. "The more often I re-live the physical life the more definite and firm will the line of the spiritual life become."[114]

This is especially reminiscent of the Quixote passage, not only by virtue of its two-track, talking-while-doing structure but also in that the narrative that Tortsov-Stanislavski improvises of the actions he is simultaneously performing literally *becomes*, as Quixote imagines his own narration eventually becoming, part of the book that will chronicle those actions for future readers—becomes, that is, a page in *Creating a Role*.

Still, such special cases notwithstanding, we normally expect improvisation to consist of enactment, not commentary. "No playwriting!" one imagines Viola Spolin hollering at Quixote from the sidelines of the Campo de Martiel. And yet, in this seemingly "too literary" improvisation, Don Quixote is directly playing a single action. One might say he is playing his objective *(to get across the plain to my next adventure)* in the context of his superobjective *(to inscribe myself among the texts of chivalry)*. But, in fact, the relation between Quixote's doing and telling is even more intimate than that between objective and superobjective.

Occasionally, Quixote permits himself to fantasize about "the wise magician . . . to whom shall fall the task of chronicling this extraordinary history of mine" (31). And yet, when in part 2 just such chronicles of his history begin to reach him, he is notably incurious as to their contents: He briefly checks the spurious continuator's version for errors of fact and does not even deign to dip into the genuine (i.e., Cervantes's own) account (895–98, 525–31). For, ultimately, Quixote regards the task of inscribing his "deeds . . . in the book of fame" (131) as properly no one's job but his own—as, indeed, only another name for *doing* the deeds.[115] One of the first things we learn about Quixote as reader is that often "he was tempted to take up his pen and literally finish the tale" (26). In a way this could stand as a description of his entire subsequent career. The scene of simultaneous doing/chronicling with which we began is only an unusually explicit instance of Quixote's fundamental project: His "heroic" actions are themselves so many attempts to write himself into the book of fame.

Nor is such "writing oneself in" the special case that it may at first appear. In a typical Montaigne essay the opinion of one after another ancient author will be summarized or quoted; then, by way of some such phrase as "if I must bring myself into this,"[116] Montaigne inscribes himself among the other scribes. What we see in Quixote is a more than usually explicit case of the usual case. Every writer seeks to inscribe himself among the scribes; all writing is a writing in.

So, of course, is all improvising.[117] Far from being simply a performance without text, improvisation enacts a whole series of essentially textual ambitions: to write oneself in; to write oneself; to be oneself the author of a text that is, also, oneself; to be a self-writing text.[118]

Our subject, however, is not acting as writing. To have established a link between improvisation and textuality will not do us much good if we cannot extend it to reading. But where would reading enter the picture? A scriptless actor seems to have nothing to read—except, possibly, himself. Could it be that the self-writing text is also a self-reading one?

In a more literal sense than any improvisatory actor Don Quixote gives rise to a text of his own actions: the authorized and spurious accounts of his adventures. But, as we have seen, when these accounts eventually fall into Quixote's hands, he scarcely vouchsafes them a glance, i.e., he passes up the opportunity for self-reading. Mallarmé described Hamlet as "reading in the book of himself"[119] (an image no doubt suggested by Hamlet's own "book and volume of my brain");[120] Proust promised to make his audience "fit readers of themselves";[121] and Keats put forward a view of the self-as-book from which the self-as-reader draws nourishment: "the Heart . . . is the Mind's Bible, . . . the teat from which the Mind or intelligence sucks its identity."[122] Particularly this last passage, with its imagery of oral self-sustenance, suggests that, if acting is reading in the books of others, improvisatory acting might well be reading in the book of the self. Such an approach sounds promising, but I think Don Quixote is right to be skeptical.

For one thing, what manner of "book" would the self present to the actor-reader? The poststructuralists have argued that, yes, the self is a text—but a wholly *stereotyped* one. According to Roland Barthes, "subjectivity is . . . only [a] wash of codes"; what seems to us our "personal core" is no more than "the track or the furrow left by the experience of texts of all kinds."[123] In short, if we are a text, "we are . . . an already-read text."[124] But to read in the book of an "already-read" self is not to read anything new, hence, it would seem, not to improvise.[125]

But perhaps the poststructuralists are wrong and the "book of the self" is not stereotyped but "original": Then would "reading in the book of the self" be a good description of improvisation? One has only to remove this obstacle, however, to see that the quality of the reading matter was never really the issue. The difficulty with the whole conception lies not in the self's being a stale or otherwise unsatisfactory text but simply in its *being* a text, i.e., already written, *there before* the improviser. For an actor to read in the book of the self would, after all, be to treat the self as a preexisting script, *available to do,* and to do a script, even a script of one's own, is not to improvise.

If improvisation is not "reading in the book of the self," in what sense *is* it reading? Actually, the answer is already implicit in the quasi-improvisatory passage from *Don Quixote* with which we began. "No sooner had the rubicund Apollo spread over the face of the broad and spacious earth the golden filaments of his beauteous locks"—so Don Quixote writes as he goes. Only this is not really Don Quixote's writing; it is all straight out of the chivalry books: "and so he went on, stringing together absurdities, all of a kind that his books had taught him, imitating insofar as he was able the language of their authors." Such "writing" on Quixote's part amounts to no more than taking a prior writing as having reference to himself. But this is equivalent to saying that Quixote's "writing" amounts to no more than a certain "reading" of prior writing, or, at any rate, one does not know whether to *call* the activity in question "reading" or "writing." I am going to argue that it is uncertainty on this score—and not, for example, any "freshness" or "spontaneity" that may or (as here) may not be present—which marks activity as improvisatory.

It will be objected that this is a special case: Not every improviser brings forth pastiche, so not all improvisatory writing (in) can, without further ado, simply be labeled "reading (in)." This is true, but the tendency toward an equivalence between reading and writing in the improvisatory act—and, let it not be forgotten, between the passive and active oralities that reading and writing enact on this level—is not ultimately dependent, as the Quixote example somewhat misleadingly suggests, on the identity between what is written and what is read. It is the *activities* of reading and writing that improvisation sets equal. By this I do not mean that reading and writing turn out to be the same process—a perspective we considered and rejected in chapter 2—but that in certain situations, of which improvisatory acting is one, the processes of reading and writing cannot easily be told apart.

What is the distinguishing mark of such a situation? So long as there is a literal text present, the "identity" between reading and writing can only be a manner of speaking. But where "the text" is only a matter of speaking, the identity between reading and writing is free to become the literal case. It is such a situation that confronts us in improvisatory acting. *Improvisation names the identity toward which reading and writing tend in the absence of a text.*

Before going on to consider improvisation itself in this light let us orient ourselves to this perspective by examining some "middle cases" between *text present:* identity of reading and writing only figurative and *text absent:* identity of reading and writing literally the case.

Are there such middle cases? There had better be! As I noted earlier in another context, contemporary criticism abounds in assertions of the identity between reading and writing, of which the following are only a small sampling:

> Today the fundamental question no longer concerns the *writer* and the *work,* but *writing* and *reading,* and consequently it is our task to define a new space in which these two phenomena might be understood as reciprocal and simultaneous, a curved space, a medium of exchanges and reversibility in which we would at last be on the same side as our language.[126]

> One must then, in a single gesture, but doubled, read and write.[127]

> The reader writes the text.[128]

> I write my reading.[129]

If one chooses to hear such statements as expressions of *aspiration,* their purport is clear enough. But to supply a situation of which they might be the description, a level on which they might do no more than state the facts of the matter—this is not so easy. So long as the context is presumed to be one of actual texts, such equations of reading to writing seem either plainly false or plainly figurative. On the one hand, the reader did not literally conceive the word–strings or set down the marks of the writing he is reading (*Anna Karenina* was there before I bought my copy). On the other hand, if all that is meant is that readers "compose," or "realize," texts out of the signs provided, then reading = writing is just another trope for active reading, and, as I argued in chapter 2, not an especially appropriate one. The *presence* of a text, it seems, consigns all reading = writing statements to falsity; the *absence* of one, to metaphor.

But the literal and figurative possibilities having both been excluded, there seems no remaining level for the equation to make sense on, nothing left for it to mean. Fortunately, the middle is not quite so thoroughly excluded. We are not reduced to imagining *either* a reader/ writer with actual book and pen somehow both in hand *or* an empty-handed, wholly metaphorical "reader"/"writer." There is, in fact, a whole spectrum of intermediate situations with respect to which the statement "reading = writing" is neither simply metaphorical nor simply untrue.

To take a very obvious example: When we hail the appearance of a new piece of critical writing on Chekhov as a fresh reading of Chekhov, are we hailing reading or writing? Or consider acts of translation. When I render *le livre* as "book," am I reading the French word in English or writing the English word for the French?

Or imagine the following. You sneak up behind someone who claims to be reading aloud—and find that there is nothing on the pages of his book. You would say: "Oh, then he's *not* reading." Or, if you were a poststructuralist critic, you might say: "His reading is really writing." It would be quite clear that in the first case you would be using *reading* literally; in the second case, figuratively—our two original blind alleys.

But now suppose that you had formed a suspicion that the pages were blank but could not get a glimpse of the book, or, what would create the same difficulty for your inquiry, that *the reader holds no book.* There are then two possibilities: Either this self-proclaimed reader is reciting earlier, memorized *reading,* or he is *writing* the stuff as he goes along. How could you determine which?

It is tempting to say: "Well, if I could see the book he claims to be reading from, then I'd know." But not necessarily. In Dostoyevsky's *The Idiot* Aglaia recites to Prince Myshkin a poem of Pushkin's which, she feels, perfectly sums up his life. And when she comes to the lines:

In his blood he traced the letters
A. M. D. upon his shield,

she changes the letters *A*, *M*, and *D* to *N*, *F*, and *B*, the initials of the woman Myshkin is in love with.[130] Shall we say Aglaia has mis*read* or re*written* the initials? This is not a psychological question about Aglaia; it has nothing to do with whether she consciously altered the text or made a Freudian slip;[131] it cannot be settled by a better knowledge of Aglaia's motives. *But neither can it be settled by a glance at the (absent) text from which she learned the poem.* Or, rather, inspection of Aglaia's copy of Pushkin would tell us whether the departure was hers or the printer's but, assuming it to be hers, would not tell us whether to name that departure (mis)reading or (re)writing. Nor does the difficulty arise from Aglaia's not being the author of the poem. Imagine the same alteration made under the same circumstances by the poet himself. In fact, Dickens often made spur-of-the-moment changes as he read his books aloud in public;[132] were these "extempore improvements" by a reading writer acts of reading or writing?

From this series of examples we may conclude as follows: In the presence of a text the distinction between reading and writing may be sometimes clear, sometimes problematic, *but in the absence of a text the distinction between reading and writing tends toward the undecidable.*

How are we to understand this "undecidability of reading/writing in the absence of a text" when what the text is absent from is the work of an improvising actor?[133] How is a text "absent" from improvisatory work? Surely not as Aglaia's copy of Pushkin is absent from her recital, i.e., present somewhere else, temporarily unavailable. In fact, a text is neither simply absent nor simply present in a course of improvisatory work.

To improvise is to *produce* a text (of *actions,* be it understood, as well as *words*) "in the moment." But, at the same time, to improvise is to *consume*[134]—draw upon, be nourished by—that text, in the very moment of producing it. An improvisation, one might say, is no sooner produced than "produced" (in the theatrical sense), never to be produced (in either sense) again.

Shall we say improvisation produces text "only" to consume it? But this implies a time lag between two distinct moments, and there *aren't* two distinct moments, because there aren't two distinct activities: The (moment of) producing *is* the (moment of) consuming. Or to put it another way: The improvising actor makes it up as he goes along. But also: The improvising actor *uses* it up as he goes along, making it up; he uses up his making up.

Now, insofar as what the improvising actor does is to *produce* the text he consumes, we may call his activity *writing*. And insofar as what the improvising actor does is to *consume* the text he produces, we may call his activity *reading*. But, since what the improvising actor does is indistinguishably to produce and consume a text, we do not know whether to call his activity writing or reading. It is for this reason that I define improvisation as the undecidable relation that writing assumes to reading in the absence of a (prior) text.

But how does such a definition place improvisation, which has "nothing to read" until it writes something for itself, in continuity with other forms of acting as reading? The answer is as follows. In improvisation's *writing* (producing, making up) of the text, we recognize the latest displacement of that *active orality* whose nature is to expel, put forth, ex-press. In improvisation's *reading* (consuming, using up) of the text we recognize the latest displacement of that *passive orality* whose nature is to receive nourishment, draw sustenance, be fed. How, then, shall we understand improvisation's *rendering indistinguishable* of writing and reading, if not as a "setting equal" of the improviser's *orally active* and *orally passive* impulses in a single action, that of the improvisation itself, which—as no less (active) production/writing than (passive) consumption/reading—cannot help but be the enactment of both impulses? Or to restate it in our usual form:

Acting (as improvisation)

Orally Active Impulse: I produce (make up, "write") a text of actions.
Orally Passive Impulse: I consume (use up, "read") a text of actions.
"Setting Equal": I consume by my actions the text my actions produce.

Thus, to define improvisation in terms of the indistinguishability of writing and reading is ultimately to recognize the form in which improvisation continues acting's general project of "setting equal" active and passive impulses toward a text, in the limiting case where there is no text *except insofar as the attempt to continue the project generates one.*

It is precisely this absence of a literal text which enables improvisation to offer the most perfect approximation yet of the boundariless relation between text and reader. "Perfect" here is of course not a value judgment. The point is not to exalt improvisatory performance over other kinds but to recognize improvisation as a farthest limit, in aspiring toward which other kinds of acting *reveal their drift.*

For, when it comes to regaining the boundariless state, all these other kinds start at a disadvantage from which they can never really recover, in that they start in division—*here* is the actor and *there* is the text—whereas the essence of the boundariless state is to be, as yet, undivided. In improvisatory work, on the other hand, where the text is only now being produced in, through, as the activity of the actor, there is no such initial division to be overcome, for there is no way for one to arise: Here acting itself inscribes a text that is itself acting. More like a writer than like a scripted actor—I have already noted how, in improvisation, active orality assumes the dimensions of writing—the improvisational actor sets up a textual "flow" of his own that denies his dependence on any feeding source outside the self. His active orality is, thus, not merely, as with the child "spitting back" milk or the scripted actor "regurgitating" lines, a matter of being active about one's taking in; he actively *produces* his intake.

Actor and text, thus, coincide in improvisation in a way that they cannot possibly coincide in any other kind of acting: not as the result of a healed division or closed breach but as having never yet known differentiation. But *never yet to have known differentiation* is the essence of the boundariless relation, which is, thus, *given in advance* to improvisation as its structure—the very nature of the thing, there from the start.

To this relation other forms of acting aspire back, but the aspiration *back* to such a state already contains a contradiction, for it is an aspiring to something's *not* having occurred whose *having* occurred alone explains the aspiration. We seem driven to conclude that the only fully satisfactory means of reuniting actor and text in a boundariless relation is for them never to have known separation. Hopeless as this may sound, it is precisely the situation that obtains in a self-authoring pattern of improvisatory activity which has "never yet" undergone division—has, indeed, *no way* of undergoing a division—into reader and text.

The disappearance of reader and text into a pattern of bodily activity may seem a strange outcome to the tale of acting as reading. And yet, it is the usual outcome: In all theater work the text and the reader tend to disappear. The actor comes off book, the "lost" physical is recovered, the text is seen no more: How should that recovery not entail that disappearance?[135]

It is in this light that I see improvisation as the condition to which all acting aspires, less an alternative to work with a script than the limit that scripted work itself forever seeks to approach, and in so doing reveals what has been its ambition from the first. *Improvisation's claim never to have known the loss of the boundariless state is only the limiting case of all acting's claim to recover a boundariless state whose essence is never to have known loss.* As a text that has always already disappeared into bodily activity, improvisatory work seems to stand surety for the actor's fundamental confidence that *where text was there bodily activity shall* (once more) *be*—in other words, for the whole claim of acting to recover a "lost" physical of reading.

Yet the preceding account leaves two basic questions unanswered. First, given the nature of what is to be recovered, how complete can any "recovery" of it be deemed which remains the essentially solitary enterprise I have thus far made acting out to be—"solitary" both in its general nature as reading and in its ultimate outcome as a (boundariless) relation between one individual and his text? And, second, what of the fact that this solitary transaction is not, or is not primarily, between the actor and the text as such but, rather, between the actor and his *role*? Actually, these two questions—the place of role and the place of other actors—are closely related. Roles, we shall see, are so many ways to read, reading identities, "other readers"; while the other actors who assume the roles are, of course, quite literally other readers. I will, therefore, first consider the actor's work on his role as an attempt to assume (and as a resistance to assuming) the identity of another reader and then examine the work actors do with one another in rehearsal as an encounter between those who have each assumed the reading-identity of "another."

It might, I suppose, be argued that to "add" role or character to our model is not really to add anything; that to act is necessarily to act a role (however *role* may be defined in a particular theater piece or performance tradition); and that, indeed, the types of the actor-reader I have proposed already reflect this necessity: It is as "the Knight" that Don Quixote rises to enact the script of knighthood, as "Lancelot" that Paolo comes into action off the text of love. If by *role* is meant the other with whom the actor deals, have I not dwelt at length on the actor's dealings with the other? If by *role* is meant the stretch of text with which the actor is primarily concerned, have I not considered in detail the actor's transaction with the text?

But, while in general it may be acceptable to conceive of characters as "others" or "stretches of text" or in any number of other ways—say, as narrative functions (destinee, facilitator) or as literary-psychological archetypes (*miles gloriosus,* Wise Old Woman) or as imaginary persons who happen to live in *Fuente Ovejuna* rather than in Fuente Ovejuna— not all these options are available to *us.* We have been working with a particular theory of texts and reading, that of Norman Holland. If we now seek to extend the model of acting we have built on Holland's theory to acting a *character,* we must first ask what view of character is implied by the theory Holland propounds.

As for the feasibility of such an extension, here we may take some encouragement from a remark of Holland himself. According to *The Dynamics of Literary Response,* the reader's transaction with any particular character "continues and specializes" his oral transaction with the entire work.[136] This would seem to imply that the *actor*-reader's transaction with his particular character "continues and specializes" *his* oral transaction with the text as such—his *supplanting, merging, "setting equal"* of impulses toward, and achievement of a *boundariless relationship* with, it. This is not to say that all we have to do is substitute "character" for "text" in our earlier formulations. Until we say what we mean by "characters," it does not convey very much to assert that actors supplant, merge, "set equal" their impulses toward, and seek to stand in a boundariless relation with, them.

In his chapter on "Character and Identification" Holland discusses some of the characters in *Romeo and Juliet* as follows:

> A character like Romeo appeals mostly on the level of drive—he is the romantic lover, and we satisfy our wishes to love and be loved through him. The Nurse offers a distinctive pattern of drive gratification and defense. In many of her speeches she refers to something missing and offers a substitute, thus defending against or getting rid of the drive by gratifying it, rather an appropriate pattern for a wetnurse and a bawd.

Other characters we incorporate primarily as defenses: the Friar, the Prince, but notably our friend Mercutio. We do, it is true, get some vicarious gratification from the way he satisfies his narcissism, but mostly . . . he acts out for us a defense against the drives the play has stirred up.[137]

In this analysis each character is represented as working out a strategy for gratifying/managing his impulses toward the fantasy material with which *Romeo and Juliet* confronts him. But "working out a strategy for gratifying/managing their impulses toward the fantasy material with which a text confronts them" is what Holland argues *readers* do, is in fact Holland's *definition* of reading. Thus, though Holland nowhere explicitly states the equivalence, by his own definition of reading it would appear that *to be a character is to be a reader.*

Moreover, Holland seems to be implying, not only are characters in general equivalent to readers, but the identity of a *particular* character turns out to be the thing that distinguishes *the reader he is* from *other readers.*[138] What distinguishes one reader from another? To read is to solve a drive/defense conflict. To be a particular reader is to resolve a drive/defense conflict in a particular way. It is precisely on the basis of how they resolve their drive/defense conflicts that Holland distinguishes between the characters in *Romeo and Juliet*: Romeo is "mostly" drive; the Prince is "primarily" defense; Mercutio is primarily defense but also "satisfies . . . narcissism"; the Nurse offers both "drive gratification and defense," etc. But this is as much as to say: Romeo is *like a reader* who is mostly concerned with gratifying his fantasies; the Prince, *like a reader* who is primarily concerned with fantasy-management; Mercutio, *like a reader* who seeks gratification while remaining well defended, etc.

A character, in other words, is a *way* to read, a *kind* of reader. And a cast of characters comprises a collection of reading-identities, arranged along a "spectrum" from *virtually all drive/no defense* (Romeo) to *virtually all defense/no drive* (the Prince) with most of the characters falling somewhere in between, i.e., embodying, each, some *balance* of drive and defense impulses (the Nurse, Mercutio). On this spectrum of reading-identities, each character occupies a single "point," that of the particular solution to the drive/defense dilemma which he alone offers. In this sense, all characters, however complex, are "single-solution" readers.

Obviously, this does not mean that all characters are "one-dimensional" or "monotonous." Every character represents a single way to read. Whether a given character comes across as complex or simple depends on whether his particular way to read is, like Mercutio's, a complex, or, like the Prince's, a simple one. Still, even with that proviso, I would not care to defend such a model of character as a perfectly adequate or even a wonderfully suggestive one. What interests me about it from the standpoint of acting is all that it posits as *still to be done.* *Character,* as Holland presents and I have elaborated the term, is a somewhat impoverished category, but the poverty is such as an actor's work process might well be understood as an attempt to replenish.

For consider what must be the consequences for acting of conceiving character in such terms as these. If a character is a way to read, a kind of reader, then to play a character is to *agree to read* in that way, to *play at being* that kind of reader. One reads one's role first of all to learn what "reading" will mean for one in this role. I say "first of all": No one would argue that there is nothing more to acting the role of another than acting like another kind of reader. *Reading some other way* is, shall we say, acting's first stab at the problem of *being some other self.*

But immediately a question arises. The actor who, thus, undertakes to play a reader is *himself* a reader, is *already* a reader—*another* reader than the character. (Actually, as we shall see in a moment, he is another *kind* of reader, but, at very least, another one.) This being so, the implicit demand posed by the character that "henceforth you read as I do" is bound to evoke a certain resistance from the actor: What of the reader *he* formerly was, essentially is? "When reading his part," says Brecht, "the actor's attitude should be one of a man who is astounded and contradicts."[139] I would say, rather, that it cannot *but* be so, at least in part. For if on the one hand the actor seeks to assume the new reading-identity offered by the role (this is just another way of saying he wants to *play* the role), on the other hand he must also seek to assert his own identity as a reader at the expense of the character's (this is just another way of saying *he* wants to play the role).

In this ambivalence vis-à-vis the reading-identity of his character we may recognize the latest displacement of the actor's clashing active and passive oral impulses toward the other. Passive orality here manifests itself as an impulse on the part of the actor to accept as his identity that of the reader his character is, and active orality, as an impulse to impose upon the character the identity of the reader he himself is. How an actor's reading-identity differs from a character's, and how an actor goes about "imposing" his reading-identity on a character, it will be the object of the following pages to show.

When I say that a character and an actor are different kinds of
readers I do not mean simply that each is likely to have a different
understanding of the play or of the character himself, though, in fact,
this is also likely to be the case: Polonius's reading of Polonius and of the
action of *Hamlet* will in all probability diverge sharply from that of any
actor cast in the role. Nevertheless, the fundamental difference between
Polonius and the actor playing him *as readers* is not that Polonius reads
himself as wise and effective and that the actor may read him as foolish
and interfering, but that Polonius, like any character, is committed to a
single solution to the drive/defense conflicts of the text in which he
appears, whereas the actor, like any flesh-and-blood reader, is restlessly
"on the move" between the different drive/defense solutions represented
by the characters of the text.

I shall explain in a moment why such a restlessness attends reading.
Assuming that it does so, and an actor's reading no less than anyone
else's, one may ask: What becomes of this readerly need to "keep moving" *between* drive/defense solutions when the actor is confined to enacting some *one* of them, i.e., is cast in a role? Here again, as with the
overall relation of acting to reading, the pattern is one of loss and recovery. To act a character is, from one point of view, to *lose* something as
a reader. Ultimately, though, these reading losses of the actor are not
only recovered but recovered on behalf of, as a depth in, indeed, precisely as a richer *reading*-identity for, the very character on whose behalf
they were first incurred. To see how this comes about we must look
more closely at the nature of the losses a general reader sustains when
he begins to function as an actor.

Occasionally, one hears a reader say something like "I totally
identified with the uncle" (or "the rebels" or "Macduff"). This, according to Norman Holland, is not likely to have been the case:

> The work itself is a total economy of drive and management of
> drive. Some characters, like Romeo, we introject as vicarious sat-
> isfiers of drives. Others, like Mercutio or the Nurse, we introject
> because they embody defensive maneuvers for dealing with the
> anxiety-arousing aspects of the central fantasy. In short, we do not
> identify with *a* character so much as with a total interaction of
> characters in which some satisfy needs for pleasure and others sat-
> isfy our need to avoid anxiety.[140]

Holland's view is strikingly borne out by Edith Buxbaum's research on a twelve-year-old reader of detective stories:

> The boy identified not only, as we would expect, with the invincible and invulnerable heroes of the stories, but, as well, with the unsympathetically presented villains, and even with the victims in their terror, suffering and death. The boy secured the full measure of gratification, open or covert, which each of these roles afforded. . . . The identification with the detectives served to make him more secure. . . . The identification with the villains satisfied his repressed but powerful hostile feelings toward his uncle, his mother and others; that with the victims, an even more deeply repressed wish to be overcome by the uncle and be the passive victim of love-making conceived as sadistic assault.[141]

One needs *all* the solutions of the drive/defense conflict which the characters, collectively, embody, because no one solution can be more than momentarily adequate. Since, in each solution, either drive or defense must predominate, each solution is inherently unstable. Too much of Mercutio's fantasy-management, and the reader finds himself seeking out Romeo and gratification. Too much of Romeo's unwearying pursuit of pleasure, and the reader gladly takes refuge in Friar Lawrence's well-defended cell. Thus, the reader is likely to find himself reading now "with" one character, now with another. For to avail himself of the full spectrum of solutions he must be in constant motion *over* the spectrum, *between* the solutions, opening himself to the unbalance each induces for the sake of the balance that having occupied them all will produce. This empathic "lurching" is, after all, the process by which the author originally *created* the work; it is from just such a *trying on* and *shuttling between* responses to a core fantasy that the characters and conflicts of a text emerge. No wonder, then, that it should be the process by which the general reader—by which I intend no demographic or cultural stereotype but simply the nonacting, the *uncast* reader—recreates it. It cannot, however, be the process of the *actor*-reader.

In one sense, the distinction between actors and other kinds of readers is an artificial one. The actor desires from his reading what any reader desires: to appropriate a text's balance of drives and defenses for himself. But in his pursuit of this universal reading objective the actor-reader labors under a special disadvantage.

We have just seen that appropriating a text's drive/defense balance involves the reader in "lurching" empathically over a spectrum of drive/defense solutions (i.e., characters), each of which is constituted as an *im*balance of drive and defense. Imagine, then, a reader who could not "lurch," who was permanently stuck at some *one* of these unbalanced drive/defense solutions, who was obliged to read through all of (say) *Romeo and Juliet* without ever once budging off the reading-identity represented by Mercutio or Romeo or the Prince. Clearly, such a reader could not benefit from the text's balance of drive and defense impulses because such a balance can only be appropriated by movement *between* solutions—and he is "nailed" to a single one.

But there *is* such a "nonlurching" reader: *the actor*. Once cast as this or that single-solution reader, his lurching days are over. No more may he, like Edith Buxbaum's crime story enthusiast, play the detective and the victim and the villain; he must now play "the Detective" or "the Victim" or "the Villain." Or "Romeo" or "Mercutio" or "the Prince." Coming from the actor who took the role of "the Uncle," "I totally identified with the uncle" is not an implausible or inappropriate claim. To be cast in any role is to assume as one's total identity that of the reader one's character is.

We are now in a position to grasp the nature of the "losses" I spoke of actors incurring when they pass from general reading to acting. Say I am cast as Trepleff. What I got as a general reader from Trepleff—his particular solution to the drive/defense tensions of *The Sea Gull*—I still need and still get. But what about what I formerly got by *lurching away* from Trepleff to Trigorin or Arkadina or Dorn? As a reader, I still need *those* solutions, too—as correctives, as refuges, as openings; in short, as contributing toward my overall balance of defenses and drives—and where am I supposed to get *them*, "immobilized" as I now am at the single solution, Trepleff? To be cast in a role is, thus, to relinquish the very thing readers go to texts for. One cannot, it seems, read as an actor and still retain the benefits that led one to reading in the first place.

Perhaps, then, one should just let them go? Uta Hagen warns the actor against trying to hang onto the experience of general reading:

the images he conceives, and the tones and sounds he hears in his imagination on his first contact with the play must soon be discarded and not confused with the real work on the play and the part.[142]

Since I regard an actor's "real work on the play and the part" as *consisting* in an effort to recover the lost paradise of "first contact" (i.e., general reading), I do not consider this terribly good advice. But, quite apart from whether the advice is good or bad, how feasible is it? The actor now cast as Trepleff may have read *The Sea Gull* years before, with never a thought of one day playing Trepleff or even perhaps of a career in acting. But even if, already engaged as Trepleff, he only now reads the script for the first time, that first-time reading by a soon-to-be Trepleff cannot help but be *also* a general reader's first encounter with *The Sea Gull*. What is the actor supposed to do with this earlier (or concurrent) reading from the vantage of no particular role, once he has been cast in some particular role? The history of one's engagement with a text can no more than any other history be simply "discarded." How does one set about unknowing what, in fact, one knows?

Yet, insofar as "general reading" implies the freedom to "lurch" between drive/defense solutions, Hagen would appear to have a point: It is hard to see how acting can proceed without relinquishing it.[143] If the actor-reader playing Trepleff could, like the general reader of *The Sea Gull*, "lurch away" to Trigorin or Arkadina or Dorn every time Trepleff's drive/defense solution ceased to work for him, who would keep the Trepleff solution in play within *The Sea Gull*'s "total economy of drive and management of drive" till the curtain falls? Isn't it precisely the *inaccessibility* of other solutions (roles) that impels the actor to explore his own character's solution to the fullest—play it out, in every sense, to the end? But a commitment to "play it out to the end" is inherent in the commitment to play a role at all. The only "freedom" an actor sacrifices when he gives up his general reader's mobility is the freedom not to be an actor on that occasion.

This being the case, should "immobilization" in role really be regarded as a "loss" or "problem" for acting? Does it actually bother actors?

It appears to bother Janet Suzman. Cast in the title role of *Hedda Gabler*, the British actress recounts how her first move was to seek points of empathic connection with all the *other* major characters, including offstage characters.[144] For example:

> (Tesman) Tesman says: "I'm going to confess something to you, Hedda. When he'd finished reading, an ugly feeling came over me." Ugly? But that's *my* prerogative, she's thinking. I am full of ugly feelings. (95)

(Judge Brack) Having correctly gauged the extent of Brack's hypoc-
risy, can trust him with her own. When she refers to "our sort of
person," does she mean their common gentility or corruption? (94)

(Aunt Juliane) "You'll be lonely now, Miss Tesman." She understands loneliness. For a second she allows herself to sympathise with
the old lady. To be young and lonely is horrible enough. To be old
and lonely? No! (97)

(Aunt Rina) To die peacefully in bed, of old age, with your loved
ones round you, is not a vision that she can contain in her view of
things. It implies a long and comfortable life, for one thing, and
hers so far has been short and troubled. No great falls from glory?
No marks left on the world? A serene demise ending a serene existence? No! (96)

(Eilert Løvberg) He fled. She never forgave him for fleeing! (Was
she aware of a certain cowardice in him, corresponding to hers? Yet
another link in the chain of comradeship.) (100)

We have seen that characters other than one's own are the form in which
defense/drive solutions other than one's character's own are present in a
text. By thus claiming empathic rapport with each of the other characters, Suzman is implicitly claiming she can (still) occupy any of the other
points on the spectrum of drive/defense solutions which the text affords—the claim of a general reader.

That it is the general reader's freedom to "lurch" which Suzman
aims to recapture by such work is clear both from the *imagery* in which
she describes the work:

No sooner do you get a glimpse of what other paths open up to you
as you hasten round the maze of her character than the game is
over.[145] (85)

and from the *exercise* by which she physicalizes it:

Where she is left alone, and wordless, in Act I . . . Ibsen has a stage
direction, but there is no need to follow it slavishly as long as his
intention—that of showing a restless unhappy creature—is re-

spected. I saw the slippers on the carpet as I roamed around the cage of this room, and it seemed the only thing to do was to kick them out of the way, hateful things. I saw the portrait of my father and flew to it as if to draw comfort from the man who had left me in this mess; and then I felt foolish as the lifeless old boy stared back at me. I felt claustrophobia and nausea closing me in and rushed to fling aside the curtains I perversely had closed. . . . What about the piano? Why not play it? But she's too unsettled to sit down. So, I ran the butt of the gun down the keys. An ugly sound. Defiant. I wandered into the main room surveying the newly arranged furniture. It was better than it had been, but neither pleased me nor displeased me. I shoved the back of the rocking-chair as I passed. (92–93)

Both her "hasten[ing] round the maze" metaphor and her actual "hastening round the stage" exercise (in which, "restless" and "unsettled," she "wandered," "rushed," "roamed") suggest ceaseless motion over a bewildering variety of fixed positions—suggest, that is, the "lurching" of the general reader's mind over a text's spectrum of drive/defense solutions.

Should Suzman have felt the need to justify such an approach, she could always point to the example of Bottom, whose frank desire to play the lady, the tyrant, the lion, etc.,[146] appears in this context only a more frankly expressed version of Suzman's own. It might be objected that all Suzman does is sympathetically "take the part" of Tesman, Aunt Juliane, etc., for a moment, while Bottom actually proposes to take all the parts. But in the theater, where the impulse to take a character's part is customarily enacted by taking the part of the character, the impulse to take *every* character's part is, on some level, an ambition to play them all.

This is a perfectly reasonable ambition—for a reader; it is, in fact, the ambition to be a reader. When we read, Simon Lesser says, we "imaginatively act out every role," and thereby, like the lurching detective story addict described by Edith Buxbaum, secure "the full measure of gratification, open or covert, which each of these roles afford[s]."[147] Such a yearning as Bottom's, then, on the part of an actual actor "trapped" at the single reading identity of his role, might well indicate a nostalgia for the general reader's mobility of response, for the experience of general reading. Do actors know such yearnings?

(Actor) DIANE VENORA: I'm all those things, though, you see. I'm the king. I'm the adventurous knight. I'm the lover. I'm—

(Director) JOSEPH PAPP: I know, but you're doing all of that. I mean—

VENORA: I'm everything.

PAPP: You are, in my estimation. Even Rosencrantz and Guilden-stern.

VENORA: I want to play the lion, too.[148]

Bottom is a joke about what actors need and how actors work and is here invoked jestingly. But the jest is one in which a real actor may, as here, recognize the truth about what she needs and how she works. "I want to play the lion, too." . . . The actor cast as Hamlet or Hedda still yearns to move over the text's spectrum of drive/defense solutions: to be the king, the lover, the knight, "even Rosencrantz and Guilden-stern"—"everything." Bottom's dream is the actor's dream of general reading.

Granted that an actor may entertain such feelings, what's he sup-posed to do about them? He might, of course, actually try to play all the parts: I have myself seen two productions of *Hamlet* and read about one of *The Tempest* in which a single actor took every role.[149] On such occasions Bottom, and the Bottom in every actor, get their wish, and the language in which one reviewer described the solo *Tempest* confirms my understanding of the nature of that wish: "jumping around in the text, he . . . tells each character's personal story."[150] To play all the parts is to be freely in motion ("jumping around in the text") between the work's various drive/defense solutions ("each character's personal story")—in other words, is to be once again a general reader.

But one-man shows are the exception: As a rule, Snug will be along to play the lion; Suzman and Venora will be joined by their supporting casts. If the aspiration to general reader status finds expression in the impulse to be "everything"—every possible reader in the show—what expression can it hope to find in the more usual theatrical situation where each actor is confined to being "something," some *one* reader, his par-ticular character?

At first one might be inclined to answer: none. If to act a role is to agree to be a highly *specific* and *limited* kind of reader, then an impatience to get beyond or throw off this constricted reading-identity and function as a general reader once more would seem to imply restlessness or dissatisfaction with the acting process itself. (True, the one-man *Hamlets* and *Tempest* I mentioned issued in performance, but isn't it precisely the soloist's restlessness or dissatisfaction with the usual constraints of acting which such pieces perform?)

On the contrary, I am going to argue that an impulse *to act all the roles,* understood as the expression of a yearning back toward general reader status, is an essential aspect of the impulse *to act roles at all,* and that, therefore, the struggle to regain general reader status is not merely a move *within* acting but, indeed, a move *on behalf of role.* The question of how the actor "reconciles" his impulse to "act out every role" with his obligation to act some one of them is therefore badly posed. The actor acts out every role *within the project* of acting some one of them, as the elaboration of his commitment to act some one of them. He seeks to be "everything" as his way of being more adequately the something he has undertaken to be. In a word, it is *for his role* that the actor attempts to claim general reader status.

And how does one claim general reader status for the single-solution reader we have found a role to be? Briefly: by adopting an explanation of the singleness that could only be correct if the character were, in fact, a kind of "truncated" general reader. Let me explain.

I have said that to play a role is to pretend to be a certain kind of reader; for example, to play the Prince in *Romeo and Juliet* is to pretend to be an anxious-censorious reader. Now, of an *actual* reader whose every response was, like the Prince's, anxious-censorious, we wouldn't say: He's all anxious censure. We'd say: He's *repressing* or *disavowing* or *leaving unexplored* all but his anxious-censorious responses. That is, the drive/defense solutions he refused to "lurch" to we would interpret as aspects of himself he chose not to acknowledge, and his refusal to "lurch" to them, as an unwillingness to become conscious of, admit the presence of, those aspects of himself.

Of course, it would be a mistake to talk about characters in this way. Characters do not *have* "aspects," unexplored or otherwise; they are themselves only aspects, positions on a spectrum of drive/defense solutions. But it is a mistake readers cheerfully make when they wish to believe—indeed, *as their way* of believing—in the "reality" and "inner life" of characters. (Our customary praise of a credible character as "rounded" or "three-dimensional" itself reflects this tendency: To see an object as three-dimensional is to infer from a single, visible facet that other facets are present but hidden from view. By a "flat" character, on the other hand, we mean one whose single visible facet—i.e., whose basic drive/defense solution—does *not* encourage the imputation of further, "hidden" ones.) Now there is no sort of reader who more urgently needs to be able to believe in the "reality" and "inner life" of a character than the actor who is going to *play* that character with, he hopes, reality and inner life. What, then, could be more natural for the actor than to adopt the assumption that his role is no mere single drive/defense solution, but a *person,* who, though never in fact seen to "lurch" to other drive/defense solutions, must, "of course," be capable of doing so—to posit him, in short, as a general reader, 99 percent of whose response spectrum (i.e., whose consciousness and inner life) is inexplicably "missing" and will have to be supplied by the actor?

And how does one supply a single-solution reader with consciousness and inner life? But the techniques are familiar: One provides him with "motivations," "objectives," and a "superobjective," with unspoken thoughts ("subtexts"), private feelings ("emotion memory"), and a continuous mental life (a "through line"). So that the character may have a past, the actor invents incidents that the playwright did not include:

> One morning after a drinking bout, Roderigo was riding down a canal and saw, as in a dream or vision, the beauteous young Desdemona getting into a gondola to ride to church accompanied by her nurse. His breath was taken away, he stopped his gondola and blearily watched her for a long time. This caught the attention of her nurse.[151]

(He may, indeed, go so far as to compose an entire "imaginary biography.") So that the character may have experience of the physical and social worlds, the actor supplies details of milieu not indicated in the text:

> The house is *messy.* Pretentiously unpretentious living! Ugh. Scatter rugs = Prof. Alex's house = Books piled sideways on shelves. Disorder, and = *unwatered* plants. Maybe an instrument lying open? Or the record player? Yes! Hahaha. Open and ready to go. Loose records lying around. The *Eroica?* Or the *Missa Solemnis?*[152]

Much of this invented detail is of an external nature, yet it is always his character's capacity for inward experience on which the actor is at work. For to specify even the most external "given circumstances" is all the while to be specifying a *self* whose external circumstances might be these.

It is not hard to see why such devices are popular with actors. Suddenly, for the inner life of my character, in which I can never really believe because "he" is only a drive/defense solution, I am able to substitute material from my own inner life, in which I cannot *but* believe. But how can such techniques be viewed as conferring or restoring general-reader status? Since they involve a conscious turning away from or bypassing of the text for material of one's own invention, don't they, rather, represent a *refusal* to read?

On the contrary, we saw in chapter 2 that it is in just such "filling in of the blanks" of a text with material of one's own devising (thus ensuring "good continuation," "connectability of segments," etc.) that the reading process most fundamentally consists. "To end, to fill, to join, to unify—one might say that this is the basic requirement of the *readerly*," according to Roland Barthes.[153] It is also, as I noted earlier, regarded by Stanislavski as a "basic requirement" of the *acting* process: "We have to fill out what he [the playwright] leaves unsaid. Otherwise we would have only scraps and bits to offer out of the life of the persons we portray. You cannot live that way so we must create for our parts comparatively unbroken lines."[154] By insisting on his obligation to fill in the blanks of the character with objectives, motivations, etc., the actor is clearly asserting the prerogatives of, and maintaining his right to function as, a *reader*.

But not, be it noted, as the kind of reader his character is. Interpolating material *about* the character *from outside* the character on the basis of his sense of the character's place in the "total economy" of the text, the actor here behaves as something closer to the kind of reader he was before he assumed the single-solution reading-identity of the role. He reads once more as a general reader.

"Reading once more as a general reader" is certainly not the first description one would think to give of an actor engaged in composing an imaginary biography or doing subtextual analysis. More likely one would say: "He is working on the inner life of his role." But these two so different-sounding formulations are in fact equivalent. For what is the experience of inner life, moment to moment, but just such a "lurching" back and forth between different response options as we have found general reading to be? To supply a character with inner life is, thus, to supply him with the character of a general reader, to make one's own movement over a spectrum of reading responses available to be the movements of his consciousness. "Building a character," in Stanislavski's phrase, means rebuilding a reader, for one "builds" him into the very sort of lurching, full-spectrum reader one left off being in order to play him.

The actor's search for "living character" is, thus, really a search for the "lost" experience of general reading—a loss, according to Uta Hagen, to be accepted without a murmur, an experience to be discarded without a trace. But, as should now be clear, the experience is too valuable to be discarded—valuable for that very process of characterization which Hagen claims it impedes but to which I see it as providing the essential impetus. For it is precisely *his own* loss of general reader's status that impels the actor to fit out *his character* with the emotional range and mobility of a general reader, i.e., with an inner life. He expresses his dissatisfaction with having to play a single-solution reader by playing him as a full-spectrum reader capable of such a dissatisfaction. Recall in this context Janet Suzman's description of her work on Hedda as "hasten[ing] round the maze of her character." The maze, we saw, was an image of the (bewildering) variety of drive/defense solutions extended by the cast of characters as a whole. To install the *entire* maze within some one of the roles ("the maze of *her*"—i.e., Hedda's—"character") is to imply that one can do all one's former, general reader's "lurching," all one's "hastening round," within the compass of, and, indeed, as an exploration of, the inner life of a single character.

One way to summarize what I have been saying about the relation between reading and characterization is: *Bottom was right*—or, at least, on the right track. One does not play all the characters, but one plays *one's character* as "able to play all the characters," i.e., as having access to the full range of drive/defense solutions which the full spectrum of characters represents. Immobilized at a single role, the actor seeks his own former mobility of response *for the role,* so that, assuming the role, he may reassume his own former mobility of response, his "lost" status as a general reader. One might even say that an actor's whole course of work on a role is one long effort to repair the initial "disaster" of having been cast in it, and that, paradoxically, it is the very labor of rebuilding his "lost" reader's status which builds the role to which it was sacrificed.

We are now in a position to see exactly how the actor's transaction with character "continues and specializes" his transaction with the text as a whole, i.e., what form his passive and active oral impulses toward

his character assume, in what manner these are "set equal," and how
their being "set equal" brings actor and character into a boundariless
relation. Stated in our usual format, the answers to these questions are
as follows:

Acting (as a transaction with character)

Orally Passive Impulse:[155] I accept as my identity that of the (single-
solution) reader my character is.
Orally Active Impulse: I impose upon my character the identity of
the (general) reader I am.
"Setting Equal": I impose my identity as a reader upon the character
from whom I accept my identity as a reader.

The *orally passive* implications of the actor's accepting his reading-identity from another, the character, are clear enough: To accept someone
else's identity is to relinquish one's own. Henceforth another (reader)
stands in the place of the reader I was, and, in this other, the reader I
was is lost, gone, "swallowed up."[156] The *orally active* overtones of the
actor's effort to impose his reading-identity on the character should be
clear from the immediately preceding discussion of "building a character" as rebuilding a reader. So that the character may have the actor's
reading-identity for its own mental life, the actor seeks to substitute the
(general) reader he is for the (single-solution) reader the character is.
What is this but an effort on the actor's part to supplant another (reader)
with his own (reading) self—the characteristic expression sought by an
active oral impulse? Thus, in the single action of rising to portray his
character, the actor's active and passive oral impulses toward it are "set
equal." For to portray a character is simultaneously and undecidably to
portray one's acceptance of a reading-identity *from* and one's imposition
of a reading-identity *on* him.

How does such a "setting equal" of their reading-identities bring
actor and character into a boundariless relation? But the boundary to be
removed is precisely one between two different kinds of readers: *the*
(single-solution) *reader he is* and *the* (full-spectrum) *reader I am*. And in
the course of the actor's transaction with character the distinction between these two types of readers cannot help but disappear, since the
actor's portrayal cannot help but be a portrayal of both. For one thing,
since he has but a single presence to stand for the presence of either

reader, the actor necessarily represents the presence of both. But, more basically, since the actor has but a single reading *process* with which to read either *as* the character or *for* him, that reading process is undecidably the reading process of both. *My defensiveness, Mercutio as defensive, Mercutio as enacting my defensiveness, my finding Mercutio defensive*—nothing we have seen about reading as the introjection of a text's drive/defense system would encourage us to regard these "alternatives" as terribly distinct. How, then, is it possible to say whether reading is going on "in here" (in my reading activity, which I impute to the character) or "out there" (in the character's reading activity, which I experience as my own)? With the appearance of such inner/outer confusions we recognize the familiar signs of the boundariless state. It is in the loss of all distinction between his own and the character's reading processes, between himself and the character *as readers,* that the actor's boundariless relation with his character consists.

Now that we have some idea of what it means for an individual actor to assume a role, conceived as an alternative reading-identity, it is possible to take up the encounter *between* actor-readers, each of whom is engaged in such a transaction. It is thus that I would describe rehearsal; for, from the point of view of a theory of acting as reading, the whole nature of the rehearsal process follows from the fact that, in rehearsal, those who have assumed the identities of "other readers" (their characters) come up against actual, flesh-and-blood other readers (their colleagues) who have done likewise.

First, though, a word on the general possibility of extending the acting as reading model to work involving more than one person, for this is an extension that the very nature of the model seems at once to cry out for and to preclude.

I have presented acting as recovery of a "lost" situation that was, originally, not only *physical,* in that it involved eating, but *interpersonal,* in that it involved a mother and a child. How can this original situation be said to have been recovered so long as no one is involved but the single actor-reader whose transaction with the text I have thus far considered? But how introduce others into the essentially solitary transaction between an actor-reader and a text?

In practice, of course, the distinction between working alone on a script and working together with others is never absolute. Actors do not make all their discoveries about a text in solitary reading and only then come to rehearsal; rehearsal is itself a process of discovery about texts.

And, indeed, the very reading scenes I have taken as images of the actor's transaction with the text as often as not involve a transaction with "other actors." Don Quixote comes off book into action *against* his opponents; Paolo comes off book into action *with* Francesca, etc. Furthermore, we have seen that a text may *itself* be experienced as a kind of other, and one's relations with a text, as a relation with "someone else." Such considerations as these certainly seem to argue for a continuity between the actor's solitary work on the script and his rehearsal work with other actors. Yet neither an actor's experience of the text as other nor his sense of his role as "another reader" is likely to survive the arrival on the scene of the *actual* others, his colleagues, who now appear. There can be no literal *supplanting* or *merging* or *blurring of boundaries* with these flesh-and-blood new arrivals; how, then, is the paradigm to be extended to them?

But it is not really a question of "extending" anything. As I have noted, the whole acting-as-reading model traces its origins back to a self-other relation, and every subsequent displacement of the original relation preserves traces of the original "otherward" impulse. Suckling was already *by* another; introjection was *of* another; reading was the breaking down of boundaries between oneself *and* a (textual) other. If the text is itself a displacement of the maternal other, and if other actors in turn displace the text, then is not the individual actor's relationship with these others already given in his relationship with the text?

But things are not so simple. One actor cannot stand in the same relationship to another that each stands in to a "maternal" text. Actors meet as independent adults, and their relations are those of one adult with another—to which a theory of acting as reading would add: of one adult *reader* with another adult reader.

There is, of course, a long tradition of imagining relations between adults in terms of "reading."[157] "I understand you so well," Don Quixote tells Sancho, " . . . I can read you like a book."[158] Lady Capulet urges Juliet to "read o'er the volume of young Paris' face;"[159] Macbeth's face "is as a book where men / May read strange matters."[160] And the trope is still going strong. We, too, claim to be able to "read" facial expressions and body "language"; we cry out "I read you!" to those we have suddenly understood; and we describe as "a closed book" our relations with one whose behavior we no longer care to read.

One can see how such person-text confusions might be especially likely to arise in acting, where the texts to be construed present themselves in the form of persons to be related to. But, though the dramatic text is present in or through actors, actors are not present to one another as texts to be read, but as readers. If acting is reading, and the actor is a reader, then *another* actor is *another* reader. This, in turn, suggests that, if we wish to understand the nature of the interaction between actors, we must ask what sort of interaction is likely to occur between one reader and another, each of whom is imagined as having done what, over the course of this chapter, I have described individual actor-readers as doing, namely, achieved a boundariless relation with the text by "setting equal" their orally active and orally passive impulses toward it in a single act.

In other words, relations between actors on an acting-as-reading model *neither* consist in a simple extension of actor-text relations (with the other actor now standing in for the text) *nor* require the introduction of a whole new set of "interpersonal" categories. Here is an actor-reader; here is another. (Or: Here are several others. For simplicity's sake I will throughout speak in terms of *two* actors, but, clearly, the process I am about to describe can come into play among any number of performers.) All we need to understand is: How does another actor-reader's doing what I'm doing impinge on my doing it, and vice versa? What becomes of my supplant and merge impulses toward, my rising-to-enact, my boundariless relation with, a text that is now no longer present in itself but only in the reading of other actors?

In general terms the answer I shall offer is as follows. When actor meets actor in rehearsal, each actor-reader seeks to supplant the other actor's reading with his own. But at the same time each actor-reader seeks to merge into the other actor's reading. These orally active and orally passive impulses toward one another's readings of the scene both play are "set equal" in the single (inter)action of their playing it together. For this interaction—as, indistinguishably, the reading of the first into which the second "steps" and the reading of the second into which the first "steps"—simultaneously enacts *both* their readings. This "setting equal" of the actors' conflicting readings in a single, undecidable interaction thus produces boundarilessness, not as an experience for each individual actor but as the structure of the encounter between them.

Let us now look more closely at how each of the characteristic aspects of the actor-text transaction—supplantation, merger, single (inter)action, boundarilessness—is modified by being brought face-to-face with itself in the work process of another.

   1. *The individual actor's impulse to supplant the text becomes, in re-*

hearsal, an impulse to take the place of another('s) reading. There are two reasons for this displacement, of which the more basic is as follows. In his individual work each actor, as we have seen, seeks to supplant, to take the place of, the text with his own activity. But in rehearsal the text he would thus supplant is present only in, or as, others' reading of it. This means that *any* impulse he feels toward the text must now be enacted toward those other readers. And, in particular, his impulse to supplant it must be enacted as an impulse to supplant their reading, supplant them *as readers;* as a claim that *I alone* am the reader here, theirs being merely the presence of the text in which I propose to read.

But there is a further reason why actors strive to supplant each other as readers, a reason that follows directly from the nature of those roles within which, and on behalf of which, actors read. When we defined a role as a particular solution to the drive/defense tensions of the text, we didn't pause to ask what this implied about each role's view of every other, but the answer is not far to seek. Implicit in any role's claim to have solved the drive/defense problem posed by the text is a claim that the *other* roles do *not* solve it. But since "to solve the drive/defense problem posed by the text" is the very definition of reading (it was on this basis that we equated characters with readers in the first place), to deny that other roles can do this is to deny them the status of readers. Every character, qua character, irrespective of his "personality," proclaims: *"This* is what it means to be a reader; 'to read' is to do what *I* do"—and thereby denies reader status to all but himself.

It is this contesting of every character's reading claims by every other that creates the possibility of dramatic conflict in the first place. Such divisions as may arise *between* characters, i.e., the action of the play, only continues the division up of the text *into* characters, i.e., into a spectrum of competing "solutions" to the text's drive/defense problems. And it is this mutual denial by roles of one another's reading claims that ultimately provides the basis for the conflictual *supplant* aspect of relations between those who assume the roles in rehearsal. If my character's is "the only way to read," then I, who read that way, am, once again, the only reader on the scene. This has nothing to do with egotism or arrogance but simply reflects the fact that, from one point of view at least, to agree to play a character is implicitly to decline to read in all ways but that character's, to proceed on the assumption that *none here reads but I.*

Meanwhile, however, the very nature of the rehearsal situation calls in question this claim of each actor to be "the only reader in the room." Since other characters are other kinds of readers, the sudden arrival of other actors *as* those other characters literally reintroduces the possibility that other kinds of readers may be present. When other characters appear as flesh-and-blood other actors the reading options associated with those characters once again appear as possible reading options for flesh and blood. Since each of these suddenly present options implicitly denies the validity of all the rest, rehearsal assumes the aspect of a pure power struggle, a clash of readings—or, rather, the place where a clash of readings becomes the clashing of readers, each one seeking to consign the others to that very "nonreader" status to which *they*, in turn, seek to relegate *him*.

2. *The individual actor's impulse to merge with the text becomes, in rehearsal, an impulse to take his place in another('s) reading.* Clearly, no less than his impulses to supplant the text, the actor's impulse to merge with it must, in rehearsal, be displaced onto other(s') readings of it—and for the same reason: Whether for purposes of merger or supplantation, the text is now *present* only in the form of other readings and other readers. The orally passive impulse to take one's place in a text present in this wise can only be enacted by *taking one's place in another('s) reading.* But how does one "take one's place in" another('s) reading?

The picture of rehearsal I painted a moment ago as a "clash" of readings, a sort of war of each against all, is obviously one-sided. Moment by moment, rehearsal has far more the texture of adjustment, accommodation, support. Energy is sent and received; an impulse is played and played off; a climactic moment is mutually worked toward. Sam cheats a few steps upstage to allow Ellen to take a broader cross; Ellen establishes the rhythm Jeff needs to get to his next beat. From this perspective even provocations and challenges are likely to serve a purpose that is ultimately collaborative.

While such acts of mutuality can obviously be understood in purely interpersonal terms—as contributing toward the common good of the production, as producing pleasure in shared work, etc.—the impulse behind them is not, I submit, ultimately toward other persons but, rather, toward a text now only to be met with in the person of others. Whether it is merely a matter of getting out of the way of another actor's cross or of modifying one's whole portrayal of Lear so as to be more *Cordelia's* Lear, collaboration with other actors enacts the original, orally passive impulse to merge with the text in what is—now that the text is present only in the form of these potential collaborators—the one feasible way.

Here, then, is the sense in which one can speak of merging with, or taking one's place in, another('s) reading. Just as *taking the place of/ supplanting* the text could, in the suddenly interpersonal context of rehearsal, only be enacted by challenging the reader status of others, so *taking one's place in/merging with* the text can, in the new circumstances of rehearsal, only be enacted by conceding the right of others to challenge one's status as "sole reader."

3. *The single action in which the actor's orally active and orally passive impulses toward the text are set equal becomes the interaction between actors, the scene both play.* We have seen how the individual actor's supplant and merge impulses toward the text are "set equal" in his performance of it, a single action that, as at once a *taking over from* and a *taking one's place in* the text, cannot help but enact both. In the transaction *between* actors the orally active impulse has become an urge to take the place of an other('s) reading, and the orally passive impulse, an urge to take one's place in another('s) reading. What single action enacts both my taking the place of and my taking my place in another actor's reading? Clearly, his and my playing the scene together, *our interaction itself.*

My action enacts my reading. Whose reading does our interaction enact? Our interaction is not unequivocally your action into which I "step" or my action into which you "step" but—our interaction, which therefore cannot be regarded as enacting exclusively your reading of the scene or mine. Acting teachers sometimes assign two students an improvisation with radically different premises. For example: Actor 1 is told he is trying to pick up a woman in a cocktail lounge; Actor 2 is told she is being approached by a lunatic on the asylum grounds. Here, quite clearly, it is impossible to say whose "reading" the resulting improvisation enacts. One may protest that this situation is scarcely typical, there being no script to compare readings of until improvisation produces one. But, not for the first time, improvisation turns out to be presenting us with an extreme form of, rather than a clear alternative to, the scripted case. Take the interview between King Henry and Prince Hal in act 3, scene 2 of *Henry IV,* part 1. Henry "reads" his interaction with Prince Hal as: *I bring my son to an awareness of the necessity of thinking politically.* Hal "reads" his interaction with King Henry as: *I bring my father to an awareness that I have been thinking politically all along.* One may argue about which of these viewpoints the play, or a particular production of it, *endorses,* but it makes no sense to ask which of these readings the scene, or a particular performance of it, *enacts.* No less clearly with the scripted scene than with the two-premise improvisation, the mere fact that there is but one (inter)action ensures that this will be, indistinguishably, the enactment of both readings—not because the readings themselves have somehow become indistinguishable or even compatible but because there is no way of distinguishing the single action that implements both of them from itself.

But if it makes no sense to ask whether we're "in" your reading or mine of a scene we both play, then the question of whether each of us, by playing it, *asserts his own* reading or *accedes to the other's* likewise makes no sense. Taking one's place in and taking the place of another('s) reading have become, so to speak, a single taking of a common place. It is in this sense that actors' orally active and orally passive impulses toward each other's reading claims are "set equal" in the single (inter)action of their playing the scene together. It is not that the impulses to *merge* and to *supplant,* to *challenge* and to *cooperate,* are "reconciled" on some interpersonal or intrapsychic level. Their reconciliation is simply to be enacted by the same situation. The overall structure of the actor-actor transaction can therefore be summed up in our usual form as follows:

Acting (with other actors)

Orally Active Impulse: I take the place of another('s) reading.
Orally Passive Impulse: I take my place in another('s) reading.
"Setting Equal": I take the place of a reading in which I take my place.

4. *The boundariless relation of the actor with the text becomes the structure of the relation between actors.* Before asking how we might "extend" boundarilessness to inter-actor relations, it might be well to consider whether boundarilessness between actors is *desirable,* and, if so, whether it is *possible.*

Is boundarilessness a relation one actor should want or seek to stand in with another? The implied reciprocity sounds good, but actors also need to be able to assume distinct identities, pursue conflicting objectives—in a word, clash as well as collaborate. We wouldn't want a boundariless relation that excluded the possibility of contention. But if the possibility of contention is not excluded, how can we speak of a boundariless relation?

Actually, this is rather a simplification of what we have seen to be the inner structure of the boundariless relation, which, as the upshot of an unresolvable struggle between active and passive oral tendencies, far from *ruling out* contention, *presupposes* contention of the fiercest, *eat-or-be-eaten* sort—is "made" out of contention, so to speak. It is true that the original boundariless relation, that between mother and infant in the early oral stage, did not yet display a tendency toward dispute, for the not yet differentiated self of the child could not as yet comprise a distinct disputant. But all subsequent attempts to reinstate that original boundarilessness—the later oral-sadistic stage, introjection, reading, the individual actor's work on the text or role—proceed by acts of incorporation, which are always displacements of *eating another,* and by experiences of self-loss, which are always displacements of *being eaten oneself.* True, the boundariless state means the breakdown—indeed, is *accomplished* by the breaking down—of all distinction between such orally active and orally passive impulses. But the result of such a breakdown—a condition that is all eating and all being eaten, without even the possibility of distinguishing the two—sounds more like the ultimate *form* of contention than the ultimate *release* from it.

Bringing this to bear on relations between actors, it is clear that *taking one's place in* and *taking the place of* another('s) reading represent merely one more displacement of the primal eat-or-be-eaten polarity. And to revive this two-term tension, as work between actors must do, *in its original form* of a two-person situation is to revive the original question of *who eats whom.*

A boundarilessness promising at once the subtlest reciprocities and the fiercest conflicts certainly sounds like a desirable relation between actors. Is it, however, a possible one? Certainly there are going to be problems that did not arise so long as the "other" with whom boundarilessness was sought was of an introjective or textual nature. Indeed, it seems as if such boundarilessness as one may have attained with a text or role is more likely to be shattered by than passed along to these flesh-and-blood others who now appear, between whom and oneself, after all, the boundaries are clear enough. True, the boundariless relation *was* originally a relation between persons. Those persons, however, were a mother and an infant (which the two actors are not), and the boundarilessness attained was a hallucination on the part of the one of them who was not an adult (which the two actors are).

Not that boundarilessness between adults is impossible or even rare;

it is, on the contrary, a familiar dimension of the erotic. Actors, however, do not, as a rule, stand to each other as lover to lover, but as reader to reader. Is a relation of boundarilessness possible *between readers?*

We might approach this question via the example of Paolo and Francesca, who are both lovers and readers, and whose tendency to supplant/merge with their text has already encouraged us to view them as types of the actor. Paolo and Francesca certainly achieve a boundariless relation ("this one who never shall be parted from me" [l. 135]), albeit the rather sinister one ("Love brought us to one death" [l. 106]) imaged, as I have already noted, in the endlessly rotating wind that bears them and the other Lustful "hither, thither, downward, upward" (l. 43) forever. Moreover, their boundarilessness has its origins in a very literal, mouth-to-mouth "setting equal" of their orally active and orally passive impulses toward one another: namely, the kiss they exchange, which, though Paolo initiates it, is not Paolo's kiss or Francesca's kiss but, simply, Paolo-and-Francesca's kiss.[161]

Such a boundarilessness, and especially such a manner of achieving it, may not seem to have much to do with the work of actors, who, as a rule, do not build their relationships through sexual contact or remain in them forever. And yet, if we look at the moment in Paolo and Francesca's encounter when the boundary breaks, what boundary has broken—i.e., the boundary between what and what? Clearly, as in acting, it is the boundary between two *readings.* What Paolo and Francesca rise to enact is neither Paolo's reading of the Lancelot-Guinevere scene, for which Francesca merely provides the Guinevere, nor Francesca's reading of the Lancelot-Guinevere scene, for which Paolo merely provides the Lancelot. It is with them as with any two actors coming off book into action together: There being now only a single (inter)action to enact both parties' readings of the scene, it can no longer be determined—indeed, it no longer makes sense to ask—*which* or *whose* reading the interaction enacts. Neither participant can say whether in general or at any given moment he now finds himself "in here," in *his* reading of the scene, or "out there," in the other's reading of it. But it is precisely in such breaking down of the in here/out there distinction that we have repeatedly found boundarilessness to consist.

Here, then, is the form the boundariless relation assumes between actors. Their respective readings of the scene they play are "set equal" in the single (inter)action of their playing it together and, as on other levels, this "setting equal" dissolves a boundary. But the boundary it dissolves is not between one actor-reader and another but, rather, between one actor's reading and another's. No doubt there are moments when actors working well together feel running between them something like the directionless flow that links lover and lover, child and parent, reader and text. In general, though, boundarilessness is present between actors not (as with individual actors, readers, or introjectors) as the feel of an intrapsychic experience but as the structure of an interpersonal transaction, *irrespective* of the feelings toward one another of those who transact it. In this sense, a performance of our Henry-Hal scene is no less likely to issue in a boundariless relation between the actors who play it, though these actors are in conflict, than is Paolo and Francesca's "performance" of the Lancelot-Guinevere "scene," where the "actors" are at one. For the Henry-Hal interaction is no less a "setting equal" of *opposed* readings in a single enactment than the Paolo-Francesca interaction is a "setting equal" of *accordant* readings in a single enactment. In short, depending on the circumstances, a transaction between actors may or may not "feel boundariless," but on the most fundamental level what it represents is the displacement of boundarilessness from a feeling to a transaction.

It would be a mistake to view this "abandonment" of inner experience for outer situation as in any sense a loss for acting; rather, it constitutes the final stage of that recovery which, I am arguing, acting achieves. How, after all, did boundarilessness get to *be* an inner experience? In the other displacements of the mother-child relation which we examined—introjection and reading—the "setting equal" that brought on boundarilessness had to be *within* a single person (i.e., between an individual's orally active and orally passive impulses) because there *was* now only a single person: he who introjected or read. Such *inner* "setting equal" represented, precisely, an attempt to *compensate* for the absence of someone else for the reader or introjector to be in a (boundariless) relation with. Similarly, in the work of the solitary actor, as described in the earlier sections of this chapter, the intrapsychic transaction only got to *be* intrapsychic because there were no longer two psyches on hand, only a psyche and a text. Now, when another actor enters the picture, we once again have, for the first time since the Ur-situation of infant and mother, two actual persons for the transaction to run between.

It is precisely in this that the advance of actors working together over one actor's work on a script consists. An actor's solitary work restores to the reader's mentally boundariless relationship with the text its original character of physical experience. Actors' work with one another restores to that physical experience of boundarilessness *its* original character of interpersonal transaction. Since the original situation was interpersonal as well as physical, such a restoration amounts to a recovery more complete than any an actor working alone with his script could manage. I say "more complete," not "complete." The new interaction cannot literally resurrect the old one. We have to do, now, with adult readers, different actors, separate selves. Between two such, the situation cannot be as before. But simply *as* a situation, as *some* type of interpersonal encounter, it reinstates the event-status of the original: For this merely its being an event, however different a one, suffices.

It is at this point that a theory of acting as reading rejoins, or reveals itself to have been all along restating, the theatrical project as such. Recovering the "lost" physical of reading is not, after all, something acting does for reading. Acting is in the service of theater and can be of service to theater precisely because "recovering a lost physical" is the aim of theater itself. We are accustomed to speak of the action of a play as being intermittently "realized" in performance. But couldn't one as well say (in fact, wouldn't it be *truer to experience* to say) that, between occasions when it is performed, the action of a play is intermittently "derealized" in its script, that the script is where the events of the play "go" when they cannot be an event just then? Certainly, this is how dramatic texts present themselves—that is, as events that have unaccountably "lapsed" from their event-status into mere writing and are going to have to be "rescued" from this (no doubt temporary) humiliation. It is because the actor, as the restorer of *reading's* "lost" event-status, specializes in such rescues that acting can serve as, so to speak, the fundamental "technology" of theater's ambition. The actor "delivers" from their forced sojourn in textuality the once and future events of the dramatic text—and does so (reminiscent here of Quixote among the puppets) by a breathtakingly literal-minded misunderstanding of the reading process as bodily, as interpersonal, as event. Acting, in a word, offers its own recovery of the "lost" event-status of reading to be *theater's* recovery of the lost event-status of the dramatic text.

Chapter 5

Scenes of Reading as Scenes of Acting

In this chapter I am going to suggest that scenes of reading in plays tend to become images of the *actor* reading his *script* and, so, tend to raise as *their* issues, within the fiction of the play, what are in fact issues about the relation between acting and reading as that play, playwright, or era conceives those issues. If this is the case, then it might be possible to interpret a script's reading scenes as "forecasts" of the actor's eventual transaction with that script, and I shall attempt to interpret reading scenes from plays of four different periods—ancient, medieval, modern, and postmodern—along these lines.

The "acting" that, I shall argue, such scenes of reading image will not necessarily be that displaced oral process—that setting equal of opposed active and passive impulses toward a script—which I have hitherto made acting out to be. This is not because I do not find the oral structure of acting reflected in dramatic texts. On the contrary, it seems to me that the very *medium* of (most) dramatic texts, dialogue, is *itself* a displacement onto the textual plane of the orality of the process by which dramatic texts are realized. In a dialogue each speaker is orally active and orally passive in turn, now giving forth lines, now being "fed" cues. This "vacillation" between active and passive oral "roles" in the exchange recalls what we have seen to be the actor's ambivalence toward a text he must both actively supplant and passively merge with. But the point is, it more than recalls that ambivalence; it *represents* it. In a page of dialogue the oral ambivalence of the actor toward the text, and of each actor toward every other's *reading* of the text (which he likewise seeks to merge with and supplant), reappears *within* the text as an alternation of active and passive gambits—the "give" and "take" of dialogue—which, since neither speaker is definitively the giver or the taker, are "set equal" in the boundariless flow of the give-and-take.[1] From this perspective plays are "in" dialogue not because dialogue is the inevitable medium for plays (it isn't—think of Beckett's *Act without Words I and II*—and in any case the statement is tautological) but so that plays may offer themselves as images of the acting process.

Nor do the specific scenes of reading I shall consider lack oral elements; on the contrary, they generally portray reading as inextricably bound up with orality. The oral elements may be overt, as in *The Knights,* where Demosthenes simultaneously "drinks in" the good news of the tyrant Cleon's coming fall from an oracle book while drinking in some "vintage Pramnian" from a jug. Or if the scene's orality is displaced, the displacement may be of the very sort that I have argued occurs in acting. In the Coventry *Woman Taken in Adultery,* for example, the single action (flight) taken by each reader (i.e., each Accuser) in regard to the "text" (Jesus' writing in the dust) enacts both his orally passive *identification with* that text and his orally active *disavowal of* it. Indeed, given the close ties which we have seen exist between reading and eating, it would be surprising to find a reading scene in which oral motifs and tensions were *not,* in some degree, present.

If, then, I refrain from pursuing an argument for reading scenes as imaging my own particular view of acting as displaced oral process, it is not because such an argument could not be made, but, frankly, because I want to argue something more ambitious, namely, that even when reading is *not* linked with acting on the specifically oral grounds I have proposed, it is *still* likely to be linked with acting, to be seen as *imaging* acting. My contention is, essentially, that, in any scene of reading in a dramatic text, the *book* (or other reading matter) in the hands of the character tends to emerge as an image of the *script* in the hands of the actor, as that era, playwright, or play conceived of scripts; and that the *reading* of the book tends to emerge as an image of the actor reading the script, i.e., of *acting,* as that era, playwright, or play conceived of acting. In a word, I am suggesting that one may take a scene of reading from a dramatic text and argue: *As reading is here depicted, so acting was then understood.*

One *may* so argue—I affirm no more than that. The hypothesis is tentative, and the readings based on it, conjectural. I am not advancing, nor am I competent to advance, a rigorous historical argument. Rather, I seek to indicate how historical speculation might proceed in an area where strict historicist rigor is unattainable—and therefore inappropriate. What I propose is an experiment. *Suppose* one were to view scenes of reading from plays of different periods as images of the actor-script transaction in those periods: What image of the acting process in each period *might* then emerge?

The results of such an experiment will in some instances (e.g., Chekhov) lend support, in other instances (e.g., the medieval cycle drama) run counter to, what we know from other sources about acting in a given period. Of course, what we know about acting in a given period—especially about the acting process and especially for earlier periods—may well be, as I pointed out in chapter 1, next to nothing. But if this implies that what a reading scene appears to tell us about acting often cannot be cross-checked against other evidence, it also raises the possibility that reading scenes may be a source of evidence in the absence of any other; that here, perhaps, a culture reveals to us what it has revealed nowhere else, namely, its inmost experience of the acting process.

That the whole vast corpus of dramatic literature (or at least such of it as contains reading scenes) might thus be pressed into service as otherwise unavailable source material about acting is an exhilarating prospect. But what justification is there for taking scenes of reading as images of acting in the first place? Why *should* the text in a reading scene tend to become an image of the script, and the reading of it, an image of acting? Essentially, I shall argue, because such scenes, *when enacted,* necessarily become images of the actor with his script, and this "fate which awaits" such scenes in performance tends to cast its shadow back over the scenes themselves. Our first step, then, must be to consider scenes of reading in performance.

In the past of any action you see an actor perform onstage lies a prior act of reading: the actor's book-in-hand rehearsal work on the scene.[2] Occasionally, a theatrically self-conscious production forces this easily forgotten circumstance upon our attention. For example, Andrei Serban's 1983 production of *Uncle Vanya* at La Mama began with the actress playing Sonya reading Sonya's final speech—haltingly, painfully—from a book, as she might have done at an early "finding" rehearsal. When, at the close of the play, Sonya movingly *performed* the speech *sans* book, her performance was haunted by the prior act of painful, exploratory reading.[3] In fact, *any* performance is thus haunted by its own earlier rehearsal reading, but, in general, we are encouraged to ignore, rather than, as here, obliged to take note of, this basic fact.

But there is one situation in which we cannot ignore it, and that is when the action being represented onstage is *itself* "so-and-so reads a book," i.e., when the scene is a scene of reading. Here performance cannot help but recall its forgotten "past" of reading, since it now reenacts that past.

The reminder is sharpest in cases where it is clear that the present reenactment cannot be a very exact one—say, because of an obvious disparity between how reading is represented in the text and what the actor's experience of reading that text must actually have been. For example, in a fragment from Euripides' *Theseus* an illiterate coastguard, having caught sight of a sail with writing on it, proceeds to "explain the shapes" of each of the Greek letters he cannot read:

> The second one is first of all two strokes, and then another one keeping them apart in the middle [H]. The third is curly like a lock of hair [C].[4]

It would be difficult to witness this moment in performance without reflecting that, in rehearsal, all this painful nonreading must have been read. Or, again, consider the moment in Brecht's *Private Life of the Master Race* when a German scientist in secret correspondence with Einstein excitedly reads aloud to a colleague the answer to his latest query:

> For static incoherent matter, without any interaction of tension, T $= \mu$ is the only component of the tensorial density of energy which is different from 0. Consequently a static field of gravitation is formed, whose equation when the constant factor of proportionality $8\pi X$ is added gives $\Delta f = 4\pi X\mu$.[5]

Here the spectator's own consciousness of not understanding is likely to set his thoughts running on the rehearsal of this scene by an actor *who also cannot have understood*. How did the rehearsal experience of an uncomprehending reader issue in this portrayal of excited comprehension?

But it is not only in such paradoxical cases that awareness of a reading scene's "rehearsal past" is likely to obtrude. You cannot watch the Reader in *Ohio Impromptu* sit reading at his table without reflecting that this actor has sat reading this material at a table before now. You cannot listen to Oronte in *The Misanthrope* get up and read his sonnet without reflecting that this actor "has a history" of getting up and reading these lines. In short, whatever it may convey about characters or action, a performed scene of reading always conveys something else as well: *This has happened before. At another moment this person stood as now, reading these words off a page. . . .*

How, then, shall we describe what the actor playing a reading scene is doing at that moment? Is he reperforming his own past action of reading, or is he performing the present reading of the character? Clearly, its being the *same person* who plays the reader and replays the rehearsal removes all grounds for such a distinction. The actor cannot represent the character without re-presenting his own former act of reading. The page the actor reads from cannot represent the text specified as being in the character's hand at that moment—Oronte's sonnet, Einstein's letter—without re-presenting the script that was in the actor's hand when he rehearsed that moment. A reader plays a reader; reading reenacts reading.

At minimum, then, one may conclude that scenes of reading, *when performed,* necessarily become images of the actor with his script. But I want to argue more than this, namely, that some awareness of the "fate which awaits" such scenes in performance shapes the scenes themselves; that reading scenes, not merely when performed but, indeed, *as written,* are already "haunted" by foreknowledge of what is to be the actor's eventual experience of performing them; and that such scenes therefore tend to raise as "their" issues what are, in fact, aspects of the issue between an actor and a script.

There can be no single proof that all scenes of reading in plays thus foretell the acting encounter they provoke. At most one may hope to show, as I shall try to do in the remainder of this chapter, that reading scenes from a wide variety of dramatic texts are susceptible to interpretation along these lines. There is, however, one motif whose presence in a great number of reading scenes offers encouragement for such a view. Time and again in Western dramatic literature some version of the following incident is reenacted. A reader settles down to read (or is discovered at rise already reading) and is immediately broken in upon by someone who obliges him to leave off reading and interact with the newcomer. For example: Hedvig Ekdal sits reading, her thumbs in her ears to ensure privacy, and is interrupted by her mother, Gina, who wants to discuss household expenses (*The Wild Duck,* act 2). Andrei Prozoroff sits leafing through a volume of old university lectures and is interrupted by Ferapont bearing a message from Andrei's boss (*The Three Sisters,* act 2). The Elector Friedrich of Brandenburg stands at a table perusing some papers and is interrupted by his niece, Natalia, who has come to plead for her cousin's life (Kleist, *The Prince of Homburg*, act 4, sc. 1). Edmund Tyrone sits trying to concentrate on a book and is interrupted by the servant girl, Cathleen, who has come for a chat (*Long Day's Journey into Night*, act 2, sc. 1).[6] Young Christopher Columbus sits reading the *Travels of Marco Polo* and is interrupted by a man at the window who suggests he pay more heed to the life around him (Claudel, *Le Livre de Christophe Colomb*, scene 9). Richard Duke of Gloucester enters immersed in a prayer book and is interrupted by Buckingham and the Lord Mayor, who urge him to accept the crown (*Richard III*, act 3, sc. 7).[7]

It would not be difficult to add to this list. I have come upon examples of interrupted reading in plays by Aristophanes, Shakespeare, Chapman, Lillo, Kleist, Wagner, Ibsen, Chekhov, Claudel, O'Neill, Marcel Aymé, and Roger Vitrac; doubtless, there are others. In fact, so widespread is this motif that it would seem to qualify as what Ernst Curtius calls a topos: a thematic image or situation "suitable for development and modification,"[8] to which writers in every generation feel themselves drawn. Curtius identifies dozens of such topoi in Western literature: "the world as stage," "the book of nature," "straying in a wood," etc.[9] I believe Western *dramatic* literature contains one more. To Curtius's list I should like to propose the addition of a "topos of interrupted reading."

How is it that this particular situation occurs so frequently as possibly to qualify for topos status? Why is the reading of a character in a play virtually certain to be interrupted? One obvious explanation immediately suggests itself: Solitary reading can't go on for very long in a drama because it's "not dramatic."[10] The interrupting character's demand on the reading character that he set aside his volume and join the fray is, one might say, the essential demand of an action upon actors. "Come on, Dame, you are at your book / When men are at your mistress"[11]—in this reproach of a lady in a Jacobean play to her waiting woman we may hear the impatience of theater itself with those who will not *perform their part* in it. If you are going to be a self-in-action, "interrupted reading" scenes seem to say, you are going to have to come out of your *self* (as represented by your reader's solitude) and into (the) *action*.

Even interpreted no more closely than this, such scenes image rehearsal. For if there is any sort of reader whose reading seems to herald its own supersession by interaction with another, it is the *actor*-reader. And if there is any particular moment in an actor's reading which the topos situation seems to image, it is the moment when solitary work passes into rehearsal; for it is then that the actor-reader must come off book and into play. But many of these scenes have a further characteristic that even more clearly marks them as images of the rehearsal process. More often than not, the "other" who interrupts reading turns out to be either the *very* other or else a symbolic *stand-in* for the very other about whom the solitary reader was reading—a "strange coincidence," which becomes less so on the assumption that such scenes image the moment when the solitary actor-reader is joined by another *actor,* standing in for the very other *character* of whom he read but now.

To be sure, there are scenes of interrupted reading where no such continuity between the interrupting other and the reading he interrupts can be shown. Sometimes we don't know what the solitary reader is reading—this is the case with Edmund Tyrone, Hedvig Ekdal, and the Elector Friedrich—and so can't say whether the one who interrupts reading has or has not been anticipated in it. And in other instances the interrupter clearly enters in opposition to, rather than in fulfillment of, reading. The politicos who intrude upon Richard III at prayer are attempting to redirect his attention from prayer book to politics (no very formidable task). The figure at the window who interrupts Christophe Colomb seeks to rechannel his interest from the far-off wonders he reads about to the affairs of his native land. And, when Ferapont breaks in upon Andrei's reading in the book of his happy Moscow past, it is as a reminder of his unhappy provincial present.

Still, in many, if not most, topos scenes the one who interrupts reading turns out to be either the person just now being read about in the text whose reading he interrupts or else a clear surrogate for this textual figure.

Scenes where the interrupter is the very person read about are in the minority but still fairly frequent. In Aristophanes' *The Knights* Demosthenes reads an oracle text that predicts the appearance of a sausage-seller, and in walks the Sausage-Seller.[12] In Strindberg's *To Damascus* the Lady opens a book by and about the Stranger and is immediately interrupted by the Stranger.[13] In Marcel Aymé's *Clérembard* the title character sits down with a biography of Saint Francis, and "behind him . . . Saint Francis appears and comments on what he reads."[14] And in Roger Vitrac's surrealist play *Victor* the people about whom one of the characters is reading in a newspaper article suddenly materialize on the stage.[15]

More often, though, the other who interrupts solitary reading is
not the literal other read about but, instead, some kind of stand-in for
him. In act 2, scene 2, of *Cymbeline,* for example, Imogen falls asleep
reading about the treacherous violator Tereus and is immediately in-
truded upon by the treacherous violator Iachimo.[16] In George Lillo's *The
London Merchant* the condemned apprentice George Barnwell seeks con-
solation in religious reading and is interrupted by his former master,
Thorowgood, whose arrival—given the simplistic cosmos of this play,
where God is scarcely more than a being thoroughly good and Thorowgood a being scarcely less than godlike—strongly suggests the arrival
of that divine "Master" whom Barnwell has been reading about and of
whose forgiveness he receives, in Thorowgood's, a taste.[17] When, at the
opening of act 2 of *Rosmersholm,* Rebekka West breaks in upon Rosmer
as he is leafing through a pamphlet, the "interruption" fulfills the reading
it seems to terminate. For, in fact, it is Rebekka who has interrupted the
life of Rosmersholm with such new ideas as the pamphlet contains; she
herself is the "new idea" in Rosmer's life.[18] Nor, finally (if I may be
permitted an operatic example), should it surprise us that in act 3 of *Die
Meistersinger* the interruption of Hans Sachs's reading of the *Nürenberg
Chronicle* by his exuberant apprentice, David, "does not seem to have
disturbed his meditation"; for it is of just such aimless violence as
David's street brawling the night before that, Sachs informs us, the
Chronicle tells.[19] In all these instances the interrupter proves to be, if not
the identical other predicted by the text, a clear symbolic equivalent.

The most famous example of the topos at first seems to be a joke
about it—and a joke on the score of this very "continuity" that topos
scenes profess to find between reading and its interruption.

> POLONIUS: What do you read, my lord?
> HAMLET: Words, words, words.
> POLONIUS: What is the matter, my lord?
> HAMLET: Between who?
> POLONIUS: I mean the matter that you read, my lord.
> HAMLET: Slanders, sir; for the satirical rogue says here that old
> men have gray beards, that their faces are wrinkled, their eyes purg-
> ing thick amber and plumtree gum, and that they have a plentiful
> lack of wit, together with most weak hams.[20]

Hamlet's poker-faced account of his book's contents initially seems to
class this with other scenes of interrupted reading we have examined:

Here, too, the other who intrudes upon reading (gray-bearded Polonius) is identified as a stand-in for the other(s) already encountered in the text (the "old men [with] gray beards"); here, too, what interrupts reading fulfills it. But our two previous Shakespearean examples suggest that Shakespeare never uses the topos without giving it an ironic twist— Richard III *arranges* to be interrupted in his reading; Imogen *self*-interrupts (i.e., falls asleep over her book)—and the present scene is no exception.[21] For, of course, Hamlet's reply can scarcely be taken as a good faith summary of his reading matter; he is only availing himself of Polonius's question to mock him, and the mockery seems to extend to the topos as well. The promise of continuity between reading and its interruption is here treated as a mere pretext for giving one's opinion in safety. "Ah, it is you; I was just now reading about you" has become a way of saying: "What do you know, I was just reading about morons— and here you are!"

And, yet, things are not this simple. In the big scene with his father's ghost, his last appearance onstage prior to this one, Hamlet throws out a hint concerning his future reading habits which strangely corroborates the summary he here offers Polonius:

> Remember thee?
> Yea, from the table of my memory
> I'll wipe away all trivial fond records,
> All saws of books, all forms, all pressures past
> That youth and observation copied there,
> And thy commandment all alone shall live
> Within the book and volume of my brain,
> Unmixed with baser matter.
>
> (act 1, sc. 5, ll. 97–104)

When Hamlet now enters "reading on a book" (act 2, sc. 2, l. 167 s.d.), it is as if he were acting upon, or acting out, this earlier expressed resolve—in which case it is, indeed, of "old men [with] gray beards" that he reads, for we have it from his own lips that henceforth any solitary reading we see him do will be in the text of the father: "thy commandment all alone shall live / Within the book and volume of my brain." Now Polonius is one of Hamlet's prime father-surrogates—"the father of good news," Claudius calls him, in a phrase that ironically links him with the ghost of Hamlet Senior (act 2, sc. 2, l. 42)—and, thus, quite apart from all the joking about graybeards, it is clearly a surrogate for the father who up till now has *filled* Hamlet's reading who here *interrupts* it. From the "old mole" (act 1, sc. 5, l. 62) whom Hamlet will inscribe "within the . . . volume of my brain" to the "old men" in the actual book he carries, to "old Polonius" (as a second quarto stage direction refers to him [act 2, sc. 1, l. 1 s.d.]) who now accosts Hamlet, book-in-hand, it has all been one ongoing encounter with a single, paternal other. Hamlet himself seems to acknowledge as much in his willful misunderstanding of Polonius's second question:

> POLONIUS: What is the matter, my lord?
> HAMLET: Between who?
> POLONIUS: I mean the matter that you read, my lord.

The reading matter of solitude is, indeed, a matter between persons if solitary reading has already been interaction with others. For all its playing *upon,* our *Hamlet* scene thus also *plays,* the topos of interrupted reading.

The great majority of interrupted reading scenes may, then, be described as intrusions upon reading of the (literal or symbolic) "very one" forecast in the text, now appearing in flesh and blood. But "the flesh-and-blood intrusion upon reading of the very one(s) forecast in the text" is precisely the situation of rehearsal, where, to each hitherto solitary actor-reader there now appear flesh-and-blood versions of all the hitherto merely textual other characters, i.e., the other actors who play them. As for its being, in most topos scenes, a *surrogate* other who appears, this, too, makes sense on the assumption that the topos situation images rehearsal, where it is likewise "never quite the same" figure forecast in the text who now appears but always a "stand-in," an actor. In other words, the substitution, within the action of the scene, of a "slightly different other" for the other read about—Iachimo for Tereus, Polonius for the old men with gray beards, etc.—is a reflection back *within* the text of the eventual substitution of nontextual for textual others, i.e., of actors for characters in rehearsal.

But the arrival of a (nearly) identical other which our topos scenes portray is more than the literal situation of rehearsal; it is also an image of the actor's *experience* of rehearsal. By depicting this "other" with whom the actor must henceforth deal as the very other with whom he has, in his solitary reading, been dealing all along, topos scenes affirm a continuity between solitary reading and rehearsal themselves. Rehearsal, the topos seems to prophesy, will be more an *acting out* of the true situation of solitary reading as interaction with a textual other than the *substitution* of interaction for reading which it first appears. Rehearsal, topos scenes suggest, is actually the continuation by other means of a reading process it only seems to interrupt, and this is precisely what, in our chapter 4 discussion of the work actors do with one another, we found rehearsal to be.

The preceding discussion illustrates how at least *one* kind of reading scene can, as written, be what *all* reading scenes become when acted: an image of the actor with his script in rehearsal. But scenes of interrupted solitary reading are more than just one type of reading scene among others. For since, as we saw in chapter 1, *all* reading is *a solitude and its interruption*—i.e., a state of being "alone with" a (textual) other—there is a sense in which the topos situation is the situation of reading itself. If that is so, then the frequency of topos scenes in Western dramatic literature bespeaks a widespread compulsion on the part of dramatic texts to image the process by which dramatic texts are realized. Still, the fact remains that not all reading in plays is interrupted. Do other sorts of reading scenes—do reading scenes *as such*—present us with images of the actor reading his script? To answer this broader question we will have to address a broader range of examples, to which I now turn.

Aristophanes, *The Birds*

By way of introduction to our scene of reading from *The Birds,* let us look briefly at another reading scene from an earlier play of Aristophanes which raises some of the same issues in simpler form. Near the opening of *The Knights* Nicias and Demosthenes, two slaves of the demagogue Cleon ("the Paphlagonian"), get drunk and steal their master's top secret oracle book. As they read, it soon becomes clear why Cleon has been keeping this volume so closely guarded: It contains nothing less than a prediction of his eventual overthrow by a sausage-seller. No sooner do they read this than there enters—a Sausage-Seller.

Two considerations favor an interpretation of this reading scene as an image of the actor with his script. First, there is the scriptlike nature of the text being read, the oracle book. An oracle is a text that forecasts its own supersession by the events and characters it represents. In this it resembles a dramatic text, which also "comes true" when it is "super-seded" by the events and persons it foretells (i.e., when it is performed).

It is remarkable, when you consider all the different kinds of texts there are, that, in three of the five scenes of reading which occur in Aristophanes (those in *The Knights, The Birds,* and *Peace*),[22] the reading matter is an oracle book. It may just be, as Kenneth Dover suggests, that Aristophanes had a special dislike of these woolly little collections.[23] But one feature of the present scene suggests that the parallel between oracle books and scripts is more than incidental—and, indeed, more than a parallel. The oracle book predicts that the next figure to appear in the sequence of Athenian strongmen will be a sausage-seller, and the next figure who appears onstage is the Sausage-Seller. That the next event in the oracle collection is also the next event in the playscript strongly suggests that these are the same text—i.e., that the oracle book is an image occurring *within* the dramatic text of the dramatic text *itself.*

At any event—and this brings us to the second reason for taking the present scene as an image of actor and script—reading from the oracle book involves these two characters in a perplexity that also attends acting:

> NICIAS: What's the oracle say?
>
> DEMOSTHENES: *(who has finished the cup he was given a moment ago)* Pour me another.
>
> NICIAS: "Pour me another"? That's an odd thing for an oracle to say.[24]

To assume, as Nicias does, that the situation is such that whatever is said in the course of it, even what sounds like a spontaneous interpolation, is in fact being read out of a book, is to assume that the situation is acting.

Of course, it seems clear that the "reading" that Nicias jokes about does not really occur: "Pour me another" is not part of the text of the oracle book. But what about this slightly later passage in which Demosthenes reads out to the Sausage-Seller a prediction of his future glory:

> DEMOSTHENES: It's full of blessings, cleverly concealed in riddling words.
>
> *(Unrolls the scroll and recites)*
>
> When that within the great jaws of the crook-talon'd Eagle of Leather
>
> Shall be entrappèd the serpent Stupidity, drinker of swine's blood,

Then shall the tannery-brine of the Paphlagonians perish,
Then to the sellers of guts (unless they prefer to continue
Flogging their sausages still) shall the god give the power and the
glory.[25]

How do we know whether or not reading "really occurs" here? It is
tempting to reply: In each scene we know from the context. But, of
course, in neither case do we *know*—any more than Polonius *knows*
(though he may have his suspicions)—whether Hamlet is really reading
about old men with gray beards or simply having him on. To know we
would have to examine the text from which Demosthenes or Hamlet—
or the actor, insofar as the whole situation images acting—professes to
read. Well, can't we do so, and thereby determine whether the reading
that each reader represents as occurring has, in fact, occurred? Let us
keep this question in mind as we turn to our main scene of reading from
Aristophanes: *The Birds,* lines 959–91.

After the Athenian Peisthetaerus has helped the birds establish their
city in the sky ("Cloudcuckooland") he is besieged by a series of officious
busybodies—a poet, a surveyor, an inspector, etc.—all offering their
services to the new republic. With one of these, an Oracle-Monger,
Peisthetaerus has the following encounter:

ORACLE-MONGER: Forbear! touch not the goat awhile.
PEISTHETAERUS: Eh? Who are you?
ORACLE-MONGER: A soothsayer.
PEISTHETAERUS: You be hanged.
ORACLE-MONGER: O think not lightly, friend, of things divine;
Know I've an oracle of Bakis, bearing
On your Cloudcuckooburies.
PEISTHETAERUS: Eh? then why
Did you not soothsay that before I founded
My city here?
ORACLE-MONGER: The Power within forbade me.
PEISTHETAERUS: Well, well, there's nought like hearing what it
says.
ORACLE-MONGER: "Nay but if once grey crows and wolves shall
be banding together,
Out in the midway space, twixt Corinth and Sicyon, dwelling,—"

PEISTHETAERUS: But what in the world have I to do with
    Corinth?
ORACLE-MONGER: Bakis is riddling: Bakis means the Air.
"First to Pandora offer a white-fleeced ram for a victim.
Next, who first shall arrive my verses prophetic expounding,
Give him a brand-new cloak and a pair of excellent sandals."
PEISTHETAERUS: Are sandals in it?
ORACLE-MONGER: Take the book and see.
"Give him moreover a cup and fill his hands with the inwards."
PEISTHETAERUS: Are inwards in it?
ORACLE-MONGER: Take the book and see.
"Youth, divinely inspired, if thou dost as I bid, thou shalt surely
Soar in the clouds as an eagle; refuse, and thou shalt ne'er become an
Eagle or even a dove, or a woodpecker tapping the oaktree."
PEISTHETAERUS: Is all that in it?
ORACLE-MONGER: Take the book and see.
PEISTHETAERUS: O how unlike your oracle to mine,
Which from Apollo's words I copied out;
"But if a cheat, an impostor, presume to appear uninvited,
Troubling the sacred rites, and lusting to taste of the inwards,
Hit him betwixt the ribs with all your force and all your fury."
ORACLE-MONGER: You're jesting surely.
PEISTHETAERUS: Take the book and see.
"See that ye spare not the rogue, though he soar in the clouds as
    an eagle,
Yea, be he Lampon himself or even the great Diopeithes."
ORACLE-MONGER: Is all that in it?
PEISTHETAERUS: Take the book and see.
Get out! be off, confound you! *(striking him)*
ORACLE-MONGER: O! O! O!
PEISTHETAERUS: There, run away and soothsay somewhere
    else.[26]

Here, as in the *Knights* scene, we have the script-as-oracle-book predict-
ing its own supersession not merely by events in general but by the
advent of the very "actors" who now arrive to realize it:

> ORACLE-MONGER: "Who first shall arrive my verses prophetic
>   expounding,

Give him a brand new cloak."

PEISTHETAERUS: "But if a cheat, an impostor, presume to appear uninvited,

. . . .

Hit him betwixt the ribs."

But here the uncertainty that attends an actor's reading of his script—raised only glancingly in *The Knights* by Nicias's joke ("'Pour me another'? That's an odd thing for an oracle to say")—emerges as the central issue of the scene. Peisthetaerus's exchange with the Oracle-Monger raises a number of interrelated questions about reading: To what extent does a text stand behind reading? Does the text say what the reader says? Is reading always necessarily going on when it claims to be? That the scene, in presenting these issues, is presenting us with an image of the actor and the script is clear from the following consideration: As soon as one tries to describe what it is that makes reading such a questionable activity here, one finds oneself describing acting. The Oracle-Monger's "reading" seems fishy because the text conveniently provides him with just the very thing he needs to be able to say next. But to be reading from a text that conveniently provides you with just the very thing you need to be able to say next is the normal situation of the actor with the script.

Of course, anyone who professed to find acting fishy on such grounds would, rather comically, have misunderstood. There is no "mystery" about a script's readiness to supply an actor with just the words he needs at just the moment he needs them; he only needs those words at that moment because he is following the script! Aristophanes' scene, if it is in any sense an image of acting, is first of all a joke about getting the actor-script relation backwards.

Yet if such "misgivings" about the acting process seem laughable, they are not, for all that, easily disposed of. Just how do we know the actor *isn't* doing precisely what the Oracle-Monger is doing here? Or rather: How do we know our inability to say precisely what the Oracle-Monger is doing here doesn't also apply to the actor? The distinction between *actually reading* and *playing the role of a reader* seems straightforward enough. But a scene of reading necessarily conflates them and so introduces the uncertainties of reading into the heart of acting.

But (to return now to the question raised by our first Aristophanic reading scene) can't we always determine whether an actor is reading or not just by checking what he brings forth against the text from which

he professes to be bringing it? The possibility of such a check does not
fail to occur to Peisthetaerus ("Is all that really in it?"), and the Oracle-
Monger, for a presumed fraud, is surprisingly forthcoming: "Take the
book and see." He risks, however, less than might be supposed.

For what action are we to suppose accompanies this thrice-repeated
invitation? A supposition it must remain: The manuscripts contain no
stage directions for this moment,[27] so it is every director and translator
for himself. Perhaps the Oracle-Monger carries no book but is only
quoting from convenient memory.[28] Perhaps the Oracle-Monger has an
actual book but won't show it because it doesn't say what he claims.[29]
Perhaps the Oracle-Monger is truly reading from a text that he has
doctored to say what he wants.[30] Or perhaps the Oracle-Monger is truly
reading from an accurate text, which, however, he interprets to his own
ends ("Bakis means the Air"). It would seem that to settle on some one
rather than another of these four stagings is to settle the question of how
faithfully the Oracle-Monger reads, but this is not the case. For in all of
them it is the Oracle-Monger alone who controls access to the text—
either to the words themselves, as in the first three versions, or to their
interpretation, as in the last. "Take the book and see. . . ." The actor
seems constantly to be presenting us with a text against which to check
his act of reading; however, it is a text that (at least as far as performance
is concerned) can only be present in and through this very reading of the
actor's for which it is to vouch.

This is a state of affairs to which perhaps no author of dramatic texts
ever quite reconciles himself. And, while we cannot in general say how
Aristophanes felt about the attempt of the actor to put himself in the
place of reading, it is noteworthy that the Oracle-Monger, at least,
doesn't get away with it. Peisthetaerus gives him a dose of his own
medicine:

> PEISTHETAERUS: O how unlike your oracle to mine,
> Which from Apollo's words I copied out;
> "But if a cheat, an impostor, presume to appear uninvited,
> Troubling the sacred rites, and lusting to taste of the inwards,
> Hit him betwixt the ribs with all your force and your fury."
> ORACLE-MONGER: You're jesting surely.
> PEISTHETAERUS: Take the book and see.
>
> . . . .
> Get out! be off, confound you!

On one level we might interpret this turning of the tables in accordance with what we have seen to be the nature of a meeting between actor-readers. Like the Oracle-Monger at this moment, every actor will eventually have his claim to be "the only reader in the room" flung back at him by another. Another actor is another *reader,* and certainly here it is Peisthetaerus's challenge to the Oracle-Monger's "sole reader" status which marks his coming into his own *as an actor.* Up to now Peisthetaerus has confined himself to what is essentially a spectator's attempt—necessarily futile, as we have just been seeing—to "peer around" the actor's reading and see directly into the text. Now, however, in the manner of an actor, he begins to treat the text as a script, as *his* script. It is as if he had suddenly heard the Oracle-Monger's repeated admonition to "take the book *and see"* as meaning not ". . . and you'll see that it backs my claim" but rather ". . . and you'll see that it can back *your* speech as well as mine," i.e., can be a script *for you.*

And, yet, the extent to which Peisthetaerus represents any sort of alternative to the model of the actor-as-(dubious)-reader provided by the Oracle-Monger is severely qualified by the exactness with which his own behavior mirrors the Oracle-Monger's, even down to the catchphrase "take the book and see." Within the fiction of the scene, of course, this is meant for comic justice: By the very trick with which you held me helpless I shall now immobilize *you.* But the implications of this mirroring for the scene's view of reading are more problematic. Peisthetaerus's "purifying" attack on acting as dubious reading must itself be mounted as an act of dubious reading. Does this mean that acting *finds within itself* the cure of its own tendency to dubious reading? Or is the point rather that any "cure" involving reading must itself come under a doubt? Is the presence of reading in acting what enables acting to bluff a relationship to texts which it does not in fact enjoy, or does reading *call* the bluff? The ultimate indistinguishability of the Oracle-Monger's and Peisthetaerus's behavior in this scene implies that, ultimately, reading—or, at any rate, the actor's claim *to have read*—is both the falseness in, and what banishes the falseness from, acting.

Such ambivalence toward reading as both evil and cure certainly fits with what we know of Aristophanes' attitude toward the world of texts and writing in general. On the one hand, who was more contemptuous than Aristophanes of "literary" culture? One thinks of his impatience with Euripides for having introduced characters who "turn a phrase neatly . . . interpret . . . twist . . . contrive";[31] of his attacks on the Soph-

ists, who, rightly or wrongly, were held responsible for the general
proliferation of books and bookishness.[32] Indeed, taken in context, our
Birds scene is itself a moment in an episode that satirizes this proliferation. The Oracle-Monger is but one in a long procession of crackpots
peddling fraudulent writings: the wind-surveyor, with his futile calcula-
tions; the statute-seller, with his fussy ordinances; the poet, with his
empty verse. This "plague of bad *biblia* in Aristophanes' Cloud-cuckoo-
town is a satiric counterpart to conditions in Athens towards the end of
the [fifth] century [B.C.]."[33] It is a common feature of Aristophanic
structure that, at a certain point in each play, "various 'impostors' enter,
and try to share in the benefits of the new scheme, but are beaten off by
the hero."[34] We might take the fact that each impostor in *The Birds* is
associated with a text as a stage metaphor implying that the parade of
texts characteristic of a literary culture is a *succession of impostures.*

In the parabasis of *The Frogs* Aristophanes excoriates his audience
for their literary pretensions:

> But now they've learned to read
> It's real tough stuff they need;
> They don't want chicken-feed—
>   They're educated![35]

And, yet, what playwright was ever more dependent on a "literate public" than Aristophanes, whose very attacks on literary culture—presup-
posing as they do a wide familiarity with particular genres, authors, and
works[36]—can only be understood by an audience steeped in it.

In this ambivalence Aristophanes reflects the ambivalence of the
Greek mind itself toward writing and texts. On the one hand, these
were valued as providing permanence in a world of flux;[37] on the other
hand, they were mistrusted as rigid, secondary, and destructive of memory.[38] Such a split is present in Plato—Derrida juxtaposes pro- and an-
tiwriting passages from the *Laws* and the *Phaedrus,* respectively[39]—but,
more pertinent to our inquiry, it pervades Greek tragic drama.

If one has not been reading Greek tragedy lately, one may tend to
recall the Greek tragic world as pre- or illiterate. But, in fact, the plays
are full of references to reading and writing and of characters who read
and write. Even in the primal era of the *Prometheus Bound* men have already
been taught (by Prometheus) "the combining of letters as a means of
remembering all things."[40] And the still distinctly mythic milieu of Euripides' *Hippolytus* is, rather startlingly, already a "book culture":

NURSE: He who has read the writings of the ancients
and has lived much in books, he knows
that Zeus once. . . . [41]

(Aren't *they*—Hippolytus, Phaedra, Theseus—"the ancients"?)

The references to reading and writing in Greek tragedy display the same ambivalence toward these activities that characterizes Greek culture as a whole. On the plus side, once again, is the promise of stability. Characters in Aeschylus are forever being adjured to "cut" or "carve" or "inscribe" some important fact in the "tablet" of their minds or hearts.[42] (Here it is not, as in the *Phaedrus* of Plato, a question of memory versus writing but, rather, of memory as *itself* a kind of "writing" and of remembering as a kind of "reading.") The written provides a standard (and a trope) for permanence, as when, in Sophocles' *Women of Trachis,* Deinira states that she has kept the centaur's (oral) instructions in her mind "like an inscription on bronze that cannot be washed away"[43] or when Euripides' Theseus, in *The Suppliant Women,* praises writing as the guarantor of laws that, so long as they reside only in a ruler's voice, can be unvoiced at will.[44]

More often, however, Euripides is to be found on—is, indeed, after Plato, the chief spokesman for—the negative side of the quarrel. Reversing the writing = permanence trope, he tends to associate writing with false or dubious claims; in the *Hippolytus,* with those of a (supposed) religious hypocrite:

THESEUS: Go, boast that you eat no meat, that you have Orpheus
for your king. Read until you are demented
your great thick books whose substance is as smoke.[45]

in the *Iphigenia in Aulis,* with those of an untrustworthy god:

CHORUS: *(addressing* CLYTEMNESTRA) Child of the arch-necked
swan,
If the story is to be believed,
The story that Leda bore you to a winged bird,
To Zeus himself transformed!
But perhaps this is a fable
From the book of the Muses
Borne to me out of season,
A senseless tale.[46]

More important, the *action* of reading, which Euripides is the only one of the three tragic playwrights to represent onstage, he invariably represents as having bad or unintended effects. In the *Hippolytus* writing (the letter of false accusation which Phaedra orders attached to her body) bears false witness, and reading (Theseus' perusal of that letter, on the strength of which he calls down destruction on the innocent Hippolytus) brings injustice and death. In *Iphigenia in Aulis,* too, "bad writing"—a lying letter from Agamemnon to Clytemnestra, luring her and Iphigenia to Aulis on false pretenses—is at the root of all the trouble. The letter itself is sent before the action begins, but attempts in the course of the play to undo its ill effects only cast further discredit on writing. In remorse, Agamemnon writes Clytemnestra a *second* letter to countermand the first. But this letter, too, is a lie (it speaks only of postponement of the "marriage" that Iphigenia has been falsely led to believe awaits her at Aulis; in fact, she is to be sacrificed), and, in any case, it never reaches its intended reader (Menelaus intercepts the courier, reads the letter, and persuades Agamemnon to persevere in his original intent). Writing, thus, proves powerless to undo its own damage, to correct itself from within.

Nonetheless, Agamemnon's message does, eventually, reach his wife. He has taken the precaution of reading his letter aloud to the old slave who is to deliver it, and the slave, in turn, speaks its contents aloud to Clytemnestra, adding his own *spoken* account of Agamemnon's true motives. Thus, what have been revealed as the two main failings of writing—that it doesn't necessarily find its intended recipient and that it lies—are both made good when writing is entrusted to voice.

Euripides' other Iphigenia play also contains an episode in which a *written* message meant to be *read* only finds its intended reader when entrusted to voice. The famous recognition scene from *Iphigenia in Tauris* makes an especially interesting foil to our Aristophanic scene of reading because: (1) it repeats Aristophanes' ambivalence, not only toward reading as such but, specifically, toward reading's claim to be the basis of action/acting; (2) it fantasizes, as an escape from this dilemma, an acting process that would "do without" reading; and (3) it illustrates how any such fantasy must issue in a contradiction.

Let us recall the action of the scene. Iphigenia, miraculously rescued by Artemis from impending sacrifice at Aulis, now dwells among the remote Taurians who, ironically, compel her to serve as a priestess in *their* sacrificial cult. Her long lost brother, Orestes, and his friend

Pylades, traveling incognito, have been taken prisoner in Tauris and are now brought before Iphigenia to be prepared for sacrifice. Learning that the prisoners are Greeks, she promises to release one of them if he will carry to the (supposedly) far-off Orestes a letter that she dictated to another cult victim ten years earlier and has ever since been waiting for an opportunity to deliver. The prisoners accept the offer, and Pylades is given the letter. But, he asks, suppose there is a shipwreck and the letter is lost: How, then, is he to keep his end of the bargain? To guard against this contingency Iphigenia recites to Pylades the text of the very letter that he now holds sealed in his hand: "Your sister is not dead at Aulis / But is alive. . . . O brother, come and save me." "No word was ever easier to keep!" replies Pylades and, turning to his companion, hands him the tablet: "I give you this, Orestes, from your sister!" "How can I look at letters," replies Orestes, and he takes Iphigenia in his arms.[47]

As an image of the actor with his script, this is quite unlike our *Birds* example and, for that matter, all our other "scenes of reading" in being, precisely, a scene of *non*reading, of reading narrowly averted, as it were. In *The Birds* a "script" possibly absent throughout (the oracle book) is possibly read. In *Iphigenia in Tauris* a "script" definitely present throughout (the letter) is definitely not read. And, yet, except for the one "detail" of its never being read, the role that Iphigenia's letter plays in the situation unfolding between these people is very like that of a script among actors. As in acting, a text is entrusted to voice and thereby reaches its intended audience. As in acting, voice and action are substituted for a text whose prior existence is nonetheless the precondition for any such substitution. In just one respect does the whole transaction fail to resemble that of the actor with the script: *No one reads anything*. Everything that might be expected to happen "around the edges" of an act of reading happens. A text is committed to writing. A channel is found for delivering the text to its intended reader. The text is physically conveyed into the reader's hands and its contents into his mind. Only reading itself does not happen. Iphigenia's recitation of the message removes the necessity of its ever being read. And, yet, by this act of nonreading the contents of a text meant to be read are transmitted from author to reader.

On one level the action of this scene can be understood as a series of attempts to protect against the evil instability of writing, as depicted in the *Hippolytus* and the *Iphigenia in Aulis,* by means of the good stability of voice. Certainly, writing (the letter) is represented as in need of such protection at every step of the way. Its delivery must be arranged by oral bargaining, guaranteed by oral vows, safeguarded against mishap, and at length actually brought to pass, by oral repetition. Voice, in other words, is here called upon to impart to writing that stability that, in Aeschylus and Sophocles, writing is thought of as imparting to voice. When, at length, oral fulfillment of the oral vow *itself* effects delivery of the written message ("No word was ever easier to keep! / . . . / I give you this, Orestes, from your sister!"), writing drops out of the equation, so to speak, its aims achieved, and its evils averted, by the spoken word.

What significance does this elimination of reading and writing assume if we take the scene as an image of relations between actor and script? Our Aristophanes example has already suggested that acting might have its own reasons for being interested in such an elimination. In *The Birds,* as we saw, the whole acting process comes in for doubt as a result of its connection with acts of dubious reading. Such "contamination" of acting by reading there seemed inevitable because the connection itself seemed so: How could one act a script without reading it? The present scene fantasizes escape from that contamination by fantasizing away the inevitability of the acting-reading link. It purports to show how one might perform actions on the basis of a text (i.e., "act" a "script") *without ever having to read a word.*

But if we allow ourselves to imagine the experience of actors working on the *Iphigenia* scene, it soon becomes clear that the scene's fantasy of an escape from reading cannot survive the attempt to realize it—that there is, in fact, a contradiction between the scene's vision of reading-free rehearsal and any possible rehearsal work *on the scene.* Most obviously, the text of Iphigenia's letter, which, within the fiction of the scene, is never read, must, in early reading rehearsals of the scene, be read in the script, by the actor. But further: All those acts by which, within the fiction of the scene, reading is *bypassed* must *themselves* initially be accomplished by acts of reading. Oral bargain, oral summary, oral vow—all are now read. The actor's escape from reading can only be realized by an actor reading. The fantasy of doing away can only be enacted by the activity it fantasizes doing away with.

But this is precisely the situation of our Aristophanes scene, where, too, the *assault* on reading (that of the Oracle-Monger) can only be mounted as an *act* of reading (that of Peisthetaerus). It seems, then, we must revise what at first appeared a straightforward distinction between a scene where reading may or may not be going on (Aristophanes) and a scene where reading clearly is not going on (Euripides). In fact, the two scenes differ only with respect to the *stage* at which the uncertainty on this score, present in both of them, is destined to emerge. In Aristophanes the question of whether reading is going on or not is already represented within the fiction of the scene, as an issue between Peisthetaerus and the Oracle-Monger. In Euripides the question of whether reading is going on or not only first arises at the moment when actors begin to represent the scene's fiction—the moment, that is, when nonreading begins to be enacted by (rehearsal) reading. (This is not to say that the uncertainty is a product *of* rehearsal: The script is already "rigged" to produce this dilemma as surely as it is rigged to produce a performance of *Iphigenia in Tauris*.) All the Aristophanic misgivings about reading which the Euripides scene represents actors as escaping from wait down the line for them at the moment when they begin to represent it, i.e., to act.

This reappearance of the difficulties of reading *within acting* is, I submit, no coincidence. For the misgivings about reading's role in acting which come through in both our Aristophanes and Euripides passages are, it seems to me, likely to have characterized the Greek attitude toward acting itself.

From one point of view, Greek dubiousness toward reading is rather surprising. Since the Greeks esteemed voice over rigid, secondary writing, and since their reading was, for the most part, reading *aloud,* should they not, sooner than have mistrusted reading, hailed it as a cure for the silence, rigidity, and secondariness of words on a page?

The problem is that, in reading aloud, voice takes on that very characteristic of writing which made the Greeks rank writing as inferior to voice in the first place. Writing, the Greeks held, was originally only transcription of voice. Reading aloud unquestionably marks a return to what was felt to be the more primary experience of voiced sound. The voiced sound of *reading* is itself, however, now only further transcription (of the written signs back into oral signs)—a new secondariness. (In Platonic terms, if the written text is at a third remove from what it imitates—a poem about beds imitates actual beds, which themselves only imitate the Form of "the bed"—then reading aloud, which reproduces the written text in sound, would be at yet another, a *fourth,* remove from reality.)[48] Reading thus recovers the original, unmediated sound out of writing but does so by "adding on" to writing just such a new layer of mediation as writing itself once constituted with respect to voice. Reading aloud is thus, undecidably, the recovery of the unmediated *and* the most distanced act of mediation yet. No wonder the Greek attitude toward this activity was an ambivalent one!

If the ambivalence extended to acting as well, this was not only because acting involves reading but also because acting is itself structured on this very paradox. If read-aloud words re-present an original immediacy by adding yet another link to the chain of mediators between us and it, *precisely the same thing could be said of acting.* The *Agamemnon* is acted— and we stand in the unmediated presence of the *Agamemnon* events (which the script only transcribes). The *Agamemnon* is acted—and a whole new level of mediation is inserted between us and the *Agamemnon* events (the performers now transcribing into stage action the events of a script itself already transcription). Acting, too, in other words, is a paradoxical return of the immediate through the efforts of, and in the person of, the remotest mediators yet—"interpreters of [poets who are themselves only] interpreters," as Plato described actors.[49] Acting thus has the structure of—*acts out,* one might say—the very aspect of reading which made the Greeks so uncomfortable with it. It is hard to believe, though there is no way of proving it, that this structural similarity would not have influenced Greek attitudes toward acting—that, indeed, the attitude of the Greeks toward acting was not already given in their attitude toward the reading whose paradoxes acting enacts.

The Coventry *Woman Taken in Adultery* Play

And the scribes and Pharisees brought unto him a woman taken in adultery; and when they had set her in the midst,

They say unto him, Master, this woman was taken in adultery, in the very act.

Now Moses in the law commanded us, that such should be stoned: but what sayest thou?

This they said, tempting him, that they might have to accuse him. But Jesus stooped down, and with his finger wrote on the ground, as though he heard them not.

So when they continued asking him, he lifted up himself, and said unto them, He that is without sin among you, let him first cast a stone at her.

And again he stooped down, and wrote on the ground.

And they which heard it, being convicted by their own conscience, went out one by one.[50]

Two of the medieval English Corpus Christi cycles, Coventry and Chester, contain plays based on this episode from the Gospel according to St. John.[51] The Coventry play, which will be our primary concern, adds a good many elements to the biblical account: for example, an introductory scene in which a scribe and a Pharisee lament Jesus' growing influence and conspire to discredit him; a wonderful vignette of the Woman's lover escaping from her bed with his pants in his hand; and an effective exchange in which the Woman first begs to be released, then offers bribes, and at last throws herself on her Accusers' mercy.

Of these embellishments the Chester play, to which we shall often turn for purposes of comparison, contains only the first: the conspiracy scene. There are, however, two other major alterations of the biblical source, present in both cycles, which have great significance for our inquiry. In both the Coventry and Chester plays:

1. it is specified *what* Christ writes in the dust: the Accusers' sins;
2. it is these *written* words of Christ which they *read,* not *spoken* words of his which they *hear,* which put the Accusers to flight.

I am going to argue that, taken together, these two changes turn the biblical scene into a characteristically medieval image of the actor with his script.

Even taken individually, each of these changes points in the direction of the actor-script transaction. That the plays "fill in" the contents of what is, in the biblical passage, an unspecified writing recalls the actor-as-(active)-reader, "filling in" the "blanks," or "gaps," of the text.[52] Again: Each Accuser, we are told, finds *his own* sins written in the dirt—and flees (Coventry, 219). Such a script event images the situation of the actor "reading in" whatever subtextual material will, at a given moment, adequately "motivate" his character's action (in this instance, flight). Moreover, the fact that *each* Accuser reads, in the *same* writing, his own *particular* sins—a "miracle" within the fiction of the scene— seems an emblem of the script's "miraculous" power to provide each of its actor-readers with the inner truth of *his* character's life.

The other change that both Coventry and Chester make in their biblical source—the Accusers' flight being from writing they read rather than from spoken words they hear—also suggests a dimension of the actor-script transaction, for such a "flight" is paradoxical in a way we have found acting itself to be. Each Accuser flees a text that "casts" him in the "role" of a sinner. But such a flight is *already* the act of a sinner, hence, an acceptance of the role. To flee *as* sinner from the identity *of* sinner—this simultaneous *resistance* to and *acceptance* of one's relation to a text, *both* of which must be enacted by the same action (flight), explicitly recalls the *actor's* simultaneous *supplant* and *merge* impulses toward the script, both of which must likewise find expression in a single act. Like actors, the Coventry and Chester Accusers are "set in motion" by conflicting impulses toward the text they read.

Both the aspects of acting which I have argued are suggested by the Coventry version of John 8 may seem "too modern" to be present in a medieval scene of reading. Yet both connect with attitudes and practices familiar to the medieval mind. Simultaneous flight from/enactment of the "text" of one's sins recalls an essential Christian paradox: I escape from sin's being (ultimately) the story of my life by accepting sin as (initially) the story of my life. On this point the dialectic of acting shows affinities with the dialectic of repentance. As for acting as a "filling in" of textual blanks, medieval theater was from the first involved with such activity: the filling in of blanks in the liturgical texts with embellishments and expansions.[53] Then, too, it was a standard medieval devotional practice to "fill in" any circumstances, actions, and motives not specified in the scriptural text on which one was meditating.[54] It does not seem implausible that those called upon to enact these texts might have availed themselves of this technique. Indeed, I shall presently argue that, for the medieval mind, acting most fundamentally consisted in just such a "glossing" of Scripture.

While both the Accusers' *filling in of* and their *flight from* writing each by itself suggests acting, it is especially the two of these occurring *together* which marks the Coventry scene as an image of the medieval actor-script transaction. For, as I shall now attempt to show, the filling in of and the flight from a text are both, ultimately, figures for the interpretation of it. And to represent acting, in the manner of our scene, as, likewise, including both the flight from and the filling in of a text is to claim for it, too, the status of textual commentary: acting as glossing. This may seem a modest enough claim. But in a period when acting was mistrusted—this is reflected in our scene by the actor-figures (the Accusers) being sinners, Jews, "mis-representers"—and textual commentary regarded as the highest form of knowledge, the implications are startling.

On what basis can one argue that filling in and fleeing from the text are alternative descriptions of interpretation? That interpretation is a "filling in"—a supplying of material and connections not till now in evidence—seems implicit in the term itself. Furthermore, though we have hitherto come upon the terminology of filled gaps and supplied connections in modern critical writing, such language makes an especially appropriate description of medieval interpretive practice. Both in his essential project ("a constant endeavor *to fill in the lacunae* of the Biblical account . . . to establish a *continuous connection* of events")[55] and in the physical means by which he realized it (the writing in of commentary along the margins and between the lines of his text)[56] the medieval interpreter was, like the Coventry and Chester Accusers, preeminently a filler-in of blanks. *Flight* seems a less promising trope for interpretation but, in fact, picks up something essential about it. A forward-looking vocabulary is customary in these matters: one "proceeds" with an analysis, "advances" in understanding, etc. And, yet, if interpretation is generally thought of as an *approach to the meaning,* it can equally well be imagined as a *flight from the silence,* indeterminacy, openness of a still to be read text. And how does one flee silence; what does one flee? Clearly, one flees the unspecified by specifying; the indeterminate, by making a determination; the silence, by speaking a word. It is in this sense that one may regard *flight* and *filling in* not only as alternative descriptions of interpretation but, ultimately, as interchangeable ones.

Especially, for reasons that will become clear in a moment, does interpretation of a biblical passage have the character of a flight-that-specifies. I am going to propose that the Coventry Accusers' enactment of such a flight associates their activity with biblical commentary and so links acting—of which we have already found their activity to be reminiscent—with the particular sort of reading practiced by biblical commentators.

My grounds for asserting that the reading behavior of the Coventry Accusers images biblical commentary are as follows:

1. *The writing that the Accusers read and flee from is, like the Bible, divine writing.* Not only because Christ is the writer but also because within the little symbolic masque he performs in response to the Accusers' question, his gesture of writing seems to stand for *God's written law.* I arrive at this interpretation in the following manner. By their initial trick question the Accusers seek to trap Christ between the authority of the *written* Mosaic code (according to which an adulteress must die [Leviticus 12:10]) and the authority of his own *oral* teaching of mercy; between, as

the Chester play neatly puts it, "law" and "lore" (Chester, II. 220, 222, p. 396). In order to answer the question, he must, it seems, disavow either (others') writing or (his own) voice. But what happens? Jesus writes in the dirt, then interrupts his writing to speak, and then resumes writing. By which sequence of actions he seems to proclaim: "Since I am myself the source of *both* the written tradition and the 'new voice' that interrupts it, no such contradiction as your question implies can possibly arise."

A further hint of the divine character of writing in this episode lies in the overtones of the gesture itself. When Christ stoops over and writes on the ground it is reminiscent of an earlier occasion when God leaned down and imprinted his Word upon dust: the moment of Creation. For Jesus' action here the Chester Expositor uses the expression "wrott [wrote] in clay" (l. 294, p. 399)—a pun emphasizing the analogy with that other moment when this same Author "wrought in clay."[57]

As a final indication that we are watching the reenactment of some primal divine writing, consider the rather startling first reference to Jesus' action in the Coventry script: "Here, while those folk accuse the woman, Jesus ought to go on writing [*continue debet . . . scribere*] with his finger in the earth" (Coventry, 217).[58] "Ought to *go on* . . . ?" When did he *start*? This carelessly placed stage direction suggests a writing that has always been in progress, a suggestion that receives further support from the stage direction that follows: "*Jesus . . . semper scribit in terra*" (Coventry, 218). For, while the idiomatic translation of *semper scribit* is "he keeps on writing," literally the phrase means "he always writes." It is just such an absolutely prior divine writing that the divine Author himself here reenacts placing before his human readers. To find oneself with such a writing perpetually "before" one (in both senses of the word) is precisely the situation of the biblical commentator. But further:

2. *The Accusers' interpretive dilemma is that of the biblical commentator.* The Bible's being addressed to every reader means it is not addressed to any reader in particular. And, yet, to read it rightly means to read it as addressed to *me*, as the story of *my* life, the indictment of *my* sins. That is why, of all forms of interpretation, biblical commentary has most clearly the character of a flight-that-specifies. The only possible *acceptance* of Scripture's claim of universality is by way of an existential "taking personally" that, however, *rescinds* the universality in any particular case. The Coventry Accusers, who, upon reading Jesus' writing, "break apart, as if confused . . . and move off separately to three places" (Coventry,

218, translation slightly modified) enact this dilemma of the biblical interpreter, whose manner of acknowledging the general applicability of God's word must be to take it off in some direction of his own.

3. *What the Coventry and Chester Accusers do here* within *the episode is what, historically, biblical commentators have done* to *the episode: namely, given the content of Jesus' writing in the dust.* Why does St. John not tell us the words, or even the general drift, of Jesus' writing? To me the answer seems obvious: The significance lies not in *what* he writes (in the biblical version, remember, his words are not read by anyone) but, rather, as I have already suggested, in the symbolic demonstration his writing provides of the true relation between written and oral authority. This has not, however, been obvious to generations of Christian exegetes, who, since antiquity, have been trying to fill in this particular blank. Perhaps, it has been suggested, Christ is writing out an appropriate scriptural quotation, say, Exodus 23:1 ("Thou shalt not raise a false report"). Perhaps he is setting down, in an image suggested by Jeremiah 17:13 ("they that depart from me shall be written in the earth"), the names of the false Accusers. Or possibly, like a judge in a Roman court, he is making notes for the decision he is about to render.[59]

The Coventry and Chester playwrights associate themselves with this exegetical effort not only by the impulse they show to furnish a content but also in the specific content they provide. For the Coventry and Chester solution—that what the Accusers read in the dust is *their sins*—was first proposed by a biblical commentator, indeed, by the dean of all biblical commentators, St. Jerome. "We follow the venerable Jerome in the same quest for truth as his"—these are in fact the words of a twelfth-century exegete,[60] but they could as well have been spoken by the Coventry playwright, who, in developing this episode as he did, was in fact composing a Jerome-influenced "commentary" on John 8. Just how closely the dramatic and exegetical impulses might approach one another is apparent in the following examples.

"O king, I have been undone." . . . "What is the matter?" "I am pregnant. . . . The fruit of my sin grows. . . . If my husband comes to me and sees, what will I say?"

This invented dialogue is not from a medieval *play* about David and Bathsheba but, rather, from the standard medieval *gloss* on that story.[61]

[Jesus] puts his little hand to [his mother's] face, as if to prevent her from weeping.

When the nail is drawn out, John signals to Nicodemus to bring it to him inconspicuously, so that Our Lady will not be distressed by the sight of it.

These invented actions are not the stage directions of a dramatist but, rather, the "fillings in" of a biblical commentator.[62]

Now, if what the Coventry Accusers read in the dust is, in fact, what the playwright, with Jerome's help, has read in the gospel passage, this means that the text of the Coventry play is, to this extent, representing its own interpretive transaction with the biblical text. What I now want to argue is that, in doing this, the Coventry play is also representing—cannot help but represent—what will eventually be the *actor's* interpretive transaction with *it*.

I have already suggested that the very act of filling in a text is actorlike. But, further, the *specific* additions that the Coventry play makes to its biblical source, a number of which I listed at the outset of this discussion, are of the very sort that an actor might make to a script. As actors supply objectives for their characters, for example, so the Coventry play supplies objectives for the characters in the biblical account: e.g., in the Woman's case, *to bribe (or move) my captors to release me*. Or again: As actors might improvise episodes implied by, but not included in, the action, so the Coventry play fills in moments of action implied by, but not included in, the biblical text: e.g., the Accusers go to arrest the Woman; the Woman's lover reacts to her arrest. Thus, in fleeing the unspecificity of the dramatic text, the performer of the Coventry play will find *his* flight already inscribed within the Coventry script as *its* flight from the unspecificity of the biblical source. The playwright, himself following Jerome, fills in the scriptural blank *(what words did Christ write?)* with "the Accusers' sins"; the Coventry actor, in turn, fills in the script's blank *(what sins did the Accusers commit?)* with something of his own, perhaps his own sins. To "follow" such a script is to follow in the script's own path of fleeing/filling in.[63]

But if the Coventry playwright's work on the biblical text and the Coventry actor's work on the Coventry play resemble each other, it is not ultimately because of some special affinity between acting and playwriting[64] but, rather, because *both* of these activities are essentially transactions (albeit at different removes) with Holy Scripture. And for the Middle Ages there is ultimately only one transaction you can have with Holy Scripture. To *read* the Bible; to *interpret* the Bible; to *write a play* that interprets the Bible; to interpret, as an *actor,* one's *role* in such a play; and (since in the Middle Ages theatrical performances were commonly regarded as "quick [i.e., living] books" and "books for the unlearned")[65] to *be the audience* at such a play—all these are ultimately reducible to a single transaction: that *specifying flight* from the openness of the text to a meaning-for-me, which, as we have seen, is the essence of biblical interpretation.

The fundamental identity of all these activities for the medieval mind is reflected in the theatrical device of the Expositor, a single figure who, in many medieval plays, performs them all. The Expositor is basically a commentator who enters before, after, and sometimes during the action to explain its moral and theological significance to the audience. More frequent in continental than English drama[66] (cf. the French *meneur du jeu* and the Italian *festaiuolo*),[67] the Expositor nonetheless appears quite often in the English cycles as well. He is not always *called* "expositor." Indeed, the great variety of Latin names by which figures of this type are designated in the manuscripts—*expositor, doctor* [teacher, authority], *preco* [priest], *nuntius* [messenger], even *contemplacio* [(faculty of) contemplation]—itself testifies to the variety of functions these figures fulfill.[68] In fact, they function in *all* the modes that, we have seen, the "single transaction" with Holy Writ can assume, to wit:

The Expositor reads the Bible—reads it, that is, for and on behalf of the audience:

> Also [as] we read in this storie,
> God in the Mownt of Synai
> Toke [delivered to] Moises these comaundements, verely,
> Wrytten with his owne hande
> In tables of ston, as reade I.[69]

The Expositor comments on the Bible. A prophet speaks, and the Expositor speaks a gloss:

> Lordinges, this prophesie, i-wis [I know],
> Touches the Passion nothing amisse,
> For the prophet see[s] well this

What [that] shall come, as I reade:
That a childe borne of a maye [maid]
Shall suffer death, sooth to saye.[70]

or transmits others' glossing:

I will declare as it is nede [necessary],
This thing that played was.
As Augustine sayeth expressely
Of it in his Homely [homily]
Uppon St. John Evangely [the Evangelist],
Thus he sayeth in this case.

(Chester, ll. 276–81, p. 398)

As we have seen, the Coventry and Chester playwrights also see it as part of their job to transmit earlier exegetical speculation (Jerome's guess as to the contents of Christ's writing), and this leads to our next category:

The Expositor "writes the play." I do not know of a medieval play in which the Expositor literally represents the playwright. And yet, as V. A. Kolve says, he "exists . . . in order to speak for the dramatist,"[71] not only in the literal sense that he speaks the playwright's views, but, more fundamentally, in that his editing, juxtaposing, and framing of incidents amounts to a performance of the *authorial function* out there onstage for all to see.[72] At the same time, however:

The Expositor acts the biblical text. For all his authorial-interpretive "distance" from the action, and notwithstanding his lack of any individual "character" to play, the Expositor is clearly an *actor,* whom the audience sees and responds to as an element of the spectacle, part of the show. Simultaneously, though:

The Expositor is an audience for others' enactment of the biblical text. Not only in the sense that he represents the spectators' interpretive will—reading with them, and helping them to read, in the "quick book" of performance—but, more prosaically, in that he spends, and is perceived by the audience as spending, a great deal of the performance *sitting watching* the same action that they themselves sit and watch.

Though I have presented each of these functions of the Expositor separately, they tend to blur into each other. The actor who reads in the biblical script, the exegete who offers a reading of the biblical text, the playwright whose writing is an exegetical reading, the spectator who deciphers the "quick book"—all these can be represented by this single figure because, for the medieval mind, all these *comprise* a single figure engaged in the "single transaction" it is possible to have with the sacred text.

Of the two plays we are considering, one (Chester) contains an Expositor, and it is interesting to see the difference his presence makes to that play's image of the relation between acting and reading. In the Expositor-less Coventry play, all three Accusers tell us what they read in the dirt, and, miraculously, it is different in every case: each Accuser sees *his own* sins written out before him. As I suggested earlier, this may be taken as an image of each actor finding in the single writing of the script precisely the inner truth of his particular role. But suppose, remembering Peisthetaerus and the Oracle-Monger, we are inclined to view the disparity between mutually exclusive reading claims here as casting doubt on *all* of them. For no more than in Aristophanes can we *know* the content of the text these "actors" read, except in their reading of it. Should we find it a bit fishy that *one* writing can have three different contents, there is no higher authority present to rule on which, if any, of the three Accusers/actors has rightly read.

In the Chester play, when a comparable uncertainty about reading arises, such a "higher authority" seems to be at hand in the person of the Expositor. At Chester the uncertainty assumes an initially less striking, but ultimately even more perplexing, form. Instead of three Accusers, each confidently informing us that the same text says three different things, we now have two Accusers ("Secundus Jew," "Primus Pharaseus"), the first of whom informs us of what he has read:

> SECUNDUS JEW: What wrytes thou, master? Now lett see!
> Out! Alas! That wo is me!
> Here no longer dare I be—
> I see my synnes so clearly—
> For dread of worlds shame.
>
> (Chester, ll. 245–49, p. 397)

and the second of whom doesn't:

> PRIMUS PHARASEUS: Why fleest thou, fellow? By my fay [faith],
> I will see sone [soon] and assay [find out].

Alas! That I were away,
Farr behynde Fraunce!
Stand thou, Sibbel [mistress], him besyde!
No longer here I darr [dare] abyde
Against thee now for to chyde,
As I have good chaunce.

> (Chester, ll. 250–57, pp. 397–98)

It certainly seems probable that Primus Pharaseus is *also* claiming to have read *his* sins in the dust. But his not actually voicing a claim thus palpably at odds with his coreader's seems to ensure that the Coventry dilemma—how judge between actors' differing accounts of a single text?—will not arise.

Meanwhile, however, it has arisen. For the "obvious" contrast between the two Chester Accusers dissolves on examination. The Secondus Jew claims that he reads, but (as at Coventry) there is no guarantee that he is acting on the basis of his reading. The Primus Pharaseus, on the other hand, makes no such claim, but (as at Coventry) it is not improbable that he is acting on the basis of his reading. Instead of a distinction between *reading* and *not reading,* all we are left with is a distinction between a confiding and a withholding informant. But, as for the truth of what *either* the confiding informant confides *or* the withholding informant withholds, no more than in the case of Peisthetaerus and the Oracle-Monger does anything beyond the word of the readers themselves stand surety for the claims of reading.

Or so matters would stand but for the Expositor:

EXPOSITOR: For eche one of them had grace
To see theyr synnes in that place;
Yet none of [concerning] the other wyser was,
But his owne eche man knew.

> (Chester, ll. 298–301, p. 399)

An authoritative "outside" voice speaks, and all uncertainty vanishes: Each Accuser has, miraculously, read his own and only his own sins there in the dust. Behind both the doubtful claim to have read *and* the absence of such a claim lie, we are told, acts of true reading. The unverifiable has been verified; the undecidable, decided. Acting's claim to be true reading thus seems to receive validation from a higher, or at any rate an external, authority.

But, again, the reality is more complex. For in what does the Expositor's act of "conferring validity" really consist? I have already suggested that the Expositor combines the functions of actor and reader. But, what is more, the relation between his acting and his reading is the same as for any other medieval actor. The actor playing the Chester Primus Pharaseus, for example (the one who doesn't say why he flees), must decide whether and what he reads and fill in the blank accordingly. But this exactly describes what the *Expositor* does here: i.e., he decides whether and what the (actor playing the) Primus Pharaseus reads and fills in the blank accordingly. The Expositor inserts material in the openings left for interpretation in the "text" of the stage action, the "quick book," just as the actor inserts material in the openings left for interpretation in the literal text of the play. Thus, the initial impression given by the Chester Expositor of being one who validates acting's reading claims "from above" or even "from without" is a misleading one. True, the Expositor stands above or outside the fiction of the scene he expounds. But his expository activity is not superior to, or even different from, the actor's own activity as a reader. The Expositor is himself an actor-who-reads, his process of conferring validity ultimately indistinguishable from the process on which he confers it.

From this identity between Expositor and actor one can draw conflicting conclusions: on the one hand, that acting's claim to read is validated by no authority higher than its own (since the "authority" it seems to rest on is indistinguishable from itself); on the other hand, that acting *requires* no outside validation (since it is itself an instance of the procedure by which such claims as its own are validated). This ambiguity implies not only that the medieval view of acting is an ambivalent one but, further, that this ambivalence may be owing to acting's association with a reading process *itself* regarded ambivalently.

This last is surprising. To say that the Middle Ages had misgivings where acting and theater were concerned would be an understatement. From late antiquity on the overwhelming majority of writers to express an opinion on theatrical activity expressed a negative one.[73] But that these misgivings should in any measure be due to acting's tie with *reading* seems unlikely. After all, the claim to read rightly—i.e., to have read the right specifics into an authoritative text—is the basic form of a truth-claim for the medieval mind. Any involvement with reading, it seems, could do the status of the medieval actor nothing but good.

Perhaps, though, the claim of acting to be an instance of this highly regarded interpretive process was felt to be unwarranted? But with divine writing—of which the *dirt "page"* from which the Accusers read their sins, the *biblical page* from which the commentator or playwright reads the story of the Accusers, the *script page* from which the actor reads the role of the Accuser, the *performed "page"* of the "quick book" from which the Expositor and audience "read" the Accusers' significance are all displacements, *all the same page,* so to speak—only one transaction is possible. Whether it is St. Jerome fleeing from the openness of the scriptural word to a reading that specifies *the Accusers' sins* or a Coventry townsman, cast as one of those Accusers, fleeing from the openness of the script's word ("my sins") to a reading that specifies *his own sins,* it is always the same interpretive *flight-that-specifies.*[74] Thus, it need not surprise us that Peter Comestor, the greatest of medieval biblical commentators, should have allowed his students to act in liturgical dramas,[75] or that a spectator at a Cornish mystery play should have been moved to compare a clumsy actor to "a bad Clarke [scholar] in Scripture matters, cleaving more to the letter than the sense,"[76] i.e., to an ungifted commentator. When there is only a single transaction to be had with divine writing, how can acting help but be as valid an instance of it as any other?

No, it is not acting's claim to be reading which is in question but, rather, the status of reading itself—or, at least, of that blank-filling, glossing sort of reading which, for all it was the approved medieval road to knowledge, in practice came in for considerable mistrust. Glosses, it was argued, at best do no more than re-present an already present word ("if the gloss says the same as the text, then it is just redundant") and may well misrepresent it ("if it says something different, it can only be harmful"). The Latin *glosa,* a fifteenth-century scholar pointed out, is a synonym for *falsitas.*[77] And in Middle English *to gloze* means "to veil with specious comments," "to talk smoothly and speciously"[78]—to "gloss *over,*" as we still say today. Worst of all, glossing could be viewed as an act of almost inconceivable presumption. When Nicolas Manjacoria came upon a fellow-Cistercian writing sentences of commentary directly into an early manuscript of the Bible, he was horrified.[79] Yet the scribe was only doing literally what every medieval *glossator,* including Nicolas himself, claimed the right to do: "fill in the blanks" of Scripture with material of his own.

Now all these charges against biblical commentary—unwarranted doubling, misrepresentation, and presumptuousness—were also the standard medieval charges against *acting*.[80] And the defensive note that creeps into accounts given by medieval *glossators* of their practice:

> Let no one take scandal if I say something other, or otherwise, than he finds in his glosses. . . . Let it not surprise him that something has escaped the Fathers. . . . Do not ask whether what I say is new, but whether it is true.[81]

also reaches us in the writings of medieval apologists for theater:

> It is indeed a devout task to recall to the memory of Christians the wonderful gifts of God through teaching, reading aloud, and also through painting; who, then, . . . could deny it to be a work of great value to refresh these things through . . . live representation?[82]

It may be objected that to have shown a connection between medieval acting and glossing is not quite to have linked medieval acting and *reading*. Not all reading glosses (i.e., expands, interprets, connects); one can also just read what is there. And in the quotation that ends the previous paragraph it is straightforward reading aloud to others of what is there which is linked with acting ("live representation"). Now the prime medieval exemplar of straightforward reading aloud to others of what is there is the lector, that minor liturgical official charged with delivering each day's mass-readings, or *lectiones*. But, as I pointed out in chapter 1, the lector is himself a type, and possibly even a historical precursor, of the medieval actor. The faithful rendering aloud of the lector, the "reading in" of the *glossator,* the specious representation of the *glozer*—all these medieval conceptions of what a reader might be are also possible medieval conceptions of what an *actor* might be. So much is clear from our Chester and Coventry actor figures, the Accusers, who are at once purveyors of destructive fictions (insofar as they "stage" an imaginary conflict between oral and written law) and fillers in of authentic meaning (insofar as they recognize the reference to themselves in Jesus' "open" writing). Greek and medieval thought placed very different valuations on the written word: How could a civilization that found its salvation in a book ever proceed to the extreme of a Platonic mistrust of reading? But no less in the Middle Ages than in ancient Greece are the fortunes of acting linked to those of reading—*implicit* in those of reading, so to speak.

Chekhov, *The Sea Gull*

Near the opening of act 4 of *The Sea Gull* there occurs the following exchange:

> ([PAULINE] *goes to the desk. Leaning on her elbows she gazes at the manuscript. A pause.) . . .*
>
> PAULINE: *(Gazing at the manuscript)* Nobody ever thought or dreamed that some day, Kostya, you'd turn out to be a real author. But now, thank God, the magazines send you money for your stories. *(Passing her hand over his hair)* And you've grown handsome . . . dear, good, Kostya, be kind to my little Masha.
>
> MASHA: *(Making the bed)* Let him alone, Mama.
>
> PAULINE: She's a sweet little thing. *(A pause)* A woman, Kostya, doesn't ask much . . . only kind looks. As I well know.
>
> (TREPLEFF *rises from the desk and without speaking goes out.)*
>
> MASHA: You shouldn't have bothered him.
>
> PAULINE: I feel sorry for you, Masha.
>
> MASHA: Why should you?
>
> PAULINE: My heart aches and aches for you. I see it all.
>
> MASHA: It's all foolishness! Hopeless love . . . that's only in novels.[83]

Chekhov abounds in episodes of, and references to, reading; *The Sea Gull* alone provides many examples. Nina is "always reading" Trigorin's stories (act 1, p. 17). Arkadina and Dorn read Maupassant to each other (act 2, p. 23). Trigorin enters reading a book (act 2, pp. 30–31), enjoys reading proofs (act 2, p. 34), hates reading bad reviews (act 2, p. 31). Nina gives Trigorin a medal engraved with a page and line reference to a passage in his own writings (act 2, p. 38); Trigorin reads the inscription (act 2, p. 39), then looks up the passage (act 2, p. 45). Trigorin brings Trepleff a magazine containing stories by each of them, though the uncut pages reveal he has only read his own (act 4, pp. 59–60). Trepleff rereads and revises his own work-in-progress (act 4, p. 63). And so on.

With such a wealth of reading scenes to choose from it may seem perverse to focus on a scene of apparent *non*reading: Pauline merely "gazes" at Trepleff's manuscript while speaking of something else. I am going to argue, however, that such gazing on a text while speaking of something else is an image of the particular kind of reading required of an actor working on a Chekhov script—is, in fact, Chekhov's character-istic image of acting as reading. How it becomes so will perhaps be clearer if, contrary to our usual practice, we begin not with the scene itself but, instead, with an overview of reading in Chekhov's four major plays.

Though the act of reading is everywhere present in Chekhov, it is everywhere problematic, its very pervasiveness the symptom of a perva-sive cultural problem.

Sometimes the problem is clearly with the texts themselves. Tre-pleff's symbolist play (*Sea Gull,* act 1) or Kulygin's "history of our high school covering fifty years, written by me" (*Three Sisters,* act 1, p. 155), are "unreadable" exercises in self-absorption which cannot speak to a reader. Often enough, though, the texts a Chekhovian character encoun-ters have plenty to say to him. In *The Three Sisters,* especially, some text or other is constantly giving the Prozoroff family the truth of their situation. The lines of Pushkin which Masha cannot get out of her head—"By the curved seashore a green oak, a golden chain upon that oak" (act 1, pp. 144, 161)—is an image of *happiness there for the taking.* The French minister's prison diary, which Vershinin cites as an illustra-tion that "happiness we have not . . . , we only long for it" (act 2, pp. 175–76), exposes the essential emptiness of the sisters' Moscow fantasy. Even the bit of newspaper filler read out by Tchebutykin—"Balzac was married in Berdichev" (act 2, p. 173)—contains a valuable perspective. If a great writer like Balzac could find happiness in a backwater like Berdichev, how much the more should *you, here . . . ?*[84]

In all these instances—Pushkin, the minister's diary, the newspa-per—the text itself is profitable; it is the reader who fails to profit. This suggests that the problem lies not in texts but, rather, in the transaction readers have, or fail to have, with them. "I read a great deal," says Vershinin, "but don't know how to choose books, and read, perhaps, not at all what I should" (act 2, p. 172). In particular, Chekhovian characters seem to have difficulty establishing a relation between *reading* and *subsequent action.* Either the character is unable to take any action at all in response to the text he reads:

> LOPAHIN: *(turning the pages of a book)* Here I was reading a book and didn't get a thing out of it. Reading and went to sleep.
> (*Cherry Orchard,* act 1, p. 228)

Or else the character is unable to take the particular action the text prescribes:

ELENA: It is only in sociological novels they teach and cure sick peasants, and how can I suddenly for no reason go to curing and teaching them?

(Uncle Vanya, act 3, p. 105)

(Compare, in our scene, Masha's "Hopeless love . . . that's only in novels.") Or else the character reads and takes action, but some action wholly unrelated to what he reads:

(Enter MARIA VASILIEVNA *with a book; she sits down and reads; she is served tea and drinks it without looking up.) (Uncle Vanya,* act 1, p. 79)

Particularly frequent in Chekhov are moments when, as in our *Sea Gull* excerpt, the reader looks at a text and brings forth *something else.* Like the student in Kulygin's anecdote who misreads his teacher's marginal comment "Nonsense!" as "consensus" *(Three Sisters,* act 4, p. 207), Chekhovian readers are forever coming out with something other than the words on the page before them. Masha Prozoroff peers into a book—and whistles *(Three Sisters,* act 1, p. 140). Tchebutykin takes a newspaper out of his pocket—and begins to sing *(Three Sisters,* act 4, p. 222). Dorn leafs through a magazine—and announces Trepleff's suicide *(Sea Gull,* act 4, pp. 169–70). Conversely, Chekhov's characters are forever coming out with texts from which, at the moment, they do not read: for example, Kulygin's classical catchphrases, Masha's "chain on the oak" refrain, and the lines from Trigorin and Turgenev which keep flashing across Nina's mind in the midst of her final conversation with Trepleff *(Sea Gull,* act 4, pp. 65–68). The one thing that does not often happen in a Chekhov reading scene is the one thing that we are accustomed to think happens as a matter of course between an actor and a script, namely, that a reader reads of an action and performs it. "I read all kinds of remarkable books," broods Epihodoff in *The Cherry Orchard,* "but the trouble is I cannot discover my own inclinations, whether to live or to shoot myself" (act 2, p. 250). There speaks the true voice, and true dilemma, of Chekhovian reading.

Undoubtedly, such a breakdown in the reading process is an image and symptom of a larger cultural situation: a historical moment when books are no longer regarded as capable of telling people what to do now, how to act. This unfeasibility of reading "at present" is thematized in Chekhov as a banishment of authentic reading from the present of the play's action. True reading belongs to the *past:*

> TCHEBUTYKIN: Since I left the University, I haven't lifted a finger, I've not read a single book even, but just read the newspapers. . . . *(taking another newspaper out of his pocket).*
> *(Three Sisters,* act 1, p. 144)

or to the *future:*

> ANYA: We'll read in the autumn evenings, read lots of books, and a new, wonderful world will open up before us—*(daydreaming).*
> *(Cherry Orchard,* act 4, p. 289)

Even when reading takes place onstage now it tends to look ahead or back from the present moment. Uncle Vanya's mother, who "with one eye . . . looks into the grave and with the other . . . rummages through her learned books for the dawn of a new life" (act 1, p. 77), reads of a future she will never see. Andrei Prozoroff, thumbing through his old university lectures (*Three Sisters,* act 2, p. 165), reads of a past he will never see again.

But if such a crisis in reading implies a general cultural dilemma, it also has—as our Greek and medieval examples have shown us an era's view of reading tends to have—implications for acting. Or rather: In Chekhov's depictions of reading we see what acting must *become* in a cultural situation where texts can no longer be trusted to tell readers what scripts have always told actors, namely, what to do next.

That such a crisis in reading as Chekhov represents might have consequences for the actor-reader is not a mere matter of speculation. Two of the principal characters in *The Sea Gull,* Arkadina and Nina, *are* actors, and both are represented as having difficulty establishing a link between the reading they do and the actions they perform. With Arkadina this takes the form of outright denial that she so much as works from the "script" upon which her actions are plainly based. Near the beginning of act 2 she reads aloud and comments disapprovingly on a passage from Maupassant:

> ARKADINA: "And so when a woman has picked out the author she wants to entrap, she besieges him with compliments, amenities and

favors." Well, among the French that may be, but certainly here
with us there's nothing of the kind, we've no set program.

(act 2, p. 23)

Yet in act 3, faced with the prospect of Trigorin's desertion, she avails
herself of this very "set program":

> ARKADINA: Oh, it's impossible to read you without rapture! Do
> you think this is only incense? I'm flattering you? Come, look me
> in the eyes. . . . Do I look like a liar? There you see, only I can
> appreciate you; only I can tell you the truth, my lovely dar-
> ling . . . You are coming? Yes? You won't leave me?
> TRIGORIN: I have no will of my own. . . . I've never had a will of
> my own. Flabby, weak, always submitting! Is it possible that might
> please women? Take me, carry me away, only never let me be one
> step away from you.
> ARKADINA: *(to herself)* Now he's mine.

(act 3, p. 47)

Her final aside indicates that Arkadina is perfectly conscious of pursuing
the Maupassant scenario. How, then, are we to understand her earlier
disavowal of Maupassant? Arkadina claims to relish the reading aspect
of the actor's work:

> It's good to be here with you, my friends, delightful listening to
> you, but . . . sitting in my hotel room, all by myself, studying my
> part . . . how much better! (act 2, p. 26)

Yet her refusal to acknowledge the hidden "scenario" behind her "performance" with Trigorin amounts to a dismissal of the ties between
acting and reading. Her position seems to be: "Yes, I have read the text
and, yes, I now take the very action prescribed by the text. But, for all
that, I deny that I enact the text." Arkadina, in other words, installs at
the heart of *acting* that very discontinuity between reading and subsequent action which is, we have seen, the essential dilemma of
Chekhovian *reading*.

Nina's difficulties as an actor-reader at first appear quite different.
Far from seeking, like Arkadina, to deny all dependency on scripts, she
is openly trying to enact two scripts at once. On the one hand, she has

been appearing in Trigorin's drama of the abandoned girl/gull literally from the moment of its conception:

> NINA: I'm a sea gull. No, that's not it. Do you remember, you shot a sea gull? *A man comes by chance, sees it, and out of nothing else to do, destroys it.* That's not it. . . .
>
> (act 4, p. 67, italics added)

(The italicized words are those in which Trigorin first presented to Nina the idea for his not yet written story [act 2, p. 36].) On the other hand, she has never quite relinquished her act 1 role as Trepleff's symbolist earth spirit; its opening words—"Vainly now the pallid moon doth light her lamp. In the meadows the cranes wake and cry no longer" (act 1, p. 13; and, again, act 4, p. 68)—are the last words we hear Nina speak.

The situation of performing two scripts at once is already a perplexed image of the relation between acting and reading. But there is the further suggestion that, for Nina, authenticity as an actor will ultimately consist in following *neither* script, in *turning* from scripts. Her impulse to fall in with the Trigorin scenario ("I'm a sea gull") is followed by her denial: "No, that's not it. I'm an *actress*" (act 4, p. 67, italics added). And her impulse to reassume the earth spirit role in Trepleff's monodrama is followed by her departure for her next *acting* job. While Nina's decision to step free of the two male "playwrights" who between them would confine her forever to the roles of *victim* or *goddess* no doubt bodes well for her as a woman and an artist, the implications of such a move for the relation between reading and acting are not so hopeful. For, in each case, while acting *ensues* upon the impulse to follow a script, it ensues as a *cancellation* of that impulse. She will be an actress *rather than* play Trigorin's sea gull, go off to her next acting job *rather than* perform Trepleff's *Erdgeist*. To choose to act, it is implied, is to choose to have nothing further to do with the text one has been reading. As with Arkadina, the familiar Chekhovian disjunction between reading and subsequent action once again appears at the heart of, as the truth of, acting.

Unlike Arkadina and Nina, Pauline in our scene—to which, after this long detour, I now return—is not an actress. She is also, strictly speaking, not a reader: All she does is "gaze" at the text in her hand while speaking of other things. Nonetheless, I would argue that, in this apparent nonreading by an apparent nonactor, Chekhov images an acting-reading relation that gets beyond the disjunction between reading and

subsequent action so characteristic of both Chekhov's readers and his
actor-readers.

Not surprisingly, in view of all the difficulties associated with reading, *refusals to read* are quite common in *The Sea Gull*. Arkadina has not
read her son's play (act 1, p. 6), and, even after he becomes a published
author, she claims she cannot find time to read him (act 4, p. 62); Nina
declines Masha's request to read a selection from Trepleff's script (act 2,
p. 24); Trepleff asserts he has not read the works of Trigorin (act 1, p.
11), and Trigorin does not bother to read the writings of Trepleff (act 4,
p. 62). Is there any reason why Pauline's behavior with the manuscript
here should not be added to this list? On what conceivable view of
reading is gazing at a text in one's hand and speaking words other than
those it contains a possible image of reading, rather than the image of
reading *avoided,* reading *refused,* which it appears to be?

First of all, notice that the words Pauline speaks, while not those of
the Trepleff text she gazes at, are not unrelated to that text. In fact, they
reflect what she understands the significance of that text to be:

> PAULINE: *(gazing at the manuscript)* Nobody ever thought or
> dreamed that some day, Kostya, you'd turn out to be a real author.
> But now, thank God, the magazines send you money for your
> stories. . . . dear, good Kostya, be kind to my little Masha.
>
> (act 2, p. 52)

This we may paraphrase as follows: "As the latest production of a recognized author, this manuscript of yours will be treated far better than
your works used to be. In the neglect you formerly showed my daughter,
you were, I believe, 'passing on' society's neglect of you. Perhaps now
that the world is paying you more attention, you in turn will feel able
to pay more attention to her." In other words, what Pauline "reads" in
Trepleff's manuscript is a prospect of better treatment for her daughter.

Is this a "good" reading? Pauline doesn't even notice what the
manuscript says! Or, rather, "what it says" has been reduced to what the
fact of its existence "says" to her. When someone reads this way in real
life we are likely to dismiss his reading as "wholly subjective." But there
is one situation where the wholly subjective reading is the appropriate
one, and that situation is acting. Pauline is a type of the actor reading
with a stake—or, perhaps, of reading narrowed and intensified to the
finding of a stake.

Pauline, in other words, is reading for what Stanislavski was later to call the "subtext." And the mere gaze she bestows on Trepleff's manuscript is an image of the kind of attention which an actor reading for subtexts bestows on a text—attention within which the words become transparent (i.e., "disappear"), allowing the actor-reader to see through the verbal surface to "the inwardly felt expression of a human being in a part, which flows uninterruptedly beneath the words." Stanislavski's principle that "the words come from the author, the subtext from the actor," exactly describes the transaction between the "author"-character (Trepleff) and the "actor"-character (Pauline) in our scene.[85] But this amounts to saying that the Stanislavskian conception of acting as reading for subtext is already inscribed in this Chekhovian scene of reading as *its* image of reading per se. And, one must quickly add, the Chekhovian *mistrust* of acting as a reading for subtext is also already inscribed there.

This mistrust manifests itself in several ways—for one thing, in the fact that Pauline, unlike Nina and Arkadina, is *not an actor*. Conceivably, this could be taken as implying that acting has something to learn from the self-absorbed, self-seeking (but therefore, at least, *absorbed* and *seeking*) approach of the ordinary, nontheatrical "bad reader." But there is also the distinct suggestion that what she is doing *isn't acting*. A more important indication of Chekhov's mistrust of acting as subtextual reading is that Pauline never actually brings forth the text. According to Stanislavski, "It is the subtext that makes us say the words we do."[86] Pauline, however, does not get around to speaking the words on Trepleff's page. In this regard she is, as a reader, no great improvement on Masha Prozoroff gazing into a book and whistling or Tchebutykin unfolding his newspaper and bursting into song.

Now, as a critique of subtextual acting, this cannot be meant literally; even the most subtext-oriented actor does not omit to deliver his lines. Nevertheless, there is an emblematic truth here. Subtextual reading does, indeed, "make away with" the words of the script, not in the sense that they are henceforth no longer present but in the sense that they are henceforth present only as the crust or veil—the "outside"—of another, more authentic "inner" discourse. The subtext is a prime example of the Derridean *supplément*: a supposed "mere addition," which, in fact, supplants that which it claims to be only supplementing. In our scene this supplanting *in importance* of the text by the subtext becomes a *literal* supplanting of the former by the latter: Instead of delivering the text (i.e., reading Trepleff's manuscript) with the subtext somehow "behind" it, Pauline actually *delivers the subtext.*

It may seem outrageous to propose Chekhov as the source of the Stanislavskian concept of "subtext," even with the proviso that he is also a source of misgivings about it. Chekhov—who never wearied of complaining that Stanislavski's approaches distorted his work? Chekhov—who was forever telling the Moscow Art players, "you'll find it all in the text"?[87] And, yet, alongside this last dictum must be placed another very different pronouncement of Chekhov's on reading:

> When I write, I count upon my reader fully, assuming that he himself will add the subjective elements that are lacking in the telling.[88]

While Chekhov seems to be speaking primarily about readers of his fiction ("in the *telling*"), to wish for a reader who, like Pauline, will "add the subjective elements that are lacking" is to wish for the Stanislavski actor.[89] A search outside the text and inside the reader for emotional material that "makes [characters] say the words [they] do" was Chekhov's model of the reading process long before it was Stanislavski's theory of subtexts.[90]

But I want to go further and argue that the whole encounter of the Stanislavski actor with the Chekhov script is already inscribed in that script, that the actual trouble Stanislavski is known to have had as actor-reader of Chekhov's plays is anticipated in those plays' own images of troubled reading.

For all the affinity he professed to feel for them, Stanislavski did not find Chekhov's scripts easy to read. "I am used," he wrote the playwright, "to receiving rather confused impressions from the first reading of your plays." And, indeed, the first time through, *The Sea Gull* struck him as "monotonous" and insufficiently "scenic." "Are you sure," he asked Nemirovich-Danchenko, "it can be performed at all?"[91] This last comment reveals Stanislavski, as reader *of* Chekhov, grappling with what we have seen to be the characteristic dilemma of readers *in* Chekhov: inability to *imagine taking action* on the basis of what one has read. Moreover, the solution Stanislavski found to this dilemma is also anticipated in at least one moment of Chekhov's writing, namely, our scene. *Unable to read in and act from the text, one reads into the text something which, as already one's own, it is possible to act upon*—this sentence describes the Chekhovian reader, the Stanislavskian actor as forecast by Chekhov, and the figure of Pauline, in whom these meet.

In other words the "distortion" that Chekhov complained the Stanislavski actor inflicted upon his plays is nothing other than *reading itself,* as Chekhov's own plays present reading. Chekhov's misgivings about Stanislavski's techniques merely repeat the misgivings about reading which the plays themselves dramatize. Or alternately: Stanislavski's work methods merely enact the problematic view of reading already present in Chekhov's texts. Ironically, Stanislavski's actors heeded all too well Chekhov's injunction to "find it all in the text." For what they found in Chekhov's text were images of how problematic an act "finding in a text" must be, on such a view of reading as Chekhov's.

In this chapter I have advanced the conjecture that any script's scenes of reading forecast what will be the eventual rehearsal experience of actors working on that script. In the present case we possess some information on the actual rehearsal experience of a particular group of actors who worked on the material in question, and the information confirms the conjecture. The treatment that Chekhov's scenes of reading predict for themselves at the hands of actors is the very treatment they received from the Moscow Art players. The Chekhovian scene of reading has seen the future—and it is Stanislavski.

Stanislavski, *An Actor Prepares* and the Performance Piece

In the course of his long "life in art" Stanislavski had only one go at playwriting,[92] and *An Actor Prepares,* obviously, is not it. What, then, warrants the inclusion in a chapter on scenes of reading from dramatic texts of the following excerpt from this well-known acting manual?

> "Maria, come up here to me. I am going to act with you."
>
> "You!" cried Maria, and she ran up onto the stage.
>
> Again she was placed in the arm-chair, in the middle of the stage, and again she began to wait nervously, to move consciously, to pull her skirts.
>
> The Director [Tortsov] stood near her, and seemed to be looking for something very carefully in his notebook.
>
> Meantime, gradually, Maria became more quiet, more concentrated, and finally was motionless, with her eyes fixed on him. She

was afraid she might disturb him, and she merely waited for further orders. Her pose was life-like, natural. She almost seemed to be beautiful. The stage brought out her good features. Some time passed in just that way. Then the curtain fell.

"How do you feel?" the Director asked, as they returned to their places in the auditorium.

"I? Why? Did we act?"

"Of course."

"Oh! But I thought. . . . I was just sitting and waiting until you found your place in the book, and would tell me what to do. Why, I didn't act anything."

"That was the best part of it," said he. "You sat and waited, and did not act anything."[93]

With every reading scene we have examined so far, we have found the actor's eventual experience of work on the script from which it comes preinscribed in the script itself, as a relation between the in-script reader and in-script text. While *An Actor Prepares* is not a script, it is a text meant to be, in some sense, "realized" by actors; it, too, "has a future" in the hands of actor-readers; and of it, too, we may ask whether that future is anticipated in such "scenes" of reading as it may contain.

In the case of our present "scene" I would argue that this is, indeed, the case. The sort of "script" which *An Actor Prepares* presents to actors for "realization" is represented within our excerpt by Tortsov's notebook. There is some empirical basis for saying this: We know that Stanislavski did, in fact, carry around with him, and presumably from time to time consulted, a packet of notes for his textbook-in-progress. My interpretation, however, rests on no such incidental detail but on the action of the "scene" itself. *An Actor Prepares* is an acting manual. Of a person seeking to function according to the principles of an acting manual one might say: "He is not doing anything other than enacting his reading of the text, yet there is no moment when he is enacting any particular moment of the text." *But this will also stand as a description of Tortsov's behavior in our scene.* Moreover, the careful search Tortsov makes through his notebook-"script"—a search that turns out to be, itself, acting—images the actor's experience of working from *An Actor Prepares*. "Did we act?" "Of course." To train as a Stanislavski actor is to search for authentic principles of acting, but, if authentically conducted, the search is itself already acting.

It is, thus, perfectly possible to analyze our *Actor Prepares* excerpt as yet one more instance of a reading scene that forecasts the actor-reader's experience of realizing such a text as itself. But if the hypothetical "rehearsal future" of Stanislavski trainees can, thus, be found inscribed in this scene from their training manual, another less hypothetical future scene of acting also seems preinscribed there. Where have we seen this demonstration of Tortsov's before—or, rather, *since?* It is tempting to reply: "Every weekend night in the East Village since the mid-1960s." A puzzled spectator is brought into the presence of an apparent nonevent, which, by the evidence of her own responses ("Maria became more quiet, more concentrated, and finally was motionless"), she comes to recognize as a theatrical event. Tortsov has staged for his student's benefit what has subsequently come to be known as a "performance piece."

By "performance piece" I do not refer solely or even primarily to works of so-called performance art (Chris Hardman, Laurie Anderson, Ping Chong, etc.). I employ the term in a somewhat extended sense to designate works in a tradition of theatrical experiment which begins with the "happenings" of the 1960s (though these were often little more than reenactments of earlier Dada and Futurist experiments), runs through the visually composed theater pieces of Richard Foreman, Robert Wilson, and the Mabou Mines in the 1970s, and continues on into the current rash of "postmodern" productions by such companies as the Wooster Group and such directors as Andrei Serban. This is, admittedly, a pretty broad range of work to bring under a single rubric. And if that rubric is taken, as it sometimes is, to distinguish a kind of theater which is not script-centered, then certain of my examples would have to be excluded: Richard Foreman's Rhoda pieces are *plays* by Richard Foreman; Andrei Serban's Chekhov productions are realizations of Chekhov's *texts.* For my purposes, however, the distinguishing mark of a performance piece is neither a particular stand on language nor a particular theatrical style but, rather, a preoccupation with enacting the process of enactment itself. The performance piece takes acting as its subject matter, *performs* acting—as does Tortsov in our passage. Moreover, it seeks to use the spectator's own responses to shock him into an expanded, yet simplified, view of what acting can be—as does Tortsov in our passage. In short, the performance piece is an "acting class"—like Tortsov's in our passage. As surely as Stanislavski himself is forecast by the Chekhovian scene of reading, the contemporary performance piece is foreshadowed in Tortsov's classroom.[94]

If performance pieces are demonstrations of the acting process, then the kind or mode of action which predominates in a given performance piece may be taken as that work's image of acting. For example: To act is to present an enigma ("happenings"). To act is to do what one might be doing anyway (minimalist-conceptual performance). To act is to contribute an element toward a visual composition (Foreman, Wilson). To act is to manipulate objects in space (Stuart Sherman).

Assuming that the sort of thing actors do in performance pieces tends to represent acting, it is suggestive that what they seem to be doing more and more of is reading. Onstage reading is a common event and key image in the work of Richard Foreman, Andrei Serban, Daryl Chin, the Talking Band, and, above all, the Wooster Group. Even a recent light-show of a piece by the nonverbal Belgian group Le Plan K prominently featured a transaction with an open "book," whose two halves were adjacent boxes of light. I will discuss some of this work in more detail presently. But I would like to begin my consideration of acting as reading in performance pieces with an example that reveals with special clarity the preinscription of this motif in our Stanislavski passage.[95]

In 1982 the French actor Gérard Guillaumat gave a one-man reading of Victor Hugo's story *L'Homme qui rit* at La Mama. I say "gave a reading," but he did not simply read the story to the audience; nor did he "act it out"; nor did he offer a half-acted, half-told "story theater" version of the tale. Guillaumat stood behind a broad table on which a huge book rested, and, as he read, he was constantly in motion with respect to the book. Some of this movement was functional: following out a line of print with a finger, turning a page. But the great majority of Guillaumat's moves were physicalizations of events *in the reading process*. He would, for example, physically sink in upon the book as he became "absorbed" in a passage; sweep along the page as he felt himself "swept along" by events; caress the volume in a moment of empathic closeness; make passes over the page in an attempt to "evoke" the "spirit" of the work, etc. His moves, in other words, were the "moves" of a reader. What he enacted was not the text but reading itself.

Guillaumat's project, I would argue, is already present in germ in our Stanislavski passage. For what Guillaumat taught his audience is what Tortsov eventually teaches Maria. "[He] seemed to be looking for something very carefully in his notebook." The reader's exploration of a text, physicalized, is already acting.

That performance pieces conceived decades after, and by theater artists wholly out of sympathy with, Stanislavski should nonetheless be found preinscribed in a book of his may seem unlikely. (Might one not sooner expect Stanislavski's writings to contain a glimmering of, say, Lee Strasberg?) And certainly there is little in Stanislavski's attitude toward the formalistic theater experiments of his own day to suggest that he would have been sympathetic to performance work. Yet, more than anyone else, it was Stanislavski who taught us to see the true object of interest in the theater as the acting process. And it is for this reason that I view him as the hidden precursor of a whole body of subsequent work, much of it overtly un-Stanislavskian, which turns theater into a performed demonstration of its own processes—into an "acting class."

But if performance pieces are acting classes, then the function of the text in a performance piece should be comparable to that of an acting manual in an acting class, namely, to serve as a scenario for performing demonstrations of the nature of acting. One could not in general liken the function of scripts to that of acting manuals; in fact, there is an obvious contrast. A script tells you *what* to say and do but does not (except for the occasional stage direction) tell you how. Whereas an acting manual *only* tells you how to perform actions and words that, it assumes, you will come upon in some text other than itself. A performance piece script is, in this regard, no different from any other: a series of *whats*. But since (at least in the examples we are considering) to act in a performance piece is to act the *how* of reading—to impersonate, in the manner of Gérard Guillaumat, a reader's "moves"—what the actor *seeks* from the performance piece script is closer to what he seeks in the acting manual, namely, some basis on which to physicalize his reading. To act in a performance piece is (often) to enact the how of reading. An acting manual, such as *An Actor Prepares,* tells you how to enact reading. Thus, not merely in its specific events but in its very character as an acting manual, our *Actor Prepares* excerpt images the role of the text in performance work.

In the confidence, then, that what we find depicted in the acting manual we are also going to find enacted in performance pieces, let us consider the implications of the radical identity between acting and reading which our *Actor Prepares* excerpt teaches us to see. Nor is *identity* too strong a word. If our earlier play passages provided examples of scenes of reading which could not but represent acting, Tortsov's classroom provides an example of reading that cannot help but have been acting all along. A reading process indistinguishable from the acting process, a reader whose presence is already that of the actor—all this certainly sounds like good news for a view of acting as reading. And yet, such a radical identification of reading with acting as is proposed by *An Actor Prepares* and much current performance work is not without its problems.

If there is one conclusion that could be drawn from every scene of reading we have examined thus far, it is that reading introduces its own uncertainties into acting. Be the text oracle book, author's manuscript, or writing in the dust, we know the text only in the actor's reading of it, and this opens acting to all the uncertainties that attend reading itself: questions concerning the reader's good faith or lack of it, his degree of skill at construal, his propensity to add, omit, or rearrange. Reading thus installs indeterminacy at the heart of acting. But when, as in Tortsov's demonstration and in those performance pieces descended from it, acting becomes "all reading" (i.e., is identified with the enactment of reading activity), the uncertainty spreads to acting itself. No more than in the case of the Oracle-Monger do we know if Tortsov "really" reads. Only now we also do not know if he really acts, either—and this as a direct *consequence* of not knowing if he really reads. Precisely because the two activities are felt to be equivalent, any uncertainty about whether reading is in progress must become uncertainty about whether acting itself is going on. Thus, far from resolving acting's problems with reading, a radical identification of the two activities only ensures that any problem about reading will now become a problem for acting as well.

Recent performance work contains many instances of reading thus "passing on" its problems to an acting conceived as identical with itself. In Richard Foreman's 1974 piece *Vertical Mobility (Sophia = Wisdom: Part 4)*,[96] for example, the difficulties of the central character, Sophia, with reading rapidly assume the proportions of a difficulty in performing any action at all. Immediately upon entering Sophia thrusts her head into a large open book resting on two wooden props and at once finds herself virtually immobilized, capable only of "awkward movements" (41), "with crew help" (40). "How do I get out of here," she wonders (40). From this unpromising start Sophia's difficulties with reading steadily mount. She "can't get [her] pages bright enough," "can't read" (43); another character interposes a (reading?) block between her eyes and the page (43). And the more "buried in reading matter" she finds herself (43), the more incapacitated she becomes, until at last, "immersed" in her book and unable to "remember what was in the picture or if the book had a relationship to it," she makes the ultimate withdrawal from action: She goes to bed (43). In the play's final image of actor-text relations Sophia *"sits with the book on the ground beside her,"* having "forgot what I wanted to do with this book" (46). Let reading once be set aside, and, given the closeness of the two activities in Foreman's piece, it is acting itself that will be forgotten.

No such outcome seems forecast in our *Actor Prepares* excerpt. Tortsov's careful search through his notebook is untroubled (save for the trouble of knowing whether it is acting or reading). But Tortsov is not the only "character" in the "scene." Like Foreman's Sophia, Stanislavski's Maria is also ultimately immobilized by her exposure to the identity between acting and reading:

> Meantime, gradually, Maria became more quiet, more concentrated, and finally was motionless, with her eyes fixed on him. She was afraid she might disturb him, and she merely waited for further orders.

We have thus far considered Maria only as the "audience" for Tortsov's "performance." But, of course, she is also an actor, or studying to become one, and her immobilization suggests that the acting-reading identity Tortsov demonstrates may be a source of difficulties as well as opportunities for the practitioner of this art. That the first effect of his demonstration is to empty acting of any distinct *presence* or distinct *present* ("Did we act? . . . But I thought. . . . I was just sitting and waiting until you found your place in the book") gives some hint of what those difficulties might be.

As a consequence of Tortsov's lesson, Maria is jarred into abandoning two assumptions to which she, like most people, has given unthinking assent:

1. *Either acting is going on (and reading is absent) or reading is going on (and acting is absent);* i.e., the *presence* of acting is not that of reading. But Tortsov's search through his notebook turns out to have been *itself* acting.

2. *First one reads and only then, on the basis of one's reading, acts;* i.e., the *present* of acting is not that of reading. But Tortsov's search through his notebook turns out to have been *already* acting.

Obviously, both these assumptions presuppose that it is possible to distinguish acting from reading in the first place. And, therefore, it should come as no surprise to find Tortsov's challenge to both assumptions reenacted in much of the recent performance work that, like Tortsov himself, sets out to demonstrate the fundamental identity of the two activities.

Maria's first assumption, that the presence of acting means the absence of reading, rests on the fact that, when an actor internalizes a text, he "makes it disappear"—and so makes himself disappear as a reader. But, if it is a reading scene in which our actor is appearing, his own disappearance as a reader is far less conclusive. For, as we have repeatedly seen, to act a reading scene is inevitably to re-present absent (i.e., former rehearsal) reading. The difference between the two performance piece examples we shall now consider and our earlier examples of reading scenes from dramatic texts is that the performance pieces bring out in the open, *take for their subject,* this uncertain status of reading as neither simply absent from nor simply present through acting.

My first example is from Andrei Serban's production of *The Three Sisters* at the American Repertory Theatre.[97] In the original script the play opens with a long speech delivered by Olga to Irina and to Masha, who is reading silently. Serban staged the moment with *all* the sisters reading silently, while a recorded voice delivered the speech over a loudspeaker. Clearly, in such a staging it is impossible to say whether reading is simply present in or simply absent from acting. It is present as an onstage activity (whose silence, however, amounts to a kind of absence) and absent as an offstage voice-over (whose audibility yet amounts to a kind of presence). In accordance with the identity that performance work posits between reading and acting, this puzzle about the presence/absence of reading in acting reveals itself to be a puzzle about the presence/absence of acting itself. Is the actress playing Olga here absent, a mere offstage voice (which, however, as voice, claims a certain presence), or is she present in the onstage act of silent reading (which, however, as silence, suffers from a certain absence)? Whether reading is present in or (as Stanislavski's Maria assumes) absent from acting is clearly undecidable when there is no basis for distinguishing the presence or absence of acting itself.

My second example is drawn from the Wooster Group's *L.S.D.* (. . . *Just the High Points)* presented at the Performing Garage in New York in October 1984. *L.S.D.* is a prime example of a performance piece whose action is "all reading"—an "exploration of performance as acts of reading," in Elinor Fuchs's phrase. Fuchs describes how, in this production,

> the playing area has been drastically foreshortened to become the reading lectern itself, an elevated table fitted out with chairs and microphones. Correspondingly, the group's frontal, presentational style has crystallized into variations on reading, such as reading from books in the body of performance, rapid-fire recitation, and repetition from dictation.[98]

I want to focus on a single one of these "variations on reading."

Of the half-dozen or so actors who read passages from Kerouac, Burroughs, Timothy Leary, Alan Watts, etc., one, Michael Kirby, was present only via a large video monitor placed at the center of the stage-wide reading table. Throughout the piece a videotape of Kirby reading was kept running soundlessly. When it came Kirby's turn to read one of the onstage actors would announce, for example, "Michael Kirby will read Alan Watts"; the sound on the monitor would be turned up; and we would hear one taped among the several live readers.

Up to a point this device can be seen as dramatizing the fate that we have seen awaits all scenes of reading in performance: Here, too, the phantom presence of earlier, absent reading haunted the stage. Only here, in contrast with our earlier examples, there was no present act of "live" reading for the phantom to haunt. To be present as an image of absent reading was the only kind of presence this absent actor could attain.

There were, of course, other actors physically present the while. But, strangely, their literal, physical presence did not seem to confer any special solidity on them; if anything, the absent, merely represented Kirby seemed more insistently present than his flesh-and-blood colleagues. Certainly, his reading commanded a degree of attention beyond that accorded to the other actors. This may have been merely because his taped voice was harder to hear. Norman Frisch, the Wooster Group dramaturg, declared, however, that the whole production had "stabilized around the videotape of Michael," i.e., around the presence of an absent reader, and there were some misgivings that when Kirby started playing his role live again (as he was shortly expected to do) this might throw everything off.[99] It was as if the very transformation of Kirby's

performance from event to image—its literal absence—had given it a
degree of abiding presence beyond that of the merely contingent (and,
in fact, nightly changing) reading activity of the onstage cast members.
The very least one could say is that Kirby and his colleagues, the absent
and present readers, had established equal claims to represent the presence of acting. Once again, as in Serban's *Three Sisters,* the performance
piece identification of acting and reading—more radical in *L.S.D.* than
in any other work I know—removes the very basis on which Maria's
presence-of-acting/absence-of-reading distinction rests. The *L.S.D.*
stage is such that to be *present* there means to be *reading* there, whether
the reading—and the presence—be bodily or represented.

The second assumption of Maria's which Tortsov shatters—that
one *first* reads and *only then,* on the basis of that reading, acts—is also
repeatedly called into question in performance work. A one-way reading
→ enactment trajectory seems inevitable so long as acting means acting
the *content* of what one reads: Clearly, then, one must first have read it.
But if, as is assumed by Tortsov and by much subsequent experimental
work, acting means enacting the moves, the process, the activity of
reading, it may no longer be possible to set acting and reading in a
sequential relation, never mind specifying a "usual" sequence. While it
is certainly not unheard of for actors in performance pieces to be shown
moving from text to action in the customary way, performance work
also explores a whole repertoire of alternative connections between reading and action. In *L.S.D.,* for example, the actors sometimes held up
their books as they read, sometimes held up their books *after* they read,
sometimes held up their books and *didn't* read, etc. I am going to consider three alternative ways of "positioning," or "scheduling," reading
in relation to acting, each exemplified in a different recent performance
piece but all preinscribed in Tortsov's notebook.

1. *Acting precedes reading.* In November 1984 at La Mama the Talking Band presented a program of single-actor pieces called *Holding Pat-
terns.* In the last of these, *Home Remedies,* performed by Tina Shepard,
a woman was shown moving her "things" into a new space. The things
in question were mostly books, and, time and again in the course of
rearranging these, Shepard would pause, open a volume at random—a
cookbook, a Gothic romance, a Bible—and read aloud from it. And each
time her onstage activity—her "moving"—would come to a halt while
she became, depending on the nature of the text, intellectually absorbed,
sexually aroused, etc. Clearly, here the actor's reading did not, in the

usual manner of actors with scripts, lead to action but, rather, led *away* from action, provided a *refuge* from action.

Increasingly frustrated by her own immobilization—a major theme of the piece, quite apart from its expression in reading—the woman at last cried out: "What'll I do? What'll I do?" And suddenly a gleam came into her eyes: *She'd heard those words before somewhere!* Tearing across the stage to one of the not yet unpacked piles of books, she plucked forth *Waiting for Godot,* opened it to the exchange on page 54 which begins with those words,[100] and *began to read.* The performer thus discovered in a *reversal* of the usual reading-into-acting trajectory a manner of utilizing the dramatic text which made sense for her. Rather than read, rise, and enact, she first acted (came out with words that gave authentic expression to a moment of feeling), next moved (tore across the stage), and *only then read* (from *Waiting for Godot*). For those inclined to doubt the preinscription of the performance piece in Stanislavski's writings, here is an instance where a particular moment from such a piece can actually be found preinscribed there. Early in the course of work with his class on *Othello* Stanislavski takes the words of Shakespeare's text away from his student actors, with the following result:

> At first you chose, as you would in real life, the words that came to your mind and tongue. . . . Only after this preparation did we return to you the printed text of the play. . . . You grabbed [Shakespeare's words] hungrily because the author's text expressed a thought or carried out a piece of action better than your own.[101]

This eager re(?)-discovery of the playwright's words as expressing before(?)/after(?) the fact one's own thoughts better than one could do oneself is exactly Tina Shepard's experience of finding in the script of *Waiting for Godot* her own truest utterance. In neither case does the script provide the actor with the content of, or even the impetus to, action, but, rather, confers on it a retroactive validation: Surely, this must be among the authentic actions one can take, since it occurs in an authentic dramatic text.

2. *Acting alternates with reading.* The New York playwright and director Daryl Chin is no stranger to self-referential depictions of the identity between acting and reading: He is said once to have presented a piece whose script consisted entirely of reviews of his own earlier work. *The Surface Equilibrium Which Cannot be Achieved without Destruction*

(1982), written by Chin and directed jointly by him and Larry Qualls, consisted of two wholly different types of scenes in alternation with one another. In the first type three friends, a woman and two men, sat around a living room set discussing friendship, work, love. But every now and then the three actors would suddenly abandon their naturalistic set and premise, troop over to lecterns placed in a row way off to one side of the playing area, and there read out long passages of discursive writing on philosophy, politics, and art. Then, just as suddenly, the actors would leave off reading, stroll back over to the living room set, and resume their naturalistic conversation.

While they were reading out the critical prose the performers did not seem to be acting. On the other hand, the hyperrealistic chat scenes had an improvised feel to them, as if they had never been read. The *alternation* of the two kinds of scenes thus seemed to imply that theater must veer back and forth between reading that can only issue in discourse and acting that must seem never to have read. Yet, after all, this *reading that would never be acting* and this *acting that appeared never to have read* were both the product of actors reading Daryl Chin's text in rehearsal.[102] Perhaps it was for this reason that, as the play wore on, the alternation of performance modes came to seem far more a strategy for *putting some distance between* a reading and an acting process felt (feared?) to be indistinguishable than the representation of reading's stubborn distinctness from acting which it had at first appeared. By any conventional standard Chin's play "fell apart" into "two halves," but such a split here seemed less the result of poor craftsmanship than of wishful thinking, as if merely by *initiating an oscillatory motion* one might create a situation in which there were distinct "acting" and "reading" alternatives to oscillate between.

3. *An acting-reading relation exists but cannot be specified.* Here again one might cite *L.S.D.* with its text fragments chosen at random nightly by actors who then skipped around *within* each chosen text. I would prefer, however, to focus on an episode from Robert Wilson's *Einstein on the Beach* as revived in 1984 at the Brooklyn Academy of Music. In act 4, scene 1c ("Building"), an isolated reader stood down-left under a pin spot, jerking his head back and forth with incredible speed as he scanned an open book in his hand. Also downstage a broken line of figures—workers, apparently, each immobilized in a different unnatural posture—spread out across the stage away from the reader. On a scrim behind the workers and the reader was projected an immense ware-

house-fortress of a building, in the single upper window of which stood a woman, signing rapidly. Her quick, nervous hand movements seemed to echo the jerking head movement of the reader below. After a time the workers exited; a while later the reader left off reading and followed them; a little after that the hand-signing woman in the upper window, who had been the first figure to appear onstage in the scene, also disappeared.

This sequence of actions seems to me simultaneously to insist on and to refuse to disclose the basis for a connection between acting and reading. The frenetic reader bore no specifiable relation to the other actors onstage with him (the workers), among whom he nevertheless took his stand. Only the reader himself was "moved" to action by his reading and, in the usual manner of performance pieces, was moved only to the action of reading. The others scarcely moved a muscle, and, when they did, it was only to exit, leaving the reader behind. Reading, the implication was, at first outruns and at last outstays acting.

On the other hand, the figure in the window, with her actorlike hand gestures, *did* seem to bear some relation to the down-left reader. As the only rapid movements (and at times the *only* movements) onstage, the hand motions of the one and the head-and-eye motions of the other leapt into alignment with each other. But what, exactly, was the basis of the alignment? There was no direct contact between the window signer and the onstage reader; spatially, they were on different levels and at an immense distance from one another. Nor was there any hint of a causal link between the acting/signing of the one and the reading of the other. The signer was at her window before the reader arrived and was still there gesturing (acting?) after the reader had departed. Acting, the implication was, at first outruns and at last outstays reading. The spectator was left contemplating an image of acting and reading linked by ties they will never discover across a gap they can never bridge.

We may seem to have come a long way since Aristophanes, and so we have—but not along a road that leads from straightforwardness to complexity. Tortsov's notebook and Peisthetaerus's oracle book—both texts that may or may not warrant the moves of a reader whose struggle with this uncertainty is already acting—are equivalent images of the script, are, so to speak, the "same book." The movement from Old Comedy to Next Wave[103] is an evolution not from untroubled to troubled reading but, rather, from troubled reading as an overtone of the fictional situation to troubled reading as itself the dramatic event. It is not that, with performance work, the relation between acting and reading has suddenly become problematic; it is that, suddenly, the problem has become the show.

Chapter 6

The Audience as Read To

It will now be necessary to introduce two new elements into the discussion, or, rather, to take cognizance of two elements that have been present from the start. So far in this book, whether my subject has been the acting process itself (chaps. 1–4) or depictions of that process in dramatic texts (chap. 5), I have treated the actor-script transaction as wholly a matter between actors and their scripts. And yet, of course, the text an actor reads comes to the actor from an author and goes forth from the actor to an audience. The source and destination of the reading actors do must have some place in a theory of acting as reading. In this and the following chapter I will show what role is implied for the *audience* and for the *author* by the model of acting as reading presented in chapters 1 through 5.

Clearly, to extend the model in this way will entail asking: "What is the relation of an audience to acting conceived as reading?" (the subject of the present chapter) and "What is the relation of the author to acting so conceived?" (the subject of the following one). But there is the further question of the relation in which the two new elements, the author and the audience, stand to one another in an acting-as-reading model, which is to say: with an actor-reader standing between *them*. And here I must acknowledge a hidden agenda. It is this last question—the issue of author-audience relations in the theater—that I shall all the while be exploring, even as I address myself to its two "halves": the actor-audience and the author-actor transactions. Why not address author-audience relations directly? My reasons for this two-phase approach to the problem of what one might call (*pace* Eric Bentley) *the playwright as writer* will, I trust, emerge from the discussion itself, but this much in advance:

To think of the playwright as an *author* seeking *readers* is possibly not the best and certainly not the only way to think of him. One may, for example, believe like Artaud that the business of a dramatic author is not so much to produce words as "to handle the scenic material directly."[1] But even where the playwright's function clearly *includes* supplying texts, it is not necessarily *conceived* as the supplying of a text. The Greeks, for example, did not describe what a playwright does as "write" plays; in their view, he "created" or "produced" or "taught" or "directed" them.[2] "With and through words" the playwright necessarily works, yet, for all that, playwriting is perhaps less a kind of writing than "an art of composing in the medium of the actor—of composing in action," to quote Michael Goldman's suggestive and exhilarating formulation.[3]

One difficulty in particular seems to attend a view of playwriting as an author-reader transaction: Between *this* author and *these* readers there is always interposed a "third," the actor-reader, whom it would be perverse to characterize as an "obstacle" to author-reader relations, but who, since he is already a reader himself, is no simple "channel" to readers, either. And even to the extent that actors *can* be viewed as "intermediaries" of some sort, writers of essays, novels, and poems are not read in the reading of intermediaries. How, then, assimilate the playwright-audience transaction to any general model of writer-reader relations?

But, I shall argue, it is precisely on this point that seems to *differentiate* it from the general case that the playwright-public transaction *models* the general case. To be read in the interposed reading of others is the destiny of *all* writing, and it is this state of affairs that theater, with its bevy of actual interposed "other readers" (i.e., the cast), acts out.

Here, then, is the explanation of why one cannot simply approach the playwright-public relation as a binary transaction between playwright and public. It is not just that the actor stands always between; his *standing* always between is, itself, the key to the relation. In fact, the audience-playwright transaction can only *occur* as a transaction between the audience and the actor, on the one hand, and the actor and the playwright, on the other. If I now proceed to discuss the playwright-public transaction in this divided way—actor-audience relations in the remainder of the present chapter, actor-playwright relations in the following one—this reflects not so much a decision to handle the topic in a certain way as a recognition of the structure of the topic itself.

"And then, I suppose, the audience reads the performance?"—so asked a friend to whom I was describing this book at an early stage. Many suppose so. In fact, under the influence of semiotics, "reading" has become a pervasive figure for the theater audience's experience of theater. Stage action, we are told, not only displays "textuality" but is itself a "text,"[4] a "performance text,"[5] written in "scenic writing";[6] and, as such, is available for "performance reading" by the "spectator/reader," who seeks not only to "read the performance"[7] as a whole but also to "'read' bits of . . . action or mime,"[8] read gestures—in a word, to *read acting,* on the assumption that "the body [of the actor] can be read like a text."[9]

Despite its up-to-date ring and its popularity with contemporary critics, "reading" is in fact one of the oldest tropes for theatergoing, the product not of our own obsession with textuality but, rather, of the one era that might give ours some competition for the title of "most text-obsessed," namely, the Middle Ages. Long before the Federal Theatre described its productions as "living newspapers" (thus implying that they were to be read), long before Coleridge declared that "to see Kean was to read Shakespeare by flashes of lightning" (thus implying that to see more commonplace acting was to read by some less spectacular light source),[10] the author of the late medieval *Treatise of Miracles* had characterized dramatic performances as "quick [i.e., living] books," in which even the illiterate might "read the will of God."[11] The very word for the mobile stage on which the individual segments of a medieval mystery cycle were performed, *pagina,* can mean either "pageant" or "page of a book."[12]

More impressive than the mere antiquity of the theatergoing-as-reading metaphor, however, is its employment by some of theater's most distinguished practitioners. In a formulation that directly alludes to the medieval view Strindberg characterized theater as "a *Biblia Pauperum,* a Bible in pictures for those who cannot read what is written or printed."[13] It is perhaps not so surprising that Brecht, with his aesthetic of audience detachment, should urge on the spectator "an attitude corresponding roughly to the reader's method of thumbing through a book and checking back."[14] But one is startled to come upon the same imagery in Stanislavski:

> Difficult as it may be to have to deal with a badly printed book or poor handwriting, you still can reach, if you try hard enough, some

understanding of the thought behind the words. The printed or written matter lies before you; you can take the time to go over it again and again and unriddle the incomprehensible.

But what recourse have you in the theatre when the actors pronounce the text in a fashion comparable to your badly printed book, when they drop out whole letters, words, phrases which are of cardinal importance to the basic structure of the play?[15]

For the watching of a sloppy performance to resemble *obstructed* reading the watching of performances must resemble reading in the first place. Still less could one have anticipated the appeal of reading imagery to opponents of a text-centered theater. Yet the (scenic) "poetry *of* the theatre" with which Cocteau proposed to replace a (merely verbal) "poetry *in* the theatre" is, no less than what it replaces, "poetry," i.e., a "text" to be, in some sense, "read."[16] And the same could be said of those "living, moving hieroglyphs" that Artaud (who has always seemed to me to owe more to Cocteau than to Bali on this point) saw costumed actors as constituting.[17] Hieroglyphs, too, are writing, require reading. It is difficult not to see in these conceptions of Artaud and Cocteau a return of the repressed *literariness* so characteristic of French theater. Instead of a text that is the be-all and end-all of the production, we now get productions that—as (living) "hieroglyph" or (scenic) "poetry"—are "all text." The "codes" in which the "scenic writing" is written may have changed; the audience, however, goes right on reading in the "quick book."

One would not want to be in a hurry to jettison an imagery so ancient and so impressively endorsed. And, indeed, there is really no reason to jettison it. So long as *reading* is understood to be what in all the examples I have cited it so clearly is, a trope for "construal" or "interpretation," it can do no harm to speak of reading performances. We are assured that we can "read" photographs, drawings, films—even cities:[18] Why not theater?

Nevertheless, simply to pronounce theatergoing "reading" in some extended sense can in itself scarcely constitute the link we seek to establish between a model of acting as reading and the experience of the theater audience. For, though my own use of *reading,* like everyone else's, has, from time to time, slid toward the figurative,[19] it is nevertheless the *actual* process of reading a *literal* text which I have throughout been concerned to connect with acting. And if one attempts to see a spectator's experience of theater as, *literally,* a reading process, one immediately runs into difficulties—as those semiotically oriented critics who have made the attempt are the first to admit. Thus, one of them confesses that, while the words, gestures, colors, and spaces of the performance may function as signs, there is no such thing as a "specifically theatrical sign."[20] Another concedes that there are no "discrete units" of meaning (comparable to the morphemes, sentences, etc., of verbal language) into which a "performance text" can be broken down.[21] A third acknowledges that, while some productions may be scanned sequentially like a text, most neither enforce nor even imply any particular "reading pattern."[22] No signs, no syntax, no reading pattern—the sum of these concessions cedes away reading.

Many contemporary productions include stretches of actual, printed text for the audience to read, most often in the form of a placard or projection. Brecht ran up advance summaries of the coming scene "[so] that the right thing may be expected."[23] Richard Foreman, in his early productions, projected texts of interpretive comment and authorial guidance (e.g., "NOW WATCH. WATCH. IT'S BEING SAID").[24] In the Mabou Mines's *Wrong Guys* the manuscript of a crime story which an author sat typing onstage was simultaneously unfurled, letter by letter, on a screen overhead.[25] Or fragments of text may be worked into the stage setting. In Meyerhold's production of *The Magnanimous Cuckold* the consonants of the playwright's name (Crommelynck) were inscribed on a turning mill wheel.[26] A recent New York production of Sternheim's 1911 comedy *The Underpants* used the blown-up front page of a 1911 Berlin newspaper as a floor cloth.[27] In Stuart Sherman's performance piece *Chekhov* the "cherry orchard" was represented by a row of paper tree-shapes cut out of enlarged pages from Chekhov scripts.[28] Now, if theatergoing were in fact reading, or even all that much *like* reading, the moments when a spectator reads such actual onstage texts should feel continuous with the experiences of theatergoing within which they occur. But this is not the case. Reading Brecht's scene titles or Sherman's text snippets, one is immediately aware of shifting into a cognitive mode distinct from that of the moment previous; one feels, so to speak, "on holiday" from a specifically theatrical attentiveness.[29]

Why this should be so is suggested by Bert States:

In reading, the eye is an anesthetized organ, little more than a window to the waiting consciousness on which a world of signification

imprints itself with only the barest trace of the signifiers that carry
it. In the theater, however, the eye awakens and confiscates the
image.[30]

The force of this distinction can be clearly felt on those occasions when
a performance "text" suddenly assumes for a moment the dimensions
of an actual text. In canto 18 of Dante's *Paradiso* a host of radiant spirits
in the sixth heaven suddenly float up into the air "and as birds, risen from
the shore . . . make of themselves now a round flock, now some other
shape, so . . . [these] holy creatures . . . made of themselves now *D,* now
I, now *L.*"[31] They are, it turns out, spelling *"diligite iustitiam"* ("love
justice") against the sky. We have all witnessed a humbler version of this
trick between the halves of a football game when, after much marching,
running, crisscrossing, etc., the members of the marching band suddenly
form themselves into the initials of their school: "USC" or "LSU" or
whatever. What happens at such a moment illustrates States's point.
Suddenly, the whole complex visual pattern of group movement ceases
to matter to the eye, which now, as the eye of a mere reader, contents
itself with extracting "the barest trace of the signifiers," i.e., with reading the monogram. If what we had been doing all along was reading the
band's performance as a text, surely its suddenly becoming an *actual* text
would not be felt as producing such a distinct change of perceptual
mode.

But, it may be argued, merely to show that an audience does not
read a performance in the semioticians' sense of "decoding"[32] or "deci-
phering"[33] its signs does not, for us, amount to showing that they do
not read the performance. The reading we have sought to link with
acting, while, of course, proceeding by semiotic channels, is a displaced
oral process of defense against/absorption of fantasy.[34] Could not theater
audiences be said to "read" performances in this, our primary, sense of
reading?

Certainly, there is no difficulty in showing that the actor-audience
transaction is, whether considered from the actor's point of view or the
audience's, a displaced oral one. In the actor's case the *craving* to be *seen*
by spectators is, as I noted earlier, evidence of an oral dependency displaced at once *outward* from self to others (*they* are hungry to see *me*) and
upward from mouth to eye (they are hungry to *see* me). Further, the
actor's relation to his audience displays the very oral structure that we
have seen characterizes actor-text and actor-actor relations. The actor's

orally passive impulse (to be "sustained" and "nourished" by the audience) and his orally active impulse (to resist being swallowed up by the "primal cavity," or "open mouth," of the audience) are "set equal" in his single act of performing before them. The resulting uncertainty as to who is feeding (on) whom dissolves the boundary between, and so becomes the basis for a boundariless relation between, the audience and himself.[35]

In the present chapter, however, it is less the experience of the actor than that of the audience which concerns us. And, clearly, the audience's experience of theater—whether by this we mean their experience of the performer, of the events performed, or of the performance situation itself—is of a displaced oral kind. The oral nature of the audience's transaction with the performer himself is implicit in what has just been said about the performer's transaction with them. Obviously, a situation in which it is not clear which of two parties "feeds" the other is oral on both sides. But the theatergoer's encounter with the events portrayed is no less an oral one. As much as the books people read, the scripts they see performed confront them with fantasy material toward which they must balance conflicting oral impulses. Whatever process of absorption of/defense against fantasy is triggered by events on the page will also be triggered by those same events in performance—and, indeed, by the event of performance itself. At theater, as in reading, we sit immobilized—itself an encouragement to fantasizing[36]—before a stage that, no less than the printed page (or movie screen or picture tube), constitutes a "dream screen," which, as the latest site of fantasy experiences neither clearly "in us" nor "out there," reinstates the original site of all such boundary-blurring oral encounters: the breast.[37]

No wonder, then, that Norman Holland finds Tyrone Guthrie's musings on the spectator's experience of theater couched in the same imagery he himself has employed for reading:

> How, in the theater, is the absorption of the audience induced? What takes an audience "out" of itself and "into" the fiction?[38]

The conclusion to be drawn from this, however—and, indeed, from *all* the theatergoing-orality links we have noted—is not that theatergoing equals reading but, rather, that theatergoing and reading share a common substratum. What Holland says of the literary work—that it "finds in us a matrix reaching back through many, many experiences of gratification in fantasy to our earliest experience of passive satisfac-

tion"—is true also of theater performances, not because we "read" theater performances but because reading and spectating both come down
to (or, rather, come up from) oral experience. "To look at is to eat,"[39]
not because looking (at theater or anything else) is reading but because
both are displacements upward of eating.

Thus, it would appear that neither a semiotic nor a psychoanalytic
perspective is especially conducive to a link between audience experience
and reading. Semiotics sees the spectator as engaged in a process of
construal which is only figuratively reading. Psychoanalysis views him
as caught up in a displaced oral dialectic which is also present in reading
but whose presence does not necessarily indicate that reading is in progress, only that orality has been displaced. All this does not seem to bode
very well for opening out the acting as reading model to include the
audience. But, then, all this overlooks the rather obvious fact that, in any
actor-spectator transaction, a *literal* act of reading is all the while going
on. Whether or not the audience is, in any extended sense, "reading" the
performance, the performers are, in a quite literal sense, reading to the
audience: *They read them the script.* Even on a purely semiotic view the
actor is no mere sign but also an *emitter* of signs—a "multi-channelled
transmitter-in-chief," as one semiotician inimitably puts it[40]—which
means, among other things, a reader to others (though, as we shall see,
to read to others is not *merely* to emit signs). Here, then, is the basis we
have sought for letting the audience in on acting as reading, in something
more than a figurative sense of "reading." Or, rather, here is the sense
in which they have been in on it from the first. "We pause here in our
reading of *Oedipus at Colonus*"—what production could *not* avail itself
of this formula by which Lee Breuer's *Gospel at Colonus* announced its
intermission?[41] *To act is to read to an audience; to be an audience is to be read
to by actors—to read in the reading of actors.*

This is not going to strike everyone as an uncontroversial proposition. Clearly, *some* acting is reading-to: a staged reading, a one-man or
one-woman show based on a writer's texts, etc. But I pointed out in
chapter 1 that such reading performances are far from the special cases
they seem, that the apparently self-evident distinction between "reading
from a text *to* an audience" and "giving a performance *of* a text *for* an
audience"[42] begins to dissolve when one reflects that the "off-book"
performance, too, is a performance of (earlier, internalized) reading.

Granted that what actors in performance are doing is giving a reading, are they necessarily giving it *to the audience?* Are they not, rather, reading the script to each other? In a sense, of course, they are. But, as we saw in chapter 4, it is truer to speak of actors as reading *against* each other, that is, as asserting *through* reading the claim already implicit in the roles they assume that *none here truly reads but I.*

But, even assuming that it is to the audience, if anyone, that the performing actor reads, there is still the question of how adequate an account "reading to the audience" gives of his "multi-channelled" activity. Samuel Johnson's definition of performance as "a book recited with concomitants that increase or diminish its effects" was not necessarily acceptable even to his own contemporaries[43]—"people come to see characters acted, not read," observed the eighteenth-century theater critic Aaron Hill[44]—and its limitations have, if anything, only grown clearer with time. Actors don't *just* "recite," a script isn't *merely* a "book," the physical resources of theater aren't *only* "concomitants," etc. Clearly, a performance isn't just reading-to, any more than acting is just reading. But here as elsewhere my aim is to develop the implications of viewing acting as reading, not to argue that this is the only way of viewing it.

If acting isn't all reading aloud, it is equally clear that not all reading aloud is acting. This raises the possibility that some of what I shall say about the *actor's* reading aloud may also characterize other, or even all, reading aloud situations and so fail sufficiently to distinguish it from them. In fact, the possibility of common ground between actors and other kinds of readers aloud will prove extremely helpful when we come, in the next chapter, to consider the relation between actors and authors. But, even insofar as such an overlap creates difficulties, the sorts of difficulties it creates are scarcely unique to a view of acting as reading. If one treats acting as primarily a gestural art, one will inevitably say things about it that could equally well be said of mimes or dancers. If one treats acting in terms of ritual practice, one is going to wind up making assertions that also apply to shamans and priests.

Yet, even as one is thus conscientiously distinguishing acting as reading-to from reading-to as such, one cannot but be struck by how even *non*theatrical reading-to situations tend to assume the dimensions of an actor-audience encounter. Both our nontheatrical types of the actor are conspicuous readers aloud: Our literary prototype, Don Quixote, on many occasions reads to the illiterate Sancho;[45] and our historical prototype, the ecclesiastical lector, is specifically a reader *to* the congre-

gation. Even in the technical psychological literature such a link is acknowledged: An article on "Hearing Children Read" discusses classroom
reading in terms of a "performance" kept going by "cues."[46]

To some extent, of course, the resemblance is only a matter of
overlapping skills. The parent reading before a crib, no less than the
actor reading before a public, must impersonate characters, "do voices,"
etc. But the similarities go beyond externals. The *experience* as well as
the *activity* of the reader aloud often recalls acting. That strangely dou-
bled consciousness, for example, which Diderot held to be characteristic
of the actor ("he must have in himself an unmoved and disinterested
onlooker")[47] may also come to the fore in reading aloud:

> How does one continue not only to think but apparently to lose
> oneself in thought while one is reading aloud, never missing a word
> and presumably maintaining some kind of expression? . . . Yet I can
> to a certain extent be aware of the double activity going on; catching
> the general message of the thought while I maintain the even flow
> of my lecture.[48]

Conversely, the breakdown of all barrier between self and role which
characterizes another kind of acting may equally well befall the reader
aloud. Consider the following account of a schoolboy who, reading
aloud the speech of a little girl disguised as a muskrat, misreads "I would
like to know just who you think there is" as "I would like to know *you*":

> His transformation of the story through the skipping of two words
> was an appropriate response to its essential content, which is loneliness
> and the wish of the little muskrat to form a much closer bond to her
> brother, to whom she is speaking. The boy makes this desire his
> own as he expresses his wish to form a closer tie to the person to
> whom he is speaking, i.e., reading the story. In doing so, he acts
> just like the muskrat whose feelings he is voicing as he reads the story.[49]

This total emotional identification on the part of the young reader with
the role he reads is strongly reminiscent of the method actor, who from
time to time has also been known to misread a word or two of what is,
after all, "his own" speech. How closely the psychology of reading aloud
can resemble that of acting is clear from some remarks of Kafka on the
pleasure he took in reading to his sisters:

> I am dominated by the passion to get so close to the good works I read that I merge with them . . . and therefore too, under the concealment my vanity affords me, I can share as creator in the effect which the work alone has exercised.[50]

In this "passion to merge" with texts to the point where one can feel oneself their cocreator we recognize the actor's impulse, discussed in chapter 4, to be the "source" of texts that are, in fact, the source of one's work. As was noted then, this is also a *writer's* impulse vis-à-vis his predecessors' works. And the penchant for "giving readings," which Kafka here displays, is more than a personal trait; *to give reading,* as we shall see in the next chapter, is the characteristic project of the writer as such.

Not only is the experience of the reader aloud likely to feel to him like acting; those to whom he reads may well find themselves responding in the manner of a theatrical audience. Like being at theater, being read to may seem to bring one (into) the presence of an event, as in Book 7 of *The Brothers Karamazov* where Alyosha, listening to Father Païssy read from the Gospels, suddenly feels himself to be present at the wedding at Cana:

> "But what's this, what's this? Why is the room growing wider? . . . Ah, yes . . . It's the marriage, the wedding . . . yes, of course. Here are the guests, here are the young couple sitting, and the merry crowd and . . . Where is the wise governor of the feast? But who is this? Who? Again the walls are receding. . . ."[51]

And, like the presence of the actor, the presence of the reader aloud may be experienced as that of a possessed, numinous "other," as in Sartre's autobiographical account of being read to by his mother:

> She bent forward, lowered her eyelids, fell asleep. From that statue-like face came a plaster voice. I was bewildered: who was telling what and to whom? My mother had gone off: not a smile, not a sign of complicity, I was in exile. And besides, I didn't recognize her speech. Where had she got that assurance?[52]

Admittedly, both these passages represent extreme cases: Young Sartre is in a state of magical innocence vis-à-vis reading, and Alyosha is in a state of near-exhaustion. But the theatrical dimension that the extreme cases make visible is present in more commonplace instances as well. Being read to is always, in some degree, an encounter with (to speak in the language of *The Theatrical Event*) an uncanny figure, possessed by and bringing us (into) the presence of a textual "other world."

But, beyond all such specific inducements to link acting and reading-to, one factor in particular encourages the attempt. The acting as reading process, which we now seek to extend to the audience, consists in the recovery by the actor of a "lost" physical dimension of reading. "How is the audience to be let in on this process?" thus amounts to asking "How shall an audience come to participate in this recovery?" And the answer is: *They come to participate in it by being read to.* That is: It is the psychological dynamics of the reader/read-to transaction which enable the actor-reader to "pass on" his recovery of reading's "lost" physical to those to whom he reads, i.e., his audience. Thus, if we wish to understand the share of the audience in the acting process, our first step must be to understand those dynamics.

In view of all the parallels we have observed between reading and eating it is not surprising that being read to, with its intake, outflow, and mouth involvement, should also display a connection with orality. Some such link has apparently long been felt, for in many different cultures the place where you go to be read to and the place where you go to eat turn out to be the same place: e.g., Roman banquets,[53] medieval monastic refectories, and contemporary coffeehouses. It seems to me no coincidence that the medieval refectories sometimes were, and the contemporary coffeehouses often are, also the site of *theater* performances.[54] The presentday American institution of "dinner theaters" and the immemorial Asian practice of bringing one's dinner to the theater both testify to a recognition that theater, as a place where some people read to others, is (Brecht's dislike of "culinary theatre" notwithstanding) a place of feeding and being fed. But let us leave aside a specific orality-theatergoing link for the moment and focus instead on the event of being read to itself.

That this event is a displaced oral one is acknowledged by Norman Holland when he includes being read to, along with silent reading, theatergoing, and dreaming, among those activities that have their origin in "the experience of passively being fed by a loving mother."[55] It is not, however, as Holland implies, a purely passive orality but, rather, the subsequent *conflict* between active and passive oral impulses which the experience of being read to revives.

For, in fact, this experience is a highly ambiguous one. On the one hand, the person being read to is wholly dependent on another, the reader, for his intake—an extremely passive position. On the other hand, the person being read to has this other, the reader, entirely at his disposal—an extremely active status, which the listener may assert directly by commands to "stop," "repeat," "omit," "resume," etc., but which is in any case inherent in his role in the transaction, even if he does no more than sit there and, by his silent attentiveness alone, *demand reading*.

To be read to is, thus, to have wholly at your disposal another on whom you wholly depend—precisely the ambiguous situation of the infant in its active-passive transaction with its mother. Conversely, to read *to* another is to be wholly at the disposal of one whose intake you wholly control. This sounds like being the "mother" in the transaction, and one way of describing the shift in the actor's status from rehearsal to performance is to say that he goes from the role of "infant" absorbing the text to that of "mother" nourishing the audience: from eater to feeder. By this I do *not* mean that he goes from a passive role to an active one. The infant's eating, as we have repeatedly seen, has its active side, and the mother's feeding of the infant, as we have just now seen, its passive side: that of being at another's disposal. In fact, one can speak of the actor "feeding" the audience he reads to only with two qualifications. First, although in a sense he now feeds others, the actor himself has not "left eating behind." In both his ongoing transaction with the text and his just now commencing transaction with the audience (whose approval he "craves," whose "devouring gaze" he fears, etc.) the actor continues to enact his own conflicting oral impulses. And, second, what the actor passes on to the audience he reads to is not so much "something to eat" as an opportunity to participate in his own recovery of the capacity for oral experience. In fact, these two qualifications are related. It is *because* he seeks to transmit his own capacity for oral experience to others that the actor must continue immersed in such experience himself.

Let us, however, return to the experience of the person or persons read to, the audience (not necessarily theatrical) for reading. After the first six months or so infants no longer submit to being "passively . . . fed"; they now actively feed as well. And it is in the behavior of the young child, still close to literal nursing but old enough to be read to, that the clash between the orally passive and orally active aspects of being read to can most easily be glimpsed. On the one hand, the child, unable to read himself, is wholly dependent on the reader for the "flow" of text. But, like the literal infant at the breast who bites, tears, spits back, etc., the read-to child struggles against this oral dependency by orally active attempts to assert control over the flow: "Read it again! Skip that part! More! Again!"

Another context in which the active-passive structure of being read to reveals itself is in reading classes, which generally proceed by the pupil reading aloud to a teacher who interrupts as necessary. Here the person read to, the teacher, is cast in an essentially passive role as mere recipient of the student reader's "flow." And yet, of course, to this flow the instructor opposes a steady stream of orally active countergambits: Teachers interrupt, correct, prompt, and, of course, "it is the teacher who opens and closes the encounter, who takes or allocates . . . the turns."[56]

Between adult readers and listeners, too, the clash of active and passive oral impulses sometimes comes out into the open. In *Crime and Punishment* Sonia reads to Raskolnikov, at his insistence, the New Testament account of the raising of Lazarus. The extreme oral aggressiveness with which he badgers her into reading to him ("'Read!' he cried irritably and insistently. . . . 'Read! I want you to,' he persisted")[57] only underscores his dependency on her act of reading; without her help he cannot so much as find the place of the passage he desires to hear (318–19). This pattern of aggressive-dependent behavior reveals its true character as displaced infant orality when, the reading completed, Raskolnikov informs Sonia that he has just broken with *his mother* and "I have only you now" (323).

Scenes of reading from plays also reflect the active-passive orality of being read to. Samuel Beckett's *Ohio Impromptu,* for example, specifically depicts the relationship of a Listener to a Reader—and depicts it as, precisely, an irresolvable tension between active and passive oral impulses. As he hears read aloud to him a story of lost love and deepening isolation which, it becomes increasingly clear, must be his own, the Listener repeatedly signals the Reader, by knocking on the table at which both sit, to go back, repeat, resume. It would be difficult to find a clearer image than this of how someone read to is at once *wholly dependent on reading* (the Reader seems the Listener's one contact with anything outside himself) and yet *has reading wholly at his disposal* (the Reader has not only been specially dispatched *to* the Listener but also, once arrived, has his whole reading activity regulated *by* the Listener: He stops/starts/repeats all at a rap of the Listener's hand).

I have shown that, in acting, such clashing active and passive oral impulses as beset Raskolnikov and Beckett's Listener do not simply remain in conflict; they are "set equal" in a single action, the performance of which produces a boundariless relation between actor and text. Is there any comparable upshot to the clash of warring active and passive oral impulses set going in one who listens to reading? I would argue that the experience of the read-to spectator is very close to that of the actor-reader in this regard. Read to, the audience has its intake controlled (passive orality) by an actor-reader whose outflow it commands (active orality); thus, in the single experience of listening to reading the spectator's orally active and orally passive impulses *toward the actor's reading* are "set equal." The resulting uncertainty about whether the flow is being controlled from "out there" (by the actor who reads) or "in here" (by the audience's demand for reading) produces in the one who is read to that confusion between "out there" and "in here" themselves which is characteristic of the boundariless state.

We are now in a position to see how, as I began by asserting, it is the oral dynamic of being read to which provides the audience with a way into the acting as reading process—and, specifically, which enables them to share in the actor's own recovery of a "lost" physical of reading. For the actor that recovery takes the form of a boundariless relation with material toward which his conflicting orally active and orally passive impulses have been "set equal" in a single action. But just such a boundariless relation, achieved by just such a "setting equal" of just these conflicting impulses, attends the audience's experience of being read to.

It may seem paradoxical to claim that an audience can be brought closer to physicality merely by hearing others read to them. The actor is up there enacting his active and passive oral impulses. The audience member just sits and listens. What's physical about that? But such an identification of the physical with the physically active misrepresents the sense in which the actor's own act of recovery is a physical one. The actor restores a "lost" physical dimension to reading not because he is up and doing but, rather, because *what* he does—acts out conflicting oral impulses—restores a mental process that was, originally, a *situation* (that of the infant at the breast) to its original, situational status. And in this regard *being read to,* which is no less a situation than *playing a scene* is, makes as persuasive a reinstatement of reading's "lost" physical character as does acting itself.

This is in no way to deny the difference between an actor's and an audience's experience of theater but, rather, to suggest a basis for the

relation between their different experiences. The actor's process of recovering a "lost" physical of reading is vis-à-vis the text. The audience's
experience of recovering a "lost" physical of reading is vis-à-vis the
actor's process of recovery. And it is their being read to *by* the actor
which makes such *recovery in another's recovery* possible. As he reads to
them, the actor-reader passes on to the audience his own recovered
physical relation to the text, in the form of a relation on their part to his
act of reading.

That an actor's transaction with an audience is essentially such a
passing on of renewed oral capacity must have been clear to Plato when
he included the actor in the account he gave of the Greek rhapsode
(poetry reciter) as intermediary between poet and hearer:

> SOCRATES: The Muse first of all inspires men herself; and from
> these inspired persons a chain of other persons is suspended who
> take the inspiration.
>
> . . . .
> When you produce the greatest effect upon the audience in the
> recitation of some striking passage . . . are you not carried out of
> yourself, and does not your soul in an ecstasy seem to be among the
> persons or the places of which you are speaking?
>
> . . . .
> And are you aware that you produce similar effects on most of the
> spectators?
>
> ION: Only too well; for I look down upon them from the stage,
> and behold the various emotions of pity, wonder, strangeness,
> stamped upon their countenances when I am speaking.
>
> . . . .
> SOCRATES: Do you know that the spectator is the last of the rings
> which, as I am saying, receive the power of the original magnet
> from one another? The rhapsode like yourself, *and the actor,* are
> intermediate links, and the poet himself is the first of them.
> Through all these the God sways the souls of men in any direction
> which he pleases; and makes one man hang down from an-
> other. . . . And every poet has some Muse from whom he is sus-
> pended, and by whom he is said to be possessed.[58]

In this passage the performer is described as passing on to the audience
a certain "magnetism" that he has himself received from the poet, who

receives it from the Muse. That magnetism here is a trope for reinstated infant orality is clear both from the maternal character of its source ("every poet has some *Muse from whom* he is *suspended*") and also from its tendency to produce oceanic experiences ("possess[ion]," "ecstasy"), in which the distinction between "in here" and "out there" is blurred ("carried out of yourself... among the persons or the places of which you are speaking"). What a rhapsode or actor passes on to his audience is, thus, the capacity for boundariless oral experience. To Plato's account I would add only that, in the case of *actor* and audience, it is *reading-to* that provides the "mechanism" for this transmission.

Here, then, is what we set out in search of: a way in which the audience can join in the actor's reading process—and thereby share in his recovery of reading's "lost" physical. They will not "read" the actor's performance, which is not a text. Rather, they will find reinstated in the situation of being read to the "lost" situational prototype of a reading long since "passed upward" into mental process. They achieve, in relation to his act of reading the text to them, the very recovery of reading's "lost" physical which the actor himself has achieved in his work on the text. It is in this sense that the actor can be described as the reader "in" whose reading others read, and an audience can be said to read "in" the reading of the actor.

There is, however, a paradox inherent in this view of the actor-audience transaction. Here is a situation that by all rights should *deprive* you of an unmediated experience of reading—the one who reads to you has the relation with the text; *your* relation is only with this mediator—and, instead, it *gives* you reading *in the form of a relation to this very mediator.*

But this is precisely the paradox that, as we have already seen, confronts us in acting itself, which, as the return of unmediated presence in the person of a present mediator, *likewise* offers the experience of a here-and-now event of mediation for the unmediated experience of an event. But the "likewise" is superfluous. As an account of theatergoing, "reading in another's reading" does no more than restate, in terms of reader and read-to, the essential paradox of actor-audience relations. At the same time it brings into view a whole new and no less paradoxical aspect of *playwright*-audience relations, considered (and once again let me stress that this is far from the only way to consider them) as the transaction between a writer and his readers.

Of all types of authors the playwright has the most strictly delimited readership. This is not necessarily to say the smallest. The script of *Death of a Salesman* has no doubt found more readers than *Scripts for the Pageant,* a volume of poetry by James Merrill. But who *are* these readers? Directors and designers working on a production of it? Students and teachers engaged in the study of it? Scholars and critics analyzing some aspect of it? Neither singly nor even in the aggregate does this add up to a very large number of people. But let the number be enormous, it is still not the readership at which the playwright aims, the readership implied by the act of playwriting itself. *To be a playwright is to seek a readership of actors.* This is not merely an empirical observation about who mostly buys scripts. It is, first of all, a statement about the nature of scripts themselves as cast-convoking, as action-prescribing, and, as we shall see in a moment, as ultimately "unreadable" from any but an actor's standpoint. Actors are a playwright's inevitable readership because *to intend a dramatic text is to intend the reading process of the actor.*

But let us confine ourselves to the empirical level for the moment. New plays are available almost exclusively in *acting* editions, which, in turn, are available almost exclusively at *theater* bookstores, where they are bought almost exclusively by *actors* doing scenes from them or appearing in productions of them.[59] This is not a matter of poor marketing on the part of the play publishers. Samuel French and Dramatists Play Service are not "publishers" in the same sense that, say, Farrar, Straus and Giroux is a publisher; they are something closer to a distribution mechanism. This is not to denigrate the usefulness or courage of these enterprises. But to be published by Dramatists Play Service is like being published in the *American Journal of Ophthalmology:* One does not thereby make a bid for general readers, however few, but, rather, avails oneself of a channel to a specialized readership, however numerous, whose needs alone explain the existence of the channel.

Of course, none of this would prevent general readers from picking up the Dramatists Play Service or Samuel French edition of the latest play, just as they pick up the Farrar Straus edition of the latest novel. But something seems to prevent it. For, despite the fact that our first recorded instance of private reading involves a dramatic text ("As I sat on deck reading the *Andromeda* [of Euripides] to myself," begins a character in Aristophanes),[60] *there are no general readers of plays.*

Why should this be so? Basically, I would argue, because, owing to the nature of dramatic texts, there is really no such thing as a general *reading* of a play. Our chapter 4 analysis of the roles in a script as, each, a claim to be its "sole authentic reader" raises the question of how a reading extrinsic to *all* roles, as the general reader's must be, can claim authenticity.[61] This is not, of course, to say that such reading cannot be attempted. On the contrary, anyone interested in dramatic literature must attempt it, and, indeed, actors themselves must attempt it, for, as I pointed out in chapter 4, it is precisely his own general reader's experience of the script which the actor draws upon to provide an inner life for that "one-string reader," his character. But, for all that, the general reading of a dramatic text runs counter to something in the nature of the text it would read.

One of the commonest explanations otherwise literate people give for never reading plays is that they find it difficult to follow a text that's "all dialogue." But these same readers take in stride the "all dialogue" sections of, say, Henry James or Ivy Compton-Burnett, which are much harder to follow than the give-and-take in most plays and which often lack speaker identifications to boot. The real difficulty, one suspects, is not with the dialogue form itself but, rather, with the claim of each speaker in a dramatic dialogue—each role—to be, uniquely, the site of an authoritative "general reading." The would-be flesh-and-blood general reader finds his credentials challenged on every hand—indeed, challenged anew with every change of speaker. The implicit paradox here—that it is only in the "partial" reading approach represented by some one (*any* one) of its roles that an authoritative reading of the dramatic text resides—has consequences for the actor-author relation to which I shall return in the next chapter.

Here, then, is my reason for identifying actors as the playwright's intended readership: not that they alone read plays (though this, too, is roughly true) but that theirs alone is the kind of reading invited and legitimized by dramatic texts.

To write such texts, it would seem—texts that can only properly be read from within role—is ipso facto to forgo seeking general readers. And, indeed, there are playwrights who do not seek them. Shakespeare may have been one such;[62] his contemporary Heywood, who claimed that "it was never any great ambition in me to be . . . voluminously read,"[63] was apparently another. And in our own time Tennessee Williams has dismissed "a play in a book" as "only the shadow of a play and not even a clear shadow of it . . . hardly more than an architect's blueprint of a house not yet built or built and destroyed."[64] There are no general readers of blueprints.

Other playwrights, however, quite clearly *do* seek general readers. Perhaps few would go so far as Hebbel in professing to seek none but them: "The final destiny of a play is always: to be read. Why shouldn't it begin the way it's going to end anyhow?"[65] Yet, even in ancient Greece,

> tragedies were read by associates of the dramatist, by those who had for some reason failed to see the play, by tragedians, comedians, and rhetoricians who wished to use and draw on an earlier tragedy, by tragedy fanatics like Dionysus [in *The Frogs*], and, probably above all, by those who wished to learn by heart parts of tragedies for private singing and recitation.[66]

And one of the medieval English mystery cycles survives exclusively in a manuscript prepared for private reading.[67] Possibly these examples say more about the avidity of readers for plays than of playwrights for readers. But there is no doubt that once the presses were running, dramatic authors joined authors of other kinds at the printshop door. Against the examples of Shakespeare and Heywood could be ranged any number of Elizabethan dramatists (e.g., Dekker, Middleton, Marston, Jonson, Chapman, Fletcher) who, clearly, *did* care about getting their plays before a general readership[68]—as do any number of their present-day successors. Plays are, after all, occasionally published by Farrar, Straus and Giroux as well as by Dramatists Play Service; in Europe plays are sometimes even published before being performed.

And, indeed, even those playwrights who profess indifference to publication do not necessarily shun it or the quest for a broader readership it implies. The Heywood comment quoted above occurs, after all, in the printed preface to one of Heywood's published plays.[69] And Tennessee Williams's "blueprint[s] of a house not yet built" are, in fact, as widely available in ordinary print as the works of comparably well-known poets or novelists. Nor is there any great inconsistency involved here. Grant a playwright sincere when he says he is "only interested in performance": Performance, we have come to see, is a *reading* to others, an extension of the opportunity to *read* in another's *reading*. To seek to have one's texts read *to* others, *in the reading* of others, is not exactly to resign from the ambition of being read, having readers—only from that of being read *by one's audience*.

This may not seem a very real distinction. In speaking of writer-public relations we often use the terms *audience* and *readership* more or less interchangeably. Walter Ong has protested against this practice, arguing that *audience* implies a present collectivity of hearers, whereas "readers do not form a collectivity, acting here and now on one another and on the speaker as members of an audience do"; thus, *readership* is "an abstraction, in a way that 'audience' is not."[70] In general usage, however, *audience* can designate a quite abstract collectivity (e.g., the audience for detective fiction) and *readership* a quite concrete one (e.g., the, say, 8,491 eye doctors who subscribe to the *American Journal of Ophthalmology*). Nor is it difficult to think of situations where the two terms might designate a single group. An author giving a reading attended by people already familiar with his works, for example, looks out over a crowd that is at once his readership and his audience.

If, however, the writer whose relations with his public we are considering is a playwright, *readership* and *audience* suddenly acquire very different—indeed, mutually exclusive—referents. One does not ordinarily think of *reading public* as an oxymoron; yet, for a playwright, it is one. Those who hold his texts in their hands and read, i.e., the actors, are not the public by whom he seeks to be known; while those by whom he seeks to be known, i.e., the theater audience, never lay an eye on his texts. In a word, a playwright's readership (of actors) is not his audience, and his audience (of theatergoers) is not his readership.

So described, the lot of the playwright seems different from that of all other writers. But I shall argue that it is just here, where the playwright-public transaction seems to depart from author-reader relations in general, that it models them.

Throughout this chapter I have presented theater audiences as readers who, since their reading is always "in" the reading of others (the actors), never read the text itself. Now I have just put forward the playwright as a writer who is never read at firsthand. Taken together, these two formulations represent the playwright-theatergoer relation to be one between a *writer* who is never read at firsthand and a *reader* who never reads the text itself. *But this is the relation between any writer and any reader whatsoever,* between the writer and the reader as such:

we never really confront a text immediately, in all its freshness as a thing-in-itself. Rather, texts come before us as the always-already-read; we apprehend them through sedimented layers of previous interpretations, or—if the text is brand-new—through the sedimented reading habits and categories developed by those inherited interpretive traditions.[71]

In specific instances the interposed reading "in" which we receive the text may be some particular individual's critical reading of that text—Jan Kott's chapter on *The Bacchae* or Leslie Fiedler's discussion of *Huckleberry Finn*—but the argument is not affected by one's not having read essays on everything: Reading in the reading of a specifiable earlier reader is merely a special case. To read a text in terms of psychoanalysis, Marxism, or deconstruction, in search of "archetypes," "irony," or "organic form"—all these are instances of reading in earlier reading. Indeed, even considered as a mere cognizing of words, reading displays this character; for the very words it cognizes are, themselves, "always-already-read"— and not merely in the trivial sense that each and every one of them has been read before. Carlyle praised his friend Emerson's latest volume of essays as "a real *word* . . . the one such, in a world all full of jargons, hearsays, echoes and vain noises, which cannot pass with me for *words!*"[72] But, as the Russian critic Mikhail Bakhtin has argued, to be "full of jargons, hearsays, echoes, and vain noises" is precisely the essence of a "real word":

> When a member of a speaking collective comes upon a word, it is not as a neutral word of language, not as a word free from the aspirations and evaluations of others, uninhabited by others' voices. No, he receives the word from another's voice and filled with that other voice. The word enters his context from another context, permeated with the interpretations of others. His own thought finds the word already inhabited.[73]

Thus, not only do words arrive before us "permeated with the interpretations of others"; their so arriving is the most fundamental thing about them, the quality that makes them capable of communicating anything at all.

From this perspective the "special dilemma" of the dramatic author, with his two "tiers" of readers, begins to look less special, begins, indeed, to look representative. No author, any more than the playwright, ever gets his work read at firsthand because there is no reading at firsthand. No reader, any more than the theater spectator, ever gets to read in the text itself because texts themselves are precisely sites of earlier reading.

There seems, however, to be one obvious difference. While both theatergoing and reading itself may involve "reading in another's reading," at theater the other earlier readers (i.e., the actors) are actually present, whereas in reading no one seems to be present but the current reader and the text. Once again, however, where theater seems obviously to differ from the general situation, it turns out to be modeling it.

At theater we seem to have nothing between us and the events of the text (there's Lear, not fifty feet away). In fact, we have a mediator, the actor (Carnovsky as Lear), but we take the present event of his mediation (Carnovsky acting Lear) as the unmediated presence of the events he mediates (the action of *Lear*). Thus, at theater, as I noted earlier, the very presence of mediatory activity (i.e., acting) paradoxically obliterates all awareness of mediation, by getting itself accepted as the presence of what it mediates (i.e., the script's characters and events). *But this is exactly what happens in reading.* In scanning a page, too, we feel we have nothing between us and the text, and, again, it is the very presence of earlier readers mediating our reading which creates the illusion that nothing mediates it. For it is precisely these earlier readers and readings—whether in the form of actual earlier interpreters *of* the text or of those "reading habits and categories" inscribed *within* the text—that direct us at every turn how we are to take what is before us and, thus, create the illusion of simultaneous, effortless—in a word, unmediated—access to the text itself. In short, if acting is a mediation experienced as the unmediated presence of the text, *so is reading.* And in each case it is none other than the interposed earlier readers who one might suppose would *shatter* the illusion of direct textual presence that, in fact, *create* it by getting *their* unmediated presence accepted as that of the text itself.

Thus, theater "stages" the necessity of all reading's being in earlier reading and makes even what appears unique to itself—the physical presence in the room of the inevitable prior readers—stand for an aspect of the general situation. For, whomever he may represent in a particular dramatic fiction, the actor always also represents the earlier reader in whose reading all later readers read and whose presence they mistake for that of the text itself.

But, as we are now in a better position to see than when I first introduced the term, "reader in whose reading others read" is a highly paradoxical conception, as at once becomes clear if we consider the grounds on which the actor might lay claim to such a status. To the actor his own encounter with the text is direct, unmediated, bodily. Nothing, it seems to him—and, specifically, no earlier reader or reading—stands between him and the text, while he necessarily stands between the text and all later readers (i.e., his audience).

This refusal of the actor to acknowledge the presence of other readers between the text and himself has a familiar empirical correlative: Actors *hate* having the script read to them. Formerly, it is true, they got the script read to them quite a lot: by directors (e.g., Copeau and Belasco),[74] by literary advisers (Wilhelm Meister reads his actor-companions a script he thinks they should produce)[75], and, of course, by playwrights (e.g., Dryden, Chekhov, Shaw).[76] No doubt, there were often compelling practical reasons for this. Elizabethan companies, for example, had to hear read a new play they were considering doing and of which there existed as yet but one copy.[77] Nevertheless, it is a practice that always had its dangers ("the conception of the reader," Stanislavski warned, "may differ from that of the author and still be so . . . entrancing that the actor is carried away by it");[78] which runs counter, as I shall show in the next chapter, to the very nature of dramatic texts; and which, one suspects, was never very popular with actors themselves. (In the famous photograph of Chekhov reading to the Moscow Art Theatre company those of the actors who aren't looking conspicuously bored are peering at the text over Chekhov's shoulder, as if straining after a reading of their own.) Certainly, the practice did not long survive the advent of the mimeograph machine. Nowadays not only is the playwright or literary manager not encouraged to give a reading of the script; actors are likely to resent being given so much as a line reading by the director (for, after all, should it not be *they* who "give the reading"?) or even a dropped line by the stage manager (for—annoyance at one's own forgetfulness aside—should it not be *they* who "give the lines"?). In short, the actor recoils from being read to because to accept being read to is to accept that one reads in another's reading, whereas to act is to claim to be the reader prior to all others, the one with unmediated access to the text itself.

The trouble is that, as we have seen, there is no unmediated access to a text: *All* readers find earlier reading between the text and themselves—find it, if nowhere else, in the text itself. The conclusion seems inescapable: If all reading is in another's reading, *then so is the actor's.*

Useless for him to point to his "direct, physical approach": The text he directly, physically approaches he must read in the same "sedimented reading habits" and "inherited interpretive traditions" as anyone else. Nevertheless, despite the apparent impossibility of being the "first reader" when all reading is in earlier reading, "first reader" is what the actor sets up to be—the exception that proves the rule.

Leaving aside for a moment the question of whether the actor is it, can there be such a thing as an exception to the rule that *no reader is first?* Who might be some claimants of this elusive status? The first friend of the author to peruse the manuscript? The first customer of the bookseller to buy a copy? But there is nothing about the reading of such a customer or such a friend to constrain later readers: He may be literally first, but why should anyone else follow in his path? Perhaps, then, taking "first" in a different sense, a text's "first reader" is the preeminent authority who propounds its "definitive" interpretation? But definitive interpretations, far from commanding the assent of later readers, invite challenge by them; "first reader," in this context, is likely as not to mean "first to go."

Such attempts to answer the question literally suggest it may not be a very meaningful one. And, in a sense, it is not. For, as we have seen, the prior reading activity within which reading occurs is not, generally speaking, that of particular prior readers—never mind some *one* particular prior reader—but, rather, a prior *tendency* of interpretation, a preexisting *way* to read. And, yet, here is the actor setting up to *be* that impossible, or at least unspecifiable, "first one." With whose act of reading is he claiming his own coincides?

Let us consider one further candidate. Writing to his friend the Princess Marie von Thurn, to announce completion of the *Duino Elegies,* Rilke appends a startling postscript:

> I am *not* copying down and sending you the new elegies now: I would be jealous of your reading them. I feel as if it should be *I,* absolutely, who first reads them to you.[79]

Such a claim of first reading may seem an unusual one for an author to make. But, as I shall argue in more detail in the next chapter, it is only a more than usually explicit form of the claim that *every* author *implicitly* makes, namely, that the aims and meanings of his text being his to specify, others only receive their reading of it *from him.* Thus, if any reader of a text would seem entitled to put himself forward as that "first reader" the actor claims to be—the one in whose reading, itself unmediated, all later readers must read—it would seem to be *the author himself.* To aspire to be the reader who "comes before" all the others, who does not himself receive his reading from anyone but, instead, gives his reading to all the rest, is an essentially *authorial* ambition, is, indeed, as we shall also see in the next chapter, the very *form* of a claim of authorship.

This is not to say that such a claim is unproblematic when put forward by an author and only first causes trouble when an actor advances it. On the contrary, we shall find that the "first reader" claim introduces a paradox into the concept of authorship itself. What concerns us at present, however, is not the coherence or tenability of the claim but simply the question of whose claim it originally is. And on this point there can be no doubt. If acting hankers after an impossible "firstness" in an activity where none can be first, there is only one place it can have learned such a hankering. In claiming to be the exception to the rule that all reading of a text is in earlier reading, the actor is claiming, if not literal authorship of the text, at least something like an authorial relation to it. To be the thing he is, it appears, the actor must be (or at least must claim to be) the thing an *author* is—not merely some incidental thing authors are but the very thing that constitutes them as authors. This, in turn, suggests an affinity between the projects of actor and author which it will be the business of the next chapter to explore.

Chapter 7

The Actor–Reader as the Author, Reading

What is the relation between actor and author on a view of acting as reading? The answer seems obvious: The author *writes* what the actor *reads*. But we have already had indications that the actor-author relation is more complex than that of, simply, a consumer to a supplier of text. For one thing, we have seen that the roles of text-supplier and text-consumer themselves meet in the work of the improvising actor, who, precisely in this respect, becomes representative of the actor as such. Furthermore, we have found the actor's transaction with his audience to be governed by a dialectic of control and dependency which can also be seen as governing the author's (or any other artist's) transaction with *his* public. Most important, we noted in chapter 4 a parallel between acting and authoring on the grounds that each activity seeks to undo its orally passive dependence upon prior texts by an orally active giving forth of words. Of course, as was pointed out at the time, to produce this counterflow the author gives forth words of *his own,* whereas the actor reads the words of *another*—a pretty significant difference, it would appear. But we shall see in the present chapter that an author's emission of words of "his own" is, also, a kind of reading of the words of "another." Not only do actors not differ from authors on this score; acting may even be defined as an imitation of this aspect of authorship—that is, may be said *to reenact authoring conceived as a kind of reading.* Such, I shall argue, is the basic connection between actor and author from the standpoint of a theory of acting as reading. Let us, however, begin with some more empirical connections.

That there exist parallels between acting and authoring has occasionally been remarked on by actors and authors themselves. The actor, Stanislavski wrote, "will not get to the bottom of [a play] until he has thoroughly studied it by following the steps the author took when he wrote it."[1] I am not sure exactly what Stanislavski meant by this intriguing remark, but at very least he seems to imply a reciprocity: If the actor follows the steps the author took when writing, then presumably the author has anticipated the steps the actor will take when acting. In juxtaposition with this may be set the remark of Dickens that, for him, acting was "like writing a book in company"—an impression that came startlingly true when he found the conception for a new novel occurring to him in the course of performing a role in his and Wilkie Collins's play, *The Frozen Deep*.[2]

Beyond such incidental, if striking, remarks, do we find evidence of a felt affinity between the work of actor and author? I would argue that we do, though it is rather a mixed bag of evidence. Let me lay out some of it, without at first attempting much in the way of explanation or connection.

For one thing, authors frequently act. As we might expect, this has most often been the case with dramatic authors, from Shakespeare and Molière through Athol Fugard and Dario Fo. But it is not at all unusual for writers in nondramatic genres to give evidence of talent as actors— Sinclair Lewis played the lead in the stage adaptation of one of his novels;[3] Gustave Flaubert was an accomplished mime[4]—as actors themselves have often been the first to recognize. Macready declared that Dickens "reads as well as an experienced actor would."[5] Tennyson was told by Henry Irving that he would have made a fine actor.[6]

Conversely, actors often write—plays, memoirs, novels, acting textbooks, fitness manuals. And, even when they don't actually write, they seem to find the *role* of writer a particularly congenial one. For every one-man or one-woman show about a politician or historical figure there are perhaps half a dozen about writers: Alec McCowen as Kipling, Pat Carroll as Gertrude Stein, Zoe Caldwell as Lillian Hellman, etc. There are, of course, also roles in plays which provide actors with the opportunity to portray either actual authors ("Molière" in Molière's *Impromptu of Versailles*, "Tasso" in Goethe's *Torquato Tasso*) or, failing that, some version of authorial function or presence. As the speaker of an Aristophanic *parabasis*, as the Expositor in a medieval mystery play, as the Stage Manager in *Our Town* or the Animal Trainer in *Earth Spirit*—in all such roles as these the actor gets a crack at "playing author," so to speak. To both these phenomena—roles that are, in a general sense, "authorial" and roles of actual authors—we shall have occasion to return.

Furthermore, one might point to certain performance-like situations that seem designed to dissolve, or at least to perplex, the distinction between authors and actors: Simone Benmussa's production of Virginia Woolf's *Freshwater,* "played by writers only: E. Ionesco, N. Sarraute, A. Robbe-Grillet, etc.";[7] or the New York reading series "Selected Shorts," in which writers (e.g., Ann Beattie, Grace Paley) introduce actors (e.g., Fritz Weaver, Estelle Parsons) reading stories by other writers (e.g., Cynthia Ozick, Bernard Malamud);[8] or the group reading by half a dozen poets which bills itself as "a Reading in 6 Acts."[9]

Such overlapping or ambiguous situations as these seem predicted in the sound, and anticipated in the history, of the words "actor" and "author" themselves. The modern English words are only a little alike. Their respective Latin originals—*actor* and *auctor*—are much closer. (*Auctor* is also the standard Middle English form of *author*.) In fact, the two Latin words have quite separate roots—*actor* comes from *agire,* "to do" or "to perform"; *auctor* from *augere,* "to increase"—but this did not prevent the words (and, it sometimes seems, the concepts to which they refer) from being frequently substituted for one another in medieval texts.[10] The casual interchangeability of these two terms—one ("author") so strongly connoting origination and priority, the other ("actor") so clearly implying secondariness and representation—may seem astonishing. Over the course of this chapter we shall see in detail what it is about authoring that opens it to the secondariness of acting. For the moment I content myself with observing that *actor* and *auctor* would never have grown up thus entwined in both sense and sound if the activities that the words designate had not themselves been felt as connected.

If we seek a possible basis for this felt connection, one area of common ground immediately suggests itself. No wonder a current reading series in New York goes by the name of "Writers *in Performance*":[11] Writers *do* perform; they give readings. These occasions are always at least potentially theatrical, and sometimes—in the case of a histrionic author-reader like Richard Howard, for example—they become overtly so. Not every poet would accept Jerome Rothenberg's description of himself as "a stand-up performer of my own poetry," and Rothenberg himself sharply distinguishes a poet's performance from an actor's.[12]

Nonetheless, "I never performed better" was William Carlos Williams's verdict on a reading he had just given,[13] and "on an occasion like this the voice is an actor," remarked Wallace Stevens of a reading he was just about to give.[14] In light of such remarks it seems no coincidence that "Writers in Performance" was sponsored by, and took place at, the Manhattan *Theatre* Club: Ever since antiquity authors have been giving readings in theaters, from stages that, in Roman times at least, they routinely shared with jugglers, flute players, dancers, and singers.[15]

Perhaps, then, it is to the literal theatricality of the reading situation that accounts of writing as a sort of acting should be referred. Robert Frost characterizes the poet as a "performer" ("My whole anxiety is for myself as performer") and speaks of "the poem as performance."[16] Mallarmé describes the writer as a *"spirituel histrion."*[17] Wallace Stevens defines the task of poetic imagination as

> To construct a new stage. It has to be on that stage
> And, like an insatiable actor, slowly and
> With meditation, speak words that in the ear,
> In the delicatest ear of the mind, repeat,
> Exactly, that which it wants to hear, at the sound
> Of which, an invisible audience listens.[18]

In all such cases should we not perhaps take the theatricalizing language as a reflection back *within* the act of writing of the public reading situation? One may ask: How can the public reading situation, which, it would seem, can only occur *after* the text has been written, stand for the writing of the text? Once again, as in the case of the words *actor* and *auctor,* we find authorship somehow "contaminated" by a secondariness that the very concept of the author as source, or origin, seems to preclude. This paradox, we shall see, lies at the very heart of the actor-author relation.

The view of writing as inherently a kind of acting and of the author as fundamentally a kind of actor finds its clearest expression in the modern critical notion of the persona. Occasionally, for reasons of his or her own, a writer will play at being another: Doris Lessing submits manuscripts to her regular publisher under the pseudonym "Jane Somers";[19] a seventy-three-year-old white Anglo-Saxon playwright publishes a novel purporting to be the work of a reclusive young Chicano, "Danny

Santiago,"[20] etc. Pseudonymous authorship and false attribution are nothing new; not all the epistles of St. Paul are by St. Paul, either. What is new in twentieth-century critical thought is the presumption that such authorial role playing is the norm, that writing is *itself* a kind of role playing. For, if one starts from the New Critical premise that "the speaker of a literary work cannot be identified with the author,"[21] one is led directly to the conclusion that the author, in writing as if he *were* this speaker with whom he is not identical, is in some sense "acting":

> The voice we hear in a lyric, however piercingly real, is not Keats's or Shakespeare's; or, if it seems to be, . . . we are embarrassed and thrown off, as if an actor had stopped and spoken to the audience in his own person.[22]

The "I" of a text—even, according to Michel Foucault, the "I" of a mathematics treatise[23]—is an alter ego that the author assumes, a role he creates, a character he plays.

The term most often employed by contemporary critics to denote one of these fictive textual speakers is the Latin *persona*. Probably brought into prominence by Ezra Pound's use of it as the title for his 1919 volume of poems, *Personae,* the term itself is an ancient one. Already in antiquity we find it being used in something like its later meanings of "character" or "role" (cf. *dramatis personae*). But its root sense is "mask"—Pound chose his title because he felt that in each poem of the collection he was "casting off, as it were, complete masks of the self"[24]— and specifically an actor's stage mask. Nor is the employment of this term from theater practice to describe a writing practice a modern misappropriation. In the ancient rhetorical curriculum students were routinely set the task of composing speeches for the great figures of history and myth. This exercise of speaking for, or as, another was called "prosopopeia" ("impersonation"),[25] from the Greek *prosopon,* which, like the Latin *persona,* came to mean "role" or "character" but also originally meant "theatrical mask." But if, as the New Critics argued, "the poet is *always* wrapping himself up in some guise, if only the guise of being a poet,"[26] then not only the composition of such exercises but *all* writing is prosopopeia, im-personation, speaking as, or for, another. Even when an author speaks, as we say, in propria persona, he is still speaking in a role or as a character which happens to be his own. Not only "Jane

Somers" but also "Doris Lessing" is a mask of Doris Lessing's. This inability of the author, as author, to coincide with himself, any more than a face with a mask or an actor with a role, is a motif that will concern us further.

The evidence for some sort of affinity between acting and authoring thus converges from a number of directions: the history of the two words; the attraction of actual writers and actors to one another's disciplines; the tradition of performance-like readings by writers and of a performance terminology for writing; the penchant of actors for author-roles and of authors for role playing. But to recognize such a convergence is not yet to have explained the underlying affinity. To do that it will be necessary to examine in some detail the nature of authorial status and authorial claims. For this I ask the reader's patience. For long stretches I will not appear to be speaking of acting at all, but I hope at length it will be clear that I have been speaking about acting all along.

Actually, the basis we seek for an actor-author affinity already began to emerge at the end of the last chapter. There we saw that, if to be the reader in whose reading others read is the claim of the actor, it was also the claim of at least one author:

> Dear Princess . . . I am *not* copying down and sending you the new elegies now: I would be jealous of your reading them. I feel as if it should be *I*, absolutely, who first reads them to you.[27]

But Rilke is scarcely unique or even unusual among authors in his insistence that "it should be *I*, absolutely, who first reads . . . to you." Wordsworth read *The Prelude* to Coleridge.[28] Flaubert read *The Temptation of St. Anthony* to his friends Maxime Du Camp and Louis Bouilhet.[29] Goethe read poems in manuscript to Eckermann.[30] And Dickens read excerpts from *The Mystery of Edwin Drood* to the artist who was to illustrate it.[31]

Of course, by their nature such occasions are relatively rare: All of us do not get our reading of *The Prelude* straight from Wordsworth. Yet in another sense, all of us *do* get our reading of *The Prelude* straight from Wordsworth. The literal situation *author reads to audience* only enacts a far more general relation between writers and readers. To be the reader in whose reading others read is an ambition quintessentially authorial, is, indeed, the very form of a claim of authorship. "The teller of a story," writes Henry James, "is primarily . . . the reader of it"; his problem is

to make it out, distinctly, on the crabbed page of life, to disengage
it from the rude human character and the more or less Gothic text
in which it has been packed away.[32]

In relation to his public the author is most fundamentally, as Wallace
Stevens depicts him, a "Large Red Man Reading":

> he sat there reading, from out of the purple tabulae,
> The outlines of being and its expressings, the syllables of its law:
> *Poesis, Poesis,* the literal characters, the vatic lines,
>
> Which in those ears and in those thin, those spended hearts,
> Took on color, took on shape.[33]

We readers never get a direct glimpse of the "crabbed page" or "Gothic
text" or "purple tabulae" from which the author reads; we get only
James's or the "Large Red Man's" reading of these, i.e., the story or
poem that he writes. The literal situation between the Princess and Rilke
thus assumes the proportions of a trope for all readers' relation with any
writer: They read only in his reading to them.

But this mysterious "Gothic text" to which only the author has
access is not some earlier document "found among old papers"; rather,
the fiction of an earlier document found among old papers is itself a
narrative elaboration of the trope. Cervantes insists that he came upon
the early chapters of *Don Quixote* in "the annals of La Mancha" and the
remainder of the tale in an Arabic "history" by one "Cid Hamete."[34]
Laclos claims to have edited down his epistolary novel, *Les Liaisons
Dangéreuses,* from a "voluminous... correspondence" that has been
entrusted to him.[35] Chaucer pretends to be translating *Troilus and
Criseyde* out of the Latin of one "Lollius":

> of no sentiment [personal experience] I this endite [compose]
> But out of Latin in my tongue it write.
>
> . . . .
> For as mine auctor saide, so say I.[36]

But, of course, there is no Lollius or Cid Hamete, no "annals of La
Mancha" or Arabic history or "voluminous... correspondence." The
"crabbed page" is not some *different* page from the one to which your
copy and mine lie open. Indeed, the "Gothic text" is not *another* text at

all. It is simply the text itself, unavailable for direct inspection by the
reader in that it stands always already under the claim of authorial interpretation—is, indeed, constituted by that claim.[37] For, as Julia Kristeva
reminds us, to be an "author" is first of all to be the one who claims
author-ity over the meaning of a work,[38] and *authority over meaning* is
an essentially *interpretive* claim, the claim of a *reader*.

Thus, while to be the reader of a text, as I have at several points
argued, is not (except under special circumstances or speaking figuratively) to "write" it, to be the author of a text is, in a quite specific sense,
to read it. "I found myself," says the novelist Stanislaw Lem, "during
the writing process in the position of a reader. . . . [The action of the
novel] was divulged to me in the same manner that it becomes clear to
the reader in the course of reading the book—with the sole difference
that it was I who created the novel."[39] Nor is this merely one author's
perspective. "Anyone who writes a text," declares Paul de Man, "is at
that moment reading it, and the production of a text is as much an act
of reading as it is writing."[40] For, as Robert Crosman points out, authors
make meaning "in exactly the same way that we all make meaning: as
interpreters, as readers."[41] If we nonetheless deny authorial status to
readers in general, this is because it is only the author whose making-
meaning-as-a-reader makes the text. It is common—a virtual convention
of modern authorship—for writers to refuse to claim any special access
to their own work. But it is too late: The work itself is already such a
claim. In vain does novelist Rebecca West protest: "I only wrote this
book, which is not to say that I am the best authority on what it
means."[42] The renounced claim is inscribed in the disclaimer: To be the
author *is* to be the "best author-ity."

But recognition of the author as first reader introduces a paradox
into the very conception of an "author." To claim authorship is to claim
to be a source or origin. But to be a reader, even a *first* reader, is a
secondary role: Even "active readers" only appear on the scene subsequent
to the texts they read. Thus, the claim to be "first reader," by which the
author seeks to differentiate himself from other, merely secondary, readers, places him among them; for to come to a text as a reader, even as its
first one, is to come after it.

This unlooked-for secondariness at the very heart of the author
concept is, in fact, anticipated in the etymology of the word. *Auctor* has
its root in the Latin verb *augere,* "to increase," which implies something
already there to be increased. And, although the primary meanings of

auctor include "founder," "originator," "progenitor," etc., the word can also mean "adviser," "witness," "guarantor," and "auctioneer," all of which describe functions no less secondary than that of "reader."[43] Moreover, as Janet Coleman points out, the concept of "author," as it develops over the course of the Middle Ages, is of an essentially secondary figure: God is the true Author, whose act of ultimate origination the human author merely reenacts.[44] Such a parallel, moreover, necessarily cuts both ways: If it implies every human author is something of a "creator," it also imbues divine creative activity with something of the secondariness of human authorship. On a fifth-century Athenian *pyxis* a muse is shown giving a recitation from a book.[45] (Even the Muse is only a "first reader.") And, according to certain Islamic exegetical traditions, Allah did not speak the Koran to Mohammed but read it aloud.[46] (Even God is only a reader in whose reading others read.) The author, it appears, is always somehow both a source or origin and a "second who reads." Could this second who reads have anything to do with, or in certain circumstances be represented by, an *actor* who reads? Is it perhaps the possibility of such a substitution which is hinted at in the strange interchangeability we noted earlier between the words *auctor* and *actor?* I shall suggest that it is, indeed, this self-division within authorship which leaves the door open to acting. But for the moment let us return to what will prove a key link in making this argument: the phenomenon of the author reading his work in public.

If authorship is the status of a reader in whose reading others read, then to put oneself forward as, literally, the reader in whose reading others read—i.e., to read to them—can be a way of asserting a claim of authorship. Clearly, it is not the only way to assert such a claim: The authorial "first reader" may also appear *within* the text (as, say, an omniscient narrator or central consciousness). And, obviously, it is not—a point that will much concern us—a way limited to the author himself: If authoring is mere reading to others, then *any* reader to others—the actor, for example—is stepping into the shoes of the author. Still, one begins to understand better the importance to authors of this, as it otherwise might appear, somewhat marginal practice. One who "gives a reading" asserts that *reading is his to give,* which is, after all, the fundamental authorial claim.

And so, all through history, giving readings has been important to the author, not only (indeed, I would argue, not principally) as a method of propagating the text but also as a means of reclaiming his authorial relation to it. When Rilke finally delivered his *Duino Elegies* before the Princess, he did so standing at the very desk at which he had written them.[47] To read one's work aloud is to stand once more in the place of the authorial first reader.

This is not to say that authorial first reading originally *was* reading aloud. It may be tempting to see the author reading to his public as the "lost" physical situation between writers and readers, but few situations have less the character of an origin. We must not confuse historical earliness with originary character. The history of attempts to recover an authorial relation to one's work by reading it aloud reaches back to the dawn of Western civilization, but, in its earliest no less than its most recent instances, it is a history of recoveries. A public reading by Herodotus was as much a *re*claiming of authorial status as a public reading by John Ashbery is.

Nor is there any question of authorial reading aloud reinstating some "lost" primal situation where authors *composed* their works aloud in the presence of audiences. For one thing, reading aloud does not make a very persuasive model of oral composition: To bring forth a stretch of already existing text, while it is indisputably oral, is indisputably not composition. But even allowing that authorial reading might in some sense represent oral composition, oral composition itself, though historically prior to other modes of authorship (Homer before Sophocles), is no more primary than they. It is, as each of them will be, a displacement of orally active behavior (extrusion, spitting, etc.) from the body to language, i.e., is already reenactment.

But, even apart from such misunderstandings, there is an obvious problem with reading a text aloud as a means of asserting an authorial relation to it: *Anyone* can read a text aloud, and whatever claim to be the source of a text is asserted by reading it aloud *anyone's* reading it aloud asserts. That is, when Mrs. Siddons gave a reading of *Paradise Lost*[48] or Henry Irving of *Childe Harold*[49] or Alec McCowen of the Gospel according to St. Mark, Siddons, Irving, and McCowen were all making as strong a claim to be the authorial source of those texts as Milton, Byron, and St. Mark could have made solely by that means. Jerome Rothenberg characterizes the reading poet as "risk[ing] himself . . . to stand there as a witness to his words, he who alone can sound them."[50] But the author is scarcely "alone" in being able to "sound" his words: Any reader can sound them. Nor does his function as "witness" distinguish the author from other readers: Anyone, however unoriginal, can be a witness. (That *auctor* can, as we have seen, mean "witness" as well as "origin" rather casts doubt on the "origin-ality" of authors than establishes the "author-ity" of witnesses.) In short, in the absence of any outside information on the identity of the reader, reading aloud always leaves open the possibility that he who reads is another than the authorial figure his reading aloud proclaims him to be, i.e., is a merely secondary, rather than an authorial first, reader.

What is the effect of this potential for uncertainty in the case where the reader aloud is, and is known to be, the author himself: not McCowen reading Mark but Dickens reading Dickens? Before replying *none whatever; if it's Dickens up there, that settles it,* we might consider the comment of a Dublin newspaper reporter who attended one of Dickens's public readings: "It can honestly be said that Mr. Dickens is the greatest reader of the greatest writer of the age."[51] This orotund compliment, a poststructuralist apothegm *avant la lettre,* produces (and seems to record) a moment of vertiginous double vision. The author splits in two before our eyes: this "greatest writer" whose "greatest reader" Mr. Dickens is—is he, then, *another* than Mr. Dickens? How many novelists can you find on this platform?

With this compare Eckermann's reaction to being read to by Goethe:

> Goethe was this evening full of energy and gaiety. He brought some manuscript poems, which he read aloud. Not only did the original force and freshness of the poems excite me to a high degree; but also, by his manner of reading them, he showed himself to me in a phase hitherto unknown but highly important. What variety and force in his voice! What life and expression in the noble countenance, so full of wrinkles! And what eyes![52]

The Dublin journalist had presumably never seen Dickens before; his finding Dickens-the-reader to be "another" perhaps means merely that he found him other than expected (though, as we shall see, this impression is itself often only a displacement of the "otherness" of the reading writer). Eckermann, by contrast, was well acquainted with his author, saw him daily, etc. And, yet, hearing him read, Eckermann felt that he was seeing a "hitherto unknown" Goethe. Not only to his auditors but to himself as well the reading author may appear "another." "I don't know what got into me that day," reports Flaubert of an occasion on which he read from *L'Éducation sentimentale,* "but I delivered the last chapter in such a way that I was dazzled myself."[53] Who is this dazzling other by whom Flaubert feels himself dazzled?

Clearly, there are all sorts of situations in which someone other than the author may read in his stead. The author himself may be unable to be present, as when Jeremiah, forbidden to enter the temple, sent his scribe Baruch to read his prophecies to the people,[54] or as when, on more prosaic occasions, a scholar prevented by illness from attending a conference has a colleague read his paper for him. Or perhaps the author does not feel competent to "perform" his own work, as was the case with Pliny the Younger, who hired a freedman to do his public reading for him.[55] Or the author may wish to get some perspective on his work by hearing it delivered before an audience; this was apparently Petrarch's custom.[56] The question that our Dickens, Goethe, and Flaubert examples raise is whether such instances of the delegation of reading are anything more than unusually explicit enactments of the author becoming "someone else" when reading; whether he who reads—Jeremiah or Pliny himself, as much as Jeremiah's scribe or Pliny's freedman—is not always, in some sense, "another" than he who wrote;[57] whether, in fact, such literal doubling of the author does any more than "bring to pass" the division already implicit in the word *auctor* between the figure of a founder/progenitor (i.e., a writer) and the figure of a guarantor/witness (i.e., a first reader).

At minimum, our Dickens, Goethe, and Flaubert examples suggest that it is possible for the secondariness of the reader-aloud to the author—of, say, Henry Irving to Byron when he reads from *Childe Harold* or of Alec McCowen to St. Mark when he reads from the first gospel—*also* to characterize the relation of the reading author to himself. I would, however, go further and argue that this is not only possible but inevitable. The author as reader-aloud of his work cannot coincide with himself as author. To be an author is to claim the status of an origin. But to read aloud is only to *re*enact the oral "putting forth" upon which such a claim rests. And, as reenactment, it marks the claimant as secondary, even when the claimant is the author himself. For to *claim* something is necessarily to come after it. An author steps up to the lectern to give a reading and finds his text "before" him in both senses of the word: there before him to read but also there before he has read it. To *be* an author (now) is to *have* produced a text (earlier). The present of authoring is always some other present, i.e., is always past; the presence of an author is always the presence of "someone else," i.e., always a representation.

This inevitable secondariness of the author vis-à-vis the once completed text has not passed unnoticed in recent criticism, and the new "second" position has been named in various ways: the postwork author is henceforth the text's limit,[58] or margin, or owner,[59] or product.[60] But, essentially, there are only two things you can be to a text: its author or its reader. And, his work once complete, the author himself belongs in the latter category:

> "Do you cry when you read aloud?" a twelve-year-old American girl asked Dickens, when she waylaid him on a train. "We all do in our family. And we never read about Tiny Tim, or about Steerforth when his body is washed up on the beach, on Saturday nights, or our eyes are too swollen to go to Sunday School."—"Yes, I cry when I read about Steerforth," Dickens answered quietly.[61]

The "greatest reader" of Dickens now stands "quietly" among the other readers; there is nowhere else to stand. Recently, a Manhattan bookstore announced a reading of Tama Janowitz's *Slaves of New York* by "guest reader" Caitlin Clarke.[62] But no less than this of Clarke's, a reading by Janowitz herself would be that of a guest reader. For it is "as a guest only" that "the author . . . may visit his text."[63] Barthes is quite right to insist that "the birth of the reader must be at the cost of the death of the Author,"[64] but perhaps he takes his own image too literally when he identifies this newborn reader as, simply, someone else:

> there is one place where this multiplicity is focused and that place is the reader, not, as was hitherto said, the author. The reader is the space on which all the quotations that make up a writing are inscribed without any of them being lost; a text's unity lies not in its origin but in its destination.[65]

As with Jeremiah's scribe and Pliny's freedman, so the arrival of this Barthesian Other Who Reads reenacts a transit *within* authorship, a passing over of the *auctor* as "origin" into the *auctor* as "witness," consequent upon completion of the work. This reader born of authorial ashes, in other words, is first of all the author himself, the author *as* reader, henceforth capable of no relation to his text but that of a latecomer, a "destination," a second.

This secondariness of the author to his own text, and so to himself as source of that text, is not only, or even primarily, an effect of the public reading situation. Such secondariness already characterizes the author as "first reader" (reader being an essentially secondary role), which is to say, it characterizes the author as such. True, the public reading situation offers the writer a unique opportunity to *enact* his "first reader's" prerogative. Only when reading aloud from his works could Tennyson hope to control the reading of others with comments like "We now come to one of my best things. This has been tried before me, but not successfully."[66] And, yet, what is writing itself but the attempt to control the reading of others? Whether he gives readings or not, a writer is forever pointing out to us the beauties that lie upon the "crabbed page": *His writing* is that pointing out. In this sense, Dickens is the greatest reader of Dickens before he ever mounts a platform; for, in this sense, "greatest reader of Dickens" is just a periphrasis for "Dickens."

The argument may be summarized as follows: The author as first reader of his work cannot coincide with himself. But the author *as such,* and not merely when he happens to be reading aloud, is the first reader of his work (the typescript on the lectern only literalizes the "Gothic text" from which he was first to read). Therefore, the author *as such,* and not only when reading his work aloud, cannot coincide with himself. Giving a reading is an attempt on a writer's part to get back into his original authorial relationship with the text. But if the attempt succeeds, it is only because this "original authorial relationship" was itself the secondary one of first reader. Giving his reading, the author attempts, by reenactment of his own act of origination, to establish himself as an origin. But the result can never be more than reenactment of the origins of authorial secondariness—even though the "actor" in this case is none other than the author himself.

For here at last we arrive at the basis of that actor–author parallel that we found hinted at in the words themselves and saw illustrated in a whole spectrum of overlapping conceptions and activities. The surprise is that the *parallel* between actor and author turns out to consist precisely in what would, at first glance, appear to be the sharpest *contrast* between them. That very secondariness to text and author which seems to *differen-*

tiate a mere actor-reader from the author reading, in fact, *models* the author's own secondariness to himself as (former) source of a (present) text. The situation in which the actor ineluctably finds himself—his voice claiming to be the source of what it only reproduces, his presence claiming to be the presence of what it merely re-presents—is the situation of authorship.

I hope it is now clear why I have dwelt so long upon the secondariness to himself of the author reading. This is not another subject than acting; it is, so to speak, the subject of acting. To act is to reenact an author's self-division into an *auctor*-"origin"-writer and an *actor*-"witness"-reader. The arrival on the scene of the actor—like Pliny's freedman or Jeremiah's scribe, a second who comes to read for the author—literalizes the *author's* becoming secondary to himself when *he* comes to read, either in a literal public reading or simply as authorial first reader.

I can readily conceive two objections to any such parallel as this between acting and authoring: first, that to act isn't just to take over reading from an author; and second, that to take over reading from an author isn't necessarily to act. Certainly, there is truth in both these contentions. No one would dispute that there is more to acting than enacting authorial reading, that this is not all actors do. Still, if such a perspective isn't true enough, it's true as far as it goes. To describe the actor as formalizing the otherness-to-himself of *the author, reading,* is not meant to provide an exhaustive account of acting, only to suggest wherein the common ground between acting and authoring might lie.

The second objection, that to take over reading from an author is not necessarily to act, also has merit. Baruch the Scribe, in reading for Jeremiah, and Pliny's freedman, in reading for Pliny, did not thereby become actors. Yet it is worth noting that even these two overtly nontheatrical instances of surrogate reading display a certain theatrical dimension. From the moment Jeremiah's scroll is entrusted to a Second Who Reads it begins to acquire the characteristics of a script in the hands of an actor. Like a script, it serves as the basis for several different "performances" by different "casts" (it is read aloud twice by Baruch himself and once by the courtier, Yehudi). And, like a script, it is "used up," or "consumed," in performance (as Yehudi reads each section of the scroll aloud, the listening king snips it off and throws it in the fire).[67] The emerging theatrical parallel, it is true, concerns more the text itself than the surrogate reader. But the same can hardly be said of Pliny's surrender of authorial reading:

Now the perplexing question is, how I shall behave while he is reading; whether I shall sit silent in a fixed and indolent posture, or follow him as he pronounces, with my eyes, hands and voice; a manner which some, you know, practice. But I fancy I have as little gift for pantomime as for reading.[68]

The uncertainty here expressed about how much that belongs to acting ("pantomime") one has ceded away in relinquishing first-reader status explicitly links authorial first reading and acting.

Historically, moreover, such a link appears to exist. There are two principal theories of the emergence of the actor in ancient Greece, and each posits a figure who, in some sense, takes over reading from an author. It has recently been suggested that the so-called rhapsodes, whom Plato long since likened to actors, may in fact have played a key role in the development of Greek theater. The rhapsodes were professional reciters who, from the sixth century B.C. on, gave public performances of the Homeric and other traditional poetic texts.[69] These entertainers, who apparently employed gestures and impersonated the characters in the poems they recited, may well have constituted an intermediate stage between the Homeric poet-performer and the tragic actor.[70] Although a rhapsode did not come before his audience, "crabbed page" in hand— rhapsodes, like actors, performed from memory—he clearly did come before them as a stand-in for the author in his aspect of first reader. And the gestural, mimetic direction in which rhapsodic performance evolved therefore suggests that playing *another who reads* for the author is a step toward playing *another*—i.e., toward acting. But no less does the more familiar account of the origins of Greek acting present the actor as a surrogate first reader. "When Aeschylus added a second actor, the profession of the actor became distinct from that of the poet"[71]—on this theory, too, the arrival of a Second Who Reads for the author is the crucial first step toward acting.

The tendency for surrogate reading on an author's behalf to develop toward acting is also suggested by the presence in other performance traditions of figures who have clearly undergone such a development. The Chanter in Bunraku who, from his lectern at the side of the stage, reads the dialogue for all the puppet characters, is clearly a surrogate authorial reader functioning as an actor. The same might be said of the Expositor in the medieval mystery cycles, who, as noted earlier, performs several explicitly authorial functions—supplies background, introduces characters, offers commentary, etc.—but performs them *as an actor,* up there with the rest.[72]

In the Middle Ages it was widely believed that Terence's comedies had originally been performed by a supposed friend of his, Calliopus, who recited the entire script aloud.[73] I find this medieval misunderstanding a highly suggestive one in the present context. For Calliopus, it turns out, was not a friend or even a contemporary of Terence's but was, instead, a much later editor of his works, that is, a source of authoritative readings in which subsequent readers would read. To have conceived this other who took over authorial first reading from the author as an *actor* may have been a factual error, but it is an error that has stumbled into symbolizing the truth. The authorial claim to be the reader in whose reading others read reappears in the actor as no longer authorial—and so reveals itself as having been all along the claim of "another," in that it makes another of him who claims it, even when the claimant is the author himself. *Acting is representation by another than the author of the other-to-himself an author is bound to become as his own "first reader."*

It might seem as if, for such a relation between actor and author as I am proposing, *representation* (or *modeling,* as I called it earlier) is too mild a term. Would not the actor's attainment of first-reader status have to be at the expense of the author—more in the nature of a wresting away than a mimesis? (Certainly the sort of one-man show in which an actor plays a particular writer must have its origins at least as much in the actor's desire to supplant, displace, "be the death of," that author as in more acceptable feelings of admiration, empathy, etc.)

We have seen that the authorial first-reader claim is often expressed in the image of a "Gothic text" or "crabbed page" to which only the author himself has access, and from which he reads the work to (i.e., writes the work for) everyone else. In Buckingham's theatrical satire *The Rehearsal* (1672) one of the actors gets his hands on a literal version of this "Gothic text"—"a foul piece of papyr" on which the playwright, Bayes, has scribbled a synopsis for the not yet written fifth act—and reads it to his fellow cast members. (They pronounce it terrible and adjourn for lunch.)[74] In this instance the actor's takeover of authorial reading status assumes the form of a (literal) wresting away of an (actual) "crabbed page" from its author. Of course, the transaction here is between a *bad* author and *presumptuous* actors and issues in a *non*performance. But before dismissing the agonistic image of actor-author relations which it presents we would do well to consider the following exercise of Stanislavski's:

> The words are foreign to you; they are not created by your own imagination. How can an actor help himself in such a case? You realize very well how long it takes a writer to create the characters of his play—how many rough sketches Pushkin made for *Boris Godunov*, Gogol for *The Inspector-General*, and Griboyedov for his *Much Woe From Wisdom*, or other great writers before the final draft of their great work is completed.
>
> In order to make this text your own, each one of you must make for himself the rough sketches which Pushkin, Gogol, and Griboyedov had to make to reach the perfection of their thoughts, images and language. . . .
>
> Please, all of you, prepare right now two or three rough sketches of one of the important beats in your roles.[75]

To act here means: to read from "rough sketches" of which one is oneself the source, to which one alone has access. But this is precisely what we have found *writing* to be. The rough sketch that Stanislavski instructs his actors to produce is precisely Stevens's "purple tabulae" or James's "crabbed page": i.e., the text conceived as having its origins in an author-itative first reading/writing. This is no mere matter of "following the steps the author took when he wrote."[76] Stanislavski is here urging the actor to seize for himself a relation to the text which one might have supposed was available to its author alone.

Could Griboyedov, Pushkin, or Gogol have attended rehearsals of their work conducted on these principles, they might well have felt that their authorial first-reader status was being wrested away, rather than merely represented, or modeled, by the actors. Certainly, innumerable authors at innumerable rehearsals have felt so—and have reacted by attempting to wrest it back again. In the course of *The Rehearsal* playwright Bayes tries repeatedly to snatch back his first reader's prerogative. Sometimes he contents himself with attempting to dictate the reading of others:

> AMARILLIS: Thanks to the Powers above, for this deliverance.
> I hope its slow beginning will portend

A forward *Exit* to all future end.
BAYES: Pish, there you are out; to all Future end?
No, no; to all future End; you must lay the accent upon end, or
    else you lose the conceipt.

(act 3, sc. 3, ll. 5–10)

But on other occasions nothing will suffice but that he must literally take reading out of the actors' hands:

(to the PLAYERS)

BAYES: Zookers, why don't you read the paper?
KING PHYSICIAN: O, cry you mercy.

(goes to take the paper)

BAYES: Pish! nay you are such a fumbler. Come, I'll read it myself.

(takes a paper from off the coffin . . . Reads:)

Since death my earthly part will thus remove [etc.].

(act 4, sc. 1, ll. 112–15, 142)

And, at last, he takes it out of their collective hands altogether: He withdraws his script from production.

STAGE-KEEPER: Nay, good Sir, don't take away the Book. . . .
BAYES: My Play and I shall go together, we will not part indeed, Sir.

(act 5, sc. 1, ll. 401–6)

If, as we shall presently see, a compulsion to hold onto one's first-reader status at all costs runs counter to the playwriting impulse (Bayes, after all, is a *joke* of a playwright), a certain potential for conflict between the actor laying claim to an authorial function and an author claiming it back is, nonetheless, implicit in the theatrical process—is, indeed, often at the root of personal-seeming clashes between "arrogant" actors and "protective" playwrights—and, like all of theater's dilemmas, has a tendency to reappear as theater's subject matter.

In Simone Benmussa's recent stage adaptation of Nathalie Sarraute's *Childhood*,[77] for example, the contention between actor and author for first-reader status became a literal onstage event, indeed, ultimately emerged as the central action of the piece. In Benmussa's production the

first-person text of Sarraute's memoir was divided up between two readers: actress Glenn Close, who played the writer onstage; and an offstage
taped voice identified in the program as "the voice of Nathalie Sarraute."
Now challenging, now prompting, now joining in with the onstage
speaker, this offstage authorial voice seemed to represent a resolve on
the part of the author to win back the first-reader status, which the actor
had appropriated—or, at least, to maintain itself alongside the usurper.
The piece, rather a static one, drew what tension it possessed from the
struggle between these ironically paired contestants for authorship: one
who was indisputably the author, but not present; the other, who was
indisputably present, but not the author. (The actor-author dimension
of this conflict was further emphasized by the designation of Close's role
in the program as, simply, "Actress.") Even match though this may
sound, the piece did not end in a standoff. As *Childhood* drew to a close,
the "authorial" voice heard on the tape was more and more of the time
also that of the "Actress," Glenn Close. Such an outcome should not
surprise us. In the theater, victory in the contest between actor and
author for first-reader status must always rest with the actor, theater
being, precisely, that victory in that contest.[78]

Clearly, then, the actor-author relation displays elements of wresting away, usurpation, denial. This need not, however (to return to the
question that started us down this path), interfere with seeing what the
actor does as a modeling, or representation, of the authorial claim to
first reading. For that first-reader claim is itself a wresting away, a usurpation, a denial of priority to another (any other) reader. The reader who
claims to read "ahead" of the rest is first of all the author himself, and
his claim is the text itself. To imitate such an act of claiming, however
slavishly, is to dispute it, since what one is "imitating" is the disputing
of such a claim. And, conversely, to "dispute" such a claim, however
fiercely, is to imitate it.

Another obstacle, however, is not so easily disposed of. The authorial first reader is, by definition, a *single* figure, the one who gets to the
text before everyone else and reads it to them. But no single actor reads
us the dramatic text; except in the limiting case of the one-character play,
each actor reads us only a part—*his* part—of the "crabbed page." Perhaps
acting as a phenomenon or the cast as a group may be said to "take over"
authorial first reading. (A stronger candidate still might seem to be the
director: Is it not he, after all, who gets to the text even before the actors;
he in whose reading the actors themselves read?) But it is hard to see how

any particular actor could be said to do so—unless, perhaps, he were to read us the play himself.

In fact, solo readings of entire plays by single actors are not unheard of. Instances of the practice can be found in settings as diverse as sixteenth-century Spain[79] and postwar Hollywood.[80] But for this, as for all types of public readings, the golden age was the nineteenth century. Mrs. Siddons gave an unassisted reading of *Othello*.[81] Charles Kemble read *Hamlet* in public and *Cymbeline* before Queen Victoria and her court.[82] Kemble's daughter, Fanny, offered solo readings of no fewer than twenty-five Shakespeare plays, and her American contemporary Charlotte Cushman presented one-woman programs of selected Shakespeare scenes.[83]

Did the actors who performed dramatic texts in this manner thereby intend to assert a first reader's claim over them? It seems probable that they did, considering that, actors apart, the bulk of such readings were given by people whose aim this clearly was, to wit, educators, clergymen, and critics.[84] Still, if it is to solo play readings we must look for evidence of the actor as authorial first reader, such a view rests on shaky ground. For the solo reading is too special a case to demonstrate anything fundamental about acting, and the more general case seems rather to preclude than confirm the argument I am making. How can an actor assert the authorial claim to be, alone, the reader in whose reading all others read when he is, palpably, only one reader among several, when all he reads is his *role*?

The answer is that with dramatic texts it is *in* role, in *any* role, that the first-reader claim resides. And, therefore, it is by assuming some one, *any* one, of its roles that the claim to be the first reader of a dramatic text is asserted.

We have seen that in fiction or poetry some sort of first reader is often written in. Whatever other functions they may serve, the narrative voice of a novel or central consciousness of a poem serves to reinscribe within the text the will and claim of its author to be the reader in whose reading others must read. (That such figures do not always coincide with the author, as in the case of a poem's "speaker" or an "unreliable" narrator, is itself a reflection back into the text of the inevitable otherness of the authorial first reader with respect to the author himself.) In the case of a dramatic text, however, the first-reader claim has always already been ceded to others: Initially, to other "readers" *within* the text (i.e., its various roles) and, ultimately, to *actor*-readers. To play a role is to play the author because roles themselves are constituted as (conflicting) claims to the status of authorial first reader.

Clearly some kinds of roles are authorial: "presenter"-figures like the Animal Trainer in Wedekind's *Earth Spirit* or the Stage Manager in *Our Town* (direct descendants, both, of the medieval Expositor); contrivers of "scenarios," like Iago, Prospero, and Prince Hal; deliverers of prologues, epilogues, and Aristophanic *parabasis;* and, of course, characters who are literally writers ("Shakespear" in Shaw's *Dark Lady of the Sonnets,* "Molière" in the *Impromptu of Versailles*). But I would argue that an authorial claim is inherent in *every* role, in the very *conception* of a role. For, as we saw in chapter 4, each character in a script claims to be not merely *a* reader or a *kind* of reader but *the only reader in the room,* the one who, having alone solved the drive/defense conflicts of the text, now proffers his as the reading in which alone all others must read, all else be read—in short, claims to be what we have since come to call an authorial first reader.

There are, needless to say, difficulties with taking roles as sites of the authorial in a dramatic text: What of all the expressions of authorial will—action, structure, imagery, and, of course, relations *between* characters—that do not lie within any one role?[85] Obviously, a role is no more literally the "authorial first reader" of the text in which it appears than it is literally the "sole qualified reader" of that text. My point is not that either claim is valid, only that the two claims are equivalent—or, rather, that the two phrases denote a single claim, namely, that *to read is to do as I do; either you read with me or you do not read at all.*

Thus, while it may appear an obvious objection to the whole view of actor-author relations I am proposing that, after all, actors play *roles* not authors, this is the very distinction to which, it might be said, roles themselves are conceived as challenges. To portray Tennessee Williams in a one-man show is obviously to "play the author."[86] But to portray Tom Wingfield or Blanche DuBois or Maggie the Cat is no less to do so: Every character is, from his or her own perspective, the author of a one-man or one-woman show, in which he or she alone reads to us from a jealously guarded "crabbed page."

One way to grasp the authorial nature of roles as such is to consider plays that contain, as one of their roles, that of a literal author: for example, the sonneteer Oronte in *The Misanthrope;* the poetry-writing teenager, Val, in Caryl Churchill's *Fen;* "Shakespear" in Shaw's *Dark Lady of the Sonnets;* and the authors of the plays within such plays as *The*

Rehearsal, Sheridan's *The Critic,* Ghelderode's *Three Actors and Their Drama,* and Tieck's *Puss-in-Boots.* In none of these instances does the author-character simply "rise authorial" above the rest. Rather, in each case, the presence of an avowed author in their midst only seems to provoke all the other characters into contesting his claim—and, so, into revealing themselves as *competing* claims—of authorship. In *The Misanthrope,* for example, Alceste counters Oronte's pretensions as a versifier by bringing forth some verse of his own, a folk song.[87] In *Fen* Angelica literally wrests away first reading of her stepdaughter Val's poetry by wrestling the girl's notebook out of her hand.[88] In Tieck's *Puss-in-Boots* the court fool announces that he is going "to deliver a few words which don't actually belong to the play" and, when the author comes bounding onstage to protest, announces that the argument between the two of them "also doesn't belong to the play."[89] In *The Dark Lady of the Sonnets* one after another of the play's characters beats "Shakespear" to the punch in striking off famous Shakespearean quotations (e.g., "THE BEEFEATER: I shall not return too suddenly unless my sergeant comes prowling around. 'Tis a fell sergeant, sir: strict in his arrest").[90] And there is no character in *The Critic* or *The Rehearsal* who does not consider he knows more about writing than the writers Puff and Bayes. "We knew your script before you did," one of the actors in Ghelderode's *Three Actors and Their Drama* assures the onstage "Author,"[91] thus challenging his essential authority to be, any more than they, a source or origin. It is a challenge that, in one form or another, many a fictive "author" must endure from his fellow characters.

From few such encounters does the author-character emerge with his credentials intact. The outcome, it is true, varies. Sometimes the other characters conclusively steal away authorship, as in *The Critic* and *The Rehearsal,* where in each case the "mere spectators" show themselves to be in far firmer possession of an authorial perspective than the ostensible authors, Puff and Bayes; or as in *Puss-in-Boots,* where, having driven the author of the play-within-the-play offstage, the court fool promises the audience *he* will "sit myself down and compose a piece that will please you."[92] Sometimes the contest ends in a standoff, as in *The Misanthrope,* where, between the vacuous elegance of sonneteer Oronte and the vacuous plainness of balladeer Alceste, there seems little to choose. Occasionally, the conflict may issue in a collaboration, as in *Fen,* where the stepmother winds up completing, with her stepdaughter's enthusiastic approval, the poem whose first reading she began by snatching away;

or as in *The Dark Lady of the Sonnets,* where "Shakespear" cheerfully
accepts the (unwitting) contributions that all the other characters seem
unable to stop making to his collected works (e.g., "SHAKESPEAR: 'Strict
in his arrest'! 'Fell sergeant'! *[as if tasting a ripe plum]* O-o-o-h! *[he makes
a note of them]*").[93] Even when the original author figure prevails, his
victory is likely to prove a somewhat Pyrrhic one, as when, at the end
of *Three Actors and Their Drama,* the "Author" reestablishes his first
reader's right of specifying "who I meant" by himself committing the
suicide his script calls for.

There is one case in which an author-character might seem to have
a better than average shot at establishing his authorial credentials, and
that is when the author in question is not just, as in the preceding examples, some author or other but, rather, the author of the very play in
which he appears: "Molière" in Molière's *Impromptu of Versailles,* "Christian Grabbe" in Christian Grabbe's *Jest, Satire, Irony and Deeper
Significance,* "Seneca" in the *Octavia* of Seneca, "the Author" in Roger
Vitrac's *Mysteries of Love,* and in the epilogue to Ben Jonson's *Poetaster.*
In any script that contains such a role (especially when, as in the Molière
and, possibly, the Jonson examples, the role was originally played by the
author himself),[94] one might expect to find authorial first reading vested
firmly *there.* But, in fact, it is precisely in these plays that other,
nonauthorial characters most fiercely challenge, and most frequently
succeed in wresting away, the authorial status of the in-play author
figure, *as if it belonged to their roles no less than to his,* i.e., *to role as such.*
In the *Impromptu of Versailles,* for example, which depicts Molière and
his company in rehearsal, the other characters are constantly asserting
their right to tell "Molière" what he should have written ("Why didn't
you do that comedy on the actors that you talked to us about?"),[95] how
he should have written what he did write ("Shall I tell you what I think?
If I'd been in your place, I'd have really pressed matters" [sc. 5, pp.
227–28]), and what *they* would have written if it had been up to them
("If I were writing a comedy . . . I'd justify the wives" [sc. 1, p. 211]).

In all such cases, the upshot (and, one may conjecture, the *aim*) of
authorial self-representation is quite different from what might be supposed. The playwright who introduces "himself" into the action appears
to be appointing a viceroy, one who will assert from within the fiction
the control which the author himself can only assert from without. But,
in light of what actually befalls these various author-characters, it seems
as if the playwright who "writes himself in" is not so much *asserting* his

authorial will as *exposing* it to counterclaims of authorship from every other character in the text—and, ultimately, from every other actor on the stage.

Occasionally, one comes upon a scene in which all (or all the principal) characters are literally authors, and the conflict is literally between authorial claims: "Euripides" and "Aeschylus" vying for best tragic poet in *The Frogs* of Aristophanes; "Lenin," "Tzara," and "Joyce" each trying to get *his* writing accepted as the writing of the opening scene of Tom Stoppard's *Travesties*. It should by now be clear that this special case is less special than it appears. Any scene between any group of characters is, implicitly, what these scenes openly are: a confrontation between claimants to an authorial first-reader status, each of whose claims is in conflict with all the rest—a conflict to which we customarily give the name "dramatic action."

The question we set out to answer—how can the actor claim first-reader status when all he reads is his role?—has thus been not so much answered as superseded. The actor not only can assert his first-reader claim within the activity of playing his role; he cannot well play his role without asserting it, indeed, except as an assertion of it. To enact authorial first reading isn't some project additional to, or even distinct from, acting a role. If anything, it would be truer to define *role* as the form in which the opportunity to "claim authorship" presents itself to the individual actor.

As a further indication that the authorial first-reader function resides in role, and can therefore only be asserted from within role, consider how the author of the dramatic text himself is obliged to go about asserting it.

We have seen that authors of nondramatic texts frequently assert their first-reader claims by giving readings. For the public reading, with its elements of expulsive orality, direct presence, sounding voice, etc., makes a persuasive reenactment of authoring, or at least of certain fantasies about authoring.

It is not unheard of for a playwright to give a reading. The Hellenistic poet Antiphanes read a comedy of his to Alexander the Great;[96] and antiquity affords other examples of both comedies and tragedies being read aloud in public by their authors.[97] A character in Molière mentions the practice of playwrights reading their scripts to patrons to win support.[98] Goethe read his *Iphigenie* before the German colony in Rome.[99] Gorky gave a reading of *The Lower Depths* to benefit poor students at the Moscow Art Theatre.[100] Tennyson read his play *Harold* aloud to the assembled Gladstone household.[101] And, as recently as 1984 in New York, Harold Pinter gave a reading of scenes from his plays in the 92nd Street YM-YWHA Poetry Series.

Yet most of the preceding examples reflect some special circumstance—a benefit (Gorky), a backer's audition (Molière), an expatriate writer's effort to stay in touch with his public (Goethe)—and, even at that, they are not very numerous. Public readings by playwrights have always been the exception, and never more so than at present. Most often, a contemporary reading series will not even include a playwright. When it does the playwright will generally not do his own reading. (Marsha Norman is included in a "lecture/tour series" with various other women writers: The others read; Norman has her work read by actors.)[102] When the playwright does read it will most often not be from one of his plays. (Sam Shepard, appearing in the same series as Pinter, did a program of selections from his nondramatic writings.) In short, it is as rare for a playwright to read his work in public as it is commonplace for other kinds of authors to do so.

If you stop to think about it, this is quite surprising. Plays, after all, more than any other sort of text, are designed to be read aloud. And playwrights, more than any other sort of writer, are likely to make good readers, being so often actors or ex-actors themselves. Moreover, it would seem as if, considered as a way to reenact, and thereby reclaim, authorship of a text, giving readings ought to work as well for playwrights as for other authors. After all, the playwright's characters no less than the novelist's came into being as a spectrum of possible responses to a core fantasy. Presumably, in composing the play the playwright "lurched" from response to response: Would not his now "lurching" from role to role as single reader of them all faithfully reenact this initial imaginative act? Yet, of all playwrights past and present, the only one I can think of who regularly gave public readings is Seneca. And this is less the exception that proves the rule than a further instance of the rule. The example of Seneca, whose plays were probably never staged and were possibly written for just such solo performance,[103] only confirms that *there is an inverse relation between writing for the theater and reading one's work in public.* Nor is this a merely empirical observation; it follows from the very nature of dramatic texts.

If, as I have suggested, every role in a play is an authorial first reader, then the dramatic text may be defined as one in which authorial first reading itself has been disseminated, distributed, "dealt out." The famous opening of the *Impromptu of Versailles,* in which "Molière," alone on the stage, summons up his company of actors one by one ("Monsieur de Brécourt!" "What?" "Monsieur de La Grange!" "What is it?" "Monsieur du Croisy!" "Yes?", etc. [sc. i, p. 207]) is emblematic: Every script begins as a summoning up of the readers to (each of) whom the (full) claim of the authorial first reader must pass.

From this perspective it should be clear why playwrights don't give readings. Authors of poems and novels give readings to reclaim their authorial relation to their work. But the playwright cannot reclaim, or even represent, his initial authorial act by giving a reading because his initial authorial act consists in *giving away reading.* When the author of a play reads it he places back within a single, privileged act of reading a text which is constituted as a multiplying of this privilege, a dissemination of this act. (And here is why the director, for all the "obvious superiority" of his claim over the actor's, is not the true first reader of the dramatic text. What does the director do if not, precisely, "place back within a single, privileged act of reading"—his own—"a text constituted as a multiplying of this privilege, a dissemination of this act"?)[104] A solo reading by a playwright would, thus, not only not reenact his initial act of authorship but would, in effect, repeal it.

Thus, when it comes to claiming first-reader status, rather than the actor strengthening his claim by playing all the roles, the best hope for the author himself is to play some one of them—which is no doubt the reason why this practice is as common among playwrights as solo readings by them are rare. Cast as the Ghost, Shakespeare is (once again? at last?) the authorial first reader of *Hamlet.* For it is only in a role that one may expect to find a first reader's relation to the dramatic text, even if one happens to be the playwright himself. The answer to the question of how the author of a dramatic text can best assert a first reader's claim over it is: in the same way as anyone else, in the one way such texts allow. When James Merrill's three-character verse play *The Image-Maker* is read aloud it is by James Merrill and two other readers.[105] When Christopher Durang and Wallace Shawn take part in a joint reading, it is indeed *parts* (in a series of two-character scenes from one another's plays) which they take.[106] The reading that a playwright must give to assert his authorial relation to his text is the reading of a role.

I have already singled out the *Impromptu of Versailles* as a play that explicitly depicts the playwright ceding away reading, summoning up surrogate readers. There is, however, one moment in which the "author himself" (i.e., the "Molière" character) attempts to reclaim his surrendered authorial position, and how he goes about doing so is instructive. "Molière" and "Brécourt" (one of the other actors in "Molière's" company) are rehearsing a scene from the play within the play:

> MOLIÈRE: "But tell me, Chevalier, don't you think your Molière has run out of subjects and will find no more material to . . . ?"
> BRÉCOURT: "No more material? Ah, my poor Marquis, we'll always furnish him plenty, and we're hardly on the road to good sense, for all he does and all he says."
> MOLIÈRE: Wait, you've got to bring out this whole passage more. Just listen to me say it. "And will find no more material to . . . ?"— "No more material? Ah, my poor Marquis, we'll always furnish him plenty, and we're hardly on the road to good sense, for all he does and all he says. Do you think he has exhausted all the ridiculousness of men in his comedies? And without going outside the court, doesn't he still have twenty characters of people he hasn't touched on? Doesn't he have, for example, those who show each other the greatest friendliness in the world and who, when their backs are turned, entertain others by tearing each other apart? Doesn't he have those dispensers of all-out adulation, those insipid flatterers, who use no salt to season the praises they bestow, and whose flatteries all have a sickly sweetness that nauseates their listeners? . . . Come, come, Marquis, Molière will always have more subjects than he wants; and everything he has touched on up to now is only a trifle compared to what remains."
> That's about how that should be played.
>
> (sc. 4, pp. 221–22)

Despite the pretense of directorial guidance ("Just listen to me say it," "That's about how that should be played"), it is not as a director that "Molière" here regains author-ity over "his own" text. "Molière" manages to speak again as authorial first reader—i.e., as Molière—only at the moment when he takes over the part of "Brécourt." It may seem paradoxical that, for the playwright to *step back* into his original relation with his text, he must *step on* into (yet a further) role. But because it is in (each) role that the first-reader aspect of a dramatic text resides, the "original relation" of the playwright to his text was itself just such a stepping into role. The character "Molière's" discovery of his identity as dramatic author within the particular role of "Brécourt" recapitulates within the fiction of the play the process by which Molière himself discovered in the role of "Molière" (or "Brécourt" or any of the others) his identity as author of the play. (The *Impromptu of Versailles* is, of course, a play much given to such recapitulations of its own processes.)

The appearance of a playwright in one of his own roles—Shakespeare as the Ghost, Molière as "Molière," "Molière" as "Brécourt"—is obviously a special case. Yet it is a situation that images, far better than a solo reading by the playwright could do, his fundamental imaginative act. The passing of the author into some one role reenacts that passing of the authorial function into roles which is playwriting. The specialness of the case consists only in the focus on some *one* role.

For an image of the more general situation we might turn to another play much given to recapitulations of its own processes, Pirandello's *Each in His Own Way*. If in the *Impromptu of Versailles* the author disappears into a given role which thereby emerges as authorial, in *Each in His Own Way* the author *simply* disappears, and *every* role claims to be the one into which he has vanished—that is to say, claims authorship. Pirandello's comedy depicts a crowd of outraged, curious, puzzled spectators reacting to a fictionalized dramatization by "Pirandello" of a well-known scandal of the day. As is not surprising, given this theatricalist premise, *Each in His Own Way* contains all sorts of theater personnel: actors, ushers, technicians, administrators, etc. It does not, however, contain a dramatic author: "Pirandello," we learn at one point, may be in the theater;[107] but when he is called upon to speak (act 2, pp. 355–56), no one appears. What we get instead is a parade of quasi-authorial figures: an Old Author, a Literary Man, a Stage Manager, and no fewer than five Dramatic Critics. Indeed, even the exasperated spectator-characters must be numbered among these quasi-authors, since each of them, it turns out, has an "author-itative" reading to propose:

> [VARIOUS AUDIENCE VOICES.] First it's this, and then it's
>   something else!
> First they said one thing, but now they say the opposite!
> It's a joke on the audience!
> . . . .
> But why is he always harping on this illusion and reality string?
> That's not my view of it!

It's just a way of saying things!
Hasn't he expressed it?
Well, expression is art, and art is expression!

. . . .

But a single conception may present different phases, according as
you look at it, providing it be a whole conception of life.

. . . .

Yes, but supposing it didn't pretend to have any meaning?

(act 1, pp. 316–17)

To anyone but themselves the limitations of each of these "sole
qualified" claimants to author status are clear enough: The Old Author
has never had a play accepted; the Literary Man and the Stage Manager
do not write; the Dramatic Critics produce only readings of other texts;
the onlookers merely look on. Yet where no reader clearly comes first
every reading is equally authoritative.

> ANOTHER MAN: *(vehemently)* He took the plot out of the news-
> papers!

(act 1, p. 318)

The "crabbed page" from which only the authorial first reader may read
has become a newspaper page from which everybody may read, "each
in his own way." To play *any* character in this script is to play the
authorial first reader; in the absence of "Pirandello" every one of its roles
claims to be the role of author.

Once again, how but in explicitness does this differ from the general
case? From any dramatic text its author is absent (or, if present, is present, as we have seen, only as an illustration of his own susceptibility to
challenge by others). In every dramatic text the characters—and here,
notwithstanding the title of their quest, we must include Pirandello's
famous six—are in search not of an author but of author status for
themselves, of an opportunity to stand in the place of the authorial first
reader.

From this place the author of the play himself has necessarily with-
drawn, since it is in this withdrawal that his act of authorship fundamentally consists. Every dramatic author may read his fate in that of "the
Author" of Roger Vitrac's surrealist play *The Mysteries of Love,* who
enters in the act of shooting himself.[108] To enter upon playwriting will

be the "death" of the author as first reader. For it is precisely the play-wright's having vacated this position which sets in motion that clamor of conflicting claims to succeed him which is the dramatic text. Before it represents characters, action, or the human condition, a play represents authorial first reading in dispersal, and to write a play is *to write this dispersal*. The playwright thus defines himself as an author by relinquishing what writers of every other sort define themselves by asserting.[109] He *writes away* his first-reader claim—writes it, not out *of,* but out *over,* the dramatic text, which is to say, ultimately, out over a group of actors.

This is why, to revert to the question raised at the outset of this chapter, relations between actor and author on a view of acting as reading cannot be reduced to the commonsense formulation: The actor *reads* what the author *writes*. What the actor "reads" in the writing of the playwright is first of all the possibility of himself as a reader. To write for actors is not so much to give actors something to read as to give them to themselves as readers, to *write them into action* as readers. Ultimately, it is from the practice of playwriting that theory learns the ambition to write acting as reading.

Notes

Chapter 1

1. John McPhee, "North of the C. P. Line," *New Yorker* (November 26, 1984): 78.

2. Michael Lemonick, "Now: Driving by Satellite," *Science Digest* (December 1984): 34.

3. Paul de Man, *Allegories of Reading* (New Haven, Conn.: Yale University Press, 1979), 192.

4. Dante, *The Divine Comedy*, ed. and trans. Charles S. Singleton (Princeton, N.J.: Princeton University Press, 1975), *Paradiso* 1, canto 33, lines 85–89, 377. All subsequent references to *The Divine Comedy* are to this edition, by volume, canto, line, and page for text volumes (*Inferno* 1, *Purgatorio* 1, and *Paradiso* 1) and by volume and page alone for note volumes (*Inferno* 2, *Purgatorio* 2, and *Paradiso* 2).

5. Quoted in Ernst Robert Curtius, *European Literature and the Latin Middle Ages* (New York: Harper and Row, 1953), 323. Curtius gives further examples of this trope on pp. 321–32.

6. Eleanor J. Gibson and Harry Levin, *The Psychology of Reading* (Cambridge: MIT Press, 1975), 438.

7. Robert G. Crowder, *The Psychology of Reading* (New York: Oxford University Press, 1982), 3.

8. Bertolt Brecht, *Brecht on Theatre*, ed. and trans. John Willett (New York: Hill and Wang, 1964), 139.

9. Vsevolod Meyerhold, *Meyerhold on Theatre*, ed. and trans. Edward Braun (New York: Hill and Wang, 1969), 198.

10. Jerzy Grotowski, *Towards a Poor Theatre* (Holstebro, Denmark: Odin Teatrets Forlag, 1968), 34.

11. Antonin Artaud, *The Theater and Its Double* (New York: Grove Press, 1958), 13.

12. Quoted in *Rockaby*, a film by D. A. Pennebaker and Chris Hegedus documenting rehearsals for the American premiere of Samuel Beckett's play *Rockaby*.

13. Quoted in "Style," *New Yorker* (July 30, 1984): 25.

14. Viola Spolin, *Improvisation for the Theater* (Evanston, Ill.: Northwestern University Press, 1969), 4.

15. Toby Cole and Helen Krich Chinoy, eds., *Actors on Acting* (New York: Crown, 1962), 50, 57.

16. "Style," *New Yorker* (July 30, 1984): 25.

17. Eric A. Havelock, *The Literate Revolution in Greece and Its Cultural Consequences* (Princeton, N.J.: Princeton University Press, 1982), 280.

18. "Manuscripts . . . were read by actors" (ibid., 310); "tragedies were read by . . . tragedians, comedians" (Oliver Taplin, *The Stagecraft of Aeschylus* [Oxford: Oxford University Press, 1977], 16).

19. Henry R. Immerwahr, "Book Rolls on Attic Vases," in *Classical, Medieval and Renaissance Studies in Honor of Berthold Louis Ullman,* ed. Charles Henderson, Jr. (Rome: Edizioni di Storia e Letteratura, 1964), 46. See also the descriptions of reading scenes on individual Greek vases, pp. 29–31.

20. R. W. Ingram, ed., *Records of Early English Drama: COVENTRY* (Toronto: University of Toronto Press, 1981), 86; William Tydeman, *The Theatre in the Middle Ages* (Cambridge: Cambridge University Press, 1978), 207.

21. W. W. Greg, *Dramatic Documents from the Elizabethan Playhouses: Commentary* (Oxford: Oxford University Press, 1969), 173–75.

22. Cole and Chinoy, *Actors on Acting,* 100, 136, 406, 209.

23. Uta Hagen with Haskel Frankel, *Respect for Acting* (New York: Macmillan, 1973), 13.

24. Eileen Blumenthal, *Joseph Chaikin* (Cambridge: Cambridge University Press, 1984), 151.

25. Vasily Osipovich Toporov, *Stanislavski in Rehearsal: The Final Years* (New York: Theatre Arts Books, 1979), 42–43.

26. Johann Wolfgang von Goethe, *Wilhelm Meister's Apprenticeship,* trans. Thomas Carlyle (New York: Collier, 1962), 289–90.

27. Cole and Chinoy, *Actors on Acting,* 46.

28. Joseph A. Jungmann, *The Mass of the Roman Rite* (New York: Benziger, 1951), 1:409–10.

29. John H. Miller, *Fundamentals of the Liturgy* (Notre Dame, Ind.: Fides, 1959), 481.

30. See E. Catherine Dunn, "Voice Structure in the Liturgical Drama: Septet Reconsidered," in *Medieval English Drama: Essays Critical and Contextual,* ed. Jerome Taylor and Alan H. Nelson (Chicago: University of Chicago Press, 1972), 44–63.

31. Ibid., 56–58.

32. Jungmann, *Mass of the Roman Rite,* 432–33.

33. See chapter 5.

34. It is not always clear in a given passage (at least in English translation) whether Stanislavski is referring to the actor reading to himself, reading with others, or being read to. But this does not affect my present point. *Any* of these possibilities argues for a connection between acting and some aspect of reading.

35. Cole and Chinoy, *Actors on Acting,* 427.

36. Constantin Stanislavski, *Creating a Role*, trans. Elizabeth Reynolds Hapgood (1961; reprint, New York: Routledge/Theatre Arts Books, 1989), 208.

37. Ibid., 7. See also Constantin Stanislavski, *An Actor Prepares*, trans. Elizabeth Reynolds Hapgood (1936; reprint, New York: Routledge/Theatre Arts Books, 1989), 252. Stanislavski also compares theater*going* to reading.

38. Stanislavski, *Creating a Role*, 3, 4, 112, 5.

39. Constantin Stanislavski, *Building a Character*, trans. Elizabeth Reynolds Hapgood (1949; reprint, New York: Routledge/Theatre Arts Books, 1989), 112.

40. The phrase "illusion of the first time" is not, as is sometimes thought, Stanislavski's but, rather, William Gillette's. See Cole and Chinoy, *Actors on Acting*, 486.

41. Lee Strasberg, *Strasberg at the Actors Studio* (New York: Viking, 1965), 283.

42. Brecht, *On Theatre*, 137.

43. Grotowski, *Towards a Poor Theatre*, 23, 57.

44. David Cole, *The Theatrical Event* (Middletown, Conn.: Wesleyan University Press, 1977), 148–50.

45. Artaud, *Theatre and Its Double*, 10, 100, 99.

46. Spolin, *Improvisation for the Theater*, 75.

47. Stanislavski, *Actor Prepares*, 33, 37. See also Stanislavski, *Creating a Role*, 48–49.

48. Norman N. Holland, *The Dynamics of Literary Response* (1968; reprint, New York: Columbia University Press, 1989), 73.

49. Stanislavski, *Actor Prepares*, 97.

50. Ibid., 120. See also 44, 81–87.

51. Ibid., 82. See also 262.

52. Reuben A. Brower, "Reading in Slow Motion," in *In Defense of Reading*, ed. Reuben A. Brower and Richard Poirier (New York: Dutton, 1962), 11.

53. Stanley Fish, *Is There a Text in This Class?* (Cambridge: Harvard University Press, 1980), 14.

54. Anton Chekhov, *The Sea Gull*, in *Best Plays*, trans. Stark Young (New York: Random House, 1956), act 2, 26. Subsequent references to Chekhov plays are by act and page number of this edition.

55. J. M. Lotman, quoted in Wolfgang Iser, *The Act of Reading* (Baltimore: Johns Hopkins University Press, 1978), 66.

56. Georges Poulet, "Lecture et interprétation du texte littéraire," in *Qu'est-ce qu'un texte?* ed. Edmond Barbotin (Paris: Librairie José Corti, 1975), 65 (my translation).

57. Ibid., 64.

58. Plato, *Phaedrus*, in *Plato*, trans. Harold North Fowler (Cambridge: Harvard University Press, 1931), vol. 1, sec. 264c, 529 (translation slightly modified).

59. John O'Neill, *Essaying Montaigne: A Study of the Renaissance Institution of Reading and Writing* (London: Routledge and Kegan Paul, 1982), 84.

60. Philo, quoted in Daniel Chanan Matt, ed., *Zohar: The Book of Enlight-*

enment (New York: Paulist Press, 1983), 206. Similar remarks of Origen and Rumi, cited by Matt, suggest that such a body-and-soul view of the sacred text is also present in Christianity and Islam.

61. Georges Poulet, quoted in Iser, *Act of Reading,* 154.

62. Mariann Sanders Regan, *Love Words: The Self and the Text in Medieval and Renaissance Poetry* (Ithaca, N.Y.: Cornell University Press, 1982), 19.

63. Marcel Proust, "Sur la lecture" (On Reading), in *Pleasures and Days and Other Writings,* ed. F. W. Dupee (New York: Howard Fertig, 1978), 212–13. Dupee gives the title of this essay as "Ruskin and Others" because it first appeared in book form as the preface to Proust's translation of Ruskin's *Sesame and Lilies.* Proust's own title for his preface was "Sur la lecture."

64. B. L. Packer, *Emerson's Fall* (New York: Continuum, 1982), 120.

65. Roland Barthes, *The Pleasure of the Text* (New York: Hill and Wang, 1975), 6.

66. Harold Brodkey, "Reading, the Most Dangerous Game," *New York Times Book Review* (November 24, 1985): 1.

67. Julia Kristeva, *Desire in Language* (New York: Columbia University Press, 1980), 120.

68. Iser, *Act of Reading,* 80, 66.

69. Regan, *Love Words,* 43.

70. Ibid., 37.

71. Harold Bloom, *The Breaking of the Vessels* (Chicago: University of Chicago Press, 1982), 34.

72. For further discussion of the relation between solitary reading, its interruption, and rehearsal, see chapter 5.

73. For more on the relation between active and passive elements in acting and in reading, see discussion in chapter 4.

74. Philip Collins, ed., *Charles Dickens: The Public Readings* (Oxford: Oxford University Press, 1975), lvii (italics added).

75. For further examples, see Edwin Cohen, *Oral Interpretation* (Chicago: Science Research Associates, 1977), 126; and Mary Frances Hopkins and Brent Bouldin, "Professional Group Performance of Nondramatic Literature in New York," in *Performance of Literature in Historical Perspectives,* ed. David W. Thompson (Lanham, Md.: University Press of America, 1983), 697–717.

76. See chapter 5.

77. Georges Poulet, "Criticism and the Experience of Interiority," in *Reader-Response Criticism,* ed. Jane P. Tompkins (Baltimore: Johns Hopkins University Press, 1980), 42.

78. Ludwig Wittgenstein, *Philosophical Investigations* (New York: Macmillan, 1969), 65e.

79. Cole, *Theatrical Event,* 3–6.

80. Fredric Jameson, *The Political Unconscious* (Ithaca, N.Y.: Cornell University Press, 1981), 9.

81. Aristophanes, *The Frogs,* trans. Richmond Lattimore (New York: New American Library, 1962), ll. 52–54, 66–67, pp. 19–20. "This is the first explicit

allusion to reading as a private act," according to Havelock, *Literate Revolution in Greece*, 204, 207 nn. 42, 43.

82. That the pleasure Dionysus expects to obtain from his recovery is of a specifically gastronomic sort—"DIONYSUS: Did you ever feel a sudden longing for baked beans? [. . .] Well, that's the kind of craving that I feel . . . for Euripides" (ll. 62, 66–67, translation slightly modified)—anticipates my argument that the "lost" physical dimension of reading which acting recovers is, precisely, its *oral* aspect. See chapters 3 and 4.

Chapter 2

1. Actually, as Jane P. Tompkins points out, ancient and romantic criticism were already much concerned with questions of reader response; it is the conscious foregrounding of the reading process as a distinct object of study which is new in our era. See Tompkins, *Reader-Response Criticism*, 201–32.

2. Shoshana Felman, "Turning the Screw of Interpretation," *Yale French Studies*, nos. 55–56 (1977): 118.

3. Umberto Eco, *The Role of the Reader* (Bloomington: Indiana University Press, 1979), 18–19.

4. Vincent B. Leitch, *Deconstructive Criticism* (New York: Columbia University Press, 1983), 184.

5. Robert Moynihan, "Interview with Paul de Man," *Yale Review* 73, no. 4 (Summer 1984): 591.

6. Felman, "Turning the Screw," 142.

7. See chapter 1 n. 52.

8. Stanley Fish, *Self-Consuming Artifacts* (Berkeley: University of California Press, 1972), 389.

9. Roland Barthes, *S/Z* (New York: Hill and Wang, 1974), 12–13.

10. Brower, "Reading in Slow Motion," 6.

11. John Preston, *The Created Self: The Reader's Role in Eighteenth-Century Fiction* (London: Heinemann, 1970), 204–5.

12. Walter J. Ong, "The Writer's Audience Is Always a Fiction," *PMLA* 90, no. 1 (January 1975): 13.

13. Felman, "Turning the Screw," 114–15.

14. O'Neill, *Essaying Montaigne*, 84.

15. Poulet, "Criticism and the Experience of Interiority," 44.

16. Iser, *Act of Reading*, 19.

17. Harold Bloom, *Agon: Towards a Theory of Revisionism* (New York: Oxford University Press, 1982), 17.

18. Fish, *Self-Consuming Artifacts*, 382.

19. Virginia Woolf, *To the Lighthouse* (New York: Harcourt, Brace, 1927), 283. This passage was called to my attention by Susan Cole.

20. Fish, *Self-Consuming Artifacts*, xi.

21. Bloom, *Breaking of the Vessels*, 13.

22. Leitch, *Deconstructive Criticism*, 184, 75.

23. Vicki Mistacco, "The Theory and Practice of Reading Nouveaux Romans: Robbe-Grillet's *Topologie d'une cité fantôme*," in *The Reader in the Text,* ed. Susan R. Suleiman and Inge Crosman (Princeton, N.J.: Princeton University Press, 1980), 382; and Stanley Fish, *Surprised by Sin: The Reader in Paradise Lost* (Berkeley: University of California Press, 1971), xiii.

24. Fish, *Surprised by Sin,* 206.

25. Northrop Frye, quoted in Robert DeMaria, Jr., "The Ideal Reader: A Critical Fiction," *PMLA* 93, no. 4 (October 1978): 468.

26. Norman N. Holland, *Five Readers Reading* (New Haven, Conn.: Yale University Press, 1975), 12.

27. Barthes, *S/Z,* 10–11, 4.

28. Holland, *Five Readers Reading,* 122; Fish, *Is There a Text in This Class,* 327.

29. Stanley Fish, "Why No One's Afraid of Wolfgang Iser," *Diacritics* 11 (Spring 1981): 4.

30. Norman N. Holland, *Poems in Persons* (1973; reprint, New York: Columbia University Press, 1989), 145, 117.

31. Tompkins, *Reader-Response Criticism,* xiv.

32. The term is Roman Ingarden's. See ibid., 247.

33. Mistacco, "Theory and Practice of Reading Nouveaux Romans," 392.

34. Poulet, "Criticism and the Experience of Interiority," 47.

35. Barthes, *S/Z,* 10. Though I have earlier cited a passage from *S/Z* as illustrating structuralist attitudes, I do not now hesitate to place Barthes among the poststructuralists, since, as Elizabeth Bruss points out, "despite his identification with structuralism in the Anglo-American mind," Barthes "absorbed the implications of poststructuralism far more fully than all but a few of its local partisans" (*Beautiful Theories* [Baltimore: Johns Hopkins University Press, 1982], 284).

36. Jacques Derrida, *Dissemination* (Chicago: University of Chicago Press, 1981), 290.

37. Fish, "Why No One's Afraid of Wolfgang Iser," 3. Fish is here paraphrasing Iser's views.

38. Fish, *Self-Consuming Artifacts,* 406.

39. Bloom, *Breaking of the Vessels,* 32.

40. Leitch, *Deconstructive Criticism,* 104.

41. de Man, *Allegories of Reading,* 17.

42. Jacques Derrida, quoted in Robert Crosman, "Do Readers Make Meaning?" in Suleiman and Crosman, *Reader in the Text,* 149.

43. Barthes, *S/Z,* 10.

44. Ralph Waldo Emerson, *Emerson in His Journals,* ed. Joel Porte (Cambridge: Harvard University Press, 1982), 152.

45. Holland, *Five Readers Reading,* 122 (italics added).

46. On the other hand, there is considerable warrant for viewing the *writer's* creativity as a kind of *reading.* See chapter 7.

47. Tompkins, *Reader-Response Criticism,* 248.

48. Iser, *Act of Reading,* 168.

49. Ibid., 185.

50. Barthes, *S/Z*, 105.

51. There is, of course, a kind of acting which consists as much in a writerly "laying out" of blanks as in a readerly "filling in" of them—namely, improvisation. And, consequently, as we shall see in chapter 4, it is less of a mistake to say of improvising actors than of the general run of readers that they "write their reading," not because the reading process as such consists in writing but because in improvisation the moments of reading and writing cannot be distinguished.

52. Stanislavski, *Actor Prepares*, 257.

53. Iser, *Act of Reading*, 168.

54. Stanislavski, *Building a Character*, 113. The link between Stanislavski and at least one active reader has been pointed out by René Wellek. The Shakespearean critic A. C. Bradley, Wellek notes, "quite deliberately attempt[s] to fill out the gaps in the depiction of a character. . . . Though Bradley may not have heard of Stanislavski, his method resembles that of the Russian producer." See René Wellek, *A History of Modern Criticism* (New Haven, Conn.: Yale University Press, 1986), 5:32.

55. Eco, *Role of the Reader*, 29.

56. Stanislavski, *Actor Prepares*, 52.

57. Barthes, *S/Z*, 151.

58. Preston, *Created Self*, 207.

59. None of this is to deny that there is an overlap between *acting* and *writing* (on the contrary, my discussions of improvisation in chapter 4 and of the playwright-actor relation in chapter 7 both presuppose such an overlap), only that the resemblance is on the score of "realizing" texts or "filling in blanks." For more on reading—and, specifically, the actor's reading—as a filling in of blanks, see chapter 5.

Chapter 3

1. André Kertész, *On Reading* (Harmondsworth: Penguin, 1982).

2. Stanislavski, *Creating a Role*, 5.

3. Quoted in Robert DeMaria, Jr., " 'The Thinker as Reader': The Figure of the Reader in the Writing of Wallace Stevens," *Genre* 12 (1979): 265.

4. Quoted in Stanley Burnshaw, *The Seamless Web* (New York: Braziller, 1970), 12.

5. Jean-Paul Sartre, *The Words* (New York: Fawcett, 1969), 31.

6. Franz Kafka, *Diaries: 1910–1923*, ed. Max Brod (Harmondsworth: Penguin, 1964), 180.

7. Burnshaw, *Seamless Web*, 13.

8. Gibson and Levin, *Psychology of Reading*, 445–46.

9. Ibid., 351–52; Crowder, *Psychology of Reading*, 7.

10. Gibson and Levin, *Psychology of Reading*, 189, 352.

11. Ibid., 359.

12. Poulet, "Lecture et interprétation," 67–68.

13. As we shall see, the dialectic of *toward* and *away* impulses in interpretation, which visual saccades and regressions physicalize, can be traced back to the interplay of passive and active oral impulses on which reading itself is structured. (See chap. 4.)

14. Likewise, recovery of voice, in the acting process, is one of the surest signs that a more general recovery of "lost" physicality is underway. For the voice as "first to go, first to return," see chapter 4.

15. See, for example, Bernard M. W. Knox, "Silent Reading in Antiquity," *Greek, Roman and Byzantine Studies* 9, no. 4 (Winter 1968): 427, 432–33; F. D. Harvey, "Literacy in the Athenian Democracy," *Revue des études grecs* 79, no. 378 (December 1966): 632 n. 14; and Eric A. Havelock, *Preface to Plato* (Cambridge: Harvard University Press, 1963), 56 n. 18.

16. Knox, "Silent Reading in Antiquity," 421.

17. St. Augustine, *The Confessions,* trans. Rex Warner (New York: New American Library, 1963), 114–15. See also C. S. Lewis's discussion of this passage in *The Allegory of Love* (New York: Oxford University Press, 1958), 64–65.

18. Augustine, *Confessions,* 114–15.

19. Jean Leclercq, *The Love of Learning and the Desire for God* (New York: Fordham University Press, 1961), 19.

20. St. Benedict, *Rule for Monasteries,* trans. Leonard J. Doyle (Collegeville, Minn.: Liturgical Press, 1948), 67.

21. John Gower, *Confessio Amantis,* ll. 893–94 (my translation; italics added), quoted in Ruth Crosby, "Oral Delivery in the Middle Ages," *Speculum* 11, no. 1 (January 1936): 99.

22. Leclercq, *Love of Learning,* 19.

23. H. J. Chaytor, *From Script to Print* (Cambridge: Cambridge University Press, 1945), 145.

24. Ibid., 10. See also 13.

25. Leclercq, *Love of Learning,* 21–22.

26. Quoted in Chaytor, *From Script to Print,* 14–15.

27. Gibson and Levin, *Psychology of Reading,* 342.

28. Ibid., 340, 349.

29. Crowder, *Psychology of Reading,* 167–68, 78.

30. Gillian Cohen, "The Psychology of Reading," *New Literary History* 4, no. 1 (Autumn 1972): 82; Gibson and Levin, *Psychology of Reading,* 345.

31. Proust, "On Reading," 193, 183–84 (italics added).

32. Leclercq, *Love of Learning,* 19.

33. Quoted in Catherine M. Bauschatz, "Montaigne's Conception of Reading in the Context of Renaissance Poetics and Modern Criticism," in Suleiman and Crosman, *Reader in the Text,* 265.

34. Henry David Thoreau, *Walden* (New York: Holt, Rinehart and Winston, 1964), 82.

35. Leclercq, *Love of Learning,* 20–21, 90.

36. Harold Bloom, *A Map of Misreading* (New York: Oxford University Press, 1975), 165.

37. Brower, "Reading in Slow Motion," 11.

38. Walter J. Slatoff, *With Respect to Readers* (Ithaca, N.Y.: Cornell University Press, 1970), 6.

39. Sartre, *The Words*, 31.

40. Eugene R. Kintgen, *The Perception of Poetry* (Bloomington: Indiana University Press, 1983), 177.

41. J. Hillis Miller, quoted in Leitch, *Deconstructive Criticism*, 192. Compare Georges Poulet's toward and away "dance" of interpretation.

42. Eco, *Role of the Reader*, 33.

43. Jonathan Culler, *Structuralist Poetics* (Ithaca, N.Y.: Cornell University Press, 1975), 130.

44. Barthes, *Pleasure of the Text*, 31.

45. Barthes, *S/Z*, 93.

46. Ibid., 92.

47. Fish, *Self-Consuming Artifacts*, 42.

48. This must be understood in the context of the more general critical tendency, noted above, to view texts as "others" and relations with texts as relations with "others."

49. Leitch, *Deconstructive Criticism*, 115. Leitch is paraphrasing Barthes's *S/Z*.

50. O'Neill, *Essaying Montaigne*, 91.

51. Poulet, "Lecture et interprétation," 67.

52. Maurice Blanchot, *The Gaze of Orpheus* (Barrytown, N.Y.: Station Hill, 1981), 94, 95.

53. Barthes, *S/Z*, 82–83.

54. Holland, *Dynamics of Literary Response*, 162, 12–27 (see esp. p. 27).

55. Ibid., 67.

56. Anna Freud, *The Ego and the Mechanisms of Defense* (New York: International Universities Press, 1966), 44–53.

57. Holland, *Dynamics of Literary Response*, 58, 131, 75.

58. Ibid., 311–12.

59. Ibid., 101, 67.

60. Ibid., 36, 261.

61. Ibid., 79, 38.

62. Holland, *Poems in Persons*, 97.

63. Holland, *Dynamics of Literary Response*, 79.

64. Ibid., 89.

65. Ibid., 75.

66. Holland, *Poems in Persons*, 85; and *Five Readers Reading*, 18. I have added a couple of examples ("relishes," "savors") to Holland's list.

67. Beryl Smalley, *The Study of the Bible in the Middle Ages* (Notre Dame, Ind.: University of Notre Dame Press, 1970), 179.

68. Quoted in Fish, *Surprised by Sin*, 84.

69. Quoted in Holland, *Dynamics of Literary Response*, 75.

70. Quoted in ibid.

71. Leclercq, *Love of Learning*, 90.

72. Quoted in ibid., 42.

73. See, however, my discussion of "eating the book" in chapter 4.

74. Quoted in Holland, *Dynamics of Literary Response*, 76.

75. As for the other major class of physical activity metaphors for reading—those involving physical interaction with other people—we have already begun to see (and shall see in more detail in the final section of chapter 4) how compatible this is with an oral account of reading.

76. See, for example, Holland's essay on Lacan and Derrida, "Re-Covering 'The Purloined Letter': Reading as a Personal Transaction," in Suleiman and Crosman, *Reader in the Text*, 350–70.

77. These arguments are: (1) that Holland disregards the social nature of language (Elizabeth Wright, *Psychoanalytic Criticism* [London: Methuen, 1984], 67–68); (2) that in his later work he has "transferred the concept of unity from text to person" (Jonathan Culler, "Prolegomena to a Theory of Reading," in Suleiman and Crosman, *Reader in the Text*, 55; see also Robert Con Davis, "Lacan, Poe, and Narrative Repression," in *Lacan and Narration*, ed. Robert Con Davis [Baltimore: Johns Hopkins University Press, 1983], 1000–2); and (3) that his view of texts as balances of drives and defenses merely restates the traditional neoclassical view of art as conveying both instruction and delight (Meredith Anne Skura, *The Literary Use of the Psychoanalytic Process* [New Haven, Conn.: Yale University Press, 1981], 65–66).

78. For Holland's presentation of identity themes, see his "Unity Identity Text Self," in Tompkins, *Reader-Response Criticism*, 118–35, esp. 126–27. For critiques of this notion, see the Culler and Davis passages cited in the preceding note.

79. It is to the experience of the flesh-and-blood reader, with whose need to "lurch" back and forth between *different* strategies of anxiety-management—a need stressed elsewhere by Holland himself (e.g., at *Dynamics of Literary Response*, 313)—that the notion of a single identity theme seems inadequate. On the other hand, the view of a character in a text as a "reader" who displays some single strategy of anxiety-management will prove useful in my chapter 4 account of characters as "single-solution" readers, whose fixed reading identities actors at once assume and resist assuming.

80. Donald Pease, "J. Hillis Miller: The Other Victorian at Yale," in *The Yale Critics: Deconstruction in America*, ed. Jonathan Arac, Wlad Godzich, and Wallace Martin (Minneapolis: University of Minnesota Press, 1983), 67, 73.

81. Holland, *Dynamics of Literary Response*, 67.

82. Stanislavski, *Creating a Role*, 232.

83. J. Culler, "Prolegomena to a Theory of Reading," 56.

84. Sherry Turkle, *Psychoanalytic Politics* (New York: Basic Books, 1978), 58.

85. Malcolm Bowie, "Jacques Lacan," in *Structuralism and After*, ed. John Sturrock (Oxford: Oxford University Press, 1979), 123.

86. Turkle, *Psychoanalytic Politics*, 58.

87. See Anika Lemaire, *Jacques Lacan* (London: Routledge and Kegan Paul, 1979), 176–79.

88. Turkle, *Psychoanalytic Politics*, 58.

89. See Ellie Ragland-Sullivan, *Jacques Lacan and the Philosophy of Psychoanalysis* (Urbana: University of Illinois Press, 1986), 233–58. The young Lacan sought a still more extensive "rhetoricization" of the psyche (ibid., 233), perhaps comparable to Holland's trope/defense schema.

90. For the specific nature of Holland's link to ego psychology, see Wright, *Psychoanalytic Criticism*, 63–65, esp. 65.

91. J. Culler, "Prolegomena to a Theory of Reading," 56.

92. Quoted in Lemaire, *Jacques Lacan*, 72.

93. Holland, *Dynamics of Literary Response*, 79.

94. Augustine, *Confessions*, 114.

95. Ibid. (italics added).

96. Gustave Flaubert, *Madame Bovary*, trans. Eleanor Marx Aveling (translation revised by Paul de Man) (New York: Norton, 1965), 41.

97. Proust, "On Reading," 184, 183, 191, 182.

98. Ibid., 183.

99. In chapter 1, I suggested that solitary reading is continuous with the entrance of the other who seems to interrupt it, because reading is already interaction with another. Now I am proposing that solitary reading is likewise continuous with the eating that seems to interrupt it, because to read is already to eat. Clearly, these two continuities are related. In fact, they are ultimately equivalent, since, as will become clear in chapter 4, each finds its prototype in the infant-mother relationship, where *to eat* and *to interact* were as yet the same experience.

Chapter 4

1. Ezekiel 2:9–3:3.

2. Revelation 10:8–10.

3. The phrase is from the Book of Common Prayer, quoted in Holland, *Dynamics of Literary Response*, 75.

4. Stanislavski, *Creating a Role*, 5.

5. Holland, *Dynamics of Literary Response*, 79.

6. Albrecht Dürer, "St. John Devours the Book," from the series of woodcuts *Revelation of St. John*, in *Complete Woodcuts*, ed. Willi Kurth (New York: Crown, 1946), pl. 114.

7. We shall see in chapter 6, however, that being read to is no more simply a passive experience than is reading itself.

8. Holland, *Dynamics of Literary Response*, 79, 73.

9. Exercise devised by Tina Packer for the actors of Shakespeare and Company, as demonstrated by Packer on *Herman Badillo's Urban Journal*, New York, WPIX, Channel 11, January 17, 1984.

10. Alan W. Miller, *The God of Daniel S.* (London: Macmillan, 1969), 223.

11. Jungmann, *Mass of the Roman Rite*, 419, 444, 449–51.

12. William Shakespeare, *The Tempest*, act 2, sc. 2, lines 135, 148. This and all subsequent Shakespeare references are to *The Complete Signet Classic Shakespeare*, ed. Sylvan Barnet et al. (New York: Harcourt Brace Jovanovich, 1972).

13. Jungmann, *Mass of the Roman Rite,* 451.

14. Miguel de Cervantes, *Don Quixote,* trans. Samuel Putnam (New York: Viking, 1949), 947.

15. Crowder, *Psychology of Reading,* 195.

16. Holland, *Dynamics of Literary Response,* 310.

17. Holland, *Five Readers Reading,* 116.

18. Holland, *Poems in Persons,* 83.

19. Harold Bloom, *Kabbalah and Criticism* (New York: Seabury Press, 1975), 104.

20. Bauschatz, "Montaigne's Conception of Reading," 271 n. 10.

21. Proust, "On Reading," 206 (italics added, except for those of the word *object*).

22. Michel de Montaigne, *Complete Essays,* trans. Donald M. Frame (Stanford: Stanford University Press, 1971), 111. Montaigne is actually speaking of the ideal *tutor* here but of the tutor as active reader on behalf of his students.

23. Ezekiel 2:8.

24. Freud, quoted in Holland, *Dynamics of Literary Response,* 34.

25. Holland, *Dynamics of Literary Response,* 35.

26. Poulet, "Criticism and the Experience of Interiority," 42.

27. Stanislavski, *Creating a Role,* 232.

28. Holland, *Dynamics of Literary Response,* 37, 36–37.

29. Ibid., 37.

30. Charles Brenner, *An Elementary Textbook of Psychoanalysis* (Garden City, N.Y.: Doubleday, 1957), 104.

31. Freud, quoted in Holland, *Dynamics of Literary Response,* 278. In this and the quotation cited in the next note, it is, strictly speaking, "identification" that is being described, but for all practical purposes "the terms *introjection* and *incorporation* are . . . essentially synonymous with the term *identification*" (Brenner, *Elementary Textbook of Psychoanalysis,* 104).

32. Brenner, *Elementary Textbook of Psychoanalysis,* 104.

33. In view of this convergence, for the present I shall not carefully distinguish between the actor's transaction with the *text as a whole* and his transaction with *role* or *character.* Later in this chapter, however, it will prove necessary to do so.

34. Robert Graves, *The Greek Myths* (Baltimore: Penguin, 1966), 1:39.

35. Holland, *Dynamics of Literary Response,* 37.

36. Graves, *Greek Myths,* 1:46.

37. Jean-Pierre Vernant, "The Union with Metis and the Sovereignty of Heaven," in *Myth, Religion and Society,* ed. R. L. Gordon (Cambridge: Cambridge University Press, 1981), 2.

38. Holland, *Dynamics of Literary Response,* 35.

39. Vernant, "Union with Metis," 1.

40. Marcel Proust, *Swann's Way* (New York: Random House, 1970), 63.

41. Harold Bloom, *The Anxiety of Influence* (London: Oxford University Press, 1973), 57.

42. Cervantes, *Don Quixote,* 912, 696.

43. Dan Jacobson, *The Story of the Stories* (New York: Harper and Row, 1982), 131–32.

44. Holland, *Dynamics of Literary Response*, 80.

45. Ibid., 180, 179. See also p. 87.

46. Shakespeare, *The Tempest*, act 2, sc. 2, lines 135, 148; act 3, sc. 2, line 13.

47. *The Tempest*, act 4, sc. 1, lines 181–84; act 1, sc. 2, lines 109–10; act 5, sc. 1, lines 56–57.

48. Quoted in Barthes, *Pleasure of the Text*, 62.

49. Pease, "J. Hillis Miller," 73.

50. Holland, *Five Readers Reading*, 19; *Dynamics of Literary Response*, 81–82, 87, 90.

51. Cervantes, *Don Quixote*, 640–41.

52. Poulet, "Lecture et interprétation," 72.

53. Holland, *Five Readers Reading*, 39 (italics added).

54. Quoted in Terence Cave, *The Cornucopian Text: Problems of Writing in the French Renaissance* (Oxford: Oxford University Press, 1979), 37.

55. Preston, *Created Self*, 200.

56. Wallace Stevens, "The House Was Quiet and the World Was Calm," in *Collected Poems* (New York: Knopf, 1969), 358.

57. Poulet, "Criticism and the Experience of Interiority," 42.

58. Toby Cole and Helen Krich Chinoy, eds., *Directors on Directing* (Indianapolis: Bobbs-Merrill, 1963), 116; Stanislavski, *Creating a Role*, 232.

59. Iser, *Act of Reading*, 134.

60. Fish, *Surprised by Sin*, 107.

61. Stanislavski, *Creating a Role*, 25.

62. Slatoff, *With Respect to Readers*, 46–47.

63. Preston, *Created Self*, 5.

64. Ibid., 206. The sentences in quotation marks are from Diderot's *Paradoxe sur le comédien*. Preston quotes Diderot in the original French; the translation is mine.

65. Stanislavski, *Creating a Role*, 252.

66. Grotowski, *Towards a Poor Theatre*, 17.

67. Quoted in Collins, *Charles Dickens: The Public Readings*, 213.

68. Stanislavski, *Actor Prepares*, 295 (italics added).

69. Ibid., 289–91 (italics added).

70. See Cole, *Theatrical Event*, 41 and 30–31, respectively.

71. See n. 5.

72. What is more, if the reader in question be a reader *aloud*, he, the actor, and the shaman are all *conferring* essentially the same experience. For parallels between acting and reading aloud with respect to both inner process and effect on others, see chapter 6.

73. Cole, *Theatrical Event*, 7–8 and references there.

74. M. A. Screech, *Rabelais* (Ithaca, N.Y.: Cornell University Press, 1979), 130.

75. Artaud, *Theatre and Its Double*, 124, 123.

76. For some examples of actors' perception of themselves as children or as childlike, see Stephen Aaron, *Stage Fright: Its Role in Acting* (Chicago: University of Chicago Press, 1986), 39–40.

77. Peter Meredith and John E. Tailby, eds., *The Staging of Religious Drama in Europe in the Later Middle Ages: Texts and Documents in English Translation* (Kalamazoo, Mich.: Medieval Institute, 1983), 59.

78. Edmund Bergler, *The Writer and Psychoanalysis* (Garden City, N.Y.: Doubleday, 1950), 23.

79. Of course, an actor's conviction that his audience stands in a relation of oral dependency to him is not wholly projection. As we shall see in chapter 6, the actor in performance does, in a sense, "feed" the audience—or at least passes on to them his own ability to "feed" on the text.

80. Stanislavski, *Actor Prepares*, 52 (italics added).

81. Hagen, *Respect for Acting*, 154 (italics added).

82. Brenner, *Elementary Textbook of Psychoanalysis*, 97.

83. Ibid., 104.

84. For further examples of actors' use of eating-language in connection with their work, see Aaron, *Stage Fright*, 98.

85. Hagen, *Respect for Acting*, 217 (italics added for *digest* only).

86. This and all subsequent quotations from participants in this production are transcribed from the film *Rehearsing Hamlet*, produced and directed by Carl Charlson (ABC News, 1983).

87. It will be observed that this blanket formulation of the relation between active and passive orality in acting is given in brackets in table 1. This is because I intend to consider acting under the successive aspects of *speech, movement, improvisation, work on a role,* and *work with other actors;* and it is the specific formulations for each of these aspects of acting that I shall be working with.

88. Holland, *Dynamics of Literary Response*, 37.

89. The parallel developed in the following pages between acting and writing on the basis of the relation of each to active orality must be understood as only preliminary to the fuller account of actor-author relations to be given in chapter 7. See also n. 97.

90. As paraphrased by Holland, *Dynamics of Literary Response*, 38.

91. Bergler, *Writer and Psychoanalysis*, 70.

92. 1 Peter 2:2.

93. Cave, *Cornucopian Text*, 85.

94. Rainer Maria Rilke, *Letters, 1892–1910*, trans. Jane Bannard Greene and M. D. Herter Norton (New York: Norton, 1969), 140.

95. Dante, *Divine Comedy, Paradiso* 1, canto 33, ll. 106–8, p. 377. Cited in slightly different translation in Bergler, *Writer and Psychoanalysis*, 71.

96. Packer, *Emerson's Fall*, 120.

97. But this commonsense distinction between authors and actors on the grounds that the actor only reads the words of another, while adequate for present purposes, is not so absolute as it appears. As we shall see, there is a perspective from which the author is, no less than the actor, a "reader" of words

he has received from "another"—a parallel whose implications for actor-author relations I shall consider in chapter 7.

98. "For all good poetry is the spontaneous overflow of powerful feelings" (William Wordsworth, "Preface to the Second Edition of *Lyrical Ballads*, 1800," in *Selected Poetry* [New York: Random House, 1950], 678).

99. The form such character explorations assume on a view of acting as reading is discussed later in this chapter.

100. Johann Wolfgang von Goethe, *Faust*, trans. Peter Salm (Toronto: Bantam, 1985), pt. 1, lines 1224, 1237, p. 77.

101. Quoted in Holland, *Dynamics of Literary Response*, 76.

102. Robert Benedetti, "Notes to an Actor," in *Actor Training*, ed. Richard P. Brown (New York: Drama Book Specialists, 1972), 1:86.

103. Grotowski, *Towards a Poor Theatre*, 185. In contrast with the present line of argument, however, Grotowski makes it an "absolute rule" that "bodily activity comes first, and then vocal expression" (183).

104. Michel Serres, *The Parasite* (Baltimore: Johns Hopkins University Press, 1982), 149.

105. Stanislavski, *Creating a Role*, 49.

106. Dante, *Divine Comedy*, *Inferno* 1, canto 5, lines 127–38, 55. Subsequent line references to *Inferno*, canto 5, will appear in the text; page references to the editor's commentary volume (*Inferno* 2) will continue to appear in the notes.

107. Dante, *Divine Comedy*, *Inferno* 2, 94.

108. Cervantes, *Don Quixote*, 576. Subsequent page references appear in the text.

109. See also "Cid Hamete's" remark, ibid., 964.

110. Regan, *Love Words*, 48.

111. See translator's note 5 to Cervantes, *Don Quixote*, pt. 1, chap. 8, 475.

112. Karlheinz Stierle, "The Reading of Fictional Texts," in Suleiman and Crosman, *Reader in the Text*, 87.

113. Brecht, *On Theatre*, 162.

114. Stanislavski, *Creating a Role*, 228.

115. It is true that Quixote reads with interest and accepts without question the account of his accomplishments which he finds inscribed on a parchment in the Duke's garden (775). What gives this text authority in Quixote's eyes, however, is precisely its *not* being the work of an "outside author" but, rather, something flung up in his path by the adventure itself.

116. Montaigne, *Essays*, 59.

117. It may seem to limit the range of "improvisation" somewhat to equate it with "writing in," since writing in implies some prior text or body of texts to which new elements are added, and improvisation need not begin with a text at all. To this I would reply: (1) that in actual theater practice most improvisatory work either occurs in the course of work on a script or takes off from a verbally stated scenario or premise—and so *does* have the character of "addition to a given text"; and (2) that in any case, the definition toward which I am working—improvisation as the simultaneous production/consumption of text—renders problematic the very *distinction* between "prior text" and "addition."

118. By this I do *not* mean merely that improvisatory activity is an "inscrib-ing" of "traces" on the "blank page" of the stage, which the audience then "reads." As will appear in chapter 6, I am not generally very happy with the semiotic model of theatergoing as the "reading" of a "performance text" by an audience. And, clearly, one of the main problems with such a perspective is that it fails to distinguish improvisatory from other kinds of performance. What acting is *not* a "self-writing text," if all that is meant by "writing" is covering the "medium" of the stage/page with vocal and gestural "marks"?

119. Quoted in Jacques Scherer, *Le "Livre" de Mallarmé* (Paris: Gallimard, 1957), 40 (my translation).

120. Shakespeare, *Hamlet,* act 1, sc. 5, line 103.

121. Quoted in Culler, *Structuralist Poetics,* 129 (my translation).

122. John Keats, *Letters,* ed. Hyder Edward Rollins (Cambridge: Harvard University Press, 1958), 2:103.

123. Roland Barthes, quoted in Culler, *Structuralist Poetics,* 140. The second phrase is Culler's paraphrasing of Barthes.

124. Barbara Johnson, *The Critical Difference* (Baltimore: Johns Hopkins University Press, 1980), 3.

125. I say "it would seem" because, as we shall see, the essence of improvisa-tion consists not in the "originality" of the material brought forth, but in the uncertainty about whether this bringing forth constitutes writing or reading.

126. Phillipe Sollers, quoted in Gérard Genette, *Figures of Literary Discourse* (New York: Columbia University Press, 1982), 69–70.

127. Derrida, *Dissemination,* 64.

128. Derrida, quoted in Crosman, "Do Readers Make Meaning," 149.

129. Barthes, *S/Z,* 10.

130. Fyodor Dostoyevsky, *The Idiot,* trans. Constance Garnett (New York: Random House, 1935), 238.

131. In fact, we learn shortly that the change was intentional (ibid., 239).

132. Collins, *Charles Dickens: The Public Readings,* xxxvi.

133. I realize that in what follows I distort improvisation somewhat by focusing exclusively on the work of the individual actor, when so much impro-visatory work relies on the interchange *between* actors. But, ultimately, every word or action an improvising actor comes out with, whatever it may owe to the stimulus of others, is, *at the moment he produces it,* his product, his choice, his act; and it is this moment of production (specifically, its identity with the mo-ment of consumption) which concerns us here.

134. It may appear contradictory that in chapter 3 I gave *consume* as an example of a word that evokes the active element in eating, whereas in the present discussion I use it to mean "intake in general," or even "passive taking in." To this I would reply that: (1) *consume* does contain this range of connota-tions; and (2) I employ it here, toward the less active end of its spectrum, as the appropriate (and expected) "other term" in a *produce/consume* polarity. As a re-minder that *consume* is now to be taken in its more passive/receptive senses, I will, as here, sometimes set it in apposition with such terms as *draw upon, be nourished by, draw nourishment from,* etc.

135. See, however, my chapter 1 discussion of on-book performance and marginal cases.

136. Holland, *Dynamics of Literary Response*, 278.

137. Ibid., 276.

138. The equivalence of characters to readers, and of specific characters to specific readers, is implicit not only in the present passage but also in Holland's later concept of the "identity theme," according to which *readers* are distinguished from one another in the very way that *characters* are distinguished from one another in *The Dynamics of Literary Response*, namely, on the basis of their differing solutions to drive/defense conflicts. (See Holland, "Unity Identity Text Self," 118–35, esp. pp. 126–27.) That characters, like readers, have identity themes is explicitly stated by Holland in a later essay on the character of Hermia in *A Midsummer Night's Dream:* "Her characteristic mode of defense and adaptation [is] the providing of alternatives. . . . She creates an alternative that will amend the original possibility. That is her identity theme" (Norman N. Holland, "Hermia's Dream," in *Representing Shakespeare*, ed. Murray M. Schwartz and Coppélia Kahn [Baltimore: Johns Hopkins University Press, 1980], 1–20).

139. Brecht, *On Theatre*, 137.

140. Holland, *Dynamics of Literary Response*, 313.

141. As summarized by Simon O. Lesser, *Fiction and the Unconscious* (New York: Vintage, 1957), 201–2. See also Holland, *Dynamics of Literary Response*, 278–79.

142. Hagen, *Respect for Acting*, 147.

143. Furthermore, as we shall see, it is in the nature of dramatic texts themselves to resist the general reader. (See discussion in chap. 6.)

144. Janet Suzman, *"Hedda Gabler:* The Play in Performance," in *Ibsen and the Theatre*, ed. Errol Durbach (New York: New York University Press, 1980), 83–104. Subsequent page references will appear in the text.

145. I shall return in a moment to the significance of the maze's being "of her [Hedda's] character."

146. Shakespeare, *A Midsummer Night's Dream*, act 1, sc. 2, lines 30, 52–53, 71.

147. See n. 141.

148. Charlson, *Rehearsing Hamlet* (film).

149. One of the *Hamlets* was a performance piece by Stuart Sherman, done at the Performing Garage in 1982. (Sherman had, in fact, several stagehand assistants but was himself the only true performer.) The other, more dimly remembered solo *Hamlet* was the work of a wandering political performance artist called "Le Momo," whom I saw in a Paris club in 1974. The solo *Tempest* was performed by Fred Curchack at the Theater for the New City in New York in 1984.

150. Alisa Solomon, review of *Such Stuff as Dreams Are Made On*, a performance by Fred Curchack based on *The Tempest*, *Village Voice*, June 26, 1984, 104.

151. Preparatory work by one of Stanislavski's students on the role of Roderigo in *Othello*. See Stanislavski, *Creating a Role*, 191.

152. Preparatory work by Uta Hagen on the role of Martha in *Who's Afraid of Virginia Woolf?* See Hagen, *Respect for Acting,* 163.

153. Barthes, *S/Z,* 105.

154. Stanislavski, *Actor Prepares,* 257. We shall see, however, that "reading," precisely insofar as it consists in a filling in of blanks, is a highly problematic conception for Stanislavski. (See chap. 5.)

155. Contrary to my usual practice, I here list the passive oral impulse *before* the active one, in recognition that an actor first passively assumes the reading-identity of the character (i.e., is cast) and only then actively sets about imposing his own reading-identity upon it.

156. Recall Diane Venora's comment on Hamlet: "The part feeds on you, eating you."

157. It dates back at least to the Middle Ages. See Curtius, *European Literature and the Latin Middle Ages,* 316.

158. Cervantes, *Don Quixote,* 551.

159. Shakespeare, *Romeo and Juliet,* act 1, sc. 3, line 81.

160. Shakespeare, *Macbeth,* act 1, sc. 5, lines 62–63. For more Shakespearean examples in this vein, see Curtius, *European Literature and the Latin Middle Ages,* 335–38.

161. The blurring of active and passive oral impulses in the kiss is also reflected in the fact that, while Paolo kisses Francesca, in the text they "perform" it is Francesca's *character* (Guinevere) who kisses Paolo's character (Lancelot). (See Renato Poggioli, "Paolo and Francesca," in *Dante: A Collection of Critical Essays,* ed. John Frecero [Englewood Cliffs, N.J.: Prentice-Hall, 1965], 71.)

Chapter 5

1. Compare Stanley Cavell: "Speaking is taking and giving in your mouth the very matter others are giving and taking in theirs" ("Who Does the Wolf Love: *Coriolanus* and the Interpretations of Politics," in *Shakespeare and the Question of Theory,* ed. Patricia Parker and Geoffrey Hartman [Methuen: New York, 1985], 262). The developmental psychologist R. Spitz refers to the exchange of active and passive oral impulses between nursing mother and infant as "the precursor of dialogue . . . a primal dialogue" (quoted in Kenneth Kaye, *The Mental and Social Life of Babies* [Chicago: University of Chicago Press, 1982], 66).

2. Improvisation here is neither an "obvious exception" nor the limiting case I treated it as in the previous chapter. Consisting as it does of a one-time enactment, improvisation is simply not pertinent to a discussion of the relation between earlier and later enactments of a written text.

3. For further examples of "foregrounded" reading in experimental productions, see the final section of the present chapter.

4. Quoted in Harvey, "Literacy in the Athenian Democracy," 603–4.

5. Bertolt Brecht, *The Private Life of the Master Race,* trans. Eric Bentley (New York: New Directions, 1944), pt. 2, 40.

6. I am indebted to Susan Cole for this reference.

7. Richard, of course, is only pretending to read and requires little urging.

Shakespeare's depictions of interrupted reading almost always ring some ironic change on the basic situation. (See my discussions of *Cymbeline* and *Hamlet*.)

8. Curtius, *European Literature and the Latin Middle Ages*, 70.

9. For further examples, see ibid., index entry "topics," 653–54.

10. See, however, my discussion of Stanislavski's student audience held spellbound by a reading, in the final section of the present chapter.

11. George Chapman, *Bussy D'Ambois*, ed. Nicholas Brooke (London: Methuen, 1964), act 2, sc. 2, lines 108–9, p. 45.

12. Aristophanes, *The Knights*, in *The Birds and Other Plays*, trans. David Barrett and Alan H. Sommerstein (Harmondsworth: Penguin, 1979), lines 145–50, p. 41. Demosthenes is not, strictly speaking, a "solitary" reader here; Nicias, another slave, is also present. Only Demosthenes reads, however, and he reads to himself.

13. August Strindberg, *The Road to Damascus*, trans. Graham Rawson (London: Jonathan Cape, 1939), pt. 1, sc. 8, p. 73.

14. Marcel Aymé, *Clérembard*, in *Four Modern French Comedies*, ed. Wallace Fowlie (New York: Putnam, 1960), act 1, p. 178.

15. Roger Vitrac, *Victor*, in *L'Avant-scène*, no. 276 (November 15, 1962): act 2, sc. 11–12, p. 21.

16. Shakespeare, *Cymbeline*, act 2, sc. 2, lines 3–46.

17. George Lillo, *The London Merchant*, ed. William H. McBurney (Lincoln: University of Nebraska Press, 1965), act 5, sc. 2, pp. 68–71.

18. Henrik Ibsen, *Rosmersholm*, in *Six Plays*, trans. Eva Le Gallienne (New York: Random House, 1957), act 2, p. 283.

19. Richard Wagner, *Die Meistersinger von Nürnberg*, trans. Frederick Jameson (New York: Schirmer, 1932), act 3, sc. 1, pp. 353–54, 366.

20. Shakespeare, *Hamlet*, act 2, sc. 2, lines 191–201. Subsequent references appear in the text.

21. To the extent that scenes of interrupted reading image the acting process, it is possible that Shakespeare's self-conscious manipulation of the topos reflects his well-known penchant for self-conscious theatricality.

22. Two out of four, if the scene between Trygaeus and the Oracle-Monger in *Peace* (ll. 1052–1126) is not taken as a reading scene. The two Aristophanic scenes of reading which do not involve oracle books are Strepsiades reading from his account book (*The Clouds*, ll. 19–32) and the Secretary reading her minutes (*Thesmophoriazusae*, ll. 372–79).

23. K. J. Dover, *Aristophanic Comedy* (Berkeley: University of California Press, 1972), 76–77.

24. Aristophanes, *Knights*, lines 124–27, p. 40. The stage direction is, of course, the addition of the translator.

25. Ibid., lines 192–201, p. 43.

26. Aristophanes, *The Birds*, in *Plays*, trans. Benjamin Bickley Rogers (Cambridge: Harvard University Press, 1924), vol. 2, lines 959–91, pp. 223–27. I cite Rogers's translation of *The Birds* rather than the translation in the Barrett-Sommerstein volume cited in note 12 because, as will be seen, the absence of editorially added stage directions in Rogers is crucial to my discussion.

27. This is not surprising. In the whole surviving corpus of ancient Greek drama the total number of stage directions at all likely to be from the playwright's hand is possibly as low as four and certainly no greater than fourteen. See Taplin, *Stagecraft of Aeschylus*, 15 n. 1; and Dover, *Aristophanic Comedy*, 10.

28. Aristophanes, *Five Comedies*, trans. Benjamin Bickley Rogers (Garden City, N.Y.: Doubleday, 1955), 43–45. The stage directions which have been added to the Rogers translation (see n. 26) in this edition say nothing about any oracle book.

29. Aristophanes, *The Acharnians and Two Other Plays*, trans. J. Hookham Frere (London: Dent, n.d.), 179.

30. Aristophanes, *The Birds*, ed. Walter Kerr (San Francisco: Chandler, 1968), 35.

31. Aristophanes, *The Frogs*, in *The Wasps and Other Plays*, trans. David Barrett (Harmondsworth: Penguin, 1983), lines 956–58, p. 191. Once again, as in note 26, I quote from an Aristophanes play in another translation than that initially cited (see chap. 1 n. 81). So radically do translations of Aristophanes differ in assumptions and tone that one must, I feel, employ different translations to bring out different aspects of the Aristophanic text.

32. Rudolph Pfeiffer, *History of Classical Scholarship from the Beginnings to the End of the Hellenistic Age* (Oxford: Oxford University Press, 1968), 30–32. For Aristophanes' attack on the Sophists in *The Clouds*, see Dover, *Aristophanic Comedy*, 111.

33. Pfeiffer, *History of Classical Scholarship*, 28.

34. Cedric H. Whitman, *Aristophanes and the Comic Hero* (Cambridge: Harvard University Press, 1964), 10.

35. Aristophanes, *The Frogs*, in *The Wasps and Other Plays*, trans. David Barrett, lines 1115–18, p. 197.

36. *Genres:* for example, cultic hymn and dithyramb. *Authors:* for example, Homer, Hesiod, Pindar, Aeschylus, and, of course, Euripides. *Works: Thesmophoriazusae* is a virtual anthology of parodied scenes from Euripidean tragedies, not all of them extant. (See the editor's notes in Aristophanes, *Wasps and Other Plays*, 219–21.)

37. See references below to Aeschylus, Sophocles, Euripides' *Suppliant Women*, and Plato's *Laws*.

38. See Pfeiffer, *History of Classical Scholarship*, 32; Havelock, *Literate Revolution in Greece*, 334; and Derrida, *Dissemination*, 65–172.

39. See the discussions of *Laws*, bk. 10, sec. 891A (pro); and of *Phaedrus*, secs. 274E–275B (contra), in Derrida, *Dissemination*, 113 and 102, respectively.

40. Aeschylus, *Prometheus Bound*, lines 461–62. All references to Greek tragedy are to David Grene and Richmond Lattimore, eds., *The Complete Greek Tragedies*, 4 vols. (Chicago: University of Chicago Press, 1959). Subsequent citations will be by author, play title, and line number.

41. Euripides, *Hippolytus*, lines 452–54.

42. Aeschylus, *Libation Bearers*, line 150; *Eumenides*, line 275; *Prometheus Bound*, lines 789–90.

43. Sophocles, *Women of Trachis*, lines 682–83.

44. Euripides, *Suppliant Women,* lines 430–34.

45. Euripides, *Hippolytus,* lines 952–55.

46. Euripides, *Iphigenia in Aulis,* lines 793–801.

47. Ibid., lines 771–72, 789, 791–92.

48. Plato, *The Republic,* trans. H. D. P. Lee (Baltimore: Penguin, 1962), bk. 10, sec. 597, pp. 372–74. Or perhaps at a *fifth* remove, if, as Derrida claims, "writing down the image that poetic imitation has already made" itself introduces "a fourth degree of distance from reality" (Derrida, *Dissemination,* 138). In that case, 1 = Form of bed, 2 = actual bed, 3 = image of bed, 4 = writing of image, 5 = reading (aloud) of writing.

49. Plato, *Ion,* in *The Dialogues of Plato,* trans. B. Jowett (New York: Random House, 1937), vol. 1, sec. 535, p. 290. Plato is actually speaking of rhapsodes (poetry reciters) but leaves no doubt that his remarks apply to acting as well; e.g., "the rhapsode like yourself *and the actor* are intermediate links" (ibid., sec. 535, p. 291, italics added).

50. Gospel according to St. John, 8:3–9.

51. I quote from the Coventry play (henceforth cited in the text as "Coventry") in the modernized version in R. T. Davies, ed., *The Corpus Christi Play of the English Middle Ages* (London: Faber and Faber, 1972); and from the Chester play (henceforth cited in the text as "Chester") in the normalized spelling version in Peter Happé, ed., *English Mystery Plays* (Harmondsworth: Penguin, 1979), no modern English text being available. References to the Chester play are by page and line numbers; those to the Coventry play are by page number only, since Davies's text contains no line numbers. The Chester "play" is actually the second *half* of a play which also includes a preliminary "Temptation of Christ" episode. Though the two "halves" are thematically related (see Peter Travis, *Dramatic Design in the Chester Cycle* [Chicago: University of Chicago Press, 1982], 155–56 and Happé, *English Mystery Plays,* 388, headnote), they are wholly discrete actions, separated by a forty-eight-line speech of the Expositor; and for present purposes there seems no serious distortion involved in treating this second half as a distinct "Woman Taken in Adultery" play, comparable to the Coventry play on that subject.

52. Iser, *Act of Reading,* 168. See also note 63.

53. See Rosemary Woolf, *The English Mystery Plays* (Berkeley: University of California Press, 1972), 5–6; and Dunn, "Voice Structure in the Liturgical Drama," 61.

54. Meg Twycross, "Books for the Unlearned," in *Drama and Religion,* ed. James Richmond (Cambridge: Cambridge University Press, 1983), 69–73.

55. This is Erich Auerbach's description of St. Augustine's aims in *The City of God,* quoted in Jesse M. Gellrich, *The Idea of the Book in the Middle Ages* (Ithaca, N.Y.: Cornell University Press, 1985), 126 (italics added).

56. See Smalley, *Study of the Bible in the Middle Ages,* 56 and pl. 1.

57. The Middle English pronunciation of *wrought,* with the *gh* pronounced as a guttural, somewhat dilutes the pun.

58. The stage directions of this, as of many of the English Corpus Christi plays, are in Latin. The translation is Davies's.

59. For all these proposals, see Rudolf Schnackenburg, *The Gospel according to St. John* (New York: Crossroad, 1982), 2:165.

60. Andrew of St. Victor, quoted in Smalley, *Study of the Bible in the Middle Ages*, 124.

61. *Glossa Ordinaria* for 2 Kings 11:5, quoted in Gellrich, *Idea of the Book in the Middle Ages*, 127.

62. From the late medieval meditation manual *The Mirror of the Blessed Life of Jesu Christ*, quoted in Twycross, "Books for the Unlearned," 73 (my translation).

63. Clearly, the distinction I drew in chapter 2 between acting (or active reading) as a *filling in* of blanks and writing as a *laying out* of the blanks becomes more problematic in a medieval context, where writers—especially writers on biblical subjects—no less than readers begin with a (scriptural) pattern of "blanks" always already out before them; so that writing, no less than reading, becomes a matter of connecting and filling in.

64. It is true that in chapter 7 I argue for such an affinity, but on quite different grounds.

65. R. Woolf, *English Mystery Plays*, 85–88.

66. Ibid., 145.

67. For this latter term, see Michael Baxandall, *Painting and Experience in Fifteenth Century Italy* (Oxford: Oxford University Press, 1972), 72.

68. Travis, *Dramatic Design in the Chester Cycle*, 41; Woolf, *English Mystery Plays*, 164–65.

69. *The Chester Prophets Play*, in *Chief Pre-Shakespearean Dramas*, ed. Joseph Quincy Adams (Cambridge: Houghton-Mifflin, 1924), lines 73–77, p. 133.

70. Ibid., lines 337–44, p. 137.

71. V. A. Kolve, *The Play Called Corpus Christi* (Stanford, Calif.: Stanford University Press, 1966), 28.

72. For more on the Expositor as performing "authorial" functions, see Twycross, "Books for the Unlearned," 82–85.

73. See, for example, Woolf, *English Mystery Plays*, 77–79; and Mary H. Marshall, "Theatre in the Middle Ages: Evidence from Dictionaries and Glosses," pt. 2, *Symposium* 4, no. 2 (November 1950): 376–78.

74. This does not, of course, mean that all readers or readings were regarded as possessing equal authority. Within the single category of "biblical commentator," for example, a distinction was drawn between *expositor, glossator,* and *ordinator glose*—roughly, "patristic authority," "later commentator," and "compiler of commentaries" (Smalley, *Study of the Bible in the Middle Ages*, 225).

75. Ibid., 240.

76. A. M. Nagler, ed., *A Source Book in Theatrical History* (New York: Dover, 1952), 51.

77. Smalley, *Study of the Bible in the Middle Ages*, 216 (Smalley is paraphrasing Robert of Melun), 271.

78. *Oxford English Dictionary* (Oxford: Oxford University Press, 1971), entry *gloze*.

79. Smalley, *Study of the Bible in the Middle Ages*, 79–80.

80. See, for example, Woolf, *English Mystery Plays,* 86–91.

81. Richard of St. Victor, quoted in Smalley, *Study of the Bible in the Middle Ages,* 109.

82. Quoted in Woolf, *English Mystery Plays,* 367 n. 58. This particular text is from the sixteenth century, but the argument it makes was, as Woolf points out (86–91), current in the Middle Ages.

83. Anton Chekhov, *The Sea Gull,* in *Best Plays,* trans. Stark Young (New York: Random House, 1956), act 4, pp. 52–53. Subsequent references to this edition of Chekhov plays, by title and act and page numbers, will appear in the text.

84. David Magarshack, *Chekhov the Dramatist* (New York: Hill and Wang, 1960), 242.

85. Stanislavski, *Building a Character,* 113, 115.

86. Ibid., 113.

87. David Magarshack, *Stanislavski: A Life* (New York: Chanticleer Press, 1951), 48.

88. Quoted in Robert Brustein, *The Theatre of Revolt* (Boston: Little, Brown, 1964), 139.

89. That Chekhov did not regard learning how to read his fiction as wholly unrelated to learning how to act his plays is suggested by his having sent Stanislavski, during a period of tension between them over Stanislavski's approach to *The Sea Gull,* a complete edition of his *fictional* works (Magarshack, *Stanislavski,* 191).

90. Stanislavski, *Building a Character,* 113. Stanislavski did not begin the actual elaboration of his "system" until some eight years after the 1898 production of *The Sea Gull* (Magarshack, *Stanislavski,* 260).

91. Magarshack, *Stanislavski,* 254, 170, 168.

92. Ibid., 68.

93. Stanislavski, *Actor Prepares,* 35–36.

94. Is it, then, to Chekhov rather than Stanislavski that we should be looking for the origins of performance work? A number of the performance pieces I shall discuss display a discontinuity between reading and action which is reminiscent of Pauline gazing on Trepleff's manuscript and speaking of other things or Tchebutykin leafing through his newspaper and whistling. But that the difficulty in getting *from* reading to acting might be owing to a fundamental identity *between* reading and acting—this possibility, explored, as I shall argue, in both our Stanislavski excerpt and in performance work, is not considered by Chekhov.

95. What follows is not intended to establish Stanislavski as the *sole* precursor or source of the tendency in question. Public readings by authors (a practice common since antiquity), staged readings, the "stands and stools" productions of the 1950s and 1960s—all of these provide a precedent for the performance piece emphasis on reading as stage action. For more on this tradition of reading performances, see chapter 7.

96. The script is printed in *Drama Review* 18, no. 2 (T-62: June 1974): 38–47. Subsequent page references to this edition appear in the text.

97. My source for the Serban *Three Sisters* is a personal account. This and Foreman's *Vertical Mobility* are the only productions discussed in this section which I have not seen in the theater.

98. Elinor Fuchs, *"North Atlantic* and *L.S.D.," Performing Arts Journal* 8, no. 2 (23: 1984): 51. Fuchs's account is of an earlier version of *L.S.D.* but is also accurate for the autumn 1984 production.

99. Personal communication after October 20, 1984, performance.

100. Samuel Beckett, *Waiting for Godot* (New York: Grove Press, 1954), 54: "ESTRAGON: Ah! *(Despairing.)* What'll we do, what'll we do!"

101. Stanislavski, *Creating a Role,* 207.

102. I do not know if all or any of the discursive passages read at the lecterns were actually *by* Chin, but they were certainly part of the text which Chin-as-playwright presented to his actors.

103. The title of the Brooklyn Academy of Music series in which much recent performance work has been produced.

Chapter 6

1. Artaud, *Theatre and Its Double,* 112.

2. Taplin, *Stagecraft of Aeschylus,* 12–13.

3. Michael Goldman, *The Actor's Freedom* (New York: Viking, 1975), 101.

4. Keir Elam, *The Semiotics of Theatre and Drama* (London: Methuen, 1980), 213, 12.

5. Patrice Pavis, *Languages of the Stage: Essays in the Semiology of Theatre* (New York: Performing Arts Journal Publications, 1982), 124, 135; Elam, *Semiotics of Theatre and Drama,* 3, 7.

6. Pavis, *Languages of the Stage,* 31.

7. Ibid., 78, 73, 115.

8. Elam, *Semiotics of Theatre and Drama,* 52.

9. Pavis, *Languages of the Stage,* 55, 174.

10. Cole and Chinoy, *Actors on Acting,* 297.

11. Kolve, *Play Called Corpus Christi,* 5; R. Woolf, *English Mystery Plays,* 85–86 (spelling modernized).

12. Twycross, "Books for the Unlearned," 65; Phyllis Hartnoll, ed., *The Concise Oxford Companion to the Theatre* (London: Oxford University Press, 1972), entry *pageant.*

13. Toby Cole, ed., *Playwrights on Playwriting* (New York: Hill and Wang, 1961), 171.

14. Quoted in John Willett, *The Theatre of Bertolt Brecht* (New York: New Directions, 1968), 174.

15. Stanislavski, *Building a Character,* 86–87.

16. Jean Cocteau, Preface to *The Wedding on the Eiffel Tower,* in *Modern French Theatre: An Anthology of Plays,* ed. Michael Benedikt and George E. Wellwarth (New York: Dutton, 1966), 96–97.

17. Artaud, *Theatre and Its Double,* 61. It should be recalled that Brecht, Stanislavski, and Artaud were all also inclined to link the acting *process* with reading.

18. Such is the implication of such recent book titles as *Reading Photographs* by Jonathan Bayer, *Reading Drawings* by Susan Lambert, *How to Read a Film* by James Monaco, and *Close-up: How to Read the American City* by Grady Clay.

19. Such a slide might, for example, be discerned in my account of improvisation as the relation between "writing" and "reading" in the absence of a text or in my discussion of rehearsal as the acting out of conflicting impulses toward someone else's "reading."

20. Pavis, *Languages of the Stage*, 32.

21. Elam, *Semiotics of Theatre and Drama*, 48.

22. Michael Kirby, "On Literary Theatre," *Drama Review* 18, no. 2 (T-62: June 1974): 107.

23. Quoted in Willett, *Theatre of Bertolt Brecht*, 161.

24. Quoted in Michael Kirby, "Richard Foreman's Ontological-Hysteric Theatre," *Drama Review* 17, no. 2 (T-58: June 1973): 14.

25. New York Shakespeare Festival, 1981.

26. Meyerhold, *On Theatre*, 184 and photograph opposite p. 161.

27. Classic Stage Company, New York, 1985.

28. Performing Garage, New York, 1985.

29. The sense of cognitive shift is even clearer when one watches a subtitled movie or supertitled opera. For the perceptual tensions induced by the latter, see Will Crutchfield, "On Supertitles and the Joys of Opera," *New York Times*, November 27, 1986, C-13.

30. Bert O. States, "The Dog on the Stage: Theater as Phenomenon," *New Literary History* 14, no. 2 (Winter 1983): 377.

31. Dante, *Divine Comedy, Paradiso* 1, canto 18, lines 73–78, 91, pp. 202–5. *The Divine Comedy*, it has been suggested, "is less an allegory of history than a reflection of the reading process, with all its limitations in the uncertainty of meaning and the temporality of understanding" (Gellrich, *Idea of the Book in the Middle Ages*, 24. Gellrich is paraphrasing Giuseppe Mazzotta).

32. Elam, *Semiotics of Theatre and Drama*, 42, 56.

33. Pavis, *Languages of the Stage*, 63.

34. It is true that, as I noted earlier, even considered as pure semiotic process, reading displays some degree of oral structure, for semiotic processes are themselves forms of displaced orality. (See, for example, my earlier comments on the physical-oral antecedents of the hermeneutic circle, the role of cognitive scanning in fantasy immersion, and the link between interpretation and active orality.) If now I stress the distinction where earlier I stressed the convergence between the oral and semiotic approaches to reading, it is because at present I am concerned with the *experience* rather than the underlying structure of the processes in question; and, considered as experiences (in this case, the experiences of a theater audience), construal of signs no longer *feels* like introjection of fantasy, whatever their common oral heritage.

35. Aaron, *Stage Fright*, 98–99, 124. The characterization of the audience as a "primal cavity" is Donald Kaplan's (see ref. on p. 99).

36. Holland, *Dynamics of Literary Response*, 73–74.

37. Ibid., 88. The concept of the breast as the original of later "dream screens" is Bertram Lewin's.

38. Ibid., 64.

39. Ibid., 79, 37.

40. Elam, *Semiotics of Theatre and Drama*, 85.

41. Brooklyn Academy of Music, 1982.

42. Ted Pearson, "The Poem as Object," in *The Poetry Reading*, eds. Stephen Vincent and Ellen Zweig (San Francisco: Momo's Press, 1981), 319.

43. Samuel Johnson, "Preface to Shakespeare," in *The Norton Anthology of English Literature*, ed. M. H. Abrams et al. (New York: Norton, 1979), 2:2357.

44. Aaron Hill and William Popple, *The Prompter: A Theatrical Paper (1734–1736)*, sel. and ed. William W. Appleton and Kalman A. Burnim (New York: Benjamin Blom, 1966), no. 5 (May 6, 1735), 61.

45. See, for example, Cervantes, *Don Quixote*, 180–82, 207.

46. A. Hale and A. D. Edwards, "Hearing Children Read," in *The Social Psychology of Reading*, ed. John R. Edwards (Silver Springs, Md.: Institute of Modern Languages, 1981), 1:117–18.

47. Cole and Chinoy, *Actors on Acting*, 161.

48. J. D. Beresford, *Writing Aloud* (London: Collins, 1928), 74–75.

49. Bruno Bettelheim and Karen Zelan, *On Learning to Read* (New York: Knopf, 1982), 99.

50. Kafka, *Diaries*, 164.

51. Fyodor Dostoyevsky, *The Brothers Karamazov*, trans. Constance Garnett (New York: Random House, 1937), 379.

52. Sartre, *The Words*, 28–29.

53. John E. B. Mayor, ed., *Thirteen Satires of Juvenal* (Hildesheim, Ger.: Georg Olms, 1966), 179.

54. Marshall, "Theatre in the Middle Ages," 371, 376.

55. Holland, *Poems in Persons*, 97.

56. Hale and Edwards, "Hearing Children Read," 124.

57. Fyodor Dostoyevsky, *Crime and Punishment*, trans. Constance Garnett (New York: Random House, 1950), 319, 320. Subsequent page references to this edition will appear in the text.

58. Plato, *Ion*, secs. 533–36, pp. 289–91. The performances of actor and rhapsode are also linked by Aristotle in chapter 26 of the *Poetics* and by Plato elsewhere in his dialogues. See John Herington, *Poetry into Drama: Early Tragedy and the Greek Poetic Tradition* (Berkeley: University of California Press, 1985), 10–13, 224–25 nn. 14 and 15.

59. There are, of course, exceptions to this picture. A commercially successful playwright may be published by a trade press (e.g., David Mamet by Grove Press). Noncommercial playwrights are sometimes published by noncommercial presses (e.g., Richard Foreman by Station Hill; Len Jenkins by Sun and Moon). There are also occasional anthologies of new work by women playwrights, black playwrights, gay playwrights, etc., which seem aimed as much at the general readership for writing by women, blacks, and gays as at readers concerned with theater. My aim is not to present a scrupulously accurate

profile of the play publishing market but, rather, to sketch the outlines of a cultural situation to which the structure of that market gives clear but approximate expression.

60. Aristophanes, *The Frogs*, l. 52. See Havelock, *Literate Revolution in Greece*, 204, 207 n. 42. I quote the line in Havelock's translation.

61. Of course, the *director's* is a reading extrinsic to all roles, but this, rather than removing the difficulty about such a reading, raises some questions about directors.

62. Roland Mushat Frye, *Shakespeare: The Art of the Dramatist* (New York: Houghton-Mifflin, 1970), 22–23.

63. Richard Helgerson, *Self-Crowned Laureates* (Berkeley: University of California Press, 1983), 37.

64. Cole, *Playwrights on Playwriting*, 280.

65. Ibid., 288.

66. Taplin, *Stagecraft of Aeschylus*, 16.

67. Woolf, *English Mystery Plays*, 309, 418 n.21.

68. Frye, *Shakespeare: The Art of the Dramatist*, 22.

69. Helgerson, *Self-Crowned Laureates*, 37 n. 13.

70. Ong, "The Writer's Audience Is Always a Fiction," 11.

71. Jameson, *Political Unconscious*, 9.

72. Quoted in Agnieszka Salska, *Walt Whitman and Emily Dickinson* (Philadelphia: University of Pennsylvania Press, 1985), 23.

73. Mikhail Bakhtin, *Problems of Dostoyevsky's Poetics* (Minneapolis: University of Minnesota Press, 1984), 202.

74. Cole and Chinoy, *Directors on Directing*, 217, 130.

75. Goethe, *Wilhelm Meister's Apprenticeship*, 128.

76. Cole and Chinoy, *Actors on Acting*, 106; Cole and Chinoy, *Directors on Directing*, 194.

77. Gerald Eades Bentley, *The Profession of Dramatist in Shakespeare's Time* (Princeton, N.J.: Princeton University Press, 1971), 76–79.

78. Stanislavski, *Creating a Role*, 115.

79. Rainer Maria Rilke, *Letters, 1910–1926*, trans. Jane Bannard Greene and M. D. Herter Norton (New York: Norton, 1969), 291.

Chapter 7

1. Stanislavski, *Actor Prepares*, 252.

2. Quoted in Robert Louis Brannan, *Under the Management of Mr. Charles Dickens: His Production of "The Frozen Deep"* (Ithaca, N.Y.: Cornell University Press, 1966), 83, 88.

3. William E. Leuchtenberg, *Franklin Roosevelt and the New Deal* (New York: Harper and Row, 1963), 126.

4. Gustave Flaubert, *Letters, 1857–1880*, ed. and trans. Francis Steegmuller (Cambridge: Harvard University Press, 1982), 99, 139.

5. Collins, *Charles Dickens: The Public Readings*, lvii.

6. Philip Collins, *Reading Aloud: A Victorian Métier* (Lincoln, Eng.: Tennyson Society, 1973), 26.

7. The quoted phrase is from Simone Benmussa's biographical sketch in the program for Nathalie Sarraute's *Childhood* at the Samuel Beckett Theatre in New York, 1985. For an account of a rehearsal of this "all-writer" production, see "Bloomsbury Unbuttoned," *New Yorker* (November 21, 1983): 42–44.

8. This ongoing series was first presented at the Symphony Space in New York in 1985.

9. This reading was presented by The Poetry Group at the City University of New York Graduate Center in 1984.

10. See, for example, the instances of *actor* for *auctor* in a medieval manuscript of Sallust and of *auctor* for *actor* in a medieval manuscript of Suetonius cited in M.-D. Chenu, *"Auctor, Actor, Autor," Bulletin du Cange* 3 (1927): 82. Thomas M. Greene implies (*The Light in Troy* [New Haven, Conn.: Yale University Press, 1982], 12) that the Latin words *auctor, actor,* and *autor* were all employed more or less indiscriminately to signify "author" in the medieval sense of "cultural authority"—although, as Chenu points out (81–82), it is not always clear in a given case whether we are dealing with a felt equivalence, a scribal confusion, or a spelling error.

11. At the Manhattan Theatre Club.

12. Jerome Rothenberg, "The Poetics of Performance," in Vincent and Zweig, *Poetry Reading,* 121, 122–23.

13. William Carlos Williams, "From 'Sour Grapes,'" in Vincent and Zweig, *Poetry Reading,* 16.

14. Peter Brazeau, *Parts of a World: Wallace Stevens Remembered* (New York: Random House, 1983), 193.

15. Mayor, *Thirteen Satires of Juvenal,* 174, 179.

16. Richard Poirier, *The Performing Self* (New York: Oxford University Press, 1971), 92, 89. Note also the title of a recent critical study, *The Novel as Performance,* by Jerzy Kutnik.

17. Scherer, *Le "Livre" de Mallarmé,* 31.

18. Wallace Stevens, "Of Modern Poetry," in *Collected Poems,* 240.

19. Richard Zoglin, "The Golden Book Hoax," *Time* (October 1, 1984): 83.

20. John Gregory Dunne, "The Secret of Danny Santiago," *New York Review of Books* (August 16, 1984): 17–27.

21. M. C. Beardsley, quoted in Fabian Gudas, "Dramatism and Modern Theories of Interpretation," in Thompson, *Performance of Literature,* 606.

22. Reuben A. Brower, *The Fields of Light* (New York: Oxford University Press, 1962), 19.

23. Michel Foucault, "What Is an Author?" in *Textual Strategies,* ed. Josué V. Harari (Ithaca, N.Y.: Cornell University Press, 1979), 152.

24. Robert C. Elliott, *The Literary Persona* (Chicago: University of Chicago Press, 1982), 8.

25. A. Dwight Culler, "Monodrama and the Dramatic Monologue," *PMLA* 90, no. 2 (March 1975): 368.

26. Brower, *Fields of Light,* 20 (italics added).

27. Rilke, *Letters, 1910–1926,* 291.

28. Samuel Taylor Coleridge, "To William Wordsworth, Composed on the Night after His Recitation of a Poem on the Growth of an Individual Mind," in *Selected Poetry and Prose* (New York: Random House, 1951), 75.

29. Gustave Flaubert, *Letters, 1830–1857*, ed. and trans. Francis Steegmuller (Cambridge: Harvard University Press, 1980), 100.

30. Johann Peter Eckermann, *Conversations with Goethe* (London: Dent, 1951), 56.

31. Collins, *Charles Dickens: The Public Readings*, xix.

32. Henry James, *The Art of the Novel* (New York: Scribner's, 1937), 63.

33. Wallace Stevens, "Large Red Man Reading," in *Collected Poems*, 424.

34. Cervantes, *Don Quixote*, 32, 69–72. Not knowing Arabic, Cervantes is obliged to get "Hamete's" text translated by a "Spanish-speaking Moor" (71). Thus, it is not merely from an earlier text but from an earlier *reading* of an earlier text (the Moor's translation of Cid Hamete's "History") that Cervantes claims to be "reading" to us.

35. Chodlerlos de Laclos, *Les Liaisons Dangéreuses*, trans. P. W. K. Stone (Harmondsworth: Penguin, 1977), 19.

36. Geoffrey Chaucer, *Troilus and Criseyde*, ed. Donald R. Howard and James Dean (New York: New American Library, 1976), bk. 2, lines 13–14, 18, p. 43. See also note to bk. 2, line 14, p. 43; and note to bk. 1, line 394, p. 16. For further medieval and Renaissance instances of the fiction of a prior text, see Walter E. Stephens, "Mimesis, Mediation and Counterfeit," in *Mimesis in Contemporary Theory*, ed. Mihai Sparioso (Philadelphia: John Benjamins, 1984), 251–62. For some eighteenth- and nineteenth-century examples, see William Gass, *Habitations of the Word* (New York: Simon and Schuster, 1985), 268.

37. The present analysis should be read in the light of my earlier Holland-based account of the text as brought into being by the "lurching" of its author over a spectrum of conflicting responses to a core fantasy, a movement that the reader, "lurching" between *his* conflicting responses to the characters of the completed text, eventually repeats. First to pursue the very trajectory that others will pursue after him—in this respect, too, the author is the first of his own readers, his own first reader.

38. Kristeva, *Desire in Language*, 2.

39. Stanislaw Lem, "Chance and Order," *New Yorker* (January 30, 1984): 94.

40. Moynihan, "Interview with Paul de Man," 592.

41. Crosman, "Do Readers Make Meanings," 162.

42. Rebecca West, *The Fountain Overflows* (New York: Viking, 1956), dust jacket copy.

43. Charlton T. Lewis, *A Latin Dictionary for Schools* (New York: American Book Company, 1916), entries *auctor, auctoritas* and root *aug-;* Eric Partridge, *Origins* (New York: Greenwich House, 1983), entry *actor*. After I had written this chapter, there came to my attention a book that makes use of some of the same terminology I employ in the present discussion. In *Auctor and Actor: A Narratological Reading of Apuleius's Golden Ass* (Berkeley: University of California Press, 1985), John J. Winkler not only has recourse to an *auctor/actor* distinction,

but also introduces the term *first-reader*. In each case, however, the sense Winkler gives to the term in question is quite different from my own. He employs *actor* and *auctor* to distinguish the protagonist "then" (the *actor*) from the narrator "now" (the *auctor*) (139). And he uses *first-reader* to mean first-*time* reader, i.e., one who is only now going through a text for the first time (10).

44. Janet Coleman, *Medieval Readers and Writers: 1350–1400* (New York: Columbia University Press, 1981), 203–4.

45. Havelock, *Preface to Plato*, 53 n. 8.

46. Gerald L. Bruns, *Inventions: Writing, Textuality and Understanding in Literary History* (New Haven, Conn.: Yale University Press, 1982), 19, 183 n. 5.

47. Rilke, *Letters, 1910–1926*, 438.

48. James Broaden, *Memoirs of Mrs. Siddons* (Philadelphia: J. B. Lippincott, 1893), 463.

49. Collins, *Reading Aloud*, 14.

50. Rothenberg, "Poetics of Performance," 123.

51. Collins, *Charles Dickens: The Public Readings*, liv.

52. Eckermann, *Conversations with Goethe*, 56.

53. Flaubert, *Letters, 1857–1880*, 130.

54. Jeremiah 36:1–10. See also John Bright, *Jeremiah: A New Translation With Introduction and Commentary* (Garden City, N.Y.: Doubleday, 1981), 176–81.

55. Pliny the Younger, *Letters*, 2 vols., trans. William Melmouth (London: Heinemann, 1924–27), 2:256–57. Reading for another was apparently not an uncommon practice in ancient Rome. See Mayor, *Thirteen Satires of Juvenal*, 177, 180.

56. Crosby, "Oral Delivery in the Middle Ages," 95, esp. n. 3.

57. In the case of Jeremiah, of course, he who "reads" is quite literally another than He who "wrote": a prophet is by definition one who voices the word of Another. Prophecy thus constitutes the original case of authorial self-secondariness in Western culture, a status that seems already accorded it by the argument of the fourteenth-century biblical exegete Ralph Fitzralph that the relation in which Baruch stands to Jeremiah—that of a surrogate, an emissary, a "second who reads"—is precisely the relation of Jeremiah himself to God. See A. J. Minnis, *Medieval Theories of Authorship* (London: Scolar Press, 1984), 100–101.

58. Roland Barthes, "The Death of the Author," in *Image-Music-Text* (New York: Hill and Wang, 1982), 147.

59. Foucault, "What Is an Author," 147, 148.

60. Phillipe Sollers, *Writing and the Experience of Limits* (New York: Columbia University Press, 1983), 193.

61. Collins, *Charles Dickens: The Public Readings*, 248 n. 5.

62. This occurred at Chartwell Booksellers in New York in 1986.

63. Leitch, *Deconstructive Criticism*, 254.

64. Barthes, "Death of the Author," 148. In this characteristically post-modern theme one senses an allusion (a return?) to the medieval view of the author as one whose credentials consist first of all in his absence from the present

cultural scene, one who must be "above" us since he is no longer with us. To the medieval mind, it may almost be said, the only good author is a dead author—as at least one living medieval author was moved to lament. "My only fault," complained Walter Map, the excellence of whose writings led some of his contemporaries to doubt he could have written them, "is that I am alive." He went on to add that he had "no intention . . . of correcting this fault by my death" (Minnis, *Medieval Theories of Authorship*, 11–12)—precisely the strategy adopted by "The Author" in Roger Vitrac's surrealist play *The Mysteries of Love* (1924), in whose attempt to ensure his author status by his demise (he enters in the act of shooting himself) we may perhaps see a link between the literally dead medieval and the figuratively "dead" postmodern author.

65. Barthes, "Death of the Author," 148.

66. Collins, *Reading Aloud*, 4. "His own not quite impartial Greek chorus," one observer called him.

67. Jeremiah 36:1–32; Bright, *Jeremiah*, 176–79.

68. Pliny, *Letters*, 2:257.

69. Pfeiffer, *History of Classical Scholarship*, 8.

70. Bernard Gredley, "Greek Tragedy and the 'Discovery' of the Actor," in *Drama and the Actor*, ed. James Richmond (Cambridge: Cambridge University Press, 1984), 4–5. See also Herington, *Poetry into Drama*, 13, 39, 51–52.

71. Cole and Chinoy, *Actors on Acting*, 3.

72. See Twycross, "Books for the Unlearned," 84–87.

73. Behind this lay the "recurrent [medieval] misconception that the manner of performance of classical plays had been that one man read the text aloud, while others mimed the action" (Woolf, *English Mystery Plays*, 27). And in fact at Rome, from at least the early imperial period on, plays and other texts *do* seem to have been occasionally performed in this way (Joseph R. Jones, "Isidore and the Theater," *Comparative Drama* 16, no. 1 [Spring 1982]: 37–38); the medieval mistake lay in supposing the practice to have been universal.

74. George Villiers, Duke of Buckingham, *The Rehearsal*, ed. D. E. L. Crane (Durham, Eng.: University of Durham Publications, 1976), act 5, sc. 1, lines 364–79, pp. 63–64. All subsequent act, scene, and line references to this edition will appear in the text.

75. Nicolai M. Gorchakov, *Stanislavski Directs* (New York: Grosset and Dunlop, 1962), 176.

76. See n. 1.

77. Produced at the Samuel Beckett Theatre in New York in 1985.

78. This "victory" of actor over author in the theater is prefigured, as we have found so much of the actor-author relation to be, in the history of the words themselves. Over the course of the Middle Ages the Latin noun *actor* gradually replaced *auctor* as the customary term for "author of a work" (Chenu, *"Auctor, Actor, Autor,"* 83).

79. Ronald E. Surtz, *The Birth of a Theater* (Princeton, N.J.: Princeton University Department of Romance Languages and Literatures, 1979), 165–66.

80. Charles Laughton, according to Brecht, read both *King Lear* and *The Tempest* to small audiences of invited friends (Brecht, *On Theatre*, 165, 168 n.).

81. Broaden, *Memoirs of Mrs. Siddons*, 460.

82. Jane Williamson, *Charles Kemble, Man of the Theatre* (Lincoln: University of Nebraska Press, 1970), 81, 237.

83. David W. Thompson, "Early Actress Readers: Mowatt, Kemble, and Cushman," in Thompson, *Performance of Literature*, 635–39, 645–48.

84. For the educators and clergymen, see Collins, *Reading Aloud*, 20–25. As for critics: The great Austrian essayist Karl Kraus gave public readings of Shakespeare plays in early twentieth-century Vienna (Kari Grimstad, *Masks of the Prophet: The Theatrical World of Karl Kraus* [Toronto: University of Toronto Press, 1982], 284 n. 24).

85. See Joseph Frank's critique of Bakhtin's theory of the "polyphonic" novel on just such grounds as these. If, as Bakhtin claims, Dostoyevsky's novels are "a polyphony of independent voices," then, asks Frank, "what is the place of the author in this scheme?" ("The Voices of Mikhail Bakhtin," *New York Review of Books* [October 23, 1986]: 59).

86. As did Ray Stricklin in *Confessions of a Nightingale,* produced in New York at the Audrey Wood Playhouse in the Lawrence Theater in 1986.

87. Jean-Baptiste Poquelin de Molière, *The Misanthrope,* in *The Misanthrope and Tartuffe,* trans. Richard Wilbur (New York: Harcourt, Brace and World, 1965), act 1, sc. 2, pp. 30–43.

88. Caryl Churchill, *Fen* (London: Methuen, 1983), sc. 19, pp. 21–22.

89. Ludwig Tieck, *Puss-in-Boots,* trans. Gerald Gillespie (Austin: University of Texas Press, 1974), act 3, pp. 99–101.

90. George Bernard Shaw, *The Dark Lady of the Sonnets,* in *Complete Plays* (London: Constable, 1931), 646.

91. Michel de Ghelderode, *Three Actors and Their Drama,* in *Seven Plays,* trans. George Hauger (New York: Hill and Wang, 1960), 131.

92. Tieck, *Puss-in-Boots,* act 3, p. 103 (trans. slightly modified).

93. Shaw, *Dark Lady of the Sonnets,* 646.

94. Ben Jonson, *Works,* ed. C. H. Herford and Percy Simpson (Oxford: Oxford University Press, 1966), 9:581.

95. Jean-Baptiste Poquelin de Molière, *The Versailles Impromptu,* in *Tartuffe and Other Plays,* trans. Donald M. Frame (New York: New American Library, 1967), sc. 1, p. 211. Subsequent scene and page references appear in the text.

96. Mayor, *Thirteen Satires of Juvenal,* 173.

97. Pliny, *Letters,* 1:499; Mayor, *Thirteen Satires of Juvenal,* 174.

98. Jean-Baptiste Poquelin de Molière, *Two Precious Maidens Ridiculed [Les précieuses ridicules],* in *One-Act Comedies,* trans. Albert Bermel (Cleveland: World, 1964), 59–60.

99. Johann Wolfgang von Goethe, *Italian Journey,* trans. W. H. Auden and Elizabeth Mayer (New York: Schocken, 1968), 153.

100. Vladimir Nemirovich-Dantchenko, *My Life in the Russian Theatre* (New York: Theatre Arts Books, 1968), 236. This reference was brought to my attention by Susan Cole.

101. Collins, *Reading Aloud,* 5.

102. The series "Illustrious Women" was presented at the 92nd Street YM-YWHA in New York in 1985.

103. For an account of the scholarly debate on whether and how Seneca's plays were staged, see Gordon Braden, *Renaissance Tragedy and the Senecan Tradition* (New Haven, Conn.: Yale University Press, 1985), 230–31 n. 14.

104. This amounts to saying that, on some level, one can only direct a play in the teeth of the kind of thing a play is—or, at least, in the teeth of the kind of reading a play invites. I do not know whether to regard this inherent conflict between theater's aims and the chief agent of their realization as a "fruitful tension" or a "tragic contradiction." As a playwright, I have a vivid appreciation of all that a director can do for a text in the exercise of a function that is, nevertheless, a systematic undoing of it. Perhaps of all enterprises it should least surprise us to find theater structured on an unresolvable conflict.

105. The reading in question took place at the 92nd Street YM-YWHA in New York in 1986. For Merrill as one of the three readers of his own play, see Jordan Pecile, "James Merrill on Poetry," *State of the Arts*, no. 23 (Winter 1987): 22.

106. This reading, which I attended, took place at the 92nd Street YM-YWHA in New York in 1986. In the second half of the program each playwright read by himself, but what each read by himself was a *one-character* play, so that, here too, both playwrights were reading from within a role.

107. Luigi Pirandello, *Each in His Own Way*, trans. Arthur Livingston, in *Naked Masks* (New York: Dutton, 1958), act 1, p. 325. Subsequent references to this edition by act and page number will appear in the text.

108. Roger Vitrac, *The Mysteries of Love*, act 1, sc. 1, in Benedikt and Wellwarth, *Modern French Theatre*, 239.

109. This, of course, does not mean that the situations of dramatic and nondramatic authors may not resemble each other in other respects. See, for example, my earlier discussion of the playwright-audience relation as an "acting out" of the general structure of author-reader relations.

Index

Acting: applicability of Norman Holland's reading theory to, 44–49, 111–13; body in, 88–99; as dependence on/power over texts, 83, 91, 93; as enactment of critical approaches, 26–27; as filling in of gaps, 28–29, 94, 123, 161, 162, 163, 166, 172, 261nn. 51, 54, 59, 276n.63; film and television, 53; Greek attitudes toward, 158, 159–60; inner/outer confusions in, 46, 59, 72–73, 126, 134–35, 211; as "madness" of reading, 98–99; as mediation of reading, 18–19, 159–60, 198, 213, 219–20; medieval attitudes toward, 161–73; mix of active and passive impulses in, 14, 55, 57, 74, 90–92, 93, 113, 162; oral metaphors for, 79–82; as recovered relation between active and passive oral impulses, 60, 61–62 (table 1), 83–84, 87–88, 91–92, 93, 108–9, 124–26, 131–32, 202–3, 211; and shamanism, 76–78, 205, 267n.72; spread of orality from mouth to body in, 74, 82, 84, 88–90; supplant/merge impulses in, 94–95, 96–97, 111, 113, 128–31, 137, 162; voice in, 86–87, 88–89, 262n.14; water imagery for, 75–78. *See also* Acting problems; Acting process; Acting textbooks; Boundarilessness; Characterization; Image-

work; Improvisation; "Lost" physical of reading; Orality; Reading; Rehearsal; Scenes of reading
Acting problems, as reading problems, 3, 159–60, 169–73, 176, 177–79, 182–83, 187–89
Acting process, evidence for, in different periods, 5–7, 139, 162, 182–83
Acting textbooks: as images of the dramatic text, 183–96; as script surrogates, 4
Active reader, 25–30, 37–39, 94, 161, 230, 261n.54
Actor: as active reader, 27–29, 94, 161; affinities of, with author, 221–22, 223–53, 268–69n.97; attitudes of, toward reading, 3, 81; and audience, 197–98, 202–6, 208–9, 211–13; Bottom as type of, 119–20, 124; "childishness" of, 78, 209, 268n.76; and dislike of being read to, 220; Don Quixote as type of, 94–104; as "first reader," 4, 15, 220–22, 238, 239; "hunger" for approval of, 78, 79, 202, 209; immobilization of, 9–10; interaction of, with other actors, 11, 13–14, 126–38, 142–43, 146–47; as mediator of reading, 18–19, 159–60, 198, 213, 219–20; as modeling author's self-secondariness, 236, 237, 239; in nonverbal theater, 3–4, 77–78; in non-Western theater, 3–4; oral relation to audience of, 79, 202–